THE NATIONAL COLLEGIATE ATHLETIC ASSOCIATION
6201 College Boulevard
Overland Park, Kansas 66211-2422
913/339-1906
October 1991

Records and Research Compiled By: James M. Van Valkenburg, *Director of Statistics.*

Designed By: Wayne Davis, *Assistant Publications Production Coordinator.*

Edited By: Laura E. Bollig, *Publications Editor.*

NCAA, NCAA seal, NCAA logo and National Collegiate Athletic Association are registered marks of the Association and use in any manner is prohibited unless prior approval is obtained from the Association.

COPYRIGHT, 1989, 1990, 1991 BY THE NATIONAL COLLEGIATE ATHLETIC ASSOCIATION
PRINTED IN THE UNITED STATES OF AMERICA

Contents

Foreword... 4

Honors won and year-by-year statistics of players
  whose careers ended before 1970............................... 9

Honors won and year-by-year statistics of players
  whose careers ended after 1970................................113

All-time list by college of all first-team all-America players
  on teams used by NCAA in compiling its annual
  major-college consensus all-America teams..................191

Coaches with at least 10 major-college head-coaching
  seasons and .700 winning percentage or 200 victories;
  yearly won-lost records and bowl scores......................215

FOREWORD

No doubt you have met some or read about many "former all-America" college football players. But how many of them actually were first team selections on a team or teams composed primarily of major-college or Division I-A players and chosen with national input for national distribution?

"College Football's Finest" answers that question in terms of NCAA historical records. It lists the names, college by college, of all 2,390 players (from 148 colleges) over 101 years who made at least one first team on the selections used by the NCAA to compile its annual consensus all-America team for major-college or Division I-A players.

Consensus and unanimous choices in the all-America roster are highlighted. They are all there—all the linemen and backs, offensive, defensive and iron-man or two-way—all the way back to the first all-America team in 1889.

This book also features year-by-year statistics and honors won for 343 top runners, passers and receivers who brightened the game's first 121 years. Finally are the 63 coaches with .700-or-better winning percentages or at least 200 wins who head-coached at least 10 seasons at major or Division I-A colleges. Their yearly records and bowl scores are listed.

The 343 players are divided into two groups—198 whose careers ended before 1970 and 145 whose careers ended after 1970. This dividing line was chosen because through 1969, national statistics champions in the major categories were determined by total yards, points, completions, catches, etc., and most teams played 10-game schedules. In 1970, teams started playing 11-game schedules and the system was revamped to decide champions on a per-game basis.

That change provided a perfect starting point for the "moderns" section. Another change came in 1979 with an efficiency rating to determine the annual passing champion (It combines completetion percentage, yards per attempt, TD percentage and interception percentage; 100 points equals the average major-college (now I-A) passer for the first 14 seasons of the current two-platoon era prior to 1979 (see 1990 NCAA Football for complete formula details).

In addition, freshman eligibility, 44-game careers, platoon play and passing rules changes make it almost impossible to fairly compare total yards by the moderns to those by the oldtimers who played both offense and defense in the iron-man era. More about that later.

First, some history about the all-America roster. The first 61 years of NCAA consensus choices were published in the 1950 NCAA Football Guide, produced and distributed by the NCAA's service arm, the National Collegiate Athletic Bureau.

Selections were made at nightly meetings over a two-month span by a four-man NCAA panel. It included Homer F. Cooke Jr., NCAB director who had started the national football rankings as a private venture in 1937 in Seattle, where he was a sportswriter; H.D. Thoreau, general editor of the NCAA guides and noted track and field authority, who shortly left the NCAB to become Southern California sports information director; and NCAB statisticians Harvey Schiffer and Steve Boda Jr., NCAA associate director of statistics before his retirement in 1989. As the youngest in the group, Boda did not vote on which AA teams to use but recorded all the players and votes.

The quartet's source material came largely from the vast college football collection owned by Dr. Louis Henry Levy, then a retired New York physician and author who wrote about football under the name of Dr. L.H. Baker. The NCAB's Jack Waters, now NCAA director of licensing, prepared the manuscript. The story was written by Thoreau and credited to the collector.

The physician's collection included 150,000 newspaper and magazine clippings, 30,000 books and thousands of programs, pictures, catalogues and play diagrams, all of it cross-indexed for ready reference. Even so, there were some tiny gaps. A few AA teams the NCAB group wanted to use for its consensus teams were missing in a few seasons, so they simply did without.

As many as 10 teams were used some years by the NCAB for its NCAA consensus teams. In May, 1965, the NCAA adopted an official policy that teams used for the NCAA consensus team shall not include those "based primarily on potential as a professional player, or teams selected by representatives of professional football" (the point first had been raised in 1961 by Beano Cook, then SID at Pittsburgh). By 1975, only four teams were used—Associated Press, United Press International, Football Writers Association of America and American Football Coaches Association. In 1983, the Walter Camp Foundation team was added.

Every name on the all-time list was cross-checked against his college's AA list, all first-team claims were investigated and just one player was added. Certainly, one could argue that the very idea of trying to pick the best players is folly to begin with. But the public's fascination holds, and every fall, committees of writers and coaches devote serious study to it.

Returning to the 343 top players with yearly and career figures, they include all Heisman Trophy winners (first one chosen in 1935—two years before official NCAA statistics began in 1937) except two (some numbers not available) and all but a few consensus all-America runners, passers and receivers since 1937.

Some wartime figures are missing. A handful of consensus AAs are excluded because nearly all their career figures came in one season. In the book are 24 non-all-America players. They include quarterbacks who led their colleges to back-to-back national championships and others with outstanding numbers and/or top-10 Heisman finishes.

For all oldtimers before 1937, all figures were compiled by Boda, using only play-by-play reports he obtained in more than 100 trips from the NCAB office in New York to the Library of Congress and from newspapers and historical societies across the country. He used current statistics compilation rules. (The first rules for compiling football game statistics were drawn up before the 1941 season by a coaches' subcommittee headed by Michigan's Fielding "Hurry Up" Yost, former coaching great whose record is in the coaches' section of this book).

The pre-1937 group starts with Willie Heston, whose last season at Michigan was 1904, and goes to Sammy Baugh, Texas Christian 1936. In between are legends like Jim Thorpe of the Carlisle Indians (who played a major schedule), the Four Horsemen and George Gipp of Notre Dame, Red Grange of Illinois, Don Hutson and Dixie Howell of Alabama, Red Cagle of Army, Bobby Grayson of Stanford, Bronko Nagurski of Minnesota, Jay Berwanger of Chicago (the first Heisman winner in 1935), and many others. Largely unavailable are play-by-plays for others like Ernie Nevers, Stanford 1925, and Elmer Oliphant, Army 1917.

Colorado's Byron "Whizzer" White, who won four major statistical crowns in 1937, and little Davey O'Brien, who quarterbacked Texas Christian to the 1938 national title, are among those whose pre-1937 figures could be researched.

All figures in tables are regular-season games only. Bowl exploits are noted after honors won (some sparse because complete bowl figures are not available for many oldtimers). Season and career records set or held are not included because most are soon broken (see the record book, NCAA Football) and NCAA Football's Finest is not an annual publication.

Both playing and academic honors won are listed for each player. Playing honors include first-team all-America, consensus and unanimous AA, his rank in the Heisman voting, induction into the Hall of Fame and inclusion on the all-time team chosen by the Football Writers Association of America in 1969. National championship seasons are footnoted for each player.

Academic and career achievement honors include Academic all-America, the Academic All-America Hall of Fame, NCAA Postgraduate Scholarship winners, Rhodes Scholars, Hall of Fame scholar-athletes, and NCAA Honors Luncheon awards like the Theodore Roosevelt Award, Silver Anniversary team and Today's Top Six.

As an example of the difficulty of comparing players of different eras, let us consider Grange, whose entire career at Illinois (ending with 1925) was 20 games, and Michigan's Tom Harmon, the 1940 Heisman winner, 24 games.

In their era, the average game was 110 plays; now it is 140, and careers can go 44 games. This means games are 27.3 percent longer. To project, add 27.3 percent to an oldtimer's per-game average, then multiply that figure by 44.

Harmon, a run-pass tailback, projects to 4,916 career rushing yards (actual: 2,110), 7,945 total offense (rushing plus passing), 6,825 all-purpose yards and an astounding 552 points scored (he also kicked extra points and field goals). Grange's career projects to 5,799 rushing (actual: 2,071), 7,408 total offense and an amazing 9,828 all-purpose yards, not to mention 521 points. The current career records are 7,172 all-purpose yards and 393 points.

Of course, both Harmon and Grange played both ways, thus had yardage in kick, punt and interception runbacks. Could they keep up the same pace over 44 games as they did over 24 and 20? Who knows? But could the moderns keep up the same pace while playing both ways?

Rules can make a lot of difference—hash marks, for instance. In the 1920s, if the runner was tackled a yard from the sideline, the next play started there, so half the offensive line had to line up out of bounds. Then everyone in the stadium knew which direction the next play was going.

Changes in the passing game are even more drastic. At one time, an incomplete pass into the end zone automatically turned the ball over to the defense. The football did not take its present bullet shape until 1934. The passer had to be at least five yards behind the line until 1945. Many other changes affecting pass blocking and receiving have come in the last two decades.

Another oldtimer unquestionably is the most-honored player in history. He is Colorado's White, who won the Theodore Roosevelt Award, the NCAA's top award, and the Gold Medal, the top award of the National Football Foundation and Hall of Fame. He was Phi Beta Kappa as a junior, first in his class at Colorado, a Rhodes Scholar and was No. 1 in his class at Yale Law School. He won two Bronze Stars in Pacific combat, and in 1962 at the age of 45 he became the youngest man to be appointed to the U.S. Supreme Court. On the field, he was a consensus all-America, second in the Heisman voting, won four NCAA statistics titles in 1937 (his all-purpose yards per game record stood until Oklahoma State's Barry Sanders came along in 1988) and twice was National Football League rushing champion.

Now for the national championship seasons footnoted. From 1883 to 1923, we are using the Athletic Foundation teams picked in 1941 after extensive research by the late Bill Schroeder (the foundation was established in 1936 by Paul Helms, Los Angeles sportsman). For 1924 to 1935, we use the Dickinson System, devised by Frank Dickinson, a professor of economics at Illinois. In 1936 came the first Associated Press poll, in 1950 United Press International, in 1954 the FWAA champion and in 1959, the NFFHF champion. Every team that won one of these titles is footnoted as a national champion. The last 11 seasons, one team swept all four titles, thanks to the current poll-bowl system. But before that, some final polls came before the bowls, thus multiple national champions. In all, there have been 68 national champions since 1936.

James M. Van Valkenburg

1901-1969

FRANKIE ALBERT
STANFORD QB, 5-9, 170 Glendale, Calif. (Glendale HS)

Consensus all-America 40 and 41. Heisman 3rd in 41, 4th in 40. Hall of Fame.

Bowls: Rose 41—threw 41-yard TD pass, kicked 3 extra points (Beat Nebraska, 21-13).

Yr.	Team			Rushing			Passing			
	W	L	T	Car.	Yds.	Att.	Cmp.	Int.	Pct.	Yds.	TD
39	1	7	1	36	65	92	29	12	.315	438	7
40	9	0	0	39	56	99	36	12	.364	648	4
41	6	3	0	46	66	113	50	13	.442	709	4
Totals	16	10	0	121	187	304	115	37	.378	1795	15
Avg.					1.5		5.9 per Att.			15.6 per Cmp.	

Yr.		Total Offense			Scoring	
	Plays	Yds.	TDR	TD	XP	Pts.
39	128	503	9	2	6	18
40	138	704	7	3	18	36
41	159	775	8	4	13	37
Totals	425	1982	24	9	37	91
Avg.		4.7				

Other career figures: 12 int. for 125 yds., 82 punts for 37.2 avg., 11 punt ret. for 90 yds.

LANCE ALWORTH
ARKANSAS HB, 6-0, 178 Brookhaven, Miss. (Brookhaven HS)

All-America 61. Academic all-America 61. Hall of Fame.

Bowls: Gator 60—rushed 40 yards; 36.5 punting avg. (Beat Georgia Tech, 14-7). Cotton 61—scored TD on 49-yard punt return (Duke won, 7-6). Sugar 62—caught 2 passes for 55 yards (Alabama won, 10-3).

Yr.	Team			Rushing				Receiving		
	W	L	T	Car.	Yds.	Avg.	No.	Yds.	TD	Avg.
59	8	2	0	85	366	4.3	7	82	1	11.7
60	8	2	0	106	375	3.5	13	264	2	20.3
61	8	2	0	110	516	4.7	18	320	3	17.8
Totals	24	6	0	301	1257	4.2	38	666	6	17.5

Yr.	Punting		Punt Returns		K.O. Returns		Scoring		
	No.	Avg.	No.	Yds.	No.	Yds.	TD	XP	Pts.
59	37	35.5	5	47	4	112	2	2	14
60	48	33.4	18	*307	14	328	3	0	18
61	32	35.3	*28	*336	13	300	5	0	30
Totals	117	34.6	51	690	31	740	10	2	62
Avg.				13.5		23.9			

Other career figures: 14 passes att., 5 cmp. for 116 yds., 1 had int.; 2 int. by for 35 yards.

* This figure led the nation.

ALAN AMECHE
WISCONSIN
FB, 6-0, 215
Kenosha, Wis. (Kenosha HS)

Unanimous all-America 54, all-America 53. Heisman winner 54, 6th in 53. Academic all-America 53 and 54. Hall of Fame. Silver Anniversary Award, NCAA Honors Luncheon 80.
Bowl: Rose 53—rushed for 133 yards on 28 carries, one of 54 yards (Southern Cal won, 7-0).

	Team			Rushing			K.O. Returns		Scoring	
Yr.	W	L	T	Car.	Yds.	Avg.	No.	Yds.	TD	Pts.
51	7	1	1	157	824	5.2	1	18	4	24
52	6	2	1	*205	946	4.6	0	0	7	42
53	6	2	1	165	801	4.9	1	18	5	30
54	7	2	0	146	641	4.4	2	13	9	54
Totals	26	7	3	673	3212	4.8	4	49	25	150
Avg.								12.3		

Other career figures: 4 catches for 8 yds.
* This figure led the nation.

BOB ANDERSON
ARMY   HB, 6-2, 200   Cocoa, Fla. (Cocoa HS)

Consensus all-America 57, all-America 58. Heisman 7th in 57.

	Team			Rushing			Passing					Total Offense		
Yr.	W	L	T	Car.	Yds.	Avg.	Att.	Cmp.	Int.	Pct.	Yds.	TD	Plays	Yds.	TDR
57	7	2	0	153	983	*6.4	11	6	2	.545	30	1	164	1013	15
58	8	0	1	126	564	4.5	15	10	1	.667	143	4	141	707	7
59	4	4	1	76	340	4.5	17	8	3	.471	112	0	93	452	7
Totals	19	6	2	355	1887	5.3	43	24	6	.558	285	5	398	2172	29
Avg.							6.6 per Att.			11.9 per Cmp.			5.5		

	Receiving			Int.		Punting		Punt Ret.		K.O. Ret.		Scoring		
Yr.	No.	Yds.	TD	Avg.	No.	Yds.	No.	Avg.	No.	Yds.	No.	Yds.	TD	XP	Pts.
57	6	82	2	13.7	4	39	6	29.5	2	0	4	44	14	0	84
58	14	138	1	9.9	3	0	1	23.0	4	78	1	24	6	6	42
59	4	25	1	6.3	0	0	0	0.0	3	16	2	17	4	0	24
Totals	24	245	4	10.2	7	39	7	28.6	9	94	7	85	24	6	150
Avg.						5.6				10.4		12.1			

* This figure led the nation.

BOB ANDERSON
COLORADO   QB-HB, 6-0, 208   Boulder, Colo. (Boulder HS)

Consensus all-America 69.

Bowls: Bluebonnet 67—scored 2 TDs, one a 38-yard rush; rushed for 108 yards, completed 5 passes for 49 (Beat Miami, Fla., 31-21). Liberty 69—rushed for a Liberty Bowl record of 254 yards, scored 3 TDs (Beat Alabama, 47-33).

Yr.	Team W	L	T	Rushing Car.	Yds.	Avg.	Att.	Cmp.	Passing Int.	Pct.	Yds.	TD	Total Offense Plays	Yds.	TDR
67	8	2	0	166	625	3.8	110	63	5	.573	733	2	276	1358	9
68	4	6	0	183	787	4.3	222	112	12	.505	1341	7	405	2128	16
69	7	3	0	219	954	4.4	43	13	4	.302	124	0	262	1078	19
Totals	19	11	0	568	2366	4.2	375	188	21	.501	2198	9	943	4564	44
Avg.										5.9 per Att.	11.7 per Cmp.			4.8	

Yr.	Receiving No.	Yds.	Punt Returns No.	Yds.	K.O. Returns No.	Yds.	Scoring TD	XP	Pts.
67	0	0	0	0	0	0	7	0	42
68	0	0	0	0	1	16	9	2	56
69	4	68	5	56	11	193	19	0	114
Totals	4	68	5	56	12	209	35	2	212
Avg.		17.0		11.2		17.4			

Other career figures: 4 punts for 33.5 avg.

DONNY ANDERSON
TEXAS TECH
HB, 6-3, 210
Stinnett, Texas (Stinnett HS)

Consensus all-America 65, all-America 64. Heisman 4th in 65. Hall of Fame.

Bowls: Sun 65—Georgia won 7-0. Gator 66—rushed 85 yards, scored one TD, caught 9 passes for 138 yards (Georgia Tech won, 31-21).

Yr.	Team W	L	T	Rushing Car.	Yds.	Avg.	Receiving No.	Yds.	TD	Avg.
63	5	5	0	146	609	4.2	13	154	1	11.8
64	6	3	1	211	966	4.6	32	396	4	12.4
65	8	2	0	169	705	4.2	60	797	7	13.3
Totals	19	10	1	526	2280	4.3	105	1347	12	12.8

Yr.	Punting No.	Avg.	Punt Returns No.	Yds.	K.O. Returns No.	Yds.	Scoring TD	Pts.
63	51	38.5	2	5	18	448	4	24
64	54	38.3	2	28	16	320	7	42
65	43	38.5	5	64	22	541	17	102
Totals	148	38.4	9	97	56	1309	28	168
Avg.				10.8		23.4		

Other career figures: 5 passes att., 0 cmp., 1 int.; 3 int. by for 0 yds.

JON ARNETT
SOUTHERN CALIFORNIA
HB, 5-11, 190
Los Angeles, Calif. (Manual Arts HS)

All-America 55. Heisman 10th in 55.

Bowl: Rose 55—rushed 123 yards on 9 carries, including runs of 70 and 31, for 13.7 average in rain and mud; averaged 61.0 yards on two punts; completed 2 of 2 passes for 6 yards; returned 1 kickoff 19 yards; lost 1 fumble (Ohio State won, 20-7).

	Team				Rushing			Passing					Total Offense			Scoring		
Yr.	W	L	T	G	Car.	Yds.	Avg.	Att.	Cmp.	Int.	Yds.	TD	Plays	Yds.	Avg.	TD	XP-XPA	Pts.
54	8	3	0	10	87	478	5.5	30	17	2	164	0	117	642	5.5	6	1-1	37
55	6	4	0	10	141	672	4.8	25	12	2	150	0	166	822	5.0	15	18-22	108
56	8	2	0	5	99	625	6.3	11	8	1	133	1	110	758	6.9	8	7-10	55
	22	9	0	25	327	1775	5.4	56	37	5	447	1	393	2222	5.7	29	26-33	200

Career avg: 8.0 yds. per pass att.; .661 cmp. pct., 12.1 yds. per cmp.
Career per game: 71.0 rush yds.; 88.9 tot. off. yds.; 8.0 pts.

	Receiving				Int.		Punt Ret.			K.O. Ret.			All-Purpose			
Yr.	No.	Yds.	TD	Avg.	No.	Yds.	No.	Yds.	Avg.	No.	Yds.	Avg.	Plays	Yds.	TD	Avg.
54	3	104	2	36.0	3	54	11	129	11.7	6	70	11.7	110	835	6	7.6
55	6	154	2	25.7	—	—	16	282	17.6	15	418	27.9	178	1526	15	8.6
56	2	38	0	19.0	—	—	1	25	25.0	4	122	30.5	106	810	8	7.6
Totals	11	296	4	26.9	3	54	28	436	15.6	25	610	24.4	394	3171	29	8.0

Career per game: 55.8 yds. receiving and all runbacks; 126.8 yds. all-purpose.
Other career figures: 42.0-yard avg. on 16 punts.

BILLY AUSTIN
RUTGERS TB, 5-11, 170 Fanwood, N.J. (Scotch Plains HS)
All-America 58. Heisman 6th in 58.

	Team			Rushing			Passing						Total Offense		
Yr.	W	L	T	Car.	Yds.	Avg.	Att.	Cmp.	Int.	Pct.	Yds.	TD	Plays	Yds.	TDR
56	3	7	0	123	380	3.1	41	17	3	.415	230	2	164	610	6
57	5	4	0	193	946	4.9	80	38	3	.475	479	3	273	1425	15
58	8	1	0	145	747	5.2	43	22	3	.512	284	8	188	1031	*24
Totals	16	12	0	461	2073	4.5	164	77	9	.470	993	13	625	3066	45
Avg.							6.1 per Att.			12.9 per Cmp.				4.9	

	Receiving		Int.		Punting		Punt Ret.		K.O. Ret.		Scoring		
Yr.	No.	Yds.	No.	Yds.	No.	Avg.	No.	Yds.	No.	Yds.	TD	XP	Pts.
56	1	29	3	62	29	36.3	11	113	6	107	4	0	24
57	2	64	4	181	24	33.6	12	77	6	119	12	2	74
58	1	22	6	128	14	35.1	9	74	4	142	16	10	106
Totals	4	115	13	371	67	35.1	32	264	16	368	32	12	204
Avg.		28.8		28.5				8.3		23.0			

* This figure led the nation.

FRANCIS "REDS" BAGNELL
PENNSYLVANIA HB, 6-0, 178 Philadelphia, Pa. (West Catholic HS)

All-America 50. Heisman 3rd in 50. Hall of Fame.

	Team		Rushing			Passing					Total Offense		
Yr.	W	L	T	Car.	Yds.	Avg.	Att.	Cmp.	Int.	Pct.	Yds.	TD	Plays	Yds.	TDR
48	5	3	0	71	167	2.4	64	31	3	.484	445	5	135	612	7
49	4	4	0	61	65	1.1	111	53	6	.477	637	6	172	702	8
50	6	3	0	157	672	4.3	125	63	4	.504	931	7	282	1603	16
Totals	15	10	0	289	904	3.1	300	147	13	.490	2013	18	589	2917	31
Avg.							6.7 per Att.			13.7 per Cmp.			5.0		

	Interceptions		Punt Returns		K.O. Returns		Scoring	
Yr.	No.	Yds.	No.	Yds.	No.	Yds.	TD	Pts.
48	2	41	4	43	4	63	2	12
49	6	102	14	185	3	20	2	12
50	0	0	0	0	1	15	9	54
Totals	8	143	18	228	8	98	13	78
Avg.		17.9		12.7		12.3		

Other career figures: 2 punts for 33.0 avg.

TERRY BAKER
OREGON STATE
QB, 6-3, 191
Portland, Ore. (Jefferson HS)

Unanimous all-America 62. Heisman winner 62. Academic all-America 62. Hall of Fame. Silver Anniversary Award, NCAA Honors Luncheon 88. Hall of Fame Scholar-Athlete 62.

Bowl: Liberty 62—99-yard record rush (Beat Villanova, 6-0).

	Team		Rushing			Passing					Total Offense		
Yr.	W	L	T	Car.	Yds.	Avg.	Att.	Cmp.	Int.	Pct.	Yds.	TD	Plays	Yds.	TDR
60	6	3	1	111	610	5.5	117	60	12	.513	863	3	228	1473	8
61	5	5	0	73	355	4.9	134	61	8	.455	875	5	207	1230	7
62+	8	2	0	115	538	4.7	203	112	5	.552	*1738	*15	318	*2276	*24
Totals	19	10	1	299	1503	5.0	454	233	25	.513	3476	23	753	4979	39
Avg.							7.7 per Att.			14.9 per Cmp.			6.6		

	Receiving		Punting		K.O. Returns		Scoring		
Yr.	No.	Yds.	No.	Avg.	No.	Yds.	TD	XP	Pts.
60	0	0	13	42.2	2	44	5	4	34
61	5	64	23	29.7	0	0	2	0	12
62	0	0	33	37.4	0	0	9	4	58
Totals	5	64	69	35.7	2	44	16	8	104
Avg.		12.8				22.0			

+ National leader in passing efficiency in 1962 (min. 15 att. per game) at 146.5.

* This figure led the nation.

DICK BASS
PACIFIC   HB, 5-11, 189   Vallejo, Calif. (Vallejo HS)

Heisman 8th in 58.

	Team			Rushing			Passing					Total Offense		
Yr.	W	L	T	Car.	Yds.	Avg.	Att.	Cmp.	Int.	Pct.	Yds.	TD	Plays	Yds.	TDR
56	6	3	1	104	611	5,9	1	1	0	1.000	68	0	105	679	7
58	6	4	0	205	*1361	*6.6	13	4	2	.308	79	0	218	*1440	18
59	5	4	0	139	742	5.3	22	11	1	.500	216	2	161	958	10
Totals	17	11	1	448	2714	6.1	36	16	3	.444	363	2	484	3077	35
Avg.										10.1 per Att.		22.7 per Cmp.		6.4	

	Receiving				Int.		Punting		Punt Ret.		K.O. Ret.		Scoring		
Yr.	No.	Yds.	TD	Avg.	No.	Yds.	No.	Avg.	No.	Yds.	No.	Yds.	TD	XP	Pts.
56	8	71	0	8.9	4	56	0	0	10	138	5	114	7	0	42
58	6	121	1	20.2	2	5	14	27.8	13	164	10	227	*18	8	*116
59	7	116	1	16.6	1	0	1	19.0	5	58	9	196	8	2	50
Totals	21	308	2	14.7	7	61	15	27.2	28	360	24	537	33	10	208
Avg.							8.7			12.9		22.4			

* This figure led the nation.

SAMMY BAUGH
TEXAS CHRISTIAN
QB, 6-2, 180
Sweetwater, Texas (Sweetwater HS)

Consensus all-America 36, all-America 35. Heisman 4th in 36. Hall of Fame. FWAA all-time team.

Bowls: Sugar 36—44.6 punting avg., 52-yard rush, 2 interceptions (Beat Louisiana St., 3-2). Cotton 37—50-yard TD pass (Beat Marquette, 16-6).

	Team			Rushing			Passing						Total Offense		
Yr.	W	L	T	Car.	Yds.	Avg.	Att.	Cmp.	Int.	Pct.	Yds.	TD	Plays	Yds.	TDR
34	8	4	0	44	114	2.6	171	69	19	.404	883	11	215	997	13
35	11	1	0	60	195	3.3	210	97	17	.462	1240	18	270	1435	21
36	8	2	2	54	63	1.2	206	104	18	.505	1261	10	260	1324	10
Totals	27	7	2	158	372	2.4	587	270	54	.460	3384	39	745	3756	44
Avg.							5.8 per Att.			12.5 per Cmp.			5.0		

	Receiving		Int.		Punting			Punt Ret.		K.O. Ret.		Scoring	
Yr.	No.	Yds.	No.	Yds.	No.	Yds.	Avg.	No.	Yds.	No.	Yds.	TD	Pts.
34	3	23	3	51	43	1821	42.3	13	140	1	22	2	12
35	0	0	2	25	66	2837	43.0	28	394	1	6	3	18
36	0	0	5	77	89	3450	38.8	39	457	0	0	0	0
Totals	3	23	10	153	198	8108	40.9	80	991	2	28	5	30
Avg.		7.7		15.3					12.4		14.0		

RON BEAGLE
NAVY E, 6-0, 186 Covington, Ky. (Purcell HS)

Unanimous all-America 55, Consensus all-America 54. Heisman 7th in 55.
Bowl: Sugar 55—Beat Mississippi, 21-0.

Yr.	Team			No.	Receiving		Avg.	Scoring	
	W	L	T		Yds.	TD		TD	Pts.
53	4	3	2	14	146	1	10.4	1	6
54	7	2	0	20	243	3	12.2	3	18
55	6	2	1	30	451	4	15.0	4	24
Totals	17	7	3	64	840	8	13.1	8	48

GARY BEBAN
UCLA
QB, 6-0, 191
Redwood City, Calif. (Sequoia HS)

Unanimous all-America 67. Heisman winner 67, 4th in 66. Hall of Fame.
Bowl: Rose 66—2 TDs rushing (Beat Michigan St., 14-12).

Yr.	Team			Rushing			Passing					
	W	L	T	Car.	Yds.	Avg.	Att.	Cmp.	Int.	Pct.	Yds.	TD
65	7	2	1	169	576	3.4	131	70	6	.534	1336	9
66	9	1	0	123	454	3.7	157	78	10	.497	1245	6
67	7	2	1	145	227	1.6	156	87	8	.558	1359	8
Totals	23	5	2	437	1257	2.9	444	235	24	.529	3940	23
Avg.							8.9 per Att.	16.8 per Cmp.		133.8 efficiency		

Yr.	Total Offense				Scoring		
	Plays	Yds.	TDR	TD	XP		Pts.
65	300	1912	21	12	0		72
66	280	1699	16	10	4		64
67	301	1586	19	11	0		66
Totals	881	5197	56	33	4		202
Avg.		5.9					

JOE BELLINO
NAVY
HB, 5-9, 181
Winchester, Mass. (Winchester HS)

Unanimous all-America 60. Heisman winner 60. Hall of Fame.
Bowl: Orange 61—Missouri won, 21-14.

Yr.	Team			Rushing			Receiving			
	W	L	T	Car.	Yds.	Avg.	No.	Yds.	TD	Avg.
58	6	3	0	63	266	4.2	19	240	3	12.6
59	5	4	1	99	564	5.7	9	82	1	9.1
60	9	1	0	168	834	5.0	17	280	3	16.5
Totals	20	8	1	330	1664	5.0	45	602	7	13.4

Yr.	Punt Returns		K.O. Returns		Scoring		
	No.	Yds.	No.	Yds.	TD	XP	Pts.
58	3	36	4	203	5	10	40
59	6	123	6	88	8	0	48
60	6	97	13	286	18	2	110
Totals	15	256	23	577	31	12	198
Avg.		17.1		25.1			

Other career figures: 16 passes att., 5 cmp. for 112 yds. and 2 TDs, 1 had int.

ANGELO BERTELLI
NOTRE DAME   QB, 6-1, 173   West Springfield, Mass. (Cathedral HS)

Consensus all-America 43, all-America 42. Heisman winner 43, 2nd in 41, 6th in 42. Hall of Fame.

Yr.	Team			Rushing		Passing				
	W	L	T	Car.	Yds.	Att.	Cmp.	Int.	Pct.	Yds.	TD
41	8	0	1	40	40	123	70	10	*.569	1027	8
42	7	2	2	21	-14	159	72	16	.453	1039	10
43	#9	1	0	14	12	36	25	4	.694	512	10
Totals	24	3	3	75	38	318	167	30	.525	2578	28
Avg.						8.1 per Att.	15.4 per Cmp.		130.8 efficiency		

Yr.	Total Offense			Scoring		
	Plays	Yds.	TDR	TD	XP	Pts.
41	163	1067	8	0	3	3
42	180	1025	12	2	16	28
43	50	524	14	4	21	45
Totals	393	2616	34	6	40	76
Avg.		6.7				

Other career figures: 12 int. by for 60 yds., 64 punts for 35.8 avg., 1 kickoff ret. for 17 yds.
National champions. * This figure led the nation.

JAY BERWANGER
CHICAGO
HB, 6-1, 195
Dubuque, Iowa (Dubuque HS)

Consensus all-America 35, all-America 34. Heisman winner 35. Hall of Fame, FWAA all-time team.

Yr.	Team W	L	T	Rushing Car.	Yds.	Avg.	Att.	Passing Cmp.	Int.	Pct.	Yds.
33	3	3	2	183	667	3.6	34	11	4	.324	219
34	4	4	0	137	595	4.3	45	14	4	.311	297
35	4	4	0	119	577	4.8	67	25	9	.373	405
Totals	11	11	2	439	1839	4.2	146	50	17	.342	921
Avg.								6.3 per Att.		18.4 per Cmp.	

Yr.	Total Offense Plays	Yds.	K.O. Returns No.	Yds.	TD	Scoring XP	Pts.
33	217	886	8	167	8	7	55
34	182	892	13	347	8	8	56
35	186	982	13	359	6	5	41
Totals	585	2760	34	873	22	20	152
Avg.	4.7			25.7			

Other career figures: 223 punts for 37.3 avg.

FRED BILETNIKOFF
FLORIDA STATE FL, 6-1, 186 Erie, Pa. (Tech Memorial HS)

Consensus all-America 64.

Bowl: Gator 65—caught 13 passes for Gator Bowl records of 192 yards and 4 TDs of 15, 14, 10, 7 yards (Beat Oklahoma, 36-19).

Yr.	Team W	L	T	No.	Receiving Yds.	TD	Avg.	Int. No.	Yds.
62	4	3	3	6	118	1	19.7	0	0
63	4	5	1	24	358	4	14.9	3	99
64	8	1	1	57	987	11	17.3	0	0
Totals	16	9	5	87	1463	16	16.8	3	99

Yr.	Punt Returns No.	Yds.	K.O. Returns No.	Yds.	TD	Scoring XP	Pts.
62	0	0	0	0	1	0	6
63	3	20	1	27	5	0	30
64	4	54	3	42	11	2	68
Totals	7	74	4	69	17	2	104
Avg.		10.6		17.3			

Other career figures: 3 rushes for 14 yds.

FELIX "DOC" BLANCHARD
ARMY
FB, 6-0, 205
Bishopville, S.C. (St. Stanislaus HS, Bay St. Louis, Miss.)

Unanimous all-America 45 and 46, all-America 44. Heisman winner 45, 3rd in 44, 4th in 46. Hall of Fame.

Yr.	Team W	L	T	Rushing Car.	Yds.	Avg.	Receiving No.	Yds.	TD	Avg.
44	#9	0	0	61	335	5.5	8	203	3	25.4
45	#9	0	0	101	718	7.1	4	166	0	41.5
46	9	0	1	120	613	5.1	7	166	1	23.7
Totals	27	0	1	282	1666	5.9	19	535	4	28.2

Yr.	Interceptions No.	Yds.	Punting No.	Avg.	K.O. Returns No.	Yds.	Scoring TD	XP	Pts.
44	3	39	11	38.8	0	0	9	0	54
45	4	150	21	33.7	0	0	*19	1	*115
46	0	0	0	0.0	3	133	10	2	62
Totals	7	189	32	35.5	3	133	38	3	231
Avg.		27.0				44.3			

National champions. * This figure led the nation.

VIC BOTTARI
CALIFORNIA HB, 5-9, 182 Vallejo, Calif. (Vallejo HS)

Consensus all-America 38. Heisman 5th in 38, 8th in 37. Hall of Fame.
Bowl: Rose 38—rushed for 137 yards on 34 carries, two for TDs (Beat Alabama, 13-0).

Yr.	Team W	L	T	Rushing Car.	Yds.	Avg.	Passing Att.	Cmp.	Int.	Pct.	Yds.	TD	Total Offense Plays	Yds.
36	6	5	0	62	187	3.0	14	8	1	.571	198	3	76	385
37	9	0	1	135	585	4.3	36	11	6	.306	269	2	171	854
38	10	1	0	159	578	3.6	62	25	6	.403	466	7	221	1044
Totals	25	6	1	356	1350	3.8	112	44	13	.393	933	12	468	2283
Avg.							8.3 per Att.			21.2 per Cmp.			4.9	

Yr.	Int. No.	Yds.	Punting No.	Avg.	Punt Ret. No.	Yds.	K.O. Ret. No.	Yds.	Scoring TD	XP	Pts.
36	0	0	0	0.0	5	51	1	27	2	2	14
37	4	94	0	0.0	22	196	5	79	12	0	72
38	2	24	4	41.3	21	231	1	10	8	13	61
Totals	6	118	4	41.3	48	478	7	116	22	15	147
Avg.		19.7				10.0		16.6			

JOHNNY BRIGHT
DRAKE
HB, 6-0, 195
Fort Wayne, Ind. (Central HS)
All-America 50. Heisman 5th in 51. Hall of Fame.

	Team			Rushing				Passing			
Yr.	W	L	T	Car.	Yds.	Avg.	Att.	Cmp.	Int.	Pct.	Yds.	TD
49	6	2	1	170	975	5.7	105	43	15	.410	975	7
50	6	2	1	183	1232	6.7	137	81	9	.591	1168	12
51	7	2	0	160	927	5.8	70	33	7	.471	626	5
Totals	19	6	2	513	3134	6.1	312	157	31	.503	2769	24
Avg.							8.9 per Att.	17.6 per Cmp.		130.4 efficiency	

	Total Offense			Punt Returns		K.O. Returns		Scoring	
Yr.	Plays	Yds.	TDR	No.	Yds.	No.	Yds.	TD	Pts.
49	275	*1950	15	1	16	8	173	8	48
50	320	*2400	*30	5	71	11	301	18	108
51	230	1553	19	2	16	5	105	14	84
Totals	825	5903	64	8	103	24	579	40	240
Avg.		7.2			12.9		24.1		

* This figure led the nation.

JOHN BRODIE
STANFORD   QB, 6-1, 190   Oakland, Calif. (Oakland Tech HS)
Consensus all-America 56. Heisman 7th in 56.

	Team			Rushing		Passing					
Yr.	W	L	T	Car.	Yds.	Att.	Cmp.	Int.	Pct.	Yds.	TD
54	4	6	0	26	-63	163	81	*16	.497	937	2
55	6	3	1	35	20	133	76	7	.571	1024	5
56	4	6	0	55	9	*240	*139	14	*.579	*1633	*12
Totals	14	15	1	116	-34	536	296	37	.552	3594	19
Avg.						6.7 per Att.			12.1 per Cmp.		

	Total Offense			Scoring		
Yr.	Plays	Yds.	TDR	TD	XP	Pts.
54	189	874	5	3	1	19
55	168	1044	9	4	0	24
56	*295	1642	14	2	0	12
Totals	652	3560	28	9	1	55
Avg.		5.5				

Other career figures: 3 int. by for 28 yds., 63 punts for 35.6 avg., 2 punt ret. for 8 yds., 3 kickoff ret. for 34 yards.

* This figure led the nation.

JIM BROWN
SYRACUSE
HB, 6-2, 212
Manhasset, N.Y. (Manhasset HS)

Unanimous all-America 56. Heisman 5th in 56. Silver Anniversary Award, NCAA Honors Luncheon 82.
Bowl: Cotton 57—132 yards rushing on 26 carries, scored 21 points (Texas Christian won, 28-27).

Yr.	Team			Rushing			Passing				Total Offense	
	W	L	T	Car.	Yds.	Avg.	Att.	Cmp.	Yds.	TD	Plays	Yds.
54	4	4	0	75	439	5.9	0	0	0	0	75	439
55	5	3	0	128	666	5.2	2	0	0	0	130	666
56	7	1	0	158	986	*6.2	4	3	76	1	162	1062
Totals	16	8	0	361	2091	5.8	6	3	76	1	367	2167
Avg.												5.9

Yr.	Receiving				Int.		Punt Ret.		K.O. Ret.		Scoring		
	No.	Yds.	TD	Avg.	No.	Yds.	No.	Yds.	No.	Yds.	TD	XP	Pts.
54	1	20	0	20.0	3	14	4	49	4	122	4	2	26
55	6	80	1	13.3	2	13	7	198	10	320	7	13	55
56	5	56	1	11.2	3	72	4	15	7	169	14	22	106
Totals	12	156	2	13.0	8	99	15	262	21	611	25	37	187
Avg.						12.4		17.5		29.1			

* This figure led the nation.

CHRIS BURFORD
STANFORD E, 6-3, 198 Oakland, Calif. (Oakland HS)

All-America 59.

Yr.	Team			Receiving				Punt Ret.		K.O. Ret.		Scoring		
	W	L	T	No.	Yds.	TD	Avg.	No.	Yds.	No.	Yds.	TD	XP	Pts.
57	6	4	0	1	12	1	12.0	1	7	0	0	1	0	6
58	2	8	0	45	493	2	11.0	0	0	0	0	2	2	14
59	3	7	0	*61	*756	6	12.4	1	9	2	30	6	0	36
Totals	11	19	0	107	1261	9	11.8	2	16	2	30	9	2	56
Avg.									8.0		15.0			

Other career figures: 1 rush for 0 yds., 2 passes att., 2 cmp. for 66 yds.
* This figure led the nation.

GEORGE CAFEGO
TENNESSEE
TB, 6-0, 174
Scarbro, W. Va. (Scarbro HS)

Consensus all-America 39, all-America 38. Heisman 4th in 39, 7th in 38. Hall of Fame.
Bowls: Orange 39—Beat Oklahoma, 17-0. Rose 40—injured (Southern Cal won, 14-0).

Yr.	Team W	L	T	Rushing Car.	Yds.	Avg.	Passing Att.	Cmp.	Int.	Pct.	Yds.	TD	Total Offense Plays	Yds.
37	6	3	1	72	501	7.0	50	28	1	.560	317	3	122	818
38	10	0	0	113	645	5.7	35	13	2	.371	141	0	148	786
39	10	0	0	74	443	6.0	20	8	1	.400	92	0	94	535
Totals	26	3	1	259	1589	6.1	105	49	4	.467	550	3	364	2139
Avg.										5.2 per Att.	11.2 per Cmp.		5.9	

Yr.	Interceptions No.	Yds.	Punting No.	Avg.	Punt Ret. No.	Yds.	K.O. Ret. No.	Yds.	Scoring TD	XP	Pts.
37	3	0	59	42.0	21	286	2	109	4	1	25
38	2	27	34	31.5	24	344	6	144	3	6	24
39	0	0	22	38.9	19	253	4	138	2	4	16
Totals	5	27	115	38.3	64	883	12	391	9	11	65
Avg.		5.4				13.8		32.6			

CHRIS "RED" CAGLE
ARMY   HB, 5-9, 167   Merryville, La. (Merryville HS)

Unanimous all-America 28, Consensus all-America 27 and 29. Hall of Fame.

Yr.	Team W	L	T	Rushing Car.	Yds.	Avg.	Passing Att.	Cmp.	Int.	Pct.	Yds.	TD	Total Offense Plays	Yds.	TDR
26	7	1	1	69	393	5.7	9	3	0	.333	42	0	78	435	5
27	9	1	0	100	681	6.8	50	16	3	.320	353	2	150	1034	8
28	8	2	0	105	759	7.2	70	22	8	.314	470	1	175	1229	6
29	6	4	2	140	836	6.0	70	25	14	.357	567	3	210	1403	14
Totals	30	8	2	414	2669	6.4	199	66	25	.332	1432	6	613	4101	33
Avg.							7.2 per Att.			21.7 per Cmp.			6.7		

Yr.	Receiving No.	Yds.	TD	Int. No.	Yds.	Punting No.	Avg.	Punt Ret. No.	Yds.	K.O. Ret. No.	Yds.	Scoring TD	XP	Pts.
26	1	32	1	2	10	0	0.0	0	0	3	63	5	2	32
27	1	32	1	2	41	0	0.0	9	134	4	116	6	3	39
28	1	5	0	2	14	9	33.2	4	73	8	270	5	0	30
29	1	10	0	3	80	0	0.0	6	97	12	263	11	2	68
Totals	4	79	2	9	145	9	33.2	19	304	27	712	27	7	169
Avg.		19.8			16.1		33.2		16.0		26.4			

Also played at Southwestern Louisiana, 1923-25.

PAUL CAMERON
UCLA
TB, 6-0, 185
Burbank, Calif. (Burbank HS)

Consensus all-America 53, all-America 52. Heisman 3rd in 53, 6th in 52.

Bowl: Rose 54—Scored TD; 13- and 28-yard TD passes; passed for 152 yards; 59- and 52-yard punts; intercepted two passes; returned 5 kicks 95 yards (Michigan St. won, 28-20).

Yr.	Team W	L	T	Rushing Car.	Yds.	Avg.	Att.	Cmp.	Passing Int.	Pct.	Yds.	TD	Total Offense Plays	Yds.	TDR
51	5	3	1	159	597	3.8	134	66	9	.493	885	10	293	1482	15
52	8	1	0	75	189	2.5	96	36	5	.375	518	8	171	707	9
53	8	1	0	134	672	5.0	84	30	8	.357	326	5	218	998	17
Totals	21	5	1	368	1458	4.0	314	132	22	.420	1729	23	682	3187	41
Avg.							5.5 per Att.			13.1 per Cmp.			4.7		

Yr.	Interceptions No.	Yds.	Punting No.	Avg.	Punt Ret. No.	Yds.	K.O. Ret. No.	Yds.	Scoring TD	XP	Pts.
51	0	0	0	0.0	0	0	3	74	5	0	30
52	0	0	5	49.0	0	0	0	0	1	0	6
53	3	42	31	41.3	21	284	6	105	12	0	72
Totals	3	42	36	42.4	21	284	9	179	18	0	108
Avg.		14.0				13.5		19.9			

BILLY CANNON
LOUISIANA STATE   HB, 6-1, 208   Baton Rouge, La. (Istrouma HS)

Unanimous all-America 58, Consensus all-America 59. Heisman winner 59, 3rd in 58.

Bowls: Sugar 59—threw 9-yard TD pass, rushed 51 yards (Beat Clemson, 7-0). Sugar 60—Mississippi won, 21-0.

Yr.	Team W	L	T	Rushing Car.	Yds.	Avg.	Att.	Cmp.	Passing Int.	Yds.	Scoring TD	XP	Pts.
57	5	5	0	105	583	5.6	16	7	1	84	6	0	36
58	#10	0	0	115	686	6.0	4	3	0	17	11	8	74
59	9	1	0	139	598	4.3	6	2	2	20	7	2	44
Totals	24	6	0	359	1867	5.2	26	12	3	121	24	10	154
Avg.							4.7 per Att.	10.1 per Cmp.					

Yr.	Receiving No.	Yds.	TD	Avg.	Int. No.	Yds.	Punting No.	Avg.	Punt Ret. No.	Yds.	K.O. Ret. No.	Yds.
57	11	199	1	18.1	0	0	43	34.8	7	39	11	343
58	9	162	1	18.0	3	10	24	34.5	9	89	2	82
59	11	161	0	14.6	4	145	44	39.9	15	221	8	191
Totals	31	522	2	16.8	7	155	111	36.7	31	349	21	616
Avg.						22.1				11.3		29.3

National champions.

FRANK CARIDEO
NOTRE DAME   QB, 5-7, 175   Mt. Vernon, N.Y. (Mt. Vernon HS, Dean Acad., Franklin, Mass.)

Unanimous all-America 29 and 30. Hall of Fame.

Yr.	Team W	L	T	Rushing Car.	Yds.	Avg.	Att.	Cmp.	Passing Int.	Pct.	Yds.	TD	Total Offense Plays	Yds.
28	5	4	0	15	23	1.5	6	1	0	.167	15	0	21	38
29	#9	0	0	11	15	1.4	19	5	3	.263	83	1	30	98
30	#10	0	0	13	52	4.0	3	1	1	.333	4	0	16	56
Totals	24	4	0	39	90	2.3	28	7	4	.250	102	1	67	192
Avg.														2.9

Yr.	Receiving No.	Yds.	Int. No.	Yds.	Punting No.	Avg.	Punt Ret. No.	Yds.	K.O. Ret. No.	Yds.	Scoring TD	XP	Pts.
28	0	24	1	14	23	37.7	22	239	1	14	2	3	15
29	0	0	5	151	51	34.7	33	405	2	31	2	13	25
30	4	64	1	7	38	30.7	37	303	1	13	2	27	39
Totals	4	88	7	172	112	34.0	92	947	4	58	6	43	79
Avg.		22.0		24.6				10.3		14.5			

National champions.

J. C. CAROLINE
ILLINOIS
HB, 6-0, 184
Columbia, S.C. (Booker T. Washington HS)

Consensus all-America 53. Heisman 7th in 53. Hall of Fame.

Yr.	Team W	L	T	G	Rushing Car.	Yds.	Avg.	TD	Receiving No.	Yds.	Avg.	All-Purpose Plays	Yds.	Avg.
53	7	1	1	9	194	1256	6.5	5	7	52	7.4	217	1670	7.7
54	1	8	0	7	93	440	4.7	6	1	12	12.0	111	730	6.6
Totals	8	9	1	16	287	1696	5.9	11	8	64	8.0	328	2400	7.3

Career: 106.0 rush yds. per game; 150.0 all-purpose yds. per game.

Yr.	Punting No.	Yds.	Avg.	Int. No.	Yds.	Punt Ret. No.	Yds.	Avg.	K.O. Ret. No.	Yds.	Avg.	Scoring TD	XP-XPA	Pts.
53	9	344	38.2	—	—	7	129	8.4	9	233	25.9	5	1-1	31
54	16	621	38.8	3	44	3	36	12.0	11	198	18.0	6	1-1	37
Totals	25	965	38.6	3	44	10	165	16.5	20	431	21.6	11	2-2	68

BILL CARPENTER
ARMY E, 6-2, 210 Springfield, Pa. (Springfield HS)

Consensus all-America 59. Hall of Fame. Silver Anniversary Award, NCAA Honors Luncheon 85.

Yr.	Team W	L	T	No.	Receiving Yds.	TD	Avg.	Int. No.	Yds.	K.O. Ret. No.	Yds.	Scoring TD	XP	Pts.
57†	7	2	0	0	0	0	0	0	0	0	0	0	0	0
58	8	0	1	22	453	2	20.6	1	22	1	7	2	0	12
59	4	4	1	43	591	3	13.7	0	0	12	218	4	2	26
Totals	19	6	2	65	1044	5	16.1	1	22	13	225	6	2	38
Avg.									22.0		17.3			

† Injured most of season.

HOWARD "HOPALONG" CASSADY
OHIO STATE
HB, 5-10, 172
Columbus, Ohio (Central HS)

Unanimous all-America 54 and 55. Heisman winner 55, 3rd in 54. Hall of Fame.

Bowl: Rose 55—rushed 92 yards on 21 carries (Beat Southern Cal, 20-7).

Yr.	Team W	L	T	Car.	Rushing Yds.	Avg.	Receiving No.	Yds.
52	6	3	0	65	293	4.5	13	192
53	6	3	0	86	514	6.0	16	273
54	#9	0	0	102	609	6.0	12	137
55	7	2	0	161	958	6.0	1	6
Totals	28	8	0	414	2374	5.7	42	608
Avg.								14.5

Yr.	Interceptions No.	Yds.	Punt Returns No.	Yds.	K.O. Returns No.	Yds.	Scoring TD	Pts.
52	1	3	1	7	8	166	6	36
53	3	74	6	43	15	343	8	48
54	4	109	9	80	7	136	8	48
55	2	44	17	205	10	313	15	90
Totals	10	230	33	335	40	958	37	222
Avg.		23.0		10.2		24.0		

Other career figures: 19 passes att., 8 cmp. for 81 yds. and 1 TD, 3 had int.

National champions.

LYNN CHANDNOIS
MICHIGAN STATE
HB, 6-2, 195
Flint, Mich. (Central HS)
All-America 49.

	Team			Rushing				Passing					Total Offense		
Yr.	W	L	T	Car.	Yds.	Avg.	Att.	Cmp.	Int.	Pct.	Yds.	TD	Plays	Yds.	TDR
46	5	5	0	44	193	4.4	5	0	3	.000	0	0	49	193	6
47	7	2	0	51	240	4.7	1	0	1	.000	0	0	52	240	2
48	6	2	2	91	678	7.5	3	0	1	.000	13	1	94	691	13
49	6	3	0	129	885	6.9	9	3	0	.333	34	0	138	919	10
Totals	24	12	2	315	1996	6.3	18	3	5	.167	47	1	333	2043	31
Avg.														6.1	

	Receiving				Int.		Punt Ret.		K.O. Ret.		Scoring	
Yr.	No.	Yds.	TD	Avg.	No.	Yds.	No.	Yds.	No.	Yds.	TD	Pts.
46	10	175	3	17.5	3	53	0	0	6	106	6	36
47	0	0	0	0.0	6	88	3	52	3	77	2	12
48	4	107	2	26.8	4	86	5	142	4	80	12	72
49	7	127	0	18.1	7	*183	9	144	3	43	10	60
Totals	21	409	5	19.5	20	410	17	338	16	306	30	180
Avg.						20.5		19.9		19.1		

BOB CHAPPUIS
MICHIGAN   HB, 6-0, 180   Toledo, Ohio (De Vilbus HS)
Unanimous all-America 47. Heisman 2nd in 47. Hall of Fame.

Bowl: Rose 48—set Rose Bowl records of 279 total-offense yards, 188 yards passing on 14 of 24 for 2 TDs of 13 and 11 yards (Beat Southern Cal, 49-0).

	Team			Rushing				Passing					Total Offense		
Yr.	W	L	T	Car.	Yds.	Avg.	Att.	Cmp.	Int.	Pct.	Yds.	TD	Plays	Yds.	TDR
42	7	3	0	52	220	4.2	63	30	4	.476	358	2	115	578	3
46	6	2	1	102	531	5.2	78	44	8	.564	734	6	180	1265	10
47	9	0	0	113	419	3.7	84	48	5	.571	976	11	197	1395	16
Totals	22	5	1	267	1170	4.4	225	122	17	.542	2068	19	492	3238	29
Avg.							9.2 per Att.	17.0 per Cmp.		144.2 efficiency				6.6	

	Receiving		Punting		Punt Ret.		K.O. Ret.		Scoring	
Yr.	No.	Yds.	No.	Avg.	No.	Yds.	No.	Yds.	TD	Pts.
42	2	30	0	0.0	0	0	0	0	1	6
46	1	12	4	27.3	12	147	7	165	4	24
47	1	10	3	42.0	8	88	5	105	5	30
Totals	4	52	7	33.6	20	235	12	270	10	60
Avg.		13.0				11.8		22.5		

PAUL CHRISTMAN
MISSOURI TB, 6-0, 195   Maplewood, Mo. (Maplewood HS)

All-America 39. Heisman 3rd in 39, 5th in 40. Hall of Fame.
Bowl: Orange 40—scored TD, 143 total-offense yards (Georgia Tech won, 21-7).

	Team			Rushing				Passing		
Yr.	W	L	T	Car.	Yds.	Avg.	Att.	Cmp.	Int.	Pct.	Yds.	TD
38	6	3	0	111	388	3.5	145	63	19	.434	1087	7
39	8	1	0	94	418	4.4	136	63	12	.463	677	5
40	6	3	0	68	181	2.7	154	69	14	.448	*1131	*13
Totals	20	7	0	273	987	3.6	435	195	45	.448	2895	25
Avg.										6.7 per Att.	14.8 per Cmp.	

	Total Offense			Scoring	
Yr.	Plays	Yds.	TDR	TD	Pts.
38	256	1475	14	7	42
39	230	1095	12	7	42
40	222	1312	18	5	30
Totals	708	3882	44	19	114
Avg.	5.5				

Other career figures: 7 int. by for 49 yds., 54 punts for 36.4 avg., 11 punt ret. for 128 yds.
* This figure led the nation.

CHARLEY CONERLY
MISSISSIPPI HB, 6-0, 184   Clarksdale, Miss. (Clarksdale HS)

Consensus all-America 47. Heisman 4th in 47. Hall of Fame.
Bowl: Delta 47—completed 12 passes for 187 yards and 2 TDs (Beat Texas Christian, 13-9).

	Team			Rushing			Passing						Total Offense		
Yr.	W	L	T	Car.	Yds.	Avg.	Att.	Cmp.	Int.	Pct.	Yds.	TD	Plays	Yds.	TDR
42	2	7	0	—	—	—	56	22	8	.393	305	5	—	—	—
46	2	7	0	86	216	2.5	124	64	13	.516	641	3	210	857	7
47+	8	2	0	104	417	4.0	*233	*133	7	*.571	1367	*18	*337	1784	*27
Totals	12	16	0	—	—	—	413	219	28	.530	2313	26	—	—	—
Avg.									5.6 per Att.		10.6 per Cmp.				

	Int.		Punting			Punt Ret.		K.O. Ret.		Scoring	
Yr.	No.	Yds.	No.	Yds.	Avg.	No.	Yds.	No.	Yds.	TD	Pts.
42	—	—	—	—	—	1	88	—	—	1	6
46	3	30	57	2333	40.9	19	152	5	102	4	24
47	0	0	58	2324	40.1	8	118	0	0	9	54
Totals	—	—	—	—	—	28	358	—	—	14	84
Avg.					12.8						

(In 1942, no rushing figures available; one game missing in passing; no figures available for interceptions, punting and kickoff returns.)
+ National leader in passing efficiency (min. 155 att. per game) in 1947 at 125.8.
* This figure led the nation.

JOHN DAVID CROW
TEXAS A&M
HB, 6-2, 214
Springhill, La. (Springhill HS)

Unanimous all-America 57. Heisman winner 57. Hall of Fame.
Bowl: Gator 58—Tennessee won, 3-0.

Yr.	Team W	L	T	Rushing Car.	Yds.	Avg.	Passing Att.	Cmp.	Yds.	TD	Scoring XP	Pts.
55	7	2	1	66	332	5.0	0	0	0	3	0	18
56	9	0	1	101	561	5.6	7	2	12	10	0	60
57	8	2	0	129	562	4.4	9	5	68	6	1	37
Totals	24	4	2	296	1455	4.9	16	7	80	19	1	115

Yr.	Receiving No.	Yds.	TD	Avg.	Int. No.	Yds.	Punt Ret. No.	Yds.	K.O. Ret. No.	Yds.
55	5	101	1	20.2	1	1	5	57	7	129
56	6	117	2	19.5	2	5	8	136	2	58
57	2	62	0	31.0	5	39	8	55	2	49
Totals	13	280	3	21.5	8	45	21	248	11	236
Avg.						5.6		11.8		21.5

Other career figures: 1 punt for 29 yds.

JIM CROWLEY
NOTRE DAME HB, 5-11, 162 Green Bay, Wis. (East HS)

Consensus all-America 24. Hall of Fame.
Bowl: Rose 25—rushed 59 yards, caught 30-yard pass, kicked three extra points (Beat Stanford, 27-10).
One of the Four Horsemen.

Yr.	Team W	L	T	Rushing Car.	Yds.	Avg.	Passing Att.	Cmp.	Int.	Pct.	Yds.	TD	Total Offense Plays	Yds.
22	8	1	1	75	566	7.5	21	10	1	.476	154	1	96	720
23	9	1	0	88	536	6.1	36	13	4	.361	154	1	124	690
24 #	9	0	0	131	739	5.6	26	14	1	.538	236	2	157	975
Totals	26	2	1	294	1841	6.3	83	37	6	.446	544	4	377	2385
Avg.							6.6 per Att.				14.7 per Cmp.			6.3

Yr.	Receiving No.	Yds.	TD	Avg.	Int. No.	Yds.	Punting No.	Avg.	Punt Ret. No.	Yds.	K.O. Ret. No.	Yds.	Scoring TD	XP	Pts.
22	0	0	0	0.0	2	9	3	36.7	4	36	0	0	5	4	34
23	1	44	0	44.0	4	31	3	23.3	0	0	4	89	4	15	39
24	12	265	3	22.1	0	0	2	43.0	0	0	4	52	9	17	71
Totals	13	309	3	23.8	6	40	8	33.3	4	36	8	141	18	36	144
Avg.				6.7				9.0				17.6			

National champions.

LARRY CSONKA
SYRACUSE FB, 6-3, 230 Stow, Ohio (Stow HS)

Unanimous all-America 67, all-America 66. Heisman 4th in 67. Hall of Fame.
Bowl: Gator 67—scored 1 TD (Tennessee won, 18-12).

Yr.	Team			Rushing			Receiving				K.O. Ret.		Scoring		
	W	L	T	Car.	Yds.	Avg.	No.	Yds.	TD	Avg.	No.	Yds.	TD	XP	Pts.
65	7	3	0	136	795	5.8	2	13	0	6.5	0	0	4	0	24
66	8	2	0	197	1012	5.1	7	48	0	6.9	0	0	7	0	42
67	8	2	0	261	1127	4.3	11	125	2	11.4	4	89	10	2	62
Totals	23	7	0	594	2934	4.9	20	186	2	9.3	4	89	21	2	128
Avg.												22.3			

Other career figures: 8 passes att., 1 cmp. for 21 yds. and 1 int.

BILL DALEY
MICHIGAN HB, 6-2, 206 St. Cloud, Minn. (St. Cloud HS)

Unanimous all-America 43. Heisman 7th in 43.

Yr.	Team			Rushing			Scoring		
	W	L	T	Car.	Yds.	Avg.	TD	XP	Pts.
40	#8	0	0	42	307	7.3	3	0	18
41	#8	0	0	*158	685	4.3	9	0	54
42	5	4	0	86	492	5.7	8	0	48
43	8	1	0	120	817	*6.8	9	3	57
Totals	29	5	0	406	2301	5.7	29	3	177

(Played at Minnesota 1940-41-42.)
National champions (Minnesota). * This figure led the nation.

ERNIE DAVIS

SYRACUSE   HB, 6-2, 210   Elmira, N.Y. (Elmira Free Acad.)

Unanimous all-America 61, Consensus all-America 60. Heisman winner 61. Hall of Fame.

Bowls: Cotton 60—caught 87-yard TD pass for a major-bowl record, scored 14 points (Beat Texas, 23-14). Liberty 61—rushed 140 yards, one TD (Beat Miami, Fla., 15-14).

Yr.	Team W	L	T	Rushing Car.	Yds.	Avg.	Passing Att.	Cmp.	Yds.	TD	Total Offense Plays	Yds.	TDR
59	#10	0	0	98	686	7.0	2	2	13	0	100	699	10
60	7	2	0	112	877	7.8	4	2	23	0	116	900	10
61	7	3	0	150	823	5.5	1	1	74	1	151	897	16
Totals	24	5	0	360	2386	6.6	7	5	110	1	367	2496	36
Avg.												6.8	

Yr.	Receiving No.	Yds.	TD	Avg.	Int. No.	Yds.	Punt Ret. No.	Yds.	K.O. Ret. No.	Yds.	Scoring TD	XP	Pts.
59	11	94	0	8.5	2	33	6	67	3	36	10	4	64
60	11	141	2	12.8	1	0	9	98	4	87	10	2	62
61	16	157	2	9.8	2	73	7	72	3	62	15	4	94
Totals	38	392	4	10.3	5	106	22	237	10	185	35	10	220
Avg.						21.2		10.8		18.5			

National champions.

GLENN DAVIS

ARMY
HB, 5-9, 170
Claremont, Calif. (Bonita HS)

Unanimous all-America 45 and 46, consensus all-America 44. Heisman winner 46, 2nd in 44, 2nd in 45. Hall of Fame.

Yr.	Team W	L	T	Rushing Car.	Yds.	Avg.	Passing Att.	Cmp.	Int.	Pct.	Yds.	TD	Total Offense Plays	Yds.	TDR
43	7	2	1	95	634	6.7	49	21	5	.429	394	4	144	1028	12
44	#9	0	0	58	667	*11.5	10	6	1	.600	129	2	68	796	*22
45	#9	0	0	82	944	*11.5	20	11	3	.550	253	2	102	1197	*20
46	9	0	1	123	712	5.8	47	19	5	.404	396	4	170	1108	17
Totals	34	2	2	358	2957	8.3	126	57	14	.452	1172	12	484	4129	71
Avg.						9.3 per Att.			20.6 per Cmp.					8.5	

Yr.	Receiving No.	Yds.	TD	Avg.	Int. No.	Yds.	Punting No.	Avg.	Punt Ret. No.	Yds.	K.O. Ret. No.	Yds.	Scoring TD	Pts.
43	7	68	1	9.7	3	7	3	27.7	22	264	2	28	8	48
44	13	221	4	17.0	4	92	0	0.0	16	294	4	118	20	*120
45	5	213	0	42.6	2	18	0	0.0	22	230	2	55	18	108
46	20	348	5	17.4	5	30	19	34.7	24	272	2	77	13	78
Totals	45	850	10	18.9	14	147	22	33.7	84	1060	10	278	59	354
Avg.						10.5				12.6		27.8		

National champions. * This figure led the nation.

ERNIE DAVIS

PETE DAWKINS

ARMY   HB, 6-1, 197   Royal Oak, Mich. (Cranbrook School, Bloomfield Hills, Mich.)

Unanimous all-America 58. Heisman winner 58. Academic all-America 57 and 58. Hall of Fame. Silver Anniversary Award, NCAA Honors Luncheon 84. Academic All-America Hall of Fame.

Yr.	Team W	L	T	Rushing Car.	Yds.	Avg.	Passing Att.	Cmp.	Int.	Yds.	Scoring TD	XP	Pts.
56	5	3	1	6	30	5.0	0	0	0	0	3	0	18
57	7	2	0	124	665	5.4	0	0	0	0	11	0	66
58	8	0	1	78	428	5.5	4	2	1	12	12	2	74
Totals	20	5	2	208	1123	5.4	4	2	1	12	26	2	158

Yr.	Receiving No.	Yds.	TD	Avg.	Interceptions No.	Yds.	Punt Ret. No.	Yds.	K.O. Ret. No.	Yds.
56	0	0	0	0.0	0	0	0	0	0	0
57	11	225	3	20.5	3	0	8	80	6	140
58	16	494	6	*30.9	1	33	10	162	7	132
Totals	27	719	9	26.6	4	33	18	242	13	272
Avg.						8.3		13.4		20.9

* This figure led the nation.

LEN DAWSON

PURDUE   QB, 6-0, 180   Alliance, Ohio (Alliance HS)

Academic all-America 56.

Yr.	Team W	L	T	Rushing Car.	Yds.	Passing Att.	Cmp.	Int.	Pct.	Yds.	TD	Total Offense Plays	Yds.	TDR
54+	5	3	1	37	-80	167	87	8	.521	1464	*15	204	1384	16
55	5	3	1	40	-40	155	87	14	.561	1005	7	195	965	7
56	3	4	2	44	23	130	69	10	.531	856	7	174	879	7
Totals	13	10	4	121	-97	452	243	32	.538	3325	29	573	3228	30
Avg.						7.4 per Att.				13.7 per Cmp.		5.6		

Yr.	Interceptions No.	Yds.	Punt Returns No.	Yds.	K.O. Returns No.	Yds.	Scoring TD	XP	Pts.
54	1	0	1	9	2	22	1	14	20
55	1	17	2	10	1	13	0	10	10
56	2	54	1	12	2	20	0	14	14
Totals	4	71	4	31	5	55	1	38	44
Avg.		17.8		7.8		11.0			

+ National leader in passing efficiency in 1954 (min. 15 att. per game) at 145.8.
* This figure led the nation.

MIKE DITKA
PITTSBURGH   E, 6-3, 215   Aliquippa, Pa (Aliquippa HS)
Unanimous all-America 60. Heisman 6th in 60.

	Team			Receiving			Punting		K.O. Ret.		Scoring		
Yr.	W	L	T	No.	Yds.	TD	Avg.	No.	Avg.	No.	Yds.	TD	XP	Pts.
58	5	4	1	18	252	1	14.0	14	42.5	2	22	1	2	8
59	6	4	0	16	249	4	15.6	23	38.3	1	7	4	0	24
60	4	3	3	11	229	2	20.8	7	38.6	3	25	2	2	14
Totals	15	11	4	45	730	7	16.2	44	39.7	6	54	7	4	46
Avg.										9.0				

Other career figures: 2 rushes for minus 16 yds.

GLENN DOBBS
TULSA
TB, 6-3, 195
Frederick, Okla. (Frederick HS)

All-America 42. Heisman 9th in 42. Hall of Fame.

Bowls: Sun 42—threw 30-yard TD pass; 86-yard punt (Beat Texas Tech, 6-0). Sugar 43—76-yard punt and 9 consecutive pass cmp. set Sugar Bowl records, threw TD pass (Tennessee won, 14-7.)

	Team			Rushing			Passing				
Yr.	W	L	T	Car.	Yds.	Avg.	Att.	Cmp.	Int.	Pct.	Yds.
40	7	3	0	74	291	3.9	83	37	6	.446	407
41	7	2	0	65	232	3.6	69	34	10	.493	507
42	10	0	0	72	361	5.0	107	67	4	*.626	1066
Totals	24	5	0	211	884	4.2	259	138	20	.533	1980
Avg.							7.6 per Att.	14.3 per Cmp.			

	Total Offense		Punting		
Yr.	Plays	Yds.	No.	Yds.	Avg.
40	157	698	66	2567	38.9
41	134	739	44	1631	37.1
42	179	1427	26	1256	48.3
Totals	470	2864	136	5454	40.1
Avg.		6.1			

Other career figures: 9 catches for 201 yds., 4 int. by for 34 yds, 4 kickoff ret. for 81 yards, scored 6 TDs, 3 extra points—total 39 points.

* This figure led the nation.

BRIAN DOWLING
YALE   QB, 6-2, 195   Cleveland Heights, Ohio (St. Ignatius HS)

Heisman 9th in 68.

Yr.	Team W	L	T	Rushing Car.	Yds.	Avg.	Att.	Cmp.	Passing Int.	Pct.	Yds.	TD
66	4	5	0	10	51	5.1	22	12	0	.545	89	2
67	8	1	0	45	207	4.6	98	44	10	.449	684	9
68+	8	0	1	82	313	3.8	160	92	9	.575	1554	19
Totals	20	6	1	137	571	4.2	280	148	19	.529	2327	30
Avg.							8.3 per Att.		15.7 per Cmp.	144.5 efficiency		

Yr.	Plays	Total Offense Yds.	TDR	TD	Scoring XP	Pts.
66	32	140	2	0	0	0
67	143	891	13	4	0	24
68	242	1867	26	7	4	46
Totals	417	2898	41	11	4	70
Avg.		6.9				

Other career figures: 3 catches for 98 yds. and 2 TDs, 10 punts for 36.9 avg., 3 punt ret. for 38 yds.

+ National leader in passing efficiency in 1968 (min. 15 att. per game) at 165.8.

BILL DUDLEY
VIRGINIA
HB, 5-10, 175
Bluefield, Va. (Bluefield HS)

Consensus all-America 41. Heisman 5th in 41. Hall of Fame.

Yr.	Team W	L	T	Rushing Car.	Yds.	Avg.	Att.	Cmp.	Passing Int.	Pct.	Yds.	TD	Total Offense Plays	Yds.	TDR
39	5	4	0	48	194	4.0	41	16	1	.390	167	0	89	361	2
40	4	5	0	106	469	4.4	140	67	9	.479	722	4	246	1191	9
41	8	1	0	155	968	*6.2	107	57	8	.533	856	11	262	1824	*29
Totals	17	10	0	309	1631	5.3	288	140	18	.486	1745	15	597	3376	40
Avg.							6.1 per Att.		12.5 per Cmp.		5.7				

Yr.	Receiving No.	Yds.	Avg.	Int. No.	Yds.	Punting No.	Avg.	Punt Ret. No.	Yds.	K.O. Ret. No.	Yds.	TD	Scoring XP	FG	Pts.
39	7	88	12.6	0	0	12	34.0	7	102	5	160	2	9	0	21
40	9	60	6.7	6	83	*73	34.8	19	210	14	356	5	3	0	33
41	6	60	10.0	4	76	61	35.8	28	481	4	89	*18	23	1	*134
Totals	22	208	9.5	10	159	146	35.2	54	793	23	605	25	35	1	188
Avg.					15.9				14.7		26.3				

* This figure led the nation.

RANDY DUNCAN
IOWA QB, 6-0, 180 Des Moines, Iowa (Roosevelt HS)

Unanimous all-America 58. Heisman 2nd in 58.

Bowls: Rose 57—Beat Oregon St., 35-19. Rose 59—scored one TD, threw TD pass, completed 5 of 7 passes, injured in first half (Beat California, 38-12).

Yr.	Team			Rushing		Passing					
	W	L	T	Car.	Yds.	Att.	Cmp.	Int.	Pct.	Yds.	TD
56	8	1	0	10	-14	36	15	3	.417	144	2
57	7	1	1	35	59	119	70	12	.588	1124	10
58+	7	1	1	35	59	172	101	9	*.587	*1347	*11
Totals	22	3	2	80	104	327	186	24	.569	2615	23
Avg.						8.0 per Att.	14.1 per Cmp.		132.6 efficiency		

Yr.	Total Offense			Scoring	
	Plays	Yds.	TDR	TD	Pts.
56	46	130	2	0	0
57	154	1183	15	5	30
58	207	1406	15	4	24
Totals	407	2719	32	9	54
Avg.		6.7			

Other career figures: 2 int. by for 32 yds., 1 punt ret. for 4 yds., 5 kickoff ret. for 103 yds.

+ National leader in passing efficiency in 1958 (min. 15 att. per game) at 135.1.
* This figure led the nation.

NICK EDDY
NOTRE DAME HB, 6-0, 195 Lafayette, Calif. (Tracy HS)

Unanimous all-America 66. Heisman 3rd in 66.

Yr.	Team			Rushing			Receiving			K.O. Ret.		Scoring		
	W	L	T	Car.	Yds.	Avg.	No.	Yds.	TD	Avg.	No.	Yds.	TD	XP	Pts.
64	9	1	0	98	490	5.0	16	352	2	22.0	7	148	7	2	44
65	7	2	1	115	582	5.1	13	233	2	17.9	3	63	6	0	36
66	#9	0	1	78	553	7.1	15	123	0	8.2	4	193	10	0	60
Totals	25	3	2	291	1625	5.6	44	708	4	16.1	14	404	23	2	140
Avg.											28.9				

National champions.

LARRY ELKINS
BAYLOR
FL-HB, 6-1, 187
Brownwood, Texas (Brownwood HS)

Consensus all-America 63 and 64.
Bowl: Bluebonnet 63—Beat Louisiana St., 14-7.

Yr.	Team W	L	T	Receiving No.	Yds.	TD	Avg.	Punt Ret. No.	Yds.	K.O. Ret. No.	Yds.	Scoring TD	XP	Pts.
62	4	6	0	24	370	4	15.4	7	154	3	56	5	0	30
63	7	3	0	*70	*873	8	12.5	12	106	4	82	8	2	50
64	5	5	0	50	851	7	17.0	13	126	0	0	7	8	50
Totals	16	14	0	144	2094	19	14.5	32	386	7	138	20	10	130
Avg.									12.1		19.7			

Other career figures: 11 rushes for 38 yds., 2 int. by for 78 yds., 5 punts for 32.0 avg.
* This figure led the nation.

RAY EVANS
KANSAS HB, 6-1, 191 Kansas City, Kan. (Wyandotte HS)

All-America 47. Hall of Fame. Silver Anniversary Award, NCAA Honors Luncheon 73.
Bowl: Orange 48—2 TDs on 12-yard rush, 12-yard catch (Georgia Tech won, 20-14).

Yr.	Team W	L	T	Rushing Car.	Yds.	Avg.	Passing Att.	Cmp.	Int.	Pct.	Yds.	TD	Total Offense Plays	Yds.	TDR
41	3	6	0	75	193	2.6	48	21	7	.438	232	0	123	425	1
42	2	8	0	111	293	2.6	*200	*101	9	.505	1117	7	311	1410	9
46	7	2	1	112	459	4.1	39	17	4	.436	379	5	151	838	12
47	8	0	2	94	420	4.5	60	30	0	.500	598	4	154	1018	11
Totals	20	16	3	392	1365	3.5	347	169	20	.487	2326	16	739	3691	33
Avg.							6.7 per Att.			13.8 per Cmp.			5.0		

Yr.	Receiving No.	Yds.	Avg.	Int. No.	Yds.	Punting No.	Avg.	Punt Ret. No.	Yds.	K.O. Ret. No.	Yds.	Scoring TD	XP	Pts.
41	18	235	13.1	0	0	4	33.5	12	114	9	195	1	1	7
42	0	0	0.0	*10	76	62	35.0	18	185	12	268	2	1	13
46	3	107	35.7	3	8	0	0.0	14	155	6	146	7	0	42
47	1	11	11.0	3	59	0	0.0	14	230	4	105	7	0	42
Totals	22	353	16.0	16	143	66	34.9	58	684	31	714	17	2	104
Avg.					8.9				11.8		23.0			

* This figure led the nation.

MEL FARR
UCLA   HB, 6-2, 208   Santa Monica, Calif. (Hebert HS, Beaumont, Texas)

Consensus all-America 66. Heisman 7th in 66.

Bowl: Rose 66—rushed 36 yards, caught 22-yard pass (Beat Michigan St., 14-12).

Yr.	Team W	L	T	Rushing Car.	Yds.	Avg.	Receiving No.	Yds.	TD	Avg.	K.O. Ret. No.	Yds.	Scoring TD	XP	Pts.
64	4	6	0	27	86	3.2	3	21	1	7.0	2	35	1	2	8
65	7	2	1	112	785	7.0	7	158	1	22.6	5	63	8	0	48
66	9	1	0	138	809	5.9	12	225	1	18.8	4	77	10	2	62
Totals	20	9	1	277	1680	6.1	22	404	3	18.4	11	175	19	4	118
Avg.												15.9			

Other career figures: 1 pass att., 1 cmp. for 28 yds.

BEATTIE FEATHERS
TENNESSEE
HB, 5-10, 180
Bristol, Va. (Bristol HS)

Consensus all-America 33. Hall of Fame.

Yr.	Team W	L	T	Rushing Car.	Yds.	Avg.	Passing Att.	Cmp.	Int.	Pct.	Yds.	Total Offense Plays	Yds.
31	9	0	1	85	609	7.2	2	1	0	.500	9	87	618
32	9	0	1	112	616	5.5	22	7	3	.318	40	134	656
33	7	3	0	112	663	5.9	16	6	0	.375	77	128	740
Totals	25	3	2	309	1888	6.1	40	14	3	.350	126	349	2014
Avg.							3.2 per Att.			9.0 per Cmp.		5.8	

Yr.	Receiving No.	Yds.	Avg.	Int. No.	Yds.	Punting No.	Avg.	K.O. Ret. No.	Yds.	Scoring TD	Pts.
31	1	12	12.0	5	90	34	36.2	4	98	8	48
32	5	64	12.8	1	0	70	39.4	2	66	12	72
33	9	120	13.3	0	0	74	40.4	2	99	13	78
Totals	15	196	13.1	6	90	178	39.2	8	263	33	198
Avg.					15.0				32.9		

BOB FENIMORE
OKLAHOMA STATE
HB, 6-2, 188
Woodward, Okla. (Woodward HS)

Consensus all-America 45, all-America 44. Heisman 3rd in 45, 9th in 44. Hall of Fame.

Bowls: Cotton 45—2 TDs (Beat Texas Christian, 34-0). Sugar 46—2 TDs, 28-yard TD pass, 125 rushing in 25 carries (Beat St. Mary's, Calif., 33-13).

Yr.	Team W	L	T	Rushing Car.	Yds.	Avg.	Passing Att.	Cmp.	Int.	Pct.	Yds.	TD	Total Offense Plays	Yds.	TDR
43	3	4	0	56	252	4.5	79	32	5	.405	316	5	135	568	8
44	7	1	0	162	897	5.5	79	49	5	*.620	861	4	241	*1758	16
45	8	0	0	142	*1048	*7.4	61	31	7	.508	593	6	203	*1641	18
46	3	7	1	70	163	2.3	78	39	8	.500	497	1	148	660	7
Totals	21	12	1	430	2360	5.5	297	151	25	.508	2267	16	727	4627	49
Avg.							7.6 per Att.			15.0 per Cmp.			6.4		

Yr.	Receiving No.	Yds.	Int. No.	Yds.	Punting No.	Avg.	Punt Ret. No.	Yds.	K.O. Ret. No.	Yds.	Scoring TD	XP	Pts.
43	1	11	6	110	6	41.7	16	227	2	29	3	5	23
44	1	1	3	128	34	37.3	12	86	2	117	12	5	77
45	1	12	7	129	23	39.0	15	157	8	231	12	0	72
46	0	0	2	40	12	31.7	10	135	9	227	6	2	38
Totals	3	24	18	407	75	37.3	53	605	21	604	33	12	210
Avg.		8.0		22.6				11.4		28.8			

* This figure led the nation.

BOB FERGUSON
OHIO STATE   FB, 6-0, 217   Troy, Ohio (Troy HS)

Unanimous all-America 60 and 61. Heisman 2nd in 61.

Yr.	Team W	L	T	Rushing Car.	Yds.	Avg.	Receiving No.	Yds.	TD	Scoring XP	Pts.
59	3	5	1	61	371	6.1	1	3	2	0	12
60	7	2	0	160	853	5.3	3	42	13	0	78
61	#8	0	1	202	938	4.6	1	0	11	2	68
Totals	18	7	2	423	2162	5.1	5	45	26	2	158
Avg.								9.0			

Other career figures: 1 punt ret. for 3 yds., 4 kickoff ret. for 78 yds.
National champions.

CHARLES FLOWERS
MISSISSIPPI FB, 6-0, 198 Marianna, Ark. (Marianna HS)

Consensus all-America 59. Heisman 5th in 59. Academic all-America 59.
Bowls: Sugar 58—Beat Texas, 39-7. Gator 59—injured during game (Beat Florida, 7-3). Sugar 60—Beat Louisiana St., 21-0.

Yr.	Team			Rushing			Receiving		Punting		K.O. Ret.		Scoring	
	W	L	T	Car.	Yds.	Avg.	No.	Yds.	No.	Avg.	No.	Yds.	TD	Pts.
57	8	1	1	59	438	7.4	0	0	0	0.0	1	22	0	0
58	8	2	0	108	546	5.1	5	52	10	44.7	5	89	2	12
59	9	1	0	141	733	5.2	4	68	3	37.0	2	24	11	66
Totals	25	4	1	308	1717	5.6	9	120	13	42.9	8	135	13	78
Avg.								13.3				16.9		

DAN FOLDBERG
ARMY E, 6-1, 185 Dallas, Texas (Sunset HS)

Unanimous all-America 50, all-America 49. Heisman 8th in 50.

Yr.	Team			Rushing		Receiving			Scoring	
	W	L	T	Car.	Yds.	No.	Yds.	TD	Avg.	TD	Pts.
48	8	0	1	0	0	15	212	1	14.1	1	6
49	9	0	0	0	0	20	308	5	15.4	5	30
50	8	1	0	8	57	22	304	5	13.8	5	30
Totals	25	1	1	8	57	57	824	11	14.5	11	66
Avg.					7.1						

Other career figures: 1 kickoff ret. for 7 yds.

GEORGE FRANCK

MINNESOTA HB, 6-0, 175 Davenport, Iowa (Davenport HS)

Consensus all-America. Heisman 3rd in 40.

Yr.	Team W	L	T	Rushing Car.	Yds.	Avg.	Passing Att.	Cmp.	Int.	Pct.	Yds.	Total Offense Plays	Yds.	TDR
38	6	2	0	73	280	3.8	0	0	0	.000	0	73	280	3
39	3	4	1	73	382	5.2	6	3	1	.500	42	79	424	5
40	#8	0	0	99	415	4.2	16	5	2	.313	46	115	461	8
Totals	17	6	1	245	1077	4.4	22	8	3	.364	88	267	1165	16
Avg.													4.4	

Yr.	Receiving No.	Yds.	Int. No.	Yds.	Punting No.	Yds.	Avg.	Punt Ret. No.	Yds.	K.O. Ret. No.	Yds.	Scoring TD	Pts.
38	0	0	4	36	22	934	42.5	11	105	2	42	3	18
39	0	0	4	113	33	1293	39.2	14	166	5	136	5	30
40	3	97	2	29	50	1978	39.6	17	164	6	305	8	48
Totals	3	97	10	178	105	4205	40.0	42	435	13	483	16	96
Avg.		32.3		17.8					10.4		37.2		

National champions.

TUCKER FREDERICKSON

AUBURN TB, 6-2, 210 Hollywood, Fla. (South Broward HS)

Consensus all-America 64. Heisman 6th in 64.
Bowl: Orange 64—outstanding on defense (Nebraska won, 13-7).

Yr.	Team W	L	T	Rushing Car.	Yds.	Avg.	Receiving No.	Yds.
62	6	3	1	54	192	3.6	9	104
63	9	1	0	77	311	4.0	5	34
64	6	4	0	129	571	4.4	14	101
Totals	21	8	1	260	1074	4.1	28	239
Avg.								8.5

Yr.	Interceptions No.	Yds.	Punt Returns No.	Yds.	K.O. Returns No.	Yds.	Scoring TD	Pts.
62	0	0	7	37	9	214	2	12
63	4	31	0	0	4	79	3	18
64	0	0	1	1	6	137	5	30
Totals	4	31	8	38	19	430	10	60
Avg.		7.8		4.8		22.6		

BENNY FRIEDMAN
MICHIGAN   QB, 5-8, 172   Cleveland, Ohio (East Tech HS and Glenville HS)

Consensus all-America 25 and 26. Hall of Fame.

		Team				Passing			
Yr.	W	L	T	Att.	Cmp.	Int.	Pct.	Yds.	TD
24	6	2	0	55	18	6	.327	366	5
25	7	1	0	83	34	8	.410	760	13
26	7	1	0	95	34	12	.358	562	9
Totals	20	4	0	233	86	26	.369	1688	27
Avg.					7.2 per Att.		19.6 per Cmp.		

ROMAN GABRIEL
NORTH CAROLINA STATE
QB, 6-4, 225
Wilmington, N.C. (New Hanover HS)

All-America 60 and 61. Heisman 9th in 61. Academic all-America 60. Hall of Fame.

		Team		Rushing				Passing			
Yr.	W	L	T	Car.	Yds.	Att.	Cmp.	Int.	Pct.	Yds.	TD
59	1	9	0	54	-44	134	81	7	*.604	832	4
60	6	3	1	98	164	186	105	7	.565	1176	8
61	4	6	0	97	196	186	99	6	.532	937	8
Totals	11	18	1	249	316	506	285	20	.563	2945	20
Avg.					1.3		5.8 per Att.			10.3 per Cmp.	

	Total Offense			Scoring		
Yr.	Plays	Yds.	TDR	TD	XP	Pts.
59	188	788	8	4	0	24
60	284	1340	15	7	0	42
61	283	1133	12	4	2	26
Totals	755	3261	35	15	2	92
Avg.		4.3				

Other career figures: 1 int. by for 0 yds.

* This figure led the nation.

ARNOLD GALIFFA

ARMY   QB, 6-2, 190   Donora, Pa. (Donora HS)

Consensus all-America 49. Heisman 4th in 49. Hall of Fame.

Yr.	Team W	L	T	Rushing Car.	Yds.	Avg.	Att.	Cmp.	Passing Int.	Pct.	Yds.	TD
46	9	0	1	8	17	2.1	21	3	3	.143	43	0
47	5	2	2	34	71	2.1	49	22	4	.449	295	3
48	8	0	1	31	101	3.3	95	44	9	.463	701	5
49	9	0	0	51	201	3.9	97	50	5	.515	887	13
Totals	31	2	4	124	390	3.1	262	119	21	.454	1926	21
Avg.							7.4 per Att.				16.2 per Cmp.	

Yr.	Plays	Total Offense Yds.	TDR	Scoring TD	Pts.
46	29	60	0	0	0
47	83	366	5	2	12
48	126	802	8	3	18
49	148	1088	17	4	24
Totals	386	2316	30	9	54
Avg.		6.0			

Other career figures: 7 int. by for 111 yds., 3 punts for 37.7 avg., 1 punt ret. for 12 yds., 3 kickoff ret. for 40 yds.

MIKE GARRETT

SOUTHERN CALIFORNIA   HB, 5-9, 185   Los Angeles, Calif. (Roosevelt HS)

Unanimous all-America 65, all-America 64. Heisman winner 65. Hall of Fame.

Yr.	Team W	L	T	Rushing Car.	Yds.	Avg.	Receiving No.	Yds.	TD
63	7	3	0	128	833	6.5	10	78	2
64	7	3	0	217	948	4.4	17	225	1
65	7	2	1	*267	*1440	*5.4	9	94	1
Totals	21	8	1	612	3221	5.3	36	397	4
Avg.								11.0	

Yr.	Punt Returns No.	Yds.	K.O. Returns No.	Yds.	TD	Scoring XP	Pts.
63	13	90	15	342	4	2	26
64	17	173	10	253	10	2	62
65	13	235	5	105	16	0	96
Totals	43	498	30	700	30	4	184
Avg.		11.6		23.3			

Other career figures: 6 passes att., 3 cmp. for 48 yds. and 2 TDs.

* This figure led the nation.

JAKE GIBBS
MISSISSIPPI   QB, 6-0, 185   Grenada, Miss. (Grenada HS)

Unanimous all-America 60. Heisman 3rd in 60.
Bowls: Gator 59—Beat Florida, 7-3. Sugar 60—threw 43-yard TD pass (Beat Louisiana St., 21-0). Sugar 61—scored 2 TDs (Beat Rice, 14-6).

	Team			Rushing			Passing					Total Offense		
Yr.	W	L	T	Car.	Yds.	Avg.	Att.	Cmp.	Int.	Pct.	Yds.	TD	Plays	Yds.	TDR
58	8	2	0	26	86	3.3	18	7	1	.389	125	1	44	211	3
59	9	1	0	62	228	3.7	94	46	2	.489	755	6	156	983	13
60	#9	0	1	78	246	3.2	109	66	4	.606	970	12	187	1216	17
Totals	26	3	1	166	560	3.4	221	119	7	.538	1850	19	387	2410	33
Avg.						8.4 per Att.		15.5 per Cmp.		149.3 efficiency				6.2	

	Interceptions		Punting		Punt Ret.		K.O. Ret.		Scoring	
Yr.	No.	Yds.	No.	Avg.	No.	Yds.	No.	Yds.	TD	Pts.
58	0	0	0	0.0	8	262	6	75	2	12
59	3	33	25	37.7	5	27	0	0	7	42
60	0	0	26	38.0	9	70	0	0	5	30
Totals	3	33	51	37.9	22	359	6	75	14	84
Avg.		11.0				16.3		12.5		

National champions.

PAUL GIEL
MINNESOTA   HB, 5-11, 185   Winona, Minn. (Winona HS)

Unanimous all-America 53, all-America 52. Heisman 2nd in 53, 3rd in 52. Hall of Fame.

	Team			Rushing			Passing					Total Offense		
Yr.	W	L	T	Car.	Yds.	Avg.	Att.	Cmp.	Int.	Pct.	Yds.	TD	Plays	Yds.	TDR
51	2	6	1	152	789	5.2	124	56	19	.452	689	3	276	1478	9
52	4	3	2	201	650	3.2	100	42	10	.420	643	5	301	1293	10
53	4	4	1	*198	749	3.8	93	50	7	.538	590	4	291	1339	13
Totals	10	13	4	551	2188	4.0	317	148	36	.467	1922	12	868	4110	32
Avg.						6.1 per Att.		13.0 per Cmp.					4.7		

	Receiving				Int.		Punting		Punt Ret.		K.O. Ret.		Scoring		
Yr.	No.	Yds.	TD	Avg.	No.	Yds.	No.	Avg.	No.	Yds.	No.	Yds.	TD	XP	Pts.
51	10	133	1	13.3	1	64	46	34.5	1	5	0	0	6	2	38
52	8	129	1	16.1	0	0	56	37.7	0	0	9	149	5	0	30
53	2	19	0	9.5	5	60	24	34.8	17	*288	6	130	9	0	54
Totals	20	281	2	14.1	6	124	126	36.0	18	293	15	279	20	2	122
Avg.								20.7		16.3		18.6			

* This figure led the nation.

CHRIS GILBERT
TEXAS TB, 5-11, 176 Spring Branch, Texas (Spring Branch HS)

Consensus all-America 68. Heisman 8th in 68.

Bowls: Bluebonnet 66—156 yards rushing on 26 carries, one TD (Beat Mississippi, 19-0). Cotton 69—one TD (Beat Tennessee, 36-13).

Yr.	Team W	L	T	Rushing Car.	Yds.	Avg.	Receiving No.	Yds.	Avg.	K.O. Ret. No.	Yds.	Scoring TD	XP	Pts.
66	6	4	0	206	1080	5.2	2	16	8.0	7	154	6	0	36
67	6	4	0	205	1019	5.0	2	33	16.5	9	221	9	0	54
68	8	1	1	184	1132	6.2	3	75	25.0	4	78	13	4	82
Totals	20	9	1	595	3231	5.4	7	124	17.7	20	453	28	4	172
Avg.											22.7			

Other career figures: 1 punt ret. for 1 yd.

HARRY GILMER
ALABAMA HB, 6-0, 160 Birmingham, Ala. (Woodlawn HS)

All-America 45. Heisman 5th in 45, 7th in 46, 5th in 47.

Bowls: Sugar 45—completed 8 of 8 passes, gains of 41 and 48 and one 10-yard TD (Duke won, 29-26). Rose 46—rushed 116 yards in 16 carries, one of 36 yards, scored one TD, threw 24-yard TD pass (Beat Southern Cal, 34-14). Sugar 48—Texas won, 27-7.

Yr.	Team W	L	T	Rushing Car.	Yds.	Avg.	Passing Att.	Cmp.	Int.	Pct.	Yds.	TD	Total Offense Plays	Yds.	TDR
44	5	1	2	67	319	4.8	71	36	3	.507	449	3	138	768	8
45	9	0	0	79	552	7.0	88	57	3	*.648	905	*13	167	1457	*22
46	7	4	0	133	497	3.7	*160	69	10	.431	930	5	293	1427	8
47	8	2	0	115	305	2.7	93	57	6	.613	610	5	208	915	12
Totals	29	7	2	394	1673	4.2	412	219	22	.532	2894	26	806	4567	50
Avg.							7.0 per Att.				13.2 per Cmp.		5.7		

Yr.	Interceptions No.	Yds.	Punting No.	Avg.	Punt Ret. No.	Yds.	K.O. Ret. No.	Yds.	Scoring TD	Pts.
44	0	0	34	34.4	13	161	7	217	5	30
45	—	—	—	—	12	141	1	50	9	54
46	*8	79	56	38.5	*37	*436	9	230	3	18
47	3	15	29	36.4	21	381	3	77	7	42
Totals	—	—	—	—	83	1119	20	574	24	122
Avg.						13.5		28.7		

(1945 interceptions and punting figures unavailable.)

* This figure led the nation.

GEORGE GIPP

NOTRE DAME HB, 6-0, 180 Laurium, Mich. (Calumet HS)

Consensus all-America 20. Hall of Fame.

	Team			Rushing			Passing					Total Offense		
Yr.	W	L	T	Car.	Yds.	Avg.	Att.	Cmp.	Int.	Pct.	Yds.	TD	Plays	Yds.	TDR
17	6	1	1	63	244	3.9	8	3	2	.375	40	1	71	284	1
18	3	1	2	98	541	5.5	45	19	1	.422	293	1	143	834	7
19	9	0	0	106	729	6.9	72	41	4	.569	727	3	178	1456	10
20	9	0	0	102	827	8.1	62	30	9	.484	709	3	164	1536	11
Totals	27	2	3	369	2341	6.3	187	93	16	.497	1769	8	556	4110	29
Avg.								9.5 per Att.			19.0 per Cmp.			7.4	

	Interceptions		Punting		Punt Ret.		K.O. Ret.			Scoring		
Yr.	No.	Yds.	No.	Avg.	No.	Yds.	No.	Yds.	TD	XP	FG	Pts.
17	0	0	13	34.2	8	99	0	0	0	0	0	0
18	1	10	43	38.2	0	0	3	80	6	7	0	43
19	3	32	12	38.8	1	12	8	166	7	4	1	49
20	1	10	28	40.6	7	106	11	208	8	16	0	64
Totals	5	52	96	38.4	16	217	22	454	21	27	1	156
Avg.		10.4				13.6		20.6				

PAUL GIPSON

HOUSTON FB, 6-0, 205 Conroe, Texas (Washington HS)

All-America 68.

	Team			Rushing			Passing				K.O. Ret.		Scoring		
Yr.	W	L	T	Car.	Yds.	Avg.	Att.	Cmp.	Yds.	TD	No.	Yds.	TD	XP	Pts.
66	8	2	0	18	119	6.6	0	0	0	0	0	0	1	0	6
67	7	3	0	187	1100	5.9	0	0	0	0	8	137	11	2	68
68	6	2	2	242	1550	*6.4	3	2	74	1	8	227	14	0	84
Totals	21	7	2	447	2769	6.2	3	2	74	1	16	364	26	2	158
Avg.												22.8			

* This figure led the nation.

MARSHALL GOLDBERG
PITTSBURGH
HB, 6-0, 190
Elkins, W. Va. (Elkins HS)

Unanimous all-America 38, consensus all-America 37. Heisman 2nd in 38, 3rd in 37. Hall of Fame.
Bowl: Rose 37—Beat Washington, 21-0.

Yr.	Team W	L	T	Rushing Car.	Yds.	Avg.	Passing Att.	Cmp.	Int.	Pct.	Yds.	Total Offense Plays	Yds.
36	7	1	1	177	886	5.0	19	7	2	.368	92	196	978
37	#9	0	1	115	701	6.1	11	6	1	.545	76	126	777
38	8	2	0	90	374	4.2	15	8	1	.533	102	105	476
Totals	24	3	2	382	1961	5.1	45	21	4	.467	270	427	2231
Avg.							6.0 per Att.		12.9 per Cmp.			5.2	

Yr.	Interceptions No.	Yds.	Punt Ret. No.	Yds.	K.O. Ret. No.	Yds.	Scoring TD	Pts.
36	1	18	12	111	5	148	6	36
37	1	55	10	84	2	78	5	30
38	0	0	0	0	1	53	7	42
Totals	2	73	22	195	8	279	18	108
Avg.		36.5		8.9		34.9		

National champions.

PAUL GOVERNALI
COLUMBIA   HB, 5-11, 186   New York, N.Y. (Evander HS)

Consensus all-America 42. Heisman 2nd in 42.

Yr.	Team W	L	T	Rushing Car.	Yds.	Avg.	Passing Att.	Cmp.	Int.	Pct.	Yds.	TD	Total Offense Plays	Yds.	TDR
40	5	2	2	65	211	3.2	52	18	6	.346	261	3	117	472	4
41	3	5	0	138	477	3.5	167	70	11	.419	810	3	305	1287	9
42	3	6	0	103	168	1.6	165	87	*18	.527	*1442	*19	268	1610	22
Totals	11	13	2	306	856	2.8	384	175	35	.456	2513	25	690	3369	35
Avg.							6.5 per Att.		14.4 per Cmp.				4.9		

Yr.	Interceptions No.	Yds.	Punting No.	Avg.	Punt Ret. No.	Yds.	K.O. Ret. No.	Yds.	Scoring TD	Pts.
40	5	55	45	38.0	21	226	3	31	1	6
41	5	45	54	37.7	3	31	8	114	6	36
42	2	46	56	40.0	19	156	6	104	3	18
Totals	12	146	155	38.6	43	413	17	249	10	60
Avg.		12.2				9.6		14.6		

* This figure led the nation.

PAUL GOVERNALI

JIM GRABOWSKI
ILLINOIS FB, 6-2, 211 Chicago, Ill. (Taft HS)

Unanimous all-America 65, all-America 64. Heisman 3rd in 65. Academic all-America 64 and 65.

Bowl: Rose 64—rushed 125 yards on 23 carries (Beat Washington, 17-7).

Yr.	Team W	L	T	Car.	Rushing Yds.	Avg.	Receiving No.	Yds.	Avg.	K.O. Ret. No.	Yds.	Scoring TD	Pts.
63	7	1	1	118	491	4.2	3	21	7.0	2	33	6	36
64	6	3	0	186	1004	*5.4	8	89	11.1	0	0	10	60
65	6	4	0	252	1258	5.0	3	22	7.3	0	0	7	42
Totals	19	8	1	556	2753	5.0	14	132	9.4	2	33	23	138
Avg.											16.5		

OTTO GRAHAM
NORTHWESTERN
HB, 6-1, 190
Waukegan, Ill. (Waukegan HS)

All-America 43. Heisman 3rd in 43. Hall of Fame.

Yr.	Team W	L	T	Car.	Rushing Yds.	Avg.	Att.	Cmp.	Passing Int.	Pct.	Yds.	TD	Plays	Total Offense Yds.	TDR
41	5	3	0	87	259	3.0	74	36	12	.486	599	8	161	858	15
42	1	9	0	136	235	1.7	182	89	*18	.489	1092	3	318	1327	5
43	6	2	0	88	329	3.7	64	32	4	.500	490	4	152	819	13
Totals	12	14	0	311	823	2.6	320	157	34	.491	2181	15	631	3004	33
Avg.							6.8 per Att.			13.9 per Cmp.			4.8		

Yr.	Interceptions No.	Yds.	Punting No.	Avg.	Punt Ret. No.	Yds.	K.O. Ret. No.	Yds.	Scoring TD	XP	Pts.
41	3	59	23	35.7	12	152	5	125	7	0	42
42	2	28	49	35.0	17	193	2	54	2	0	12
43	4	52	18	41.4	12	236	3	76	9	7	61
Totals	9	139	90	36.5	41	581	10	255	18	7	115
Avg.		15.4				14.2		25.5			

* This figure led the nation.

HAROLD "RED" GRANGE
ILLINOIS
HB, 5-10, 170
Wheaton, Ill. (Wheaton HS)

Unanimous all-America 24, consensus all-America 23 and 25. Hall of Fame. Unanimous choice FWAA all-time team.

Yr.	Team W	L	T	Rushing Car.	Yds.	Avg.	Att.	Cmp.	Passing Int.	Pct.	Yds.	TD	Total Offense Plays	Yds.	TDR
23	#8	0	0	129	723	5.6	9	4	0	.444	36	0	138	759	12
24	6	1	1	113	743	6.6	44	26	4	.591	433	2	157	1176	15
25	5	3	0	146	605	4.1	29	10	7	.345	106	1	175	711	7
Totals	19	4	1	388	2071	5.3	82	40	11	.488	575	3	470	2646	34
Avg.								7.0 per Att.			14.4 per Cmp.			5.6	

Yr.	Receiving No.	Yds.	TD	Avg.	Int. No.	Yds.	Punting No.	Avg.	Punt Ret. No.	Yds.	K.O. Ret. No.	Yds.	Scoring TD	Pts.
23	10	178	1	17.8	3	140	1	42.0	15	212	1	7	12	72
24	2	40	0	20.0	2	24	0	0.0	11	83	4	136	13	78
25	2	35	1	17.5	6	83	1	26.0	22	191	10	310	6	36
Totals	14	253	2	18.1	11	247	2	34.0	48	486	15	453	31	186
Avg.						22.5				10.1		30.2		

National champions.

BOBBY GRAYSON
STANFORD   FB, 5-11, 190   Portland, Ore. (Jefferson HS)

Unanimous all-America 35, consensus all-America 34. Hall of Fame.

Bowls: Rose 34—152 yards rushing (Columbia won, 7-0). Rose 35—scored TD, rushed for 59 yards (Alabama won, 29-13). Rose 36—Beat Southern Methodist, 7-0.

Yr.	Team W	L	T	Rushing Car.	Yds.	Avg.	Att.	Cmp.	Passing Int.	Pct.	Yds.	TD	Total Offense Plays	Yds.	TDR
33	8	1	1	113	350	3.1	29	14	1	.483	233	2	142	583	6
34	9	0	1	150	646	4.3	11	6	2	.545	48	0	161	694	10
35	7	1	0	142	551	3.9	41	21	5	.512	280	1	183	831	5
Totals	24	2	2	405	1547	3.8	81	41	8	.506	561	3	486	2108	21
Avg.								6.9 per Att.			13.7 per Cmp.			4.3	

Yr.	Interceptions No.	Yds.	K.O. Returns No.	Yds.	Scoring TD	Pts.
33	2	28	2	45	4	24
34	5	70	2	51	10	60
35	1	42	2	36	4	24
Totals	8	140	6	132	18	108
Avg.		17.5		22.0		

Other career figures: 1 punt ret. for 5 yds.

BOB GRIESE
PURDUE   QB, 6-1, 185   Evansville, Ind. (Rex Mundi HS)

Consensus all-America 65, all-America 66. Heisman 2nd in 66, 8th in 65. Hall of Fame.
Bowl: Rose 67—completed 10 of 18 passes for 139 yards, kicked two extra points (Purdue won, 14-13).

Yr.	Team			Rushing		Passing					
	W	L	T	Car.	Yds.	Att.	Cmp.	Int.	Pct.	Yds.	TD
64	6	3	0	82	147	156	76	10	.487	934	5
65	7	2	1	111	65	238	142	8	.597	1719	11
66	8	2	0	71	215	215	130	11	.605	1749	12
Totals	21	7	1	264	427	609	348	29	.571	4402	28
Avg.							7.2 per Att.		12.6 per Cmp.		

Yr.	Total Offense			Scoring					
	Plays	Yds.	TDR	TD	PATs Att.	Made	FGs Att.	Made	Pts.
64	238	1081	9	4	23	19	2	1	46
65	349	1784	15	4	26	23	8	5	62
66	286	1964	18	6	37	33	6	4	81
Totals	873	4829	42	14	86	75	16	10	189
Avg.		5.5				.872		.625	

Other career figures: 58 punts for 33.3 avg.

RALPH GUGLIELMI
NOTRE DAME   QB, 6-0, 185   Columbus, Ohio (Grandview HS)

Unanimous all-America 54. Heisman 4th in 54.

Yr.	Team			Rushing		Passing					
	W	L	T	Car.	Yds.	Att.	Cmp.	Int.	Pct.	Yds.	TD
51	7	2	1	21	-32	53	27	4	.509	438	0
52	7	2	1	48	31	143	62	9	.434	725	4
53	9	0	1	60	74	113	52	4	.460	792	8
54	9	1	0	79	95	127	68	7	.535	1162	6
Totals	32	5	3	208	168	436	209	24	.479	3117	18
Avg.						7.1 per Att.		14.9 per Cmp.			

Yr.	Total Offense			Scoring		
	Plays	Yds.	TDR	TD	XP	Pts.
51	74	406	1	1	0	6
52	191	756	5	1	0	6
53	173	866	14	6	5	41
54	206	1257	11	5	1	31
Totals	644	3285	31	13	6	84
Avg.		5.1				

Other career figures: 10 int. by for 97 yds., 2 kickoff ret. for 15 yds.

JOHN HADL
KANSAS   QB-HB, 6-1, 205   Lawrence, Kan. (Lawrence HS)

All-America 60 and 61. Heisman 7th in 61.
Bowl: Bluebonnet 61—completed 7 of 10 passes, 41-yard rush (Beat Rice, 33-7).

Yr.	Team			Rushing			Passing					Total Offense		
	W	L	T	Car.	Yds.	Avg.	Att.	Cmp.	Int.	Pct.	Yds.	TD	Plays	Yds.	TDR
59	5	5	0	68	348	5.1	14	5	2	.357	50	2	82	398	10
60	7	2	1	108	375	3.5	87	43	5	.494	562	3	195	937	10
61	6	3	1	128	293	2.3	93	44	6	.473	665	7	221	958	13
Totals	18	10	2	304	1016	3.3	194	92	13	.474	1277	12	498	2293	33
Avg.							6.6 per Att.			13.9 per Cmp.			4.6		

Yr.	Receiving			Int.			Punting			Punt Ret.		K.O. Ret.		Scoring		
	No.	Yds.	TD	No.	Yds.	No.	Yds.	Avg.	No.	Yds.	No.	Yds.	TD	XP	Pts.
59	7	126	1	3	105	43	1960	*45.6	10	87	10	296	8	0	48
60	2	18	0	0	0	43	1743	40.5	9	40	4	87	7	0	42
61	1	-6	0	1	3	47	1696	36.1	17	191	8	165	6	2	38
Totals	10	138	1	4	108	133	5399	40.6	36	318	22	548	21	2	128
Avg.		13.8			27.0					8.8		24.7			

* This figure led the nation.

TERRY HANRATTY
NOTRE DAME   QB, 6-1, 200   Butler, Pa. (Butler HS)

Consensus all-America 68. Heisman 3rd in 68, 8th in 66, 10th in 67.

Yr.	Team			Rushing			Passing				
	W	L	T	Car.	Yds.	Avg.	Att.	Cmp.	Int.	Pct.	Yds.	TD
66	#9	0	1	50	124	2.5	147	78	10	.531	1247	8
67	8	2	0	75	183	2.4	206	110	15	.534	1439	9
68	7	2	1	56	279	5.0	197	116	9	.589	1466	10
Totals	24	4	2	181	586	3.2	550	304	34	.553	4152	27
Avg.							7.5 per Att.			13.7 per Cmp.		

Yr.	Total Offense			Scoring		
	Plays	Yds.	TDR	TD	XP	Pts.
66	197	1371	13	5	2	32
67	281	1622	16	7	0	42
68	253	1745	14	4	0	24
Totals	731	4738	43	16	2	98
Avg.		6.5				

National champions.

TOM HARMON
MICHIGAN
HB, 6-0, 195
Gary, Ind. (Horace Mann HS)

Unanimous all-America 40, consensus all-America 39. Heisman winner 40, 2nd in 39. Hall of Fame.

Yr.	Team W	L	T	Rushing Car.	Yds.	Avg.	Att.	Cmp.	Passing Int.	Pct.	Yds.	TD	Total Offense Plays	Yds.	TDR
38	6	1	1	77	398	5.2	45	21	1	.467	310	3	122	708	6
39	6	2	0	129	868	6.7	94	37	8	.394	488	6	223	1356	*20
40	7	1	0	186	844	4.5	93	42	11	.452	502	7	279	1346	*23
Totals	19	4	1	392	2110	5.4	232	100	20	.431	1300	16	624	3410	49
Avg.										5.6 per Att.	13.0 per Cmp.			5.5	

Yr.	Receiving No.	Yds.	Int. No.	Yds.	Punting No.	Avg.	Punt Ret. No.	Yds.	K.O. Ret. No.	Yds.	TD	Scoring XP	FG	Pts.
38	0	0	0	0	0	0.0	2	11	0	0	3	0	0	18
39	4	110	3	98	2	55.0	0	0	5	132	*14	15	1	*102
40	0	0	3	20	43	38.6	21	244	6	204	16	18	1	*117
Totals	4	110	6	118	45	39.3	23	255	11	336	33	33	2	237
Avg.		27.5		19.7				11.1		30.5				

* This figure led the nation.

JIMMY HARRIS
OKLAHOMA   QB, 6-1, 170   Terrell, Texas (Terrell HS)

Bowls: Orange 56—completed 3 of 5 passes for 34 yards with no interceptions, rushed 50 yards on 9 carries and intercepted 1 pass for 12 yards (Beat Maryland, 20-6).

Yr.	Team W	L	T	G	Rushing Car.	Yds.	Att.	Cmp.	Passing Int.	Pct.	Yds.	TD	Total Offense Plays	Yds.	TDR
54	10	0	0	10	73	427	18	5	1	.278	81	0	91	508	3
55	#10	0	0	10	96	398	20	8	2	.400	148	2	116	546	6
56	#10	0	0	10	76	362	37	23	1	.622	482	8	113	844	12
Totals	30	0	0	30	245	1187	75	36	4	.480	711	10	320	1898	21

Career: 9.5 per pass att., 19.8 per cmp., 161.0 efficiency, 63.3 total offense yds. per game; 5.9 per play.

Other career figures: 96 pts. (kicked 24 extra points); 4.8 yds. per rush; 4 int. by, 76 yds. 19.0 avg.; 10 punt ret., 146 yds.

National champions.

LEON HART
NOTRE DAME
E, 6-5, 260
Turtle Creek, Pa. (Turtle Creek HS)

Unanimous all-America 49, consensus all-America 48, all-America 47. Heisman winner 49. Hall of Fame.

	Team				Receiving			Scoring	
Yr.	W	L	T	No.	Yds.	TD	Avg.	TD	Pts.
46	#8	0	1	5	107	1	21.4	1	6
47	#9	0	0	9	147	3	16.3	3	18
48	9	0	1	16	231	4	14.4	4	24
49	#10	0	0	19	257	5	13.5	5	30
Totals	36	0	2	49	742	13	15.1	13	78

National champions.

LEON HEATH
OKLAHOMA FB, 6-1, 195 Hollis, Okla. (Hollis HS)

Consensus all-America 50. Heisman 7th in 50.

Bowls: Sugar 49—rushed 56 yards (Beat North Caro., 14-6). Sugar 50—set Sugar Bowl records with 170 yards rushing and 86-yard TD rush, also 34-yard TD rush (Beat Louisiana St., 35-0). Sugar 51—rushed 121 yards on 20 carries (Kentucky won, 13-7).

	Team			Rushing			Receiving			K.O. Ret.		Scoring	
Yr.	W	L	T	Car.	Yds.	Avg.	No.	Yds.	TD	Avg.	No.	Yds.	TD	Pts.
48	9	1	0	63	379	6.0	4	93	2	23.3	4	69	7	42
49	10	0	0	75	684	*9.1	3	101	0	33.7	3	75	6	36
50	#10	0	0	102	606	5.9	11	205	2	18.6	2	26	6	36
Totals	29	1	0	240	1669	7.0	18	399	4	22.2	9	170	19	114
Avg.												18.9		

National champions. * This figure led the nation.

STAN HEATH
NEVADA-RENO   QB, 6-1, 185   Milwaukee, Wis. (Shorewood HS)

All-America 48. Heisman 5th in 48.
Bowls: Salad 48—Beat North Texas, 13-6. Harbor 49—injured in first half (Villanova won, 27-7).

Yr.	Team W	L	T	Rushing Car.	Yds.	Att.	Cmp.	Passing Int.	Pct.	Yds.	TD
46†	4	5	0	3	-25	33	7	6	.212	150	1
47	8	2	0	7	-21	134	59	9	.440	742	3
48+	9	1	0	11	-13	*222	*126	9	.568	*2005	*22
Totals	21	8	0	21	-59	389	192	24	.494	2897	26
Avg.							7.4 per Att.			15.1 per Cmp.	

Yr.	Plays	Total Offense Yds.	TDR	Scoring TD	Pts.
46†	36	125	1	0	0
47	141	721	3	0	0
48	233	*1992	*23	1	6
Totals	410	2838	27	1	6
Avg.	6.9				

† Played at Wisconsin in 46.
Other career figures: 2 punt ret. for 29 yds., 2 kickoff ret. for 27 yds.
+ National leader in passing efficiency in 1948 (min. 15 att. per game) at 157.2.
* This figure led the nation.

DON HEINRICH
WASHINGTON   QB, 6-0, 181   Bremerton, Wash. (Bremerton HS)

All-America 52 and 50. Heisman 9th in 52. Hall of Fame.

Yr.	Team W	L	T	Rushing Car.	Yds.	Att.	Cmp.	Passing Int.	Pct.	Yds.	TD
49	3	7	0	30	-28	119	64	7	.538	899	6
50	8	2	0	50	-39	221	*134	9	*.606	*1846	14
52	7	3	0	24	5	270	*137	17	.507	1647	13
Totals	18	12	0	104	-62	610	335	33	.549	4392	33
Avg.							7.2 per Att.			13.1 per Cmp.	

Yr.	Plays	Total Offense Yds.	TDR	Punting No.	Avg.	Scoring TD	Pts.
49	149	871	9	34	36.3	3	18
50	271	1807	17	40	34.5	3	18
52	294	1652	17	47	26.3	4	24
Totals	714	4330	43	121	35.7	10	60
Avg.		6.1					

* This figure led the nation.

WILLIE HESTON
MICHIGAN HB, 5-8, 190 Grants Pass, Ore. (Grants Pass HS)

Consensus all-America 03 and 04. Hall of Fame. FWAA all-time team.

Bowl: Rose 02—In 18 carries, one of 49 yards, rushed for 170 yards—a Rose Bowl record that stood for 57 years (Beat Stanford, 49-0).

	Team				Rushing†		Scoring	
Yr.	W	L	T	Car.	Yds.	Avg.	*TD	Pts.
01	#10	0	0	67	684	10.2	20	100
02	#11	0	0	56	487	8.7	15	75
03	11	0	1	102	482	4.7	16	80
04	10	0	0	54	686	12.7	21	105
Totals	42	0	1	279	2339	8.4	72	360

† Rushing statistics available for 17 of 36 career games. * TDs worth 5 pts.
# National champions.

BILL HILLENBRAND
INDIANA HB, 6-0, 195 Evansville, Ind. (Memorial HS)

Consensus all-America 42. Heisman 5th in 42.

	Team			Rushing			Passing					Total Offense		
Yr.	W	L	T	Car.	Yds.	Avg.	Att.	Cmp.	Int.	Pct.	Yds.	TD	Plays	Yds.	TDR
41	2	6	0	140	263	1.9	59	18	9	.305	412	5	199	675	12
42	7	3	0	130	498	3.8	102	50	8	.490	901	9	232	1399	15
Totals	9	9	0	270	761	2.8	161	68	17	.422	1313	14	431	2074	27
Avg.								8.2 per Att.			19.3 per Cmp.			4.8	

	Receiving			Int.		Punting		Punt Ret.		K.O. Ret.		Scoring		
Yr.	No.	Yds.	Avg.	No.	Yds.	No.	Avg.	No.	Yds.	No.	Yds.	TD	XP	Pts.
41	8	89	11.1	3	87	19	34.7	42	561	8	174	7	0	42
42	2	11	5.5	0	0	12	30.3	23	*481	5	139	6	4	40
Totals	10	100	10.0	3	87	31	33.0	65	1042	13	313	13	4	82
Avg.					29.0				16.0		24.1			

* This figure led the nation.

MIKE HOLOVAK
BOSTON COLLEGE FB, 6-2, 214 Lansford, Pa. (Seton Hall HS)

Consensus all-America 42. Heisman 4th in 42.

Bowls: Sugar 41—scored one TD (Beat Tennessee, 19-13). Orange 43—set Orange Bowl records of 158 yards rushing, 15.8 yards per carry and 18 points, on rushes of 65, 35 and 2 yards; caught 45-yard pass (Alabama won, 37-21).

	Team			Rushing				Scoring	
Yr.	W	L	T	Car.	Yds.	Avg.	TD	XP	Pts.
40	10	0	0	101	532	5.3	11	0	66
41	7	3	0	118	586	5.0	5	0	30
42	8	1	0	174	965	5.5	7	2	44
Totals	25	4	0	393	2083	5.3	23	2	140

DAVE HOPPMANN
IOWA STATE TB, 6-1, 195 Madison, Wis. (East HS)

All-America 62.

	Team			Rushing					Passing			
Yr.	W	L	T	Car.	Yds.	Avg.	Att.	Cmp.	Int.	Pct.	Yds.	TD
60	7	3	0	161	844	5.2	40	17	6	.425	214	3
61	5	5	0	*229	920	4.0	91	41	10	.451	718	8
62	5	5	0	198	798	4.0	89	40	6	.449	679	6
Totals	17	13	0	588	2562	4.4	220	98	22	.445	1611	17
Avg.										7.3 per Att.	16.4 per Cmp.	

	Total Offense			K.O. Ret.		Scoring	
Yr.	Plays	Yds.	TDR	No.	Yds.	TD	Pts.
60	201	1058	8	1	19	5	30
61	*320	*1638	13	4	59	5	30
62	287	1477	17	13	277	11	66
Totals	808	4173	38	18	355	21	126
Avg.		5.2			19.7		

Other career figures: 13 punt ret. for 100 yds., 1 int. by for 0 yds., 3 catches for 43 yds.

* This figure led the nation.

PAUL HORNUNG
NOTRE DAME
QB, 6-2, 205
Louisville, Ky. (Flaget HS)

Consensus all-America 55, all-America 56. Heisman winner 56, 5th in 55. Hall of Fame.

Yr.	Team W	L	T	Rushing Car.	Yds.	Avg.	Att.	Cmp.	Passing Int.	Pct.	Yds.	TD	Total Offense Plays	Yds.	TDR
54	9	1	0	23	159	6.9	19	5	0	.263	36	0	42	195	2
55	8	2	0	92	472	5.1	103	46	10	.447	743	9	195	1215	15
56	2	8	0	94	420	4.5	111	59	13	.532	917	3	205	1337	10
Totals	19	11	0	209	1051	5.0	233	110	23	.472	1696	12	442	2747	27
Avg.							7.3 per Att.				15.4 per Cmp.			6.2	

Yr.	Receiving No.	Yds.	Int. No.	Yds.	Punting No.	Avg.	Punt Ret. No.	Yds.	K.O. Ret. No.	Yds.	TD	Scoring XP	FG	Pts.
54	0	0	3	94	5	38.8	1	6	1	58	2	6	0	18
55	0	0	5	59	28	36.3	0	0	6	109	6	5	2	47
56	3	26	2	59	31	37.6	4	63	16	496	7	14	0	56
Totals	3	26	10	212	64	37.2	5	69	23	663	15	25	2	121
Avg.		8.7		21.2				13.8		28.8				

LES HORVATH
OHIO STATE   QB, 5-10, 167   Parma, Ohio (Parma HS)

Unanimous all-America 44. Heisman winner 44. Hall of Fame.

Yr.	Team W	L	T	Rushing Car.	Yds.	Avg.	Att.	Cmp.	Passing Int.	Pct.	Yds.	TD
41	6	1	1	33	145	4.4	0	0	0	.000	0	0
42	#9	1	0	100	481	4.8	18	11	1	.611	165	0
44	9	0	0	163	905	5.6	31	14	3	.452	345	4
Totals	24	2	1	296	1531	5.2	49	25	4	.510	510	4
Avg.							10.4 per Att.				20.4 per Cmp.	

Yr.	Total Offense Plays	Yds.	TDR	Receiving No.	Yds.	Scoring TD	Pts.
41	33	145	0	0	0	0	0
42	118	646	6	9	139	6	36
44	194	1250	16	1	17	12	72
Totals	345	2041	22	10	156	18	108
Avg.		5.9			15.6		

Other career figures: 2 int. by for 31 yds., 3 punt ret. for 42 yds., 1 kickoff ret. for 15 yds.
National champions.

MILLARD "DIXIE" HOWELL
ALABAMA   HB, 5-10, 164   Hartford, Ala. (Hartford HS)

Consensus all-America 34. Hall of Fame.
Bowl: Rose 35—completed 9 of 12 passes for 160 yards and one 59-yard TD, rushed for 79 yards including a 67-yard TD, returned four kicks 74 yards and punted six times for a 43.8 avg. (Beat Stanford, 29-13).

	Team			Rushing				Passing			
Yr.	W	L	T	Car.	Yds.	Avg.	Att.	Cmp.	Int.	Pct.	Yds.	TD
32	8	2	0	84	369	4.4	27	10	1	.370	129	1
33	7	1	1	124	630	5.1	48	20	6	.417	271	0
34	9	0	0	135	840	6.2	76	41	3	.539	597	3
Totals	24	3	1	343	1839	5.4	151	71	10	.470	997	4
Avg.								6.6 per Att.			14.0 per Cmp.	

	Total Offense			Punting		Scoring	
Yr.	Plays	Yds.	TDR	No.	Avg.	TD	Pts.
32	111	498	4	15	39.0	3	18
33	172	901	9	81	39.7	9	54
34	211	1437	13	40	42.1	10	60
Totals	494	2836	26	136	40.3	22	132
Avg.		5.7					

BILLY HOWTON
RICE   E, 6-2, 180   Plainview, Texas (Plainview HS)

All-America 51.
Bowl: Cotton 50—Beat North Caro., 27-13.

	Team				Receiving			Int.		K.O. Ret.		Scoring	
Yr.	W	L	T	No.	Yds.	TD	Avg.	No.	Yds.	No.	Yds.	TD	Pts.
49	9	1	0	7	97	0	13.9	0	0	0	0	0	0
50	6	4	0	24	445	5	18.5	0	0	0	0	6	36
51	5	5	0	33	747	7	*22.6	2	17	5	47	7	42
Totals	20	10	0	64	1289	12	20.1	2	17	5	47	13	78
Avg.								8.5		9.4			

Other career figures: 1 punt for 28 yds., 7 rushes for 12 yds.
* This figure led the nation.

JOHN HUARTE
NOTRE DAME
QB, 6-0, 180
Anaheim, Calif. (Mater Dei HS, Santa Ana, Calif.)

Consensus all-America 64. Heisman winner 64.

	Team			Rushing		Passing					
Yr.	W	L	T	Car.	Yds.	Att.	Cmp.	Int.	Pct.	Yds.	TD
62	5	5	0	4	-14	8	4	0	.500	38	0
63	2	7	0	11	-53	42	20	0	.476	243	1
64	#9	1	0	37	7	205	114	11	.556	2062	16
Totals	16	13	0	51	-60	255	138	11	.541	2343	17
Avg.						9.2 per Att.	17.0 per Cmp.		144.7 efficiency		

		Total Offense			Scoring	
Yr.	Plays	Yds.	TDR		TD	Pts.
62	11	24	0		0	0
63	53	190	1		0	0
64	242	2069	19		3	18
Totals	306	2283	20		3	18
Avg.		7.5				

Other career figures: 1 catch for 11 yds.
National champions.

DON HUTSON
ALABAMA   E, 6-1, 185   Pine Bluff, Ark. (Pine Bluff HS)

Consensus all-America 34. Hall of Fame. FWAA all-time team.

Bowl: Rose 35—caught 6 passes for 165 yards, including TDs of 59 and 54 yards (Beat Stanford, 29-13).

	Team			Rushing		Receiving				Scoring	
Yr.	W	L	T	Car.	Yds.	No.	Yds.	TD	Avg.	TD	Pts.
32	8	2	0	0	0	3	30	0	10.0	0	0
33	7	1	1	0	0	4	48	0	12.0	0	0
34	9	0	0	8	47	19	326	3	17.2	3	18
Totals	24	3	1	8	47	26	404	3	15.5	3	18
Avg.					5.9						

VIC JANOWICZ
OHIO STATE
HB, 5-9, 189
Elyria, Ohio (Elyria HS)

Unanimous all-America 50. Heisman winner 50. Hall of Fame.
Bowl: Rose 50—intercepted 2 passes, returned one 46 yards (Beat California, 17-14).

Yr.	Team W	L	T	Rushing Car.	Yds.	Avg.	Passing Att.	Cmp.	Int.	Pct.	Yds.	TD	Total Offense Plays	Yds.	TDR
49	6	1	2	30	112	3.7	4	2	0	.500	50	0	34	162	2
50	6	3	0	114	314	2.8	77	32	7	.416	561	11	191	875	16
51	4	3	2	106	376	3.5	25	7	3	.280	74	2	131	450	3
Totals	16	7	4	250	802	3.2	106	41	10	.387	685	13	356	1487	21
Avg.										6.5 per Att.		16.7 per Cmp.		4.2	

Yr.	Receiving No.	Yds.	Int. No.	Yds.	Punting No.	Avg.	Punt Ret. No.	Yds.	K.O. Ret. No.	Yds.	Scoring TD	XP	FG	Pts.
49	1	24	0	0	4	34.3	10	120	7	144	2	2	0	14
50	1	17	1	18	54	36.5	8	107	0	0	5	26	3	65
51	7	126	1	0	62	39.5	4	32	1	34	1	9	3	24
Totals	9	167	2	18	120	37.9	22	259	8	178	8	37	6	103
Avg.		18.6		9.0				11.8		22.3				

JACK JENSEN
CALIFORNIA   FB, 5-11, 195   Oakland, Calif. (Oakland HS)

Consensus all-America 48. Heisman 4th in 48. Hall of Fame.
Bowl: Rose 49—scored on 67-yard rush, injured in 3rd quarter (Northwestern won, 20-14).

Yr.	Team W	L	T	Rushing Car.	Yds.	Avg.	Passing Att.	Cmp.	Int.	Pct.	Yds.	TD	Total Offense Plays	Yds.	TDR
46	2	7	0	51	189	3.7	20	6	3	.300	105	2	71	294	5
47	9	1	0	86	434	5.0	22	11	1	.500	271	3	108	705	6
48	10	0	0	137	1010	7.4	26	6	6	.231	150	1	163	1160	7
Totals	21	8	0	274	1633	6.0	68	23	10	.338	526	6	342	2159	18
Avg.										7.7 per Att.		22.9 per Cmp.		6.3	

Yr.	Receiving No.	Yds.	TD	Int. No.	Yds.	Punting No.	Avg.	Punt Ret. No.	Yds.	K.O. Ret. No.	Yds.	Scoring TD	Pts.
46	4	111	1	0	0	27	35.1	10	125	3	94	3	18
47	0	0	0	7	102	43	37.1	2	21	2	37	3	18
48	1	23	0	1	19	24	37.0	3	32	7	158	6	36
Totals	5	134	1	8	121	94	36.5	15	178	12	289	12	72
Avg.		26.8			15.1				11.9		24.1		

CHARLEY JOHNSON
NEW MEXICO STATE   QB, 6-1, 190   Big Spring, Texas (Big Spring HS)

Bowls: Sun 60—threw TD passes of 57 and 15 yards (Beat North Texas, 28-8). Sun 61—completed 18 of 26 passes for 180 yards and 2 TDs (Beat Utah St., 20-13).

Yr.	Team W	L	T	Rushing Car.	Yds.	Avg.	Att.	Cmp.	Passing Int.	Pct.	Yds.	TD
58	4	6	0	14	159	1.4	179	97	11	.542	1184	9
59+	7	3	0	52	186	3.6	199	105	9	.528	1449	*18
60#	10	0	0	63	123	2.0	199	109	6	.548	1511	*13
Totals	21	9	0	229	468	2.0	577	311	26	.539	4144	40
Avg.							7.2 per Att.	13.3 per Cmp.			129.1 efficiency	

Yr.	Plays	Total Offense Yds.	TDR	Scoring TD	Pts.
58	293	1343	9	0	0
59	251	1635	*18	0	0
60	262	1634	14	1	6
Totals	806	4612	41	1	6
Avg.		5.7			

Other career figures: 5 int. by for 55 yds., 104 punts for 34.8 avg., 3 kickoff ret. for 35 yds.
+ National leader in passing efficiency in 1959 (min. 15 att. per game) at 135.7.
# National leader in passing efficiency in 1960 (min. 15 att. per game) at 134.1.
* This figure led the nation.

RON JOHNSON
MICHIGAN   HB, 6-1, 205   Detroit, Mich. (Northwestern HS)

All-America 68. Heisman 6th in 68.

Yr.	Team W	L	T	Car.	Rushing Yds.	Avg.	Total Offense Plays	Yds.
66	6	4	0	12	44	3.7	12	44
67	4	6	0	220	1005	4.6	220	1005
68	8	2	0	255	1391	5.5	256	1391
Totals	18	12	0	487	2440	5.0	488	2440
Avg.								5.0

Yr.	No.	Receiving Yds.	TD	Avg.	K.O. Returns No.	Yds.	TD	Scoring XP	Pts.
66	0	0	0	0.0	5	42	0	0	0
67	13	179	1	13.8	26	498	8	0	48
68	14	166	0	11.9	9	150	19	2	116
Totals	27	345	1	12.8	40	690	27	2	164
Avg.						17.3			

Other career figures: 1 pass att., 1 had int.

CLINT JONES
MICHIGAN STATE HB, 6-0, 206 Cleveland, Ohio (Cathedral Latin HS)

Consensus all-America 66, all-America 65. Heisman 6th in 66.
Bowl: Rose 66—rushed 113 yards on 20 carries (UCLA won, 14-12).

Yr.	Team W	L	T	Rushing Car.	Yds.	Avg.	Receiving No.	Yds.	TD	Avg.	K.O. Ret. No.	Yds.	Scoring TD	XP	Pts.
64	4	5	0	72	350	4.9	1	15	1	15.0	5	83	5	0	30
65	10	0	0	165	787	4.8	26	308	2	11.8	2	24	12	2	74
66	#9	0	1	159	784	4.9	6	85	0	14.2	2	55	6	0	36
Totals	23	5	1	396	1921	4.9	33	408	3	12.4	9	162	23	2	140
Avg.												18.0			

Other career figures: 1 int. by for 32 yds., 1 punt ret. for 21 yds., 1 pass att.
National champions.

CHARLIE "CHOO-CHOO" JUSTICE
NORTH CAROLINA
TB, 5-10, 165
Asheville, N.C. (Lee Edwards HS)

Consensus all-America 48, all-America 49. Heisman 2nd in 48 and 49. Hall of Fame.

Bowls: Sugar 47—(Georgia won, 20-10). Sugar 49—(Oklahoma won, 14-6). Cotton 50—passed for one TD, lateraled for another (Rice won, 27-13). 3 bowls combined: 303 total-offense yards, 42.7 punting avg.

Yr.	Team W	L	T	Rushing Car.	Yds.	Avg.	Passing Att.	Cmp.	Int.	Pct.	Yds.	TD	Total Offense Plays	Yds.	TDR
46	8	1	1	131	943	7.2	50	19	9	.380	270	1	181	1213	13
47	8	2	0	135	548	4.1	50	27	5	.540	382	6	185	930	14
48	9	0	1	147	766	5.2	122	62	11	.508	854	12	269	1620	*23
49	7	3	0	123	377	3.1	99	51	7	.515	731	6	222	1108	14
Totals	32	6	2	536	2634	4.9	321	159	32	.495	2237	25	857	4871	64
Avg.							7.0 per Att.			14.1 per Cmp.			5.7		

Yr.	Receiving No.	Yds.	TD	Avg.	Int. No.	Yds.	Punting No.	Avg.	Punt Ret. No.	Yds.	K.O. Ret. No.	Yds.	Scoring TD	Pts.
46	2	39	1	19.5	0	0	45	39.9	18	228	10	344	12	72
47	6	119	3	19.8	2	23	61	41.6	24	285	7	156	8	48
48	4	46	1	11.5	1	10	62	*44.0	19	332	5	141	11	66
49	6	28	1	4.7	0	0	63	44.1	7	124	9	184	8	48
Totals	18	232	6	12.9	3	33	231	42.6	68	969	31	825	39	234
Avg.				11.0				14.3			26.6			

* This figure led the nation.

JOE KAPP

CALIFORNIA QB, 6-2, 205 Newhall, Calif. (Hart HS)

All-America 58. Heisman 5th in 58.

Bowl: Rose 59—threw 17-yard TD pass (Iowa won, 38-12).

Yr.	Team			Rushing			Passing					Total Offense		
	W	L	T	Car.	Yds.	Avg.	Att.	Cmp.	Int.	Pct.	Yds.	TD	Plays	Yds.	TDR
56	3	7	0	55	152	2.8	112	52	13	.464	667	1	167	819	2
57	1	9	0	77	197	2.6	77	38	10	.494	581	4	154	778	6
58	7	3	0	142	582	4.1	97	56	5	.577	649	2	239	1231	7
Totals	11	19	0	274	931	3.4	286	146	28	.510	1897	7	560	2828	15
Avg.								6.6 per Att.		13.0 per Cmp.			5.1		

Yr.	Interceptions		Punting		Punt Ret.		K.O. Ret.		Scoring		
	No.	Yds.	No.	Avg.	No.	Yds.	No.	Yds.	TD	XP	Pts.
56	2	70	2	38.5	0	0	6	105	1	0	6
57	2	23	14	36.4	4	33	5	96	2	2	14
58	2	33	9	31.3	7	65	5	104	5	2	32
Totals	6	126	25	34.8	11	98	16	305	8	4	52
Avg.		21.0				8.9		19.1			

KEN KAVANAUGH

LOUISIANA STATE E, 6-3, 203 Little Rock, Ark. (Central HS)

Consensus all-America 39. Heisman 7th in 39. Hall of Fame.

Bowl: Sugar 38—Santa Clara won, 6-0.

Yr.	Team			Receiving				Scoring		
	W	L	T	No.	Yds.	TD	Avg.	TD	XP	Pts.
37	9	1	0	11	310	4	*28.2	5	0	30
38	6	4	0	17	298	*5	17.5	5	1	31
39	4	5	0	*30	*467	*8	15.6	9	0	54
Totals	19	10	0	58	1075	17	18.5	19	1	115

* This figure led the nation.

DICK KAZMAIER
PRINCETON
TB, 5-11, 171
Maumee, Ohio (Maumee HS)

Unanimous all-America 51, all-America 50. Heisman winner 51. Hall of Fame. Silver Anniversary Award, NCAA Honors Luncheon 77.

Yr.	Team W	L	T	Rushing Car.	Yds.	Avg.	Att.	Cmp.	Passing Int.	Pct.	Yds.	TD
49	6	3	0	100	382	3.8	94	51	6	.543	773	7
50	9	0	0	119	707	5.9	72	44	7	.611	665	15
51+	9	0	0	149	861	5.8	123	77	5	*.626	966	13
Totals	24	3	0	368	1950	5.3	289	172	18	.595	2404	35
Avg.							8.3 per Att.		14.0 per Cmp.		156.9 efficiency	

Yr.	Plays	Total Offense Yds.	TDR	TD	Scoring XP	Pts.
49	194	1155	10	3	2	20
50	191	1372	22	7	1	43
51	272	*1827	*22	9	0	54
Totals	657	4354	54	19	3	117
Avg.	6.6					

+ National leader in passing efficiency in 1951 (min. 11 att. per game) at 155.3.
* This figure led the nation.

LEROY KEYES
PURDUE   HB-DB, 6-3, 205   Newport News, Va. (Carver HS)

Unanimous all-America 67 and 68. Heisman 2nd in 68, 3rd in 67.
Bowl: Rose 67—Beat Southern Cal, 14-13.

Yr.	Team W	L	T	Rushing Car.	Yds.	Avg.	Att.	Cmp.	Passing Int.	Pct.	Yds.	TD	Total Offense Plays	Yds.	TDR
66	8	2	0	12	101	8.4	3	3	0	1.000	41	2	15	142	5
67	8	2	0	149	986	6.6	10	5	0	.500	59	3	159	1045	22
68	8	2	0	193	1003	5.2	9	4	1	.444	81	3	202	1084	18
Totals	24	6	0	354	2090	5.9	22	12	1	.545	181	8	376	2271	45
Avg.							8.2 per Att.		15.1 per Cmp.				6.0		

Yr.	No.	Receiving Yds.	TD	Avg.	Interceptions No.	Yds.	Punt Ret. No.	Yds.	K.O. Ret. No.	Yds.	Scoring TD	Pts.
66	2	18	0	9.0	4	161	3	18	7	183	3	18
67	45	758	6	16.8	1	5	1	9	5	112	*19	*114
68	33	428	1	13.0	0	0	0	0	0	0	15	90
Totals	80	1204	7	15.1	5	166	4	27	12	295	37	222
Avg.						33.2		6.8		24.6		

* This figure led the nation.

BILLY KILMER
UCLA HB, 6-0, 186 Azuza, Calif. (Citrus HS)

All-America 60. Heisman 5th in 60.

	Team			Rushing			Passing				Total Offense		
Yr.	W	L	T	Car.	Yds.	Avg.	Att.	Cmp.	Int.	Pct.	Yds.	TD	Plays	Yds.	TDR
58	3	6	1	50	195	3.9	25	4	0	.160	93	0	75	288	1
59	5	4	1	94	388	4.1	101	41	5	.406	702	7	195	1090	10
60	7	2	1	163	803	4.9	129	64	8	.496	1086	8	292	*1889	16
Totals	15	12	3	307	1386	4.5	255	109	13	.427	1881	15	562	3267	27
Avg.								7.4 per Att.			17.3 per Cmp.			5.8	

	Punting			Punt Returns		K.O. Returns		Scoring			
Yr.	No.	Yds.	Avg.	No.	Yds.	No.	Yds.	TD	XP	Pts.
58	13	515	39.6	1	8	2	29	1	2	8
59	27	1128	41.8	5	21	5	129	3	0	18
60	35	1480	42.3	0	0	0	0	8	4	52
Totals	75	3123	41.6	6	29	7	158	12	6	78
Avg.					4.8		22.6			

Other career figures: 1 int. by for 9 yds.

* This figure led the nation.

JOHN KIMBROUGH
TEXAS A&M FB, 6-2, 221 Haskell, Texas (Haskell HS)

Unanimous all-America 40, consensus all-America 39. Heisman 2nd in 40, 5th in 39. Hall of Fame.

Bowls: Sugar 40—rushed 152 yards on 26 carries, scored 2 TDs, one on 10-yard run at end of 18-yard pass-lateral play (Beat Tulane, 14-13). Cotton 41—scored one TD, rushed 58 yards (Beat Fordham, 13-12).

	Team			Rushing			Passing			
Yr.	W	L	T	Car.	Yds.	Avg.	Att.	Cmp.	Pct.	Yds.
38	4	4	1	70	271	3.9	0	0	.000	0
39	#10	0	0	143	475	3.3	2	1	.500	30
40	8	1	0	162	611	3.8	12	4	.333	52
Totals	22	5	1	375	1357	3.6	14	5	.357	82

	Receiving		Interceptions		Scoring	
Yr.	No.	Yds.	No.	Yds.	TD	Pts.
38	9	83	2	21	4	24
39	5	39	5	59	10	60
40	10	75	5	127	7	42
Totals	24	197	12	198	21	126
Avg.		8.2		16.5		

National champions.

NILE KINNICK
IOWA
QB-HB, 5-8, 167
Omaha, Neb. (Benson HS)

Consensus all-America 39. Heisman winner 39. Hall of Fame.

Yr.	Team			Rushing			Passing					Total Offense		
	W	L	T	Car.	Yds.	Avg.	Att.	Cmp.	Int.	Pct.	Yds.	TD	Plays	Yds.	TDR
37	1	7	0	95	214	2.3	87	36	15	.414	566	1	182	780	3
38	1	6	1	53	136	2.6	49	21	8	.429	241	1	102	377	0
39	6	1	1	106	374	3.5	93	31	13	.333	638	11	199	1012	16
Totals	8	14	2	254	724	2.9	229	88	36	.384	1445	13	483	2169	19
Avg.										6.3 per Att.		16.4 per Cmp.		4.5	

Yr.	Interceptions		Punting			Punt Ret.		K.O. Ret.		Scoring		
	No.	Yds.	No.	Yds.	Avg.	No.	Yds.	No.	Yds.	TD	XP	Pts.
37	3	0	55	2346	42.7	36	322	4	114	2	0	12
38	7	39	41	1686	41.1	11	72	3	72	0	0	0
39	8	52	71	2834	39.9	19	227	15	*377	5	11	41
Totals	18	91	167	6866	41.1	66	621	22	563	7	11	53
Avg.	5.1					9.4		25.6				

WALT KOWALCZYK
MICHIGAN STATE   HB, 6-0, 205   Westfield, Mass. (Westfield HS)

Consensus all-America 57. Heisman 3rd in 57.
Bowl: Rose 56—rushed 88 yards in 13 carries, completed 25-yard pass (Beat UCLA, 17-14).

Yr.	Team			Rushing			Receiving		
	W	L	T	Car.	Yds.	Avg.	No.	Yds.	TD	Avg.
55	8	1	0	82	584	7.1	0	0	0	0.0
56	7	2	0	42	128	3.0	3	59	1	19.7
57	8	1	0	101	545	5.4	7	128	0	18.3
Totals	23	4	0	225	1257	5.6	10	187	1	18.7

Yr.	Punt Returns		K.O. Returns		Scoring	
	No.	Yds.	No.	Yds.	TD	Pts.
55	5	75	4	99	6	36
56	2	26	2	13	2	12
57	4	39	1	20	9	54
Totals	11	140	7	132	17	102
Avg.		12.7		18.9		

Other career figures: 2 int. by for 35 yds.

RON KRAMER
MICHIGAN E, 6-3, 220 East Detroit, Mich. (East Detroit HS)

Unanimous all-America 56, consensus all-America 55. Heisman 6th in 56, 8th in 55. Hall of Fame.

Yr.	Team W	L	T	Rushing Car.	Yds.	No.	Receiving Yds.	TD	Avg.
54	6	3	0	4	17	23	303	2	13.2
55	7	2	0	5	29	12	224	4	18.7
56	7	2	0	5	19	19	361	2	19.0
Totals	20	7	0	14	65	54	888	8	16.4
Avg.					4.6				

Yr.	Punting No.	Avg.	TD	Scoring XP	FG	Pts.
54	19	41.3	3	13	0	31
55	10	36.5	4	12	0	36
56	2	56.0	2	17	2	35
Totals	31	40.7	9	42	2	102

Other career figures: 3 passes att., 1 cmp., 1 int. for 23 yds.; 2 int. by for 7 yds.; 3 punt ret. for 43 yds.; 1 kickoff ret. for 25 yds.

TED KWALICK
PENN STATE E, 6-4, 230 McKees Rocks, Pa. (Montour HS)

Unanimous all-America 68, all-America 67. Heisman 4th in 68. Hall of Fame.

Bowls: Gator 68—started at wingback, caught 12-yard TD pass (Tied Florida St., 17-17). Orange 69—caught 6 passes for 74 yards (Beat Kansas, 15-14).

Yr.	Team W	L	T	Rushing Car.	Yds.	No.	Receiving Yds.	TD	Avg.
66	5	5	0	0	0	22	377	4	17.1
67	8	2	0	5	19	33	563	4	17.1
68	10	0	0	14	96	31	403	2	13.0
Totals	23	7	0	19	115	86	1343	10	15.6
Avg.					6.1				

Yr.	Punt Returns No.	Yds.	K.O. Returns No.	Yds.	TD	Scoring XP	Pts.
66	0	0	1	5	4	2	26
67	7	34	1	0	4	4	28
68	0	0	1	53	4	2	26
Totals	7	34	3	58	12	8	80
Avg.		4.9		19.3			

PAUL LARSON
CALIFORNIA   HB-QB, 5-11, 180   Turlock, Calif. (Turlock HS)

All-America 54. Heisman 5th in 54.

Yr.	Team W	L	T	Rushing Car.	Yds.	Avg.	Att.	Cmp.	Passing Int.	Pct.	Yds.	TD	Total Offense Plays	Yds.	TDR
51	8	2	0	8	100	12.5	0	0	0	.000	0	0	8	100	0
52	7	3	0	57	362	6.4	2	0	0	.000	0	0	59	362	5
53	4	4	2	91	141	1.5	171	85	16	.497	1431	6	262	*1572	11
54	5	5	0	86	-52	-0.6	195	*125	8	*.641	*1537	10	281	1485	15
Totals	24	14	2	242	551	2.3	368	210	24	.571	2968	16	610	3519	31
Avg.								8.1 per Att.		14.1 per Cmp.			5.8		

Yr.	Receiving No.	Yds.	TD	Int. No.	Yds.	Punting No.	Avg.	Punt Ret. No.	Yds.	K.O. Ret. No.	Yds.	TD	Scoring XP	FG	Pts.
51	0	0	0	0	0	0	0.0	8	118	9	155	0	0	0	0
52	4	51	1	3	61	1	47.0	24	261	11	184	5	1	0	31
53	0	0	0	6	102	15	33.2	1	0	2	21	5	20	0	50
54	0	0	0	3	0	22	34.5	9	71	10	285	5	16	1	49
Totals	4	51	1	12	163	38	34.3	42	450	32	645	15	37	1	130
Avg.		12.8			13.6				10.7		20.2				

* This figure led the nation.

JOHN LATTNER
NOTRE DAME
HB, 6-1, 190
Chicago, Ill. (Fenwick HS)

Unanimous all-America 52 and 53. Heisman winner 53, 5th in 52. Hall of Fame.

Yr.	Team W	L	T	Rushing Car.	Yds.	Avg.	Receiving No.	Yds.	Avg.
51	7	2	1	68	341	5.0	8	157	19.6
52	7	2	1	148	732	4.9	17	220	12.9
53	9	0	1	134	651	4.9	14	204	14.6
Totals	23	4	3	350	1724	4.9	39	581	14.9

Yr.	Interceptions No.	Yds.	Punting No.	Avg.	Punt Returns No.	Yds.	K.O. Returns No.	Yds.	Scoring TD	Pts.
51	5	66	26	32.3	10	91	0	0	6	36
52	4	58	51	37.1	7	113	3	45	5	30
53	4	4	29	35.0	9	103	8	331	9	54
Totals	13	128	106	35.3	26	307	11	376	20	120
Avg.		9.8				11.8		34.2		

Other career figures: 8 passes att., 3 cmp. for 101 yds., 2 had int.

HANK LAURICELLA

TENNESSEE TB, 5-10, 169 New Orleans, La. (Holy Cross HS)

Unanimous all-America 51. Heisman 2nd in 51. Hall of Fame.

Bowls: Cotton 51—75-yard rush, 131 yards rushing (Beat Texas, 20-14). Sugar 52—Maryland won, 28-13.

Yr.	Team W	L	T	Rushing Car.	Yds.	Avg.	Passing Att.	Cmp.	Int.	Pct.	Yds.	TD	Total Offense Plays	Yds.	TDR
49	7	2	1	78	139	1.8	63	29	7	.460	430	6	141	569	7
50	10	1	0	106	443	4.2	65	21	5	.323	323	5	171	766	9
51	#10	0	0	111	881	7.9	51	24	5	.471	352	5	162	1233	13
Totals	27	3	1	295	1463	5.0	179	74	17	.413	1105	16	474	2568	29
Avg.							6.2 per Att.			14.9 per Cmp.			5.4		

Yr.	Punting No.	Avg.	Punt Returns No.	Yds.	K.O. Returns No.	Yds.	Scoring TD	Pts.
49	31	38.9	17	198	4	79	1	6
50	57	36.6	0	0	1	26	4	24
51	43	34.7	0	0	6	116	8	48
Totals	131	36.5	17	198	11	221	13	78
Avg.				11.6		20.1		

National champions.

ELMER LAYDEN

NOTRE DAME FB, 6-0, 162 Davenport, Iowa (Davenport HS)

Consensus all-America 24. Hall of Fame.

Bowl: Rose 25—scored 3 TDs including 78- and 70-yard interception returns; punted 54 and 53 yards (Beat Stanford, 27-10).

One of the Four Horsemen.

Yr.	Team W	L	T	Rushing Car.	Yds.	Avg.	Passing Att.	Cmp.	Int.	Pct.	Yds.	TD	Total Offense Plays	Yds.
22	8	1	1	80	453	5.7	17	9	2	.529	173	2	97	626
23	9	1	0	102	420	4.1	6	3	1	.500	51	0	108	471
24	#9	0	0	111	423	3.8	6	1	1	.167	18	0	117	441
Totals	26	2	1	293	1296	4.4	29	13	4	.448	242	2	322	1538
Avg.							8.3 per Att.			18.6 per Cmp.			4.8	

Yr.	Receiving No.	Yds.	TD	Avg.	Int. No.	Yds.	Punting No.	Avg.	Punt Ret. No.	Yds.	K.O. Ret. No.	Yds.	Scoring TD	XP	Pts.
22	4	57	1	14.3	2	5	18	37.6	2	27	2	38	1	3	9
23	6	78	2	13.0	3	58	61	36.0	1	1	6	110	7	5	47
24	1	10	0	10.0	2	59	34	35.3	0	0	5	111	6	4	40
Totals	11	145	3	13.2	7	122	113	36.1	3	28	13	259	14	12	96
Avg.						17.4				9.3		19.9			

National champions.

BOBBY LAYNE

TEXAS   QB, 6-0, 191   Dallas, Texas (Highland Park HS)

Consensus all-America 47. Heisman 6th in 47, 9th in 46. Hall of Fame.

Bowls: Cotton 46—threw 48 and 15-yard touchdown passes; scored 4 TDs, one a 50-yard catch; completed 11 of 12 passes; kicked four extra points (Beat Missouri, 40-27). Sugar 48—scored TD, threw TD pass, completed 11 passes for 183 yards (Beat Alabama, 27-7).

Yr.	Team			Rushing			Passing						Total Offense		
	W	L	T	Car.	Yds.	Avg.	Att.	Cmp.	Int.	Pct.	Yds.	TD	Plays	Yds.	TDR
44	5	4	0	78	264	3.4	91	50	5	.549	662	4	169	926	9
45	9	1	0	40	147	3.7	54	20	5	.370	396	3	94	543	3
46	8	2	0	81	338	4.2	140	77	*14	*.550	1122	6	221	1460	14
47+	9	1	0	43	96	2.2	115	63	7	.548	965	9	158	1061	11
Totals	31	8	0	242	845	3.5	400	210	31	.525	3145	22	642	3990	37
Avg.							7.9 per Att.			15.0 per Cmp.				6.2	

Yr.	Interceptions		Punting		Punt Ret.		K.O. Ret.			Scoring		
	No.	Yds.	No.	Avg.	No.	Yds.	No.	Yds.	TD	XP	FG	Pts.
44	3	11	1	58.0	9	142	2	35	5	6	0	36
45	2	19	12	33.5	8	101	4	111	0	7	0	7
46	6	48	12	42.1	12	142	7	152	8	0	2	54
47	0	0	0	0.0	0	0	0	0	2	5	0	17
Totals	11	78	25	38.6	29	385	13	298	15	18	2	114
Avg.		7.1				13.3		22.9				

Other career figures: 1 catch for 38 yds.

+ National leader in passing efficiency in 1947 (min. 11 att. per game) at 138.9.
* This figure led the nation.

EDDIE LeBARON

PACIFIC   QB, 5-7, 167   Oakdale, Calif. (Oakdale HS)

All-America 49. Hall of Fame.

Bowls: Optimist 46—19 net yards on 15 plays total offense; punted once for 30 yards; one 10-yard punt return (North Texas won, 14-13, in final game of Amos Alonzo Stagg's 57-season coaching career, last 14 seasons coming at Pacific). Raisin 48—completed 6 of 14 passes for 118 yards and two TDs; 12 yards on 3 rushes; 48.5-yard average on 3 punts; 36-yard interception return (Pacific won, 35-21).

Yr.	Team				Rushing			Passing						Total Offense		
	W	L	T	G	Car.	Yds.	TD	Att.	Cmp.	Int.	Pct.	Yds.	TD	Plays	Yds.	Avg.	TDR
46	5	6	0	6	15	31	1	40	24	7	.600	595	8	55	626	11.4	9
47	9	1	0	10	22	6	3	98	42	10	.429	955	14	120	961	8.0	17
48	7	1	2	10	25	11	2	111	49	12	.441	1006	11	136	1017	7.5	13
49	11	0	0	11	30	30	0	157	82	7	.522	1282	12	187	1312	7.0	15
Totals	32	8	2	37	92	78	6	406	197	36	.485	3838	45	498	3916	7.9	54

Career avg.: 9.5 pass yds. per att.; 19.5 per cmp.; 146.8 efficiency.
Career per game: 103.7 yds. passing; 105.8 total offense.
Other career figures: 38.5 avg. on 108 punts; punted out of bounds inside 10-yard line 20 times; scored 42 points, including 82-yard interception TD; ret. 4 punts 70 yds., 17.5 avg.; 7 int. for 161 yds., 23.0 avg.

(Missed first part of 1946 season with appendicitis.)

EDDIE LeBARON

JERRY LeVIAS
SOUTHERN METHODIST
FL, 5-10, 170
Beaumont, Texas (Herbert HS)

Consensus all-America 68. Academic all-America 68.
Bowls: Cotton 67—caught two 23-yard passes in 72-yard scoring drive (Georgia won, 24-9). Astro-Bluebonnet 68—caught 11-yard TD pass (Beat Oklahoma, 28-27).

Yr.	Team W	L	T	Rushing Car.	Yds.	Avg.	Passing Att.	Cmp.	Yds.	TD
66	8	2	0	8	43	5.4	9	5	89	1
67	3	7	0	22	31	1.4	8	1	5	1
68	7	3	0	14	87	6.2	6	0	0	0
Totals	18	12	0	44	161	3.7	23	6	94	2

Yr.	Receiving No.	Yds.	TD	Avg.	Punt Ret. No.	Yds.	K.O. Ret. No.	Yds.	Scoring TD	XP	Pts.
66	18	420	7	23.3	17	222	15	393	9	0	54
67	57	724	7	12.7	17	227	21	394	7	0	42
68	80	1131	8	14.1	24	261	17	293	9	4	58
Totals	155	2275	22	14.7	58	710	53	1080	25	4	154
Avg.						12.2		20.4			

SHERMAN LEWIS
MICHIGAN STATE HB, 5-8, 154 Louisville, Ky. (DuPont Manual HS)

Consensus all-America 63. Heisman 3rd in 63.

Yr.	Team W	L	T	Rushing Car.	Yds.	Avg.	Receiving No.	Yds.	TD	Avg.
61	7	2	0	64	399	6.2	5	90	1	18.0
62	5	4	0	98	590	6.0	6	79	1	13.2
63	6	2	1	90	577	6.4	11	303	5	27.5
Totals	18	8	1	252	1566	6.2	22	472	7	21.5

Yr.	Punt Returns No.	Yds.	K.O. Returns No.	Yds.	TD	Scoring XP	Pts.
61	9	117	1	23	6	2	38
62	10	84	11	202	9	4	58
63	13	154	8	155	8	0	48
Totals	32	355	20	380	23	6	144
Avg.		11.1		19.0			

Other career figures: 4 passes att., 1 cmp. for 10 yds.; 3 int. by for 29 yds.

FLOYD LITTLE

SYRACUSE   HB, 5-11, 195   New Haven, Conn. (Bordentown, N.J., Military Acad.)

All-America 64, 65 and 66. Heisman 5th in 65 and 66. Hall of Fame.

Bowls: Sugar 65—Louisiana St. won, 13-10. Gator 67—scored 1 TD, set Gator Bowl record of 216 rushing yards (Tennessee won, 18-12).

Yr.	Team			Rushing			Receiving			
	W	L	T	Car.	Yds.	Avg.	No.	Yds.	TD	Avg.
64	7	3	0	149	828	5.6	16	248	1	15.5
65	7	3	0	193	1065	5.5	21	248	1	11.8
66	8	2	0	162	811	5.0	13	86	2	6.6
Totals	22	8	0	504	2704	5.4	50	582	4	11.6

Yr.	Punt Returns		K.O. Returns		Scoring		
	No.	Yds.	No.	Yds.	TD	XP	Pts.
64	11	270	11	335	12	0	72
65	18	423	8	254	*19	0	114
66	14	152	9	208	15	2	92
Totals	43	845	28	797	46	2	278
Avg.		19.7		28.5			

Other career figures: 6 passes att., 3 cmp. for 19 yds., one TD.

* This figure led the nation.

BILLY LOTHRIDGE

GEORGIA TECH   QB, 6-1, 184   Gainesville, Ga. (Gainesville HS)

All-America 63. Heisman 2nd in 63, 8th in 62.

Bowls: Gator 62—kicked extra point (Penn St. won, 30-15). Bluebonnet 62—kicked extra point and 26-yard field goal, completed 5 passes for 68 yards (Missouri won, 14-10).

Yr.	Team			Rushing			Passing				
	W	L	T	Car.	Yds.	Avg.	Att.	Cmp.	Int.	Pct.	Yds.	TD
61	7	3	0	53	45	0.8	63	26	3	.413	371	2
62	7	2	1	128	478	3.7	156	83	8	.532	1006	6
63	7	3	0	117	223	1.9	153	76	7	.497	1017	10
Totals	21	8	1	298	746	2.5	372	185	18	.497	2394	18
Avg.							6.4 per Att.				12.9 per Cmp.	

Yr.	Total Offense				Scoring				
	Plays	Yds.	TDR	TD	PATs		FGs		Pts.
					Att.	Made	Att.	Made	
61	116	416	5	3	20	16	6	4	46
62	284	1484	15	9	24	20	10	5	89
63	270	1240	13	3	19	15	17	*12	69
Totals	670	3140	33	15	63	51	33	21	204
Avg.		4.7				.810		.636	

Other career figures: 150 punts for 37.6 avg.

* This figure led the nation.

RICHIE LUCAS
PENN STATE   QB, 6-1, 185   Glassport, Pa. (Glassport HS)

Consensus all-America 59. Heisman 2nd in 59.
Bowl: Liberty 59—Injured in 2nd quarter (Beat Alabama, 7-0).

	Team			Rushing			Passing					
Yr.	W	L	T	Car.	Yds.	Avg.	Att.	Cmp.	Int.	Pct.	Yds.	TD
57	6	3	0	39	66	1.7	59	27	4	.458	426	4
58	6	3	1	65	218	3.4	80	36	4	.450	483	3
59	8	2	0	99	325	3.3	117	58	8	.496	913	5
Totals	20	8	1	203	609	3.0	256	121	16	.473	1822	12
Avg.								7.1 per Att.			15.1 per Cmp.	

	Total Offense			Scoring		
Yr.	Plays	Yds.	TDR	TD	XP	Pts.
57	98	492	5	1	0	6
58	145	701	9	6	2	38
59	216	1238	11	6	0	36
Totals	459	2431	25	13	2	80
Avg.	5.3					

Other career figures: 7 int. by for 143 yds., 69 punts for 36.2 avg., 8 punt ret. for 63 yds., 3 kickoff ret. for 38 yds.

SID LUCKMAN
COLUMBIA   HB, 5-11, 194   New York, N.Y. (Erasmus Hall HS)

All-America 38. Heisman 3rd in 38, 6th in 37. Hall of Fame.

	Team			Rushing			Passing					
Yr.	W	L	T	Car.	Yds.	Avg.	Att.	Cmp.	Int.	Pct.	Yds.	TD
36	5	3	0	—	—	—	68	31	3	.456	492	6
37	2	5	2	—	—	—	176	83	13	.472	1065	8
38	3	6	0	92	428	4.7	132	66	10	.500	856	6
Totals	10	14	2	—	—	—	376	180	26	.479	2413	20
Avg.								6.4 per Att.			13.4 per Cmp.	

	† Total Offense			† Punting		† Scoring		
Yr.	Plays	Yds.	TDR	No.	Avg.	TD	XP	Pts.
36	—	—	8	—	—	2	0	12
37	—	—	11	—	—	3	0	18
38	224	1284	10	51	40.1	4	8	32
Totals	—	—	29	—	—	9	8	62

† No figures available for these categories in 1936 and 1937.

JOHN LUJACK
NOTRE DAME
QB, 6-0, 180
Connellsville, Pa. (Connellsville HS)

Unanimous all-America 46 and 47. Heisman winner 47, 3rd in 46. Hall of Fame.

Yr.	Team W	L	T	Rushing Car.	Yds.	Avg.	Att.	Cmp.	Passing Int.	Pct.	Yds.	TD
43	#9	1	0	46	191	4.2	71	34	8	.479	525	4
46	#8	0	1	23	108	4.7	100	49	8	.490	778	5
47	#9	0	0	12	139	11.6	109	61	8	.560	791	9
Totals	26	1	1	81	438	5.4	280	144	24	.514	2094	18
Avg.								7.5 per Att.			14.5 per Cmp.	

Yr.	Plays	Total Offense Yds.	TDR	TD	Scoring XP	Pts.
43	117	716	8	4	4	28
46	123	886	6	1	0	6
47	121	930	10	1	0	6
Totals	361	2532	24	6	4	40
Avg.	7.0					

Other career figures: 2 catches for 10 yds., 7 int. by for 106 yds., 5 punt ret. for 51 yds., 3 kickoff ret. for 33 yds., 62 punts for a 36.2 avg.

National champions.

FRANCIS "PUG" LUND
MINNESOTA HB, 5-11, 185 Rice Lake, Wis. (Rice Lake HS)

Consensus all-America 34, all-America 33. Hall of Fame.

Yr.	Team W	L	T	Rushing Car.	Yds.	Avg.	Att.	Cmp.	Passing Int.	Pct.	Yds.	TD	Total Offense Plays	Yds.	TDR
32	5	3	0	161	811	5.0	77	25	10	.325	392	3	238	1203	5
33	4	0	4	167	626	3.7	60	25	12	.417	253	0	227	879	4
34	#8	0	0	111	621	5.6	19	7	2	.368	151	2	130	772	8
Totals	17	3	4	439	2059	4.7	156	57	24	.365	796	5	595	2854	17
Avg.								5.1 per Att.		14.0 per Cmp.			4.8		

Yr.	Receiving No.	Yds.	Int. No.	Yds.	Punting No.	Avg.	Punt Ret. No.	Yds.	K.O. Ret. No.	Yds.	Scoring TD	Pts.
32	0	0	1	9	66	32,7	39	311	2	34	2	12
33	1	17	0	0	85	35.5	38	330	12	329	4	24
34	1	22	2	9	41	35.4	26	235	9	236	6	36
Totals	2	39	3	18	192	34.5	103	876	23	599	12	72
Avg.		19.5		6.0				8.5		26.0		

National champions.

ART LUPPINO
ARIZONA TB, 5-9, 178   La Jolla, Calif. (La Jolla HS)

Yr.	Team W	L	T	Rushing Car.	Yds.	Avg.	Receiving No.	Yds.	Avg.
53	4	5	1	59	382	6.5	1	12	12.0
54	7	3	0	*179	*1359	7.6	4	50	12.5
55	5	4	1	*209	*1313	6.3	7	74	10.6
56	4	6	0	66	327	5.0	4	49	12.3
Totals	20	18	2	513	3381	6.6	16	185	11.6

Yr.	Interceptions No.	Yds.	Punt Returns No.	Yds.	K.O. Returns No.	Yds.	Scoring TD	XP	Pts.
53	0	0	3	80	2	46	5	4	34
54	3	84	4	68	*20	*632	*24	22	*166
55	1	0	11	62	11	253	13	18	96
56	1	10	1	13	7	138	6	5	41
Totals	5	94	19	223	40	1069	48	49	337
Avg.		18.8		11.7		26.7			

Other career figures: 12 punts for 27.6 avg.
* This figure led the nation.

DICKY MAEGLE
RICE HB, 6-0, 175   Taylor, Texas (Taylor HS)

Consensus all-America 54. Heisman 6th in 54. Academic all-America 54. Hall of Fame.

Bowl: Cotton 54—set three all-time major bowl records, with 265 rushing yards, 24.1 yards per carry and 95-yard rush, on which Alabama fullback Tommy Lewis jumped from the bench and tackled Maegle, who was in the clear at the Alabama 41. Maegle was awarded TD. Maegle also had 79- and 34-yard TD rushes (Beat Alabama, 28-6).

Yr.	Team W	L	T	Rushing Car.	Yds.	Avg.	Receiving No.	Yds.
52	5	5	0	9	35	3.9	3	93
53	8	2	0	114	833	*7.3	5	26
54	7	3	0	144	905	6.3	18	198
Totals	20	10	0	267	1773	6.6	26	317
Avg.								12.2

Yr.	Interceptions No.	Yds.	Punt Returns No.	Yds.	K.O. Returns No.	Yds.	Scoring TD	XP	Pts.
52	0	0	1	15	0	0	0	0	0
53	3	68	17	194	3	41	10	1	61
54	2	14	15	293	6	116	12	0	72
Totals	5	82	33	502	9	157	22	1	133
Avg.		16.4		15.2		17.4			

Other career figures: 4 passes att., 1 cmp. for 9-yd. TD, 1 had int.; 12 punts for 33.5 avg.
* This figure led the nation.

JOHN MAJORS

TENNESSEE TB, 5-10, 162 Huntland, Tenn. (Huntland HS)

Unanimous all-America 56. Heisman 2nd in 56. Hall of Fame.
Bowl: Sugar 57—rushed for TD after carrying 8 times in 39-yard drive (Baylor won, 13-7).

Yr.	Team W	L	T	Rushing Car.	Yds.	Avg.	Att.	Cmp.	Passing Int.	Pct.	Yds.	TD	Total Offense Plays	Yds.	TDR
54	4	6	0	96	416	4.3	24	8	4	.333	107	1	120	523	4
55	6	3	1	183	657	3.6	65	36	5	.554	476	5	248	1133	11
56	10	0	0	108	549	5.1	59	36	3	.610	552	5	167	1101	12
Totals	20	9	1	387	1622	4.2	148	80	12	.541	1135	11	535	2757	27
Avg.						7.7 per Att.		14.2 per Cmp.		128.1 efficiency			5.2		

Yr.	Interceptions No.	Yds.	Punting No.	Avg.	Punt Ret. No.	Yds.	K.O. Ret. No.	Yds.	Scoring TD	Pts.
54	1	36	18	34.4	5	118	4	81	3	18
55	1	0	39	38.7	21	234	5	128	6	36
56	0	0	26	43.0	10	86	6	135	7	42
Totals	2	36	83	39.1	36	438	15	344	16	96
Avg.		18.0				12.2		22.9		

OLLIE MATSON

SAN FRANCISCO
FB, 6-2, 203
San Francisco, Calif. (Washington HS)

All-America 51. Heisman 9th in 51. Hall of Fame.

Yr.	Team W	L	T	Rushing Car.	Yds.	Avg.	Receiving No.	Yds.	Avg.
49	7	3	0	156	853	5.5	16	323	20.2
50	7	4	0	146	747	5.1	5	73	14.6
51	9	0	0	245	*1566	6.4	6	58	9.7
Totals	23	7	0	547	3166	5.8	27	454	16.8

Yr.	Interceptions No.	Yds.	Punt Returns No.	Yds.	K.O. Returns No.	Yds.	Scoring TD	XP	Pts.
49	3	9	17	298	11	227	7	0	42
50	5	106	24	215	3	84	13	3	81
51	3	8	9	116	7	280	*21	0	*126
Totals	11	123	50	629	21	591	41	3	249
Avg.		11.2		12.6		28.1			

Other career figures: 1 pass att., 1 cmp. for minus 12 yds.

* This figure led the nation.

BILL McCOLL
STANFORD E, 6-4, 225 San Diego, Calif. (Hoover HS)

Unanimous all-America 51. Consensus all-America 50. Heisman 4th in 51. Hall of Fame.
Bowl: Rose 52—three catches during 84-yard scoring drive (Illinois won, 40-7).

	Team				Receiving			Interceptions	
Yr.	W	L	T	No.	Yds.	TD	Avg.	No.	Yds.
49	7	3	1	25	299	3	12.0	0	0
50	5	3	2	39	671	4	17.2	2	37
51	9	1	0	42	607	7	14.5	0	0
Totals	21	7	3	106	1577	14	14.9	2	37

	Punt Returns		K.O. Returns		Scoring	
Yr.	No.	Yds.	No.	Yds.	TD	Pts.
49	0	0	3	31	3	18
50	4	60	3	36	4	24
51	0	0	3	28	7	42
Totals	4	60	9	95	14	84
Avg.		15.0		10.6		

Other career figures: 6 rushes for 11 yds., 2 passes att., 0 cmp.

TOMMY McDONALD
OKLAHOMA
HB, 5-9, 169
Albuquerque, N.M. (Highland HS)

Consensus all-America 56. All-America 55. Heisman 3rd in 56. Hall of Fame.
Bowl: Orange 56—scored TD; 33-yard punt return (Beat Maryland, 20-6).

	Team			Rushing			Passing					Total Offense		
Yr.	W	L	T	Car.	Yds.	Avg.	Att.	Cmp.	Int.	Pct.	Yds.	TD	Plays	Yds.	TDR
54	10	0	0	27	128	4.7	8	3	0	.375	123	0	35	251	2
55	#10	0	0	103	702	6.8	24	17	0	.708	265	0	127	967	16
56	#10	0	0	119	853	7.2	12	8	1	.667	183	3	131	1036	*20
Totals	30	0	0	249	1683	6.8	44	28	1	.636	571	3	293	2254	38
Avg.								13.0 per Att.			20.4 per Cmp.			7.7	

	Receiving			Interceptions		Punt Ret.		K.O. Ret.		Scoring	
Yr.	No.	Yds.	TD	Avg.	No.	Yds.	No.	Yds.	No.	Yds.	TD	Pts.
54	2	28	1	14.0	2	19	7	134	2	42	2	12
55	6	104	1	17.3	1	21	11	207	4	88	16	96
56	12	282	4	23.5	6	136	13	149	3	95	17	102
Totals	20	414	6	20.7	9	176	31	490	9	225	35	210
Avg.				19.6			15.8		25.0			

National champions. * This figure led the nation.

HUGH McELHENNY

WASHINGTON HB, 6-1, 197 Los Angeles, Calif. (Washington HS)

All-America 51. Heisman 8th in 51. Hall of Fame.

	Team			Rushing				Passing	
Yr.	W	L	T	Car.	Yds.	Avg.	Att.	Cmp.	Yds.
49	3	7	0	103	456	4.4	14	7	45
50	8	2	0	179	1107	6.2	13	4	77
51	3	6	1	169	936	5.5	2	0	0
Totals	14	15	1	451	2499	5.5	29	11	122

	Receiving				Punt Ret.		K.O. Ret.		Scoring		
Yr.	No.	Yds.	TD	Avg.	No.	Yds.	No.	Yds.	TD	XP	Pts.
49	15	184	1	12.3	5	27	9	246	4	0	24
50	16	236	1	14.8	6	79	8	240	14	0	84
51	24	339	4	14.1	7	141	13	262	17	23	125
Totals	55	759	6	13.8	18	247	30	748	35	23	233
Avg.						13.7		24.9			

Other career figures: 1 int. by for 18 yds.; 5 passes had int.

BANKS McFADDEN

CLEMSON HB, 6-5, 175 Great Falls, S.C. (Great Falls HS)

All-America 39. Heisman 8th in 39. Hall of Fame.

Bowl: Cotton 40—rushed 44 yards on 4 carries, 42.6 punting avg., knocked down two end zone passes (Beat Boston College, 6-3).

	Team			Rushing			Passing					Total Offense		
Yr.	W	L	T	Car.	Yds.	Avg.	Att.	Cmp.	Int.	Pct.	Yds.	TD	Plays	Yds.	TDR
37	4	4	1	31	183	5.9	2	0	1	.000	0	0	33	183	2
38	7	1	1	66	342	5.2	20	10	0	.500	169	3	86	511	8
39	8	1	0	72	436	6.1	67	28	6	.418	541	5	139	977	10
Totals	19	6	2	169	961	5.7	89	38	7	.427	710	8	258	1671	20
Avg.|						8.0 per Att.			18.7 per Cmp.			6.5		

	Receiving			Int.		Punting			Punt Ret.		K.O. Ret.		Scoring		
Yr.	No.	Yds.	Avg.	No.	Yds.	No.	Yds.	Avg.	No.	Yds.	No.	Yds.	TD	XP	Pts.
37	9	169	18.8	0	0	17	697	41.0	1	2	4	111	2	2	14
38	2	26	13.0	1	5	29	1139	39.3	0	0	1	14	5	0	30
39	1	23	23.0	3	29	56	2423	43.3	5	8	1	14	5	1	31
Totals	12	218	18.2	4	34	102	4259	41.8	6	10	6	139	12	3	75
Avg.			8.5							1.7		23.2			

DON MEREDITH
SOUTHERN METHODIST QB, 6-3, 195 Mt. Vernon, Texas (Mt. Vernon HS)

All-America 58 and 59. Heisman 3rd in 59, 9th in 58. Hall of Fame.

Yr.	Team			Rushing			Passing				
	W	L	T	Car.	Yds.	Avg.	Att.	Cmp.	Int.	Pct.	Yds.	TD
57	4	5	1	88	131	1.5	102	71	6	*.696	912	7
58	6	4	0	77	230	3.0	113	64	7	.566	961	7
59	5	4	1	102	25	0.2	181	105	10	.580	1266	11
Totals	15	13	2	267	386	1.4	396	240	23	.606	3139	25
Avg.							7.9 per Att.	13.1 per Cmp.		136.4 efficiency		

Yr.			Total Offense			Scoring		
	Plays		Yds.	TDR	TD		XP	Pts.
57	190		1043	11	4		4	28
58	190		1191	15	8		4	52
59	283		1291	13	2		4	16
Totals	663		3525	39	14		12	96
Avg.		5.3						

Other career figures—1 punt for 37 yds., 11 kickoff ret. for 253 yds.
* This figure led the nation.

DON MILLER
NOTRE DAME HB, 5-11, 160 Defiance, Ohio (Defiance HS)

All-America 23. Hall of Fame. One of the Four Horsemen.

Yr.	Team			Rushing			Receiving		
	W	L	T	Car.	Yds.	Avg.	No.	Yds.	TD	Avg.
22	8	1	1	87	472	5.4	6	144	1	24.0
23	9	1	0	89	698	7.8	9	149	1	16.6
24	#9	0	0	107	763	7.1	16	297	2	18.6
Totals	26	2	1	283	1933	6.8	31	590	4	19.0

Yr.	Punt Returns		K.O. Returns		Scoring	
	No.	Yds.	No.	Yds.	TD	Pts.
22	0	0	5	179	5	30
23	4	69	1	15	10	60
24	0	0	1	20	7	42
Totals	4	69	7	214	22	132
Avg.		17.3		30.6		

Other career figures—1 pass att., 1 int.; 3 int. by for 43 yds.
National champions.

GEORGE MIRA
MIAMI (FLA.)
QB, 6-0, 182
Key West, Fla. (Key West HS)

All-America 62. Heisman 5th in 62, 10th in 63.
 Bowls: Liberty 61—completed 7 passes for 94 yards; 2-point pass (Syracuse won, 15-14). Gotham 62—completed 24 of 46 passes for 321 yards, 2 for 10 and 30-yard TDs; 2-point pass (Nebraska won, 36-34).

	Team			Rushing				Passing			
Yr.	W	L	T	Car.	Yds.	Avg.	Att.	Cmp.	Int.	Pct.	Yds.	TD
61	7	3	0	62	179	2.9	151	74	6	.490	896	8
62	7	3	0	68	160	2.4	*260	122	16	.469	1572	10
63	3	7	0	59	163	2.8	*335	172	14	.513	2155	10
Totals	17	13	0	189	502	2.7	746	368	36	.493	4623	28
Avg.							6.2 per Att.				12.6 per Cmp.	

	Total Offense			Scoring	
Yr.	Plays	Yds.	TDR	TD	Pts.
61	213	1075	11	3	18
62	328	1732	13	3	18
63	394	*2318	12	2	12
Totals	935	5125	36	8	48
Avg.		5.5			

Other career figures—2 catches for 32 yds., 2 punts for 41.0 avg., 1 punt ret. for 12 yds.

* This figure led the nation.

EARL MORRALL
MICHIGAN STATE   QB, 6-1, 180   Muskegon, Mich. (Muskegon HS)

Consensus all-America 55. Heisman 4th in 55.
 Bowls: Rose 54—39-yard punting avg. (Beat UCLA, 28-20). Rose 56—threw 13-yard TD pass, 40-yard punting avg. (Beat UCLA, 17-14).

	Team			Rushing				Passing				
Yr.	W	L	T	Car.	Yds.	Avg.	Att.	Cmp.	Int.	Pct.	Yds.	TD
53	8	1	0	14	9	0.6	31	17	3	.548	279	2
54	3	6	0	32	26	0.8	99	39	8	.394	795	6
55	8	1	0	47	106	2.3	68	42	5	.618	941	5
Totals	19	8	0	93	141	1.5	198	98	16	.495	2015	13
Avg.							10.2 per Att.	20.6 per Cmp.		140.5 efficiency		

	Total Offense			Scoring		
Yr.	Plays	Yds.	TDR	TD	XP	Pts.
53	45	288	2	0	0	0
54	131	821	6	0	2	2
55	115	1047	9	4	0	24
Totals	291	2156	17	4	2	26
Avg.		7.4				

Other career figures: 4 int. by for 132 yds., 56 punts for 39.2 avg.

CRAIG MORTON
CALIFORNIA   QB, 6-4, 215   Campbell, Calif. (Campbell HS)
All-America 64. Heisman 7th in 64.

Yr.	Team			Rushing		Passing					
	W	L	T	Car.	Yds.	Att.	Cmp.	Int.	Pct.	Yds.	TD
62	1	9	0	22	-90	126	69	10	.548	905	9
63	4	5	1	87	-52	207	101	12	.488	1475	14
64	3	7	0	47	-238	308	185	9	.601	2121	13
Totals	8	21	1	156	-380	641	355	31	.554	4501	36
Avg.						7.0 per Att.				12.7 per Cmp.	

Yr.	Plays	Total Offense Yds.	TDR	TD	Scoring XP	Pts.
62	148	815	10	1	0	6
63	294	1423	18	4	4	28
64	355	1883	16	3	0	18
Totals	797	4121	44	8	4	52
Avg.		5.2				

BRONKO NAGURSKI
MINNESOTA
T-FB, 6-2, 217
International Falls, Minn. (International Falls HS)

Consensus all-America 29. Hall of Fame. FWAA all-time team.

Yr.	Team			Rushing				Scoring	
	W	L	T	Car.	Yds.	Avg.		TD	Pts.
27	6	0	2	0	0	0.0	played tackle all season	0	0
28	6	2	0	74	298	4.0	5 games at fullback	3	18
29	6	2	0	61	259	4.2	5 games at fullback	3	18
Totals	18	4	2	135	557	4.1		6	36

Other career figures: 1 int. by for 0 yds.

JOE NAMATH

ALABAMA   QB, 6-2, 194   Beaver Falls, Pa. (Beaver Falls HS)

Bowls: Orange 63—threw TD pass, completed 9 passes for 86 yards (Beat Oklahoma, 17-0). Sugar 64—did not play (Beat Mississippi, 12-7). Orange 65—threw 2 TD passes, one for 20 yards, completed 18 passes—an Orange Bowl record—for 255 yards (Texas won, 21-17).

Yr.	Team W	L	T	Rushing Car.	Yds.	Avg.	Att.	Cmp.	Passing Int.	Pct.	Yds.	TD
62	9	1	0	80	228	2.9	145	76	7	.524	1192	13
63	8	2	0	76	201	2.6	128	63	7	.492	765	7
64	#10	0	0	44	133	3.0	100	64	4	.640	757	5
Totals	27	3	0	200	562	2.8	373	203	18	.544	2714	25
Avg.							7.3 per Att.		13.4 per Cmp.		128.0 efficiency	

Yr.	Plays	Total Offense Yds.	TDR	TD	Scoring XP	Pts.
62	225	1420	17	4	2	26
63	204	966	12	5	2	32
64	144	890	11	6	0	36
Totals	573	3276	40	15	4	94
Avg.		5.7				

National champions.

HARRY NEWMAN

MICHIGAN   QB, 5-7, 175   Detroit, Mich. (Northern HS)

Unanimous all-America 32. Hall of Fame.

Yr.	Team W	L	T	Rushing Car.	Yds.	Avg.	Att.	Cmp.	Passing Int.	Pct.	Yds.	TD	Total Offense Plays	Yds.	TDR
30	8	0	1	81	237	2.9	47	17	3	.362	409	4	128	646	5
31	8	1	1	31	96	3.1	35	10	1	.286	203	3	66	299	4
32	#8	0	0	81	163	2.0	85	30	14	.353	487	5	166	650	8
Totals	24	1	2	193	496	2.6	167	57	18	.341	1099	12	360	1595	17
Avg.							6.6 per Att.		19.3 per Cmp.		4.4				

Yr.	Interceptions No.	Yds.	Punt Returns No.	Yds.	K.O. Returns No.	Yds.	TD	Scoring XP	FG	Pts.
30	4	25	24	124	2	37	1	3	1	12
31	1	35	10	67	1	27	1	7	0	13
32	1	0	52	602	11	290	3	7	2	31
Totals	6	60	86	793	14	354	5	17	3	56
Avg.		10.0		9.2		25.3				

Other career figures: 1 punt for 22 yds.

National champions.

DWIGHT NICHOLS
IOWA STATE   TB, 5-10, 164   Knoxville, Iowa (Knoxville HS)

All-America 59. Heisman 8th in 59.

Yr.	Team			Rushing			Passing					Total Offense		
	W	L	T	Car.	Yds.	Avg.	Att.	Cmp.	Int.	Pct.	Yds.	TD	Plays	Yds.	TDR
57	4	5	1	211	668	3.2	100	50	7	.500	751	7	311	1419	12
58	4	6	0	220	815	3.7	57	26	2	.456	357	0	277	1172	3
59	7	3	0	207	746	3.6	80	43	5	.538	609	8	287	1355	17
Totals	15	14	1	638	2229	3.5	237	119	14	.502	1717	15	875	3946	32
Avg.							7.2 per Att.				14.4 per Cmp.			4.4	

Yr.	Interceptions		Punting		Punt Returns		K.O. Returns		Scoring	
	No.	Yds.	No.	Avg.	No.	Yds.	No.	Yds.	TD	Pts.
57	2	5	1	46.0	11	68	3	55	5	30
58	1	0	14	29.9	18	195	5	137	3	18
59	4	70	0	0.0	12	123	9	188	9	54
Totals	7	75	15	31.0	41	386	17	380	17	102
Avg.		10.7				9.4		22.4		

DAVEY O'BRIEN
TEXAS CHRISTIAN
QB, 5-7, 150
Dallas, Texas (Woodrow Wilson HS)

Unanimous all-America 38. Heisman winner 38. Hall of Fame.

Bowls: Cotton 37—Beat Marquette, 16-6. Sugar 39—set Sugar Bowl records of 17 completions in 27 attempts for 225 yards, including 44-yard TD pass; kicked 20-yard field goal (Beat Carnegie Tech, 15-7).

Yr.	Team			Rushing			Passing					Total Offense		
	W	L	T	Car.	Yds.	Avg.	Att.	Cmp.	Int.	Pct.	Yds.	TD	Plays	Yds.	TDR
36	8	2	2	36	21	0.6	33	18	3	.545	202	2	69	223	2
37	4	4	2	166	442	2.7	*234	*94	*18	.402	969	3	*400	1411	10
38	#10	0	0	124	390	3.1	167	*93	4	.557	*1457	*19	291	*1847	*22
Totals	22	6	4	326	853	2.6	434	205	25	.472	2628	24	760	3481	34
Avg.							6.1 per Att.				12.8 per Cmp.			4.6	

Yr.	Interceptions		Punting		Punt Ret.		K.O. Ret.			Scoring			
	No.	Yds.	No.	Avg.	No.	Yds.	No.	Yds.	TD	Att.-Made		FG	Pts.
36	5	17	34	34.5	23	237	1	4	0	0	0	0	0
37	5	32	64	33.2	58	547	8	240	7	9	7	*2	55
38	6	86	7	35.8	35	402	2	56	3	*35	*28	0	46
Totals	16	135	105	33.8	116	1186	11	300	10	44	35	2	101
Avg.	8.4			33.8		10.2		27.3					

National champions. * This figure led the nation.

BOB ODELL
PENNSYLVANIA HB, 5-11, 182 Sioux City, Iowa (East HS)

Consensus all-America 43. Heisman 2nd in 43.

	Team			Rushing			Passing				Total Offense		
Yr.	W	L	T	Car.	Yds.	Avg.	Att.	Cmp.	Int.	Pct.	Yds.	Plays	Yds.
41	7	1	0	56	109	1.9	8	4	1	.500	54	64	163
42	5	3	1	83	398	4.8	10	1	1	.100	10	93	408
43	6	2	1	38	265	7.0	6	2	1	.333	2	44	267
Totals	18	6	2	177	772	4.4	24	7	3	.292	66	201	838
Avg.													4.2

	Receiving			Int.		Punting		Punt Ret.		K.O. Ret.		Scoring	
Yr.	No.	Yds.	Avg.	No.	Yds.	No.	Avg.	No.	Yds.	No.	Yds.	TD	Pts.
41	6	55	9.2	1	3	5	36.8	9	152	4	117	3	18
42	2	-4	-2.0	2	15	8	35.3	11	210	2	55	3	18
43	16	213	13.3	4	47	5	38.6	18	284	1	30	5	30
Totals	24	264	11.0	7	65	18	36.6	38	646	7	202	11	66
Avg.					9.3				17.0		28.9		

STEVE OWENS
OKLAHOMA
TB, 6-2, 215
Miami, Okla. (Miami HS)

Unanimous all-America 69. Heisman winner 69.

Bowls: Orange 68—scored TD, rushed for 61 yards. (Beat Tennessee, 26-24). Astro-Bluebonnet 68—threw 21-yard TD pass, rushed 113 yards on 36 carries (Southern Methodist won, 28-27).

	Team			Rushing			Passing			
Yr.	W	L	T	Car.	Yds.	Avg.	Att.	Cmp.	Yds.	TD
67	9	1	0	190	808	4.3	0	0	0	0
68	7	3	0	*357	1536	4.3	2	2	22	2
69	6	4	0	*358	*1523	4.3	3	2	25	0
Totals	22	8	0	905	3867	4.3	5	4	47	2

	Receiving		K.O. Returns		Scoring	
Yr.	No.	Yds.	No.	Yds.	TD	Pts.
67	2	10	1	18	12	72
68	10	94	7	112	21	126
69	4	32	1	3	*23	138
Totals	16	136	9	133	56	336
Avg.		8.5		14.8		

* This figure led the nation.

JOHNNY PAPIT
VIRGINIA   FB, 6-0, 195   Philadelphia, Pa. (Northeast HS)

All-America 49.

Yr.	Team			Rushing			Receiving		K.O. Ret.		Scoring	
	W	L	T	Car.	Yds.	Avg.	No.	Yds.	No.	Yds.	TD	Pts.
47	7	3	0	39	190	4.9	1	15	0	0	4	24
48	5	3	1	135	884	6.5	2	8	7	146	5	30
49	7	2	0	197	1214	6.2	0	0	17	397	9	54
50	8	2	0	167	949	5.7	3	62	6	108	8	48
Totals	27	10	1	538	3237	6.0	6	85	30	651	26	156
Avg.								14.2		21.7		

Other career figures: 3 passes att., 1 cmp. for 11 yds.; 1 punt ret. for 7 yds.

VITO "BABE" PARILLI
KENTUCKY   QB, 6-1, 183   Rochester, Pa. (Rochester HS)

Consensus all-America 50 and 51. Heisman 3rd in 51, 4th in 50. Hall of Fame.

Bowls: Orange 50—threw 52-yard TD pass, completed 6 passes for 128 yards (Santa Clara won, 21-13). Sugar 51—threw 22-yard TD pass, completed 9 of 12 passes for 105 yards (Beat Oklahoma, 13-7). Cotton 52—threw 2 TD passes, one for 12 yards, passed for 85 yards (Beat Texas Christian, 20-7).

Yr.	Team			Rushing		Passing					
	W	L	T	Car.	Yds.	Att.	Cmp.	Int.	Pct.	Yds.	TD
49	9	2	0	31	-142	150	81	13	.540	1081	8
50	10	1	0	31	54	203	114	12	.562	1627	*23
51+	7	4	0	30	-161	239	136	12	*.569	1643	*19
Totals	26	7	0	92	-249	592	331	37	.559	4351	50
Avg.						7.3 per Att.				13.1 per Cmp.	

Yr.	Plays	Total Offense Yds.	TDR	Scoring TD	Pts.
49	181	939	9	1	6
50	234	1681	28	5	30
51	269	1482	21	2	12
Totals	684	4102	58	8	48
Avg.		6.0			

Other career figures: 73 punts for 36.2 avg.

+ National leader in passing efficiency in 1951 (min. 15 att. per game) at 130.8.
* This figure led the nation.

JIM PHILLIPS
AUBURN E, 6-2, 205 Alex City, Ala. (Benjamin Russell HS)

Unanimous all-America 57. Heisman 6th in 57. Academic all-America 57.
Bowl: Gator 56—TD catch (Vanderbilt won, 25-13).

Yr.	Team W	L	T	No.	Receiving Yds.	TD	Avg.	K.O. Returns No.	Yds.	Scoring TD	Pts.
55	8	1	1	14	272	1	19.4	2	30	1	6
56	7	3	0	23	383	4	16.7	1	12	4	24
57	10	0	0	15	357	4	23.8	0	0	5	30
Totals	25	4	1	52	1012	9	19.5	3	42	10	60

MIKE PHIPPS
PURDUE
QB, 6-3, 206
Columbus, Ind. (Columbus HS)

Unanimous all-America 69. Heisman 2nd in 69. Academic all-America 69. NCAA Postgraduate Scholarship 70.

Yr.	Team W	L	T	Rushing Car.	Yds.	Avg.	Passing Att.	Cmp.	Int.	Pct.	Yds.	TD
67	8	2	0	86	220	2.6	243	118	7	.486	1800	11
68	8	2	0	57	22	0.4	169	88	9	.521	1096	3
69	8	2	0	97	218	2.2	321	169	18	.526	2527	23
Totals	24	6	0	240	460	1.9	733	375	34	.512	5423	37
Avg.							7.5 per Att.				14.5 per Cmp.	

Yr.	Total Offense Plays	Yds.	TDR	Scoring TD	Pts.
67	329	2020	12	1	6
68	226	1118	3	0	0
69	418	2745	31	8	48
Totals	973	5883	46	9	54
Avg.		6.0			

PETE PIHOS
INDIANA   E-FB, 6-0, 205   Chicago, Ill. (Austin HS)

All-America 43. Heisman 8th in 45. Hall of Fame.

Yr.	Team W	L	T	Rushing Car.	Yds.	Avg.	Att.	Passing Cmp.	Int.	Yds.	TD
42	7	3	0	0	0	0.0	0	0	0	0	0
43	4	4	2	16	68	4.3	0	0	0	0	0
45	9	0	1	92	410	4.5	1	1	0	12	0
46	6	3	0	76	262	3.4	12	7	1	84	1
Totals	26	10	3	184	740	4.0	13	8	1	96	1

Yr.	Receiving No.	Yds.	TD	Avg.	Scoring TD	Pts.
42	21	294	1	14.0	1	6
43	20	241	3	12.1	6	36
45	5	103	0	20.6	8	48
46	10	213	2	21.3	8	48
Totals	56	851	6	15.2	23	138

Other career figures: 3 int. by for 56 yds., 1 punt ret. for 1 yard, 3 kickoff ret. for 36 yds.

JIM "PREACHER" PILOT
NEW MEXICO STATE   HB, 5-11, 205   Kingsville, Texas (H.M. King HS)

Yr.	Team W	L	T	Rushing Car.	Yds.	Avg.	Receiving No.	Yds.
61	5	4	1	191	*1278	*6.7	4	20
62	4	6	0	*208	*1247	6.0	4	26
63	3	6	1	91	446	4.9	0	0
Totals	12	16	2	490	2971	6.1	8	46
Avg.								5.8

Yr.	Interceptions No.	Yds.	Punt Returns No.	Yds.	K.O. Returns No.	Yds.	TD	Scoring XP	Pts.
61	1	14	9	161	9	147	21	12	*138
62	0	0	5	31	10	213	*15	2	92
63	2	7	7	145	4	71	2	0	12
Totals	3	21	21	337	23	431	38	13	242
Avg.		7.0		16.0		18.7			

Other career figures: 2 passes att., 1 int.

* This figure led the nation.

EDDIE PRICE
TULANE   FB, 5-11, 190   New Orleans, La. (Warren Easton HS)

All-America 49. Hall of Fame.

	Team			Rushing			Receiving		
Yr.	W	L	T	Car.	Yds.	Avg.	No.	Yds.	Avg.
46	3	7	0	49	309	6.3	2	11	5.5
47	2	5	2	106	471	4.4	2	36	18.0
48	9	1	0	188	1178	6.3	2	7	3.5
49	7	2	1	171	1137	*6.6	7	81	11.6
Totals	21	15	3	514	3095	6.0	13	135	10.4

	Punt Returns		K.O. Returns		Scoring	
Yr.	No.	Yds.	No.	Yds.	TD	Pts.
46	3	33	3	37	5	30
47	3	26	6	148	5	30
48	0	0	7	133	10	60
49	0	0	11	219	11	66
Totals	6	59	27	537	31	186
Avg.		9.8		19.9		

* This figure led the nation.

JOHN RAUCH
GEORGIA   QB, 6-0, 185   Yeadon, Pa. (Yeadon HS)

All-America 48.

Bowls: Oil 45—Beat Tulsa, 20-6. Sugar 47—scored 2 TDs, one a 13-yard rush (Beat North Caro., 20-10). Gator 48—scored TD, threw 13-yard TD pass, completed 12 of 20 passes for 190 yards (Tied Maryland, 20-20). Orange 49—threw 37-yard TD pass, completed 11 of 17 passes for 161 yards (Texas won, 41-28).

	Team			Rushing		Passing					Total Offense		
Yr.	W	L	T	Car.	Yds.	Att.	Cmp.	Int.	Pct.	Yds.	TD	Plays	Yds.	TDR
45	8	2	0	26	-21	68	29	4	.426	566	5	94	545	6
46	10	0	0	32	69	87	48	4	.552	779	14	119	848	*21
47	7	4	0	57	-150	181	98	10	.541	1352	10	238	1202	12
48	9	1	0	37	-117	141*	71	13	.504	1307	5	178	1190	9
Totals	34	7	0	152	-219	477	246	31	.516	4004	34	629	3785	48
Avg.						8.4 per Att.	16.3 per Cmp.		132.6 efficiency			6.0		

	Receiving			Interceptions		Punting		K.O. Ret.		Scoring	
Yr.	No.	Yds.	TD	No.	Yds.	No.	Avg.	No.	Yds.	TD	Pts.
45	2	37	0	1	25	14	33.4	3	131	1	6
46	4	90	2	6	46	4	33.0	2	42	7	42
47	0	0	0	4	36	21	31.7	1	13	2	12
48	0	0	0	2	34	0	0.0	3	48	4	24
Totals	6	127	2	13	141	39	32.4	9	234	14	84
Avg.		21.2			10.8				26.0		

Other career figures: 1 punt ret. for 14 yds.

* This figure led the nation.

MEL RENFRO
OREGON HB, 5-11, 190 Portland, Ore. (Jefferson HS)

Consensus all-America 62. All-America 63.
Bowl: Sun 64—Beat Southern Methodist, 21-14.

Yr.	Team			Rushing			Passing						Total Offense		
	W	L	T	Car.	Yds.	Avg.	Att.	Cmp.	Int.	Pct.	Yds.	TD	Plays	Yds.	TDR
61	4	6	0	61	335	5.5	8	4	2	.500	99	2	69	434	6
62	6	3	1	126	753	6.0	11	4	2	.364	107	2	137	860	15
63	7	3	0	82	444	5.4	11	5	0	.455	54	0	93	498	6
Totals	17	12	1	269	1532	5.7	30	13	4	.433	260	4	299	1792	27
Avg.								8.7 per Att.			20.0 per Cmp.			6.0	

Yr.	Receiving				Int.		Punt Ret.		K.O. Ret.		Scoring		
	No.	Yds.	TD	Avg.	No.	Yds.	No.	Yds.	No.	Yds.	TD	XP	Pts.
61	7	86	0	12.3	1	8	2	49	5	199	4	0	24
62	16	298	3	18.6	2	67	6	42	10	245	13	0	78
63	18	260	2	14.4	0	0	2	38	8	170	6	3	39
Totals	41	644	5	15.7	3	75	10	129	23	614	23	3	141
Avg.						25.0		12.9		26.7			

BOBBY REYNOLDS
NEBRASKA
HB, 5-11, 180
Grand Island, Neb. (Grand Island HS)

All-America 50. Heisman 5th in 50.

Yr.	Team			Rushing			Passing						Total Offense		
	W	L	T	Car.	Yds.	Avg.	Att.	Cmp.	Int.	Pct.	Yds.	TD	Plays	Yds.	TDR
50	6	2	1	193	1342	7.0	10	4	2	.400	75	0	203	1417	22
51	2	8	0	87	424	4.9	29	12	3	.414	200	1	116	624	3
52	5	4	1	93	430	4.6	13	3	2	.231	34	0	106	464	4
Totals	13	14	2	373	2196	5.9	52	19	7	.365	309	1	425	2505	29
Avg.								5.9 per Att.			16.3 per Cmp.			5.9	

Yr.	Receiving			Int.		Punting		Punt Ret.		K.O. Ret.		Scoring			
	No.	Yds.	TD	No.	Yds.	No.	Avg.	No.	Yds.	No.	Yds.	TD	XP	FG	Pts.
50	11	173	3	0	0	36	37.3	3	28	5	88	*22	25	0	*157
51	5	55	1	1	20	29	33.8	5	71	8	153	2	0	0	12
52	0	0	0	0	0	17	35.8	4	51	0	0	4	15	1	42
Totals	16	228	4	1	20	82	35.8	12	150	13	241	28	40	1	211
Avg.		14.3			20.0				12.5		18.5				

* This figure led the nation.

JERRY RHOME

TULSA   QB, 6-0, 181   Dallas, Texas (Sunset HS)

All-America 64. Heisman 2nd in 64.

Bowl: Bluebonnet 64—threw 35-yard TD pass, scored TD, completed 22 of 36 passes for 252 yards (Beat Mississippi, 14-7).

	Team			Rushing			Passing				
Yr.	W	L	T	Car.	Yds.	Avg.	Att.	Cmp.	Int.	Pct.	Yds.	TD
61†	2	7	1	92	82	0.9	129	74	6	.574	693	5
63	5	5	0	77	67	0.9	258	150	13	.581	1909	10
64#	8	2	0	144	258	1.8	*326	*224	4	*.687	*2870	*32
Totals	15	14	1	313	407	1.3	713	448	23	.628	5472	47
Avg.							7.7 per Att.	12.2 per Cmp.		142.6 efficiency		

		Total Offense			Scoring 2-Pt. passes		
Yr.	Plays	Yds.	TDR	TD	Att.	Made	Pts.
61†	221	775	5	0	1	1	0
63	335	1976	12	2	8	7	12
64	*470	*3128	*40	8	14	8	48
Totals	1026	5879	57	10	23	16	60
Avg.	5.7						

Other career figures: 52 punts for 34.1 avg.; 3 kickoff ret. for 37 yds.

\# National leader in passing efficiency in 1964 (min. 15 att. per game) at 172.6.

* This figure led the nation.

† Played at Southern Methodist in 61.

PAT RICHTER

WISCONSIN   E, 6-5, 229   Madison, Wis. (East HS)

Consensus all-America 62. All-America 61. Heisman 6th in 62. Academic all-America 62. Silver Anniversary Award, NCAA Honors Luncheon 88.

Bowl: Rose 63—caught 11 passes for 163 yards, including 19-yard TD catch (Southern Cal won, 42-37).

	Team			Receiving				Punting		K.O. Ret.		Scoring		
Yr.	W	L	T	No.	Yds.	TD	Avg.	No.	Avg.	No.	Yds.	TD	XP	Pts.
60	4	5	0	25	362	1	14.5	6	35.0	0	0	1	2	8
61	6	3	0	47	*817	*8	17.4	0	0.0	1	12	8	0	48
62	8	1	0	38	531	5	14.0	36	39.0	0	0	5	0	30
Totals	18	9	0	110	1710	14	15.5	42	38.4	1	12	14	2	86

* This figure led the nation.

KYLE ROTE
SOUTHERN METHODIST   HB, 6-0, 190   San Antonio, Texas (Thomas Jefferson HS)

Consensus all-America 50. Heisman 2nd in 50. Hall of Fame.

Bowl: Cotton 49—36-yard TD rush; 17 carries for 93 yards rushing; 4 catches for 55 yards; set Cotton Bowl record with 84-yard punt (Beat Oregon, 21-13).

Yr.	Team W	L	T	Rushing Car.	Yds.	Avg.	Passing Att.	Cmp.	Int.	Pct.	Yds.	TD	Total Offense Plays	Yds.	TDR
48	8	1	1	115	504	4.4	0	0	0	.000	0	0	115	504	7
49	5	4	1	142	777	5.5	42	13	4	.310	158	0	184	935	12
50	6	4	0	153	757	4.9	66	27	9	.409	490	3	219	1247	16
Totals	19	9	2	410	2038	5.0	108	40	13	.370	648	3	518	2686	35
Avg.							6.0 per Att.			16.2 per Cmp.				5.2	

Yr.	Receiving No.	Yds.	TD	Avg.	K.O. Returns No.	Yds.	TD	Scoring XP	Pts.
48	19	214	3	11.3	1	19	7	0	42
49	14	298	3	21.3	6	207	12	2	74
50	28	221	1	7.9	14	336	13	0	78
Totals	61	733	7	12.0	21	562	32	2	194
Avg.						26.8			

GEORGE SAUER
NEBRASKA   FB, 6-2, 195   Lincoln, Neb. (Lincoln HS)

Consensus all-America 33. Hall of Fame.

Yr.	Team W	L	T	Rushing Car.	Yds.	Avg.	Passing Att.	Cmp.	Int.	Pct.	Yds.	TD	Total Offense Plays	Yds.	TDR
31	8	2	0	132	565	4.3	57	15	11	.298	233	1	189	798	7
32	7	1	1	128	411	3.2	50	11	5	.220	163	3	178	574	5
33	8	1	0	133	594	4.5	43	19	6	.442	305	1	176	899	7
Totals	23	4	1	393	1570	4.0	150	47	22	.313	701	5	543	2271	19
Avg.							4.7 per Att.			14.9 per Cmp.				4.2	

Yr.	Interceptions No.	Yds.	TD	Punting No.	Avg.	K.O. Returns No.	Yds.	TD	Scoring XP	FG	Pts.
31	1	70	1	61	38.8	2	49	6	0	0	36
32	6	108	2	62	32.5	2	37	2	0	0	12
33	3	37	0	67	34.6	5	118	6	1	1	40
Totals	10	215	3	190	35.2	9	204	14	1	1	88
Avg.		21.5					22.7				

Other career figures: 1 catch for 25 yds.

JAMES SAXTON
TEXAS   HB, 5-11, 160   Palestine, Texas (Palestine HS)

Unanimous all-America 61. Heisman 3rd in 61.
Bowls: Cotton 60—Syracuse won, 23-14. Bluebonnet 60—Tied Alabama, 3-3. Cotton 62—scored TD, 74-yard punt (Beat Mississippi, 12-7).

| | Team | | | Rushing | | | Passing | | | | Scoring | | |
Yr.	W	L	T	Car.	Yds.	Avg.	Att.	Cmp.	Pct.	Yds.	TD	TD	XP	Pts.
59	9	1	0	55	271	4.9	4	4	1.000	39	1	1	1	7
60	7	3	0	76	407	5.4	4	1	.250	11	0	3	0	18
61	9	1	0	107	846	*7.9	1	1	1.000	46	1	9	2	56
Totals	25	5	0	238	1524	6.4	9	6	.667	96	2	13	3	81

| | Receiving | | | | Interceptions | | Punting | | Punt Ret. | | K.O. Ret. | |
Yr.	No.	Yds.	TD	Avg.	No.	Yds.	No.	Avg.	No.	Yds.	No.	Yds.
59	0	0	0	0.0	2	18	12	43.0	4	36	0	0
60	9	185	1	20.6	3	4	15	32.5	11	163	1	16
61	7	123	0	17.6	0	0	1	54.0	5	33	6	143
Totals	16	308	1	19.3	5	22	28	37.8	20	232	7	159
Avg.						4.4				11.6		22.7

* This figure led the nation.

GALE SAYERS
KANSAS   HB, 6-0, 194   Omaha, Neb. (Central HS)

Consensus all-America 63 and 64. Heisman 12th in 64. Hall of Fame.

| | Team | | | Rushing | | | Passing | | | | | Total Offense | | |
Yr.	W	L	T	Car.	Yds.	Avg.	Att.	Cmp.	Int.	Pct.	Yds.	TD	Plays	Yds.	TDR
62	6	3	1	158	1125	*7.1	2	1	0	.500	13	0	160	1138	7
63	5	5	0	132	917	6.9	3	2	0	.667	35	1	135	952	9
64	6	4	0	122	633	5.2	15	6	1	.400	55	1	137	688	6
Totals	17	12	1	412	2675	6.5	20	9	1	.450	103	2	432	2778	22
Avg.														6.4	

| | Receiving | | | | Punt Returns | | K.O. Ret. | | | Scoring | | |
Yr.	No.	Yds.	TD	Avg.	No.	Yds.	No.	Yds.	TD	XP	Pts.
62	7	71	0	10.1	8	56	6	141	7	0	42
63	11	155	1	14.1	5	130	9	184	8	2	50
64	17	182	0	10.7	15	138	7	195	5	0	30
Totals	35	408	1	11.7	28	324	22	520	20	2	122
Avg.						11.6		23.6			

* This figure led the nation.

JACK SCARBATH
MARYLAND
QB, 6-1, 190
Baltimore, Md. (Poly HS)

Unanimous all-America 52. Heisman 2nd in 52. Hall of Fame.
Bowl: Sugar 52—scored TD (Beat Tennessee, 28-13).

Yr.	Team W	L	T	Rushing Car.	Yds.	Avg.	Passing Att.	Cmp.	Int.	Pct.	Yds.	TD
50	7	2	1	81	252	3.1	80	32	5	.400	463	4
51	9	0	0	56	156	2.8	67	34	4	.507	675	8
52	7	2	0	102	227	2.2	113	59	5	.522	1049	10
Totals	23	4	1	239	635	2.7	260	125	14	.481	2187	22
Avg.							8.4 per Att.		17.5 per Cmp.		135.9 efficiency	

Yr.	Plays	Total Offense Yds.	TDR	Scoring TD	Pts.
50	161	715	7	3	18
51	123	831	15	7	42
52	215	1276	13	3	18
Totals	499	2822	35	13	78
Avg.		5.7			

MARCHY SCHWARTZ
NOTRE DAME   HB, 5-11, 178   Bay St. Louis, Miss. (St. Stanislaus HS)

Consensus all-America 30 and 31. Hall of Fame.

Yr.	Team W	L	T	Rushing Car.	Yds.	Avg.	Passing Att.	Cmp.	Int.	Pct.	Yds.	TD
29	#9	0	0	65	326	5.0	17	3	4	.176	63	0
30	#10	0	0	124	927	7.5	56	17	9	.304	319	3
31	6	2	1	146	692	4.7	51	9	4	.176	174	3
Totals	25	2	1	335	1945	5.8	124	29	17	.234	556	6
Avg.							4.5 per Att.		19.2 per Cmp.			

Yr.	Plays	Total Offense Yds.	TDR	Scoring TD	Pts.
29	82	389	3	3	18
30	180	1246	12	9	54
31	197	866	8	5	30
Totals	459	2501	23	17	102
Avg.		5.4			

Other career figures—1 catch for 4 yds., 2 int. by for 10 yds., 79 punts for 35.3 avg., 7 punt ret. for 39 yds., 6 kickoff ret. for 169 yds.

National champions.

RON SELLERS
FLORIDA STATE   FL, 6-4, 187   Jacksonville, Fla. (Paxon HS)

Consensus all-America 67. All-America 68. Heisman 10th in 68. Hall of Fame.

Bowls: Sun 67—caught 6 passes for 170 yards, 2 TDs (Wyoming won, 28-20). Gator 68—caught Gator Bowl record of 14 passes for 145 yards, 1 TD (Tied Penn St., 17-17). Peach 69—caught 8 passes for 76 yards, 2 TDs (Louisiana St. won, 31-27).

	Team				Receiving			Scoring	
Yr.	W	L	T	No.	Yds.	TD	Avg.	TD	Pts.
66	6	4	0	56	874	3	15.6	3	18
67	7	2	1	70	*1228	8	17.5	8	48
68	8	2	0	*86	*1496	*12	17.4	12	72
Totals	21	8	1	212	3598	23	17.0	23	138

* This figure led the nation.

ORENTHAL JAMES "O.J." SIMPSON
SOUTHERN CALIFORNIA
HB, 6-2, 205
San Francisco, Calif. (Galileo HS)

Unanimous all-America 67 and 68. Heisman winner 68, 2nd in 67. Hall of Fame.

Bowls: Rose 68—scored 2 TDs, rushed 128 yards on 25 carries (Beat Indiana, 14-3). Rose 69—80-yard TD rush, rushed 171 yards on 28 carries; 8 catches for 85 yards (Ohio St. won, 27-16).

	Team				Rushing			Passing		
Yr.	W	L	T	Car.	Yds.	Avg.	Att.	Cmp.	Yds.	TD
67	#9	1	0	*266	*1415	*5.3	5	3	33	3
68	9	0	1	355	*1709	4.8	3	1	15	0
Totals	18	1	1	621	3124	5.0	8	4	48	3

	Receiving			K.O. Returns		Scoring	
Yr.	No.	Yds.	Avg.	No.	Yds.	TD	Pts.
67	10	109	10.9	7	176	11	66
68	18	126	7.0	6	131	*22	132
Totals	28	235	8.4	13	307	33	198
Avg.					26.8		

National champions.

FRANK SINKWICH
GEORGIA HB, 5-8, 185 Youngstown, Ohio (Chaney HS)

Unanimous all-America 42. Consensus all-America 41. Heisman winner 42, 4th in 41. Hall of Fame.

Bowls: Orange 42—set all-time major bowl record of 382 yards total offense; set Orange Bowl records of 243 yards passing, .692 cmp. pct. (9 of 13), and 3 TD passes of 61, 60 and 15 yards; rushed for 139 yards, one a 43-yard TD (Beat Texas Christian, 40-26). Rose 43—scored TD, injured, 71 yards total offense (Beat UCLA, 9-0).

	Team			Rushing			Passing					
Yr.	W	L	T	Car.	Yds.	Avg.	Att.	Cmp.	Int.	Pct.	Yds.	TD
40	5	4	1	63	373	5.9	44	21	2	.477	226	6
41	8	1	1	*209	*1103	5.3	115	52	7	.452	713	11
42	10	1	0	175	795	4.5	166	84	7	.506	1392	10
Totals	23	6	2	447	2271	5.1	325	157	16	.483	2331	27
Avg.							7.2 per Att.	14.8 per Cmp.		128.7 efficiency		

		Total Offense			Scoring	
Yr.	Plays	Yds.	TDR	TD	FG	Pts.
40	107	599	11	5	0	30
41	324	1816	18	7	1	45
42	*341	*2187	*26	16	0	96
Totals	772	4602	55	28	1	171
Avg.		6.0				

* This figure led the nation.

EMIL SITKO
NOTRE DAME FB-HB, 5-8, 180 Fort Wayne, Ind. (Central HS)

Unanimous all-America 49. Consensus all-America 48. Heisman 7th in 48, 8th in 49. Hall of Fame.

	Team			Rushing			Receiving			
Yr.	W	L	T	Car.	Yds.	Avg.	No.	Yds.	TD	Avg.
46	#8	0	1	53	346	6.5	3	55	0	18.3
47	#9	0	0	60	426	7.1	4	62	1	15.5
48	9	0	1	129	742	5.8	7	70	0	10.0
49	#10	0	0	120	712	5.9	2	15	0	7.5
Totals	36	0	2	362	2226	6.1	16	202	1	12.6

	Punt Returns		K.O. Returns		Scoring	
Yr.	No.	Yds.	No.	Yds.	TD	Pts.
46	2	20	1	1	3	18
47	0	0	2	52	5	30
48	0	0	1	76	9	54
49	1	23	4	89	9	54
Totals	3	43	8	218	26	156
Avg.		14.3		27.3		

National champions.

BRUCE SMITH
MINNESOTA HB, 6-0, 193   Faribault, Minn. (Faribault HS)

Consensus all-America 41. Heisman winner 41. Hall of Fame.

	Team			Rushing			Passing						Total Offense		
Yr.	W	L	T	Car.	Yds.	Avg.	Att.	Cmp.	Int.	Pct.	Yds.	TD	Plays	Yds.	TDR
39	3	4	1	66	297	4.5	0	0	0	0	0	0	66	297	6
40	#8	0	0	100	460	4.6	24	7	2	.292	155	3	124	615	8
41	#8	0	0	92	446	4.9	31	13	2	.419	320	1	123	766	6
Totals	19	4	1	258	1203	4.8	55	20	4	.364	475	4	313	1678	20
Avg.							8.6 per Att.			23.8 per Cmp.			5.4		

	Receiving		Punting		Punt Returns		K.O. Returns		Scoring		
Yr.	No.	Yds.	No.	Avg.	No.	Yds.	No.	Yds.	TD	XP	Pts.
39	6	84	0	0.0	0	0	5	105	6	0	36
40	0	0	0	0.0	0	0	0	0	5	2	32
41	0	0	19	35.2	12	121	0	0	5	0	30
Totals	6	84	19	35.2	12	121	5	105	16	2	98
Avg.		14.0				10.1		21.0			

National champions.

STEVE SPURRIER
FLORIDA
QB, 6-2, 203
Johnson City, Tenn. (Science Hill HS)

Unanimous all-America 66. All-America 65. Heisman winner 66, 9th in 65.
Bowls: Sugar 66—set Sugar Bowl records of 27 completions (in 45 attempts), 352 yards passing and 344 total offense; threw 21- and 22-yard TD passes, scored TD (Missouri won, 20-18). Orange 67—completed 14 passes for 160 yards, 36.1 punting avg. (Beat Georgia Tech, 27-12).

	Team			Rushing		Passing					
Yr.	W	L	T	Car.	Yds.	Att.	Cmp.	Int.	Pct.	Yds.	TD
64	7	3	0	102	146	114	65	10	.570	943	6
65	7	3	0	125	230	287	148	13	.516	1893	14
66	8	2	0	76	66	291	179	8	.615	2012	16
Totals	22	8	0	303	442	692	392	31	.566	4848	36
Avg.					1.5	7.0 per Att.				12.4 per Cmp.	

	Total Offense			Scoring		
Yr.	Plays	Yds.	TDR	TD	FG	Pts.
64	216	1089	7	1	0	6
65	412	2123	16	2	0	12
66	367	2078	17	1	3	15
Totals	995	5290	40	4	3	33
Avg.	5.3					

Other career figures—3 catches for 5 yds.; 130 punts for 40.3 avg.

ROGER STAUBACH
NAVY
QB, 6-2, 190
Cincinnati, Ohio (Purcell HS)

Unanimous all-America 63. Heisman winner 63. Hall of Fame. Silver Anniversary Award, NCAA Honors Dinner 90.
Bowl: Cotton 64—set Cotton Bowl records of 21 completions (in 31 attempts) and 228 yards passing (Texas won, 28-6).

	Team			Rushing		Passing					
Yr.	W	L	T	Car.	Yds.	Att.	Cmp.	Int.	Pct.	Yds.	TD
62	5	5	0	85	265	98	66	3	*.673	966	7
63	9	1	0	156	418	161	107	6	*.665	1474	7
64	3	6	1	104	-1	204	119	10	.583	1131	4
Totals	17	12	1	345	682	463	292	19	.631	3571	18
Avg.					2.0	7.7 per Att.	12.2 per Cmp.		133.1 efficiency		

		Total Offense		Scoring		
Yr.	Plays	Yds.	TDR	TD	XP	Pts.
62	183	1231	14	7	0	42
63	317	1892	15	8	2	50
64	308	1130	6	2	0	12
Totals	808	4253	35	17	2	104
Avg.		5.3				

* This figure led the nation.

SANFORD "SANDY" STEPHENS
MINNESOTA   QB, 6-0, 215   Uniontown, Pa. (Uniontown HS)

Consensus all-America 61. Heisman 4th in 61.
Bowls: Rose 61—Washington won, 17-7. Rose 62—scored 2 TDs, completed 7 of 11 passes for 75 yards (Beat UCLA, 21-3).

	Team			Rushing			Passing					TD	Total Offense		
Yr.	W	L	T	Car.	Yds.	Avg.	Att.	Cmp.	Int.	Pct.	Yds.		Plays	Yds.	TDR
59	2	7	0	39	140	3.6	82	24	9	.293	376	2	121	516	5
60	#8	1	0	57	164	2.9	52	20	2	.385	305	2	109	469	11
61	7	2	0	110	487	4.4	142	47	13	.331	794	9	252	1281	15
Totals	17	10	0	206	791	3.8	276	91	24	.330	1475	13	482	2266	31
Avg.							5.3 per Att.		16.2 per Cmp.				4.7		

	Int.		Punting		Punt Returns		K.O. Ret.		Scoring		
Yr.	No.	Yds.	No.	Avg.	No.	Yds.	No.	Yds.	TD	XP	Pts.
59	3	70	3	19.0	13	57	11	299	3	2	20
60	4	114	55	35.4	16	111	8	190	9	0	54
61	2	2	39	28.6	13	88	0	0	6	2	38
Totals	9	186	97	32.2	42	256	19	489	18	4	112
Avg.		20.7				6.1		25.7			

National champions.

BOB STEUBER
MISSOURI E-HB, 6-2, 195 St. Louis, Mo. (Christian Brothers College HS)

All-America 42. Hall of Fame.

Bowl: Sugar 42—barely short with 45-yard field goal attempt in closing minutes (Fordham won, 2-0).

	Team			Rushing			†Passing		
Yr.	W	L	T	Car.	Yds.	Avg.	Att.	Cmp.	Yds.
40	6	3	0	10	51	5.1	0	0	0
41	8	1	0	113	855	*7.6	17	—	111
42	8	3	1	149	1098	*7.4	50	—	356
Totals	22	7	1	272	2004	7.4	67	—	467
Avg.									7.0 per Att.

	Total Offense		†Receiving			Scoring		
Yr.	Plays	Yds.	No.	Yds.	TD	XP		Pts.
40	10	51	16	293	5	4		34
41	130	966	—	—	9	13		67
42	199	1454	—	—	*18	13		*121
Totals	339	2471	—	—	32	30		222
Avg.		7.3						

† Other passing, all receiving figures unavailable for 1942.
* This figure led the nation.

JERRY STOVALL
LOUISIANA STATE HB, 6-2, 195 West Monroe, La. (West Monroe HS)

Unanimous all-America 62. Heisman 2nd in 62.

Bowls: Orange 62—Beat Colorado, 25-7. Cotton 63—Beat Texas, 13-0.

	Team			Rushing			Receiving			Scoring	
Yr.	W	L	T	Car.	Yds.	Avg.	No.	Yds.	TD	Avg.	TD	Pts.
60	5	4	1	65	308	4.7	12	114	0	9.5	1	6
61	9	1	0	64	405	6.3	9	135	0	15.0	3	18
62	8	1	1	89	368	4.1	9	203	1	22.6	11	66
Totals	22	6	2	218	1081	5.0	30	452	1	15.1	15	90

	Punting		Interceptions		Punt Ret.		K.O. Ret.	
Yr.	No.	Avg.	No.	Yds.	No.	Yds.	No.	Yds.
60	*64	42.1	3	82	6	44	5	95
61	51	37.8	2	18	7	69	4	83
62	50	37.0	2	6	6	58	6	250
Totals	165	39.3	7	106	19	171	15	428
Avg.				15.1		9.0		28.5

* This figure led the nation.

HARRY STUHLDREHER
NOTRE DAME   QB, 5-7, 151   Massillon, Ohio (Washington HS)

Consensus all-America 24. Hall of Fame.
One of the Four Horsemen.

	Team			Rushing			Passing						Total Offense		
Yr.	W	L	T	Car.	Yds.	Avg.	Att.	Cmp.	Int.	Pct.	Yds.	TD	Plays	Yds.	TDR
22	8	1	1	26	49	1.9	15	8	3	.533	68	3	41	117	9
23	9	1	0	26	50	1.9	19	10	3	.526	205	3	45	255	6
24	#9	0	0	17	19	1.1	33	25	2	.758	471	4	50	490	7
Totals	26	2	1	69	118	1.7	67	43	8	.642	744	10	136	862	22
Avg.							11.1 per Att.			17.3 per Cmp.					

		Receiving			Punt Ret.		K.O. Ret.			Scoring	
Yr.	No.	Yds.	TD	Avg.	No.	Yds.	No.	Yds.	TD	XP	Pts.
22	6	95	1	15.8	28	199	1	10	6	0	36
23	7	63	0	9.0	38	308	0	0	3	1	19
24	5	52	0	10.4	22	194	2	13	3	1	19
Totals	18	210	1	11.7	88	701	3	23	12	2	74
Avg.						8.0		7.7			

Other career figures—3 int. by for 0 yds.
National champions.

JIM SWINK
TEXAS CHRISTIAN   HB, 6-1, 180   Rusk, Texas (Rusk HS)

Unanimous all-America 55. Heisman 2nd in 55. Academic all-America 55 and 56. Silver Anniversary Award, NCAA Honors Luncheon 82. Academic All-America Hall of Fame.

Bowls: Cotton 56—2 TDs, one a 39-yard rush, 107 yards rushing on 19 carries (Mississippi won, 14-13). Cotton 57—scored TD (Beat Syracuse, 28-27).

	Team			Rushing			Receiving			
Yr.	W	L	T	Car.	Yds.	Avg.	No.	Yds.	TD	Avg.
54	4	6	0	99	670	6.8	9	104	0	11.6
55	9	1	0	157	1283	*8.2	5	111	1	22.2
56	7	3	0	158	665	4.2	19	390	2	20.5
Totals	20	10	0	414	2618	6.3	33	605	3	18.3

	Interceptions		Punt Ret.		K.O. Ret.		Scoring		
Yr.	No.	Yds.	No.	Yds.	No.	Yds.	TD	XP	Pts.
54	2	15	8	59	2	39	6	1	37
55	2	46	10	64	9	198	*20	5	*125
56	2	25	6	28	10	171	6	3	39
Totals	6	86	24	151	21	408	32	9	201
Avg.		14.3		6.3		19.4			

Other career figures—7 passes att., 1 cmp. for 11 yds., 1 had int.
* This figure led the nation.

EDDIE TALBOOM
WYOMING   HB, 5-10, 167   South Bend, Ind. (Washington HS)

All-America 50.

Bowl: Gator 51—scored 2 TDs, threw TD pass, completed 10 of 16 passes for 143 yards, kicked 2 extra points, 39-yard punting avg. (Beat Washington & Lee, 20-7).

Yr.	Team			Rushing			Passing					
	W	L	T	Car.	Yds.	Avg.	Att.	Cmp.	Int.	Pct.	Yds.	TD
48	4	5	0	112	354	3.2	90	54	2	.600	651	8
49	9	1	0	104	405	3.9	55	30	4	.545	431	5
50	9	0	0	124	376	3.0	100	57	6	.570	920	8
Totals	22	6	0	340	1135	3.3	245	141	12	.576	2002	21
Avg.							8.2 per Att.	14.2 per Cmp.		144.7 efficiency		

Yr.	Total Offense				Scoring	PATs		
	Plays	Yds.	TDR	TD	Att.	Made	Pts.	
48	202	1005	19	11	40	28	94	
49	159	836	13	8	48	31	79	
50	224	1296	23	15	45	40	130	
Totals	585	3137	55	34	133	99	303	
Avg.		5.4						

Other career figures—77 punts for 38.7 avg., 2 int. by for 15 yds., 4 punt ret. for 14 yds., 6 kickoff ret. for 115 yds.

CLENDON THOMAS
OKLAHOMA   HB, 6-2, 188   Oklahoma City, Okla. (Southeast HS)

Consensus all-America 57. Heisman 9th in 57.

Bowls: Orange 56—Beat Maryland, 20-6. Orange 58—13-yard TD rush, rushed 62 yards on 13 carries, 12-yard catch (Beat Duke, 48-21).

Yr.	Team			Rushing			Passing						Total Offense		
	W	L	T	Car.	Yds.	Avg.	Att.	Cmp.	Int.	Pct.	Yds.	TD	Plays	Yds.	TDR
55	#10	0	0	71	485	6.8	11	3	0	.273	36	0	82	521	9
56	#10	0	0	104	817	*7.9	2	0	1	.000	0	0	106	817	18
57	9	1	0	130	816	6.3	17	5	1	.294	79	1	147	895	10
Totals	29	1	0	305	2118	6.9	30	8	2	.267	115	1	335	2233	37
Avg.														6.7	

Yr.	Receiving				Int.		Punting		Punt Ret.		K.O. Ret.		Scoring	
	No.	Yds.	TD	Avg.	No.	Yds.	No.	Avg.	No.	Yds.	No.	Yds.	No.	Yds.
55	1	21	0	21.0	1	9	16	37.8	10	199	2	51	9	54
56	12	241	4	20.1	3	50	2	38.0	1	15	5	158	*18	*108
57	3	30	0	10.0	1	12	37	37.6	7	178	4	87	9	54
Totals	16	292	4	18.3	5	71	55	37.6	18	392	12	296	36	216
Avg.				14.2				21.8			24.7			

National champions. * This figure led the nation.

JIM THORPE

CARLISLE HB, 6-1, 185 Prague, Okla. (Carlisle Indian Industrial School)

Consensus all-America 11 and 12. Hall of Fame. FWAA all-time team.

Yr.	Team W	L	T	Rushing Car.	Yds.	Avg.	Att.	Cmp.	Int.	Passing Pct.	Yds.	TD	Total Offense Plays	Yds.	TDR
07	10	1	0	16	67	4.2	0	0	0	.000	0	0	16	67	6
08	10	2	1	113	781	6.9	13	8	0	.615	212	1	126	993	5
11	11	1	0	113	899	8.0	4	1	2	.250	15	0	117	914	14
12	12	1	1	191	1869	9.8	18	8	1	.444	103	0	209	1972	29
*Totals	43	5	2	433	3616	8.4	35	17	3	.486	330	1	468	3946	54
Avg.								9.4 per Att.			19.4 per Cmp.			8.4		

Yr.	Receiving No.	Yds.	Int. No.	Yds.	Punting No.	Avg.	Punt Ret. No.	Yds.	K.O. Ret. No.	Yds.	TD	Scoring XP	FG	Pts.
07	0	0	0	0	0	—	3	10	0	0	†6	0	0	30
08	0	0	0	0	49	—	14	144	2	50	†4	13	‡6	57
11	0	0	1	0	39	—	9	108	2	34	†14	19	7	110
12	2	40	1	95	45	—	26	259	9	184	29	38	4	224
*Totals	2	40	2	95	133	—	52	521	13	268	53	70	17	421
Avg.		20.0		47.5				10.0		20.6				

* Statistics available for 29 of 44 career games in every category but scoring, which includes all 44 games.

† TDs worth 5 pts. ‡ FGs worth 4 pts.

BOB TIMBERLAKE

MICHIGAN QB, 6-4, 215 Franklin, Ohio (Franklin HS)

All-America 64. Heisman 4th in 64. Academic all-America 64. Hall of Fame Scholar-Athlete 64. Bowl: Rose 65—24-yard TD rush, completed 7 of 10 passes for 77 yards (Beat Oregon St., 34-7).

Yr.	Team W	L	T	Rushing Car.	Yds.	Avg.	Att.	Cmp.	Passing Int.	Pct.	Yds.	TD
62	2	7	0	74	108	1.5	34	16	3	.471	179	0
63	3	4	2	98	228	2.3	98	47	4	.480	593	3
64	8	1	0	144	574	4.0	127	63	5	.496	807	5
Totals	13	12	2	316	910	2.9	259	126	12	.486	1579	8
Avg.								6.1 per Att.			12.5 per Cmp.	

Yr.	Total Offense Plays	Yds.	TDR	TD	Scoring XP Att.	Made	FG	Pts.
62	108	287	1	1	5	5	1	14
63	196	821	5	2	12	12	1	27
64	271	1381	13	8	20	20	4	80
Totals	575	2489	19	11	37	37	6	121
Avg.		4.3				1.000		

Other career figures—10 catches for 160 yds., 2 int. by for 0 yds., 6 kickoff ret. for 107 yds.

JIM THORPE

ERIC TIPTON
DUKE
HB, 5-11, 181
Petersburg, Va. (Petersburg HS)

All-America 38. Hall of Fame.

Bowl: Rose 39—rushed 59 yards, passed for 84, including 24-yarder during FG drive; 38.5 punting avg. (Southern Cal won, 7-3).

Yr.	Team W	L	T	Rushing Car.	Yds.	Avg.	Att.	Cmp.	Passing Int.	Pct.	Yds.	TD
36	9	1	0	129	577	4.5	0	0	0	.000	0	0
37	7	2	1	125	594	4.8	60	16	6	.267	277	1
38	9	0	0	110	462	4.2	47	22	1	.468	275	1
Totals	25	3	1	364	1633	4.5	107	38	7	.355	552	2
Avg.									5.2 per Att.		14.5 per Cmp.	

Yr.	Total Offense Plays	Yds.	Punting No.	Yds.	Avg.	Scoring TD	XP	Pts.
36	129	577	0	0	0.0	6	0	36
37	185	871	90	3656	40.6	7	3	45
38	157	737	59	2378	40.3	4	0	24
Totals	471	2185	149	6034	40.5	17	3	105
Avg.		4.6						

CHARLEY TRIPPI
GEORGIA   HB, 5-11, 185   Pittston, Pa. (Pittston HS)

Unanimous all-America 46. Heisman 2nd in 46. Hall of Fame.

Bowls: Rose 43—rushed 115 yards on 27 carries, completed 6 of 13 passes for 88 yards, intercepted a pass, 49.0 avg. on 2 punts (Beat UCLA, 9-0). Oil 45—threw 65-yard TD pass, 68-yard TD punt return (Beat Tulsa, 20-6). Sugar 47—set Sugar Bowl record with 67-yard TD pass (Beat North Caro., 20-10).

Yr.	Team W	L	T	Rushing Car.	Yds.	Avg.	Att.	Cmp.	†Passing Int.	Pct.	Yds.	TD	Total Offense Plays	Yds.
42	10	1	0	98	672	6.9	58	—	—	—	567	—	156	1239
43	8	2	0	65	321	4.9	60	27	5	.450	576	2	125	897
46	10	0	0	115	744	6.5	70	40	3	.571	622	5	185	1366
Totals	28	3	0	278	1737	6.2	188	—	—	—	1765	—	466	3502
Avg.									9.4 per Att.					7.5

Yr.	Receiving No.	Yds.	Int. No.	Yds.	Punting No.	Avg.	Punt Ret. No.	Yds.	K.O. Ret. No.	Yds.	Scoring TD	Pts.
42	—	—	—	—	—	—	—	—	—	—	8	48
45	1	5	0	0	14	41.4	11	220	5	98	9	54
46	11	120	6	107	40	35.5	18	195	5	128	14	84
Totals	—	—	—	—	—	—	—	—	—	—	31	186

† Other passing figures unavailable in 1942 (as are those for other five categories).

DON TRULL
BAYLOR QB, 6-1, 179 Oklahoma City, Okla. (Southeast HS)

All-America 63. Heisman 4th in 63. Academic all-America 62 and 63. Hall of Fame Scholar-Athlete 63.

Bowls: Gotham 61—scored TD, completed 11 of 16 passes for 116 yards, one a 38-yard TD (Beat Utah St., 24-9). Bluebonnet 63—2 TD passes, one of 13 yards, completed 26 of 37 passes for 255 yards (Beat Louisiana St., 14-7).

	Team			Rushing			Passing					
Yr.	W	L	T	Car.	Yds.	Avg.	Att.	Cmp.	Int.	Pct.	Yds.	TD
61	5	5	0	17	103	6.1	56	26	4	.464	359	4
62	4	6	0	93	136	1.5	229	*125	12	.546	1627	11
63	7	3	0	98	119	1.2	308	*174	12	*.565	*2157	12
Totals	16	14	0	208	358	1.7	593	325	28	.548	4143	27
Avg.								7.0 per Att.			12.7 per Cmp.	

	Total Offense			Scoring	
Yr.	Plays	Yds.	TDR	TD	Pct.
61	73	462	4	0	0
62	322	1763	15	4	24
63	*406	2276	*22	10	60
Totals	801	4501	41	14	84
Avg.		5.6			

* This figure led the nation.

HOWARD TWILLEY
TULSA
E, 5-10, 180
Galena Park, Texas (Galena Park HS)

Unanimous all-America 65. Heisman 2nd in 65. Academic all-America 64 and 65.

Bowls: Bluebonnet 64—kicked two extra points (Beat Mississippi, 14-7). Bluebonnet 65—8 catches for 87 yards (Tennessee won, 27-6).

	Team				Receiving				PATs		Scoring 2-Pt. Passes		
Yr.	W	L	T	No.	Yds.	TD	Avg.	TD	Att.	Made	Caught	X-Pts.	Pts.
63	5	5	0	32	386	3	12.1	3	0	0	2	4	22
64	8	2	0	*95	*1178	*13	12.4	13	24	20	6	32	110
65	8	2	0	*134	*1179	*16	13.3	16	29	23	4	31	127
Totals	21	9	0	261	3343	32	12.8	32	53	43	12	67	259
Avg.										.811			

Other career figures—1 kickoff ret. for 6 yds.

* This figure led the nation.

NORM VAN BROCKLIN
OREGON   QB, 6-2, 190   Walnut Creek, Calif. (Alcanes HS)

All-America 48. Heisman 6th in 48. Hall of Fame.

Bowl: Cotton 49—completed 8 passes for 145 yards, one a 21-yard TD (Southern Methodist won, 21-13).

Yr.	Team W	L	T	Rushing Car.	Yds.	Att.	Cmp.	Passing Int.	Pct.	Yds.	TD
46	4	4	1	0	0	9	0	3	.000	0	0
47	7	3	0	13	-9	168	76	12	.452	939	9
48	9	1	0	8	-52	139	68	7	.489	1010	7
Totals	20	8	1	21	-61	316	144	22	.456	1949	16
Avg.						6.2 per Att.				13.5 per Cmp.	

Yr.	Plays	Total Offense Yds.	TDR	Punting No.	Avg.	Scoring XP	Pts.
46	9	0	0	1	36.0	0	0
47	181	930	9	66	40.1	0	0
48	147	958	7	49	34.8	10	10
Totals	337	1888	16	116	37.8	10	10
Avg.		5.6					

BILLY VESSELS
OKLAHOMA   HB, 6-0, 185   Cleveland, Okla. (Cleveland HS)

Consensus all-America 52. Heisman winner 52. Hall of Fame.

Bowl: Sugar 51—threw 17-yard TD pass, rushed 68 yards on 17 carries (Kentucky won, 13-7).

Yr.	Team W	L	T	Rushing Car.	Yds.	Avg.	Att.	Cmp.	Passing Int.	Pct.	Yds.	TD
50	#10	0	0	135	870	6.4	13	5	1	.385	78	3
51	8	2	0	27	143	5.3	6	2	1	.333	40	0
52	8	1	1	161	1072	6.7	20	7	3	.350	209	2
Totals	26	3	1	323	2085	6.5	39	14	5	.359	327	5
Avg.							8.4 per Att.				23.4 per Cmp.	

Yr.	Receiving No.	Yds.	K.O. Returns No.	Yds.	Scoring TD	Pts.
50	11	229	13	309	15	90
51	3	39	4	74	2	12
52	7	165	9	145	*18	108
Totals	21	433	26	528	35	210
Avg.		20.6		20.3		

Other career figures—4 int. by for 39 yds., 13 punt ret. for 221 yds.

National champions. * This figure led the nation.

DOAK WALKER
SOUTHERN METHODIST
HB, 5-11, 168
Dallas, Texas (Highland Park HS)

Unanimous all-America 48. Consensus all-America 47 and 49. Heisman winner 48, 3rd in 47 and 49. Hall of Fame.

Bowls: Cotton 48—threw 53-yard TD pass, completed 5 of 9 passes for 69 yards; rushed 56 yards on 18 carries, one a TD; kicked extra point (Tied Penn St., 13-13). Cotton 49— rushed 66 yards on 14 carries, one a TD; completed 6 of 10 passes for 79 yards; 79-yard punt; kicked two extra points (Beat Oregon, 21-13).

Yr.	Team W	L	T	Rushing Car.	Yds.	Avg.	Passing Att.	Cmp.	Int.	Pct.	Yds.	TD	Total Offense Plays	Yds.	TDR
45	5	6	0	58	289	5.0	65	38	4	.585	387	1	123	676	6
47	9	0	1	163	653	4.0	52	30	3	.577	344	2	215	997	13
48	8	1	1	109	537	4.9	47	26	5	.553	318	6	156	855	17
49	5	4	1	130	449	3.5	58	34	6	.586	605	5	188	1054	16
Totals	27	11	3	460	1928	4.2	222	128	18	.577	1654	14	682	3582	52
Avg.							7.5 per Att.			12.9 per Cmp.					

Yr.	Receiving No.	Yds.	TD	Avg.	Int. No.	Yds.	Punting No.	Avg.	Punt Ret. No.	Yds.	K.O. Ret. No.	Yds.	Scoring TD	XP	FG	Pts.
45	2	32	0	16.0	2	58	11	30.5	15	238	5	115	5	0	0	30
47	8	132	0	16.5	2	32	11	34.4	20	258	10	*387	11	18	1	87
48	14	264	3	18.9	3	75	35	42.1	10	169	5	161	11	22	0	88
49	3	26	1	8.7	1	11	23	41.7	5	87	6	101	11	17	0	83
*Totals	27	454	4	16.8	8	176	80	39.3	50	752	26	764	38	57	1	288
Avg.						22.0				15.0		29.4				

* This figure led the nation.

KENNY WASHINGTON
UCLA HB, 6-1, 195 Los Angeles, Calif. (Lincoln HS)

All-America 39. Heisman 6th in 39. Hall of Fame.

Yr.	Team W	L	T	Rushing Car.	Yds.	Avg.	Passing Att.	Cmp.	Int.	Pct.	Yds.	TD	Total Offense Plays	Yds.	TDR
37	2	6	1	138	530	3.8	72	34	6	.472	495	4	210	1025	8
38	7	4	1	147	573	3.9	65	21	11	.323	214	2	212	787	12
39	6	0	4	168	811	4.8	91	37	8	.407	559	7	259	*1370	12
Totals	15	10	6	453	1914	4.2	228	92	25	.404	1268	13	681	3182	32
Avg.							5.6 per Att.			13.8 per Cmp.				4.7	

Yr.	Receiving No.	Yds.	Avg.	Int. No.	Yds.	Punt Returns No.	Yds.	K.O. Ret. No.	Yds.	Scoring TD	Pts.
37	2	30	15.0	2	*124	0	0	6	160	4	24
38	5	47	9.4	3	74	1	10	7	161	10	60
39	2	51	25.5	1	28	1	18	6	107	5	30
Totals	9	128	14.2	6	226	2	28	19	428	19	114
Avg.					37.7		14.0		22.5		

* This figure led the nation.

HERMAN WEDEMEYER
ST. MARY'S (CAL.)   HB, 5-10, 173   Honolulu, Hawaii (St. Louis HS)

Unanimous all-America 45. Heisman 4th in 45, 5th in 46. Hall of Fame.

Bowl: Sugar 46—threw 46-yard TD pass, kicked extra point (Oklahoma St. won, 33-13). Oil 47—scored 2 TDs (Georgia Tech won, 41-19).

Yr.	Team			Rushing			Passing					Total Offense		
	W	L	T	Car.	Yds.	Avg.	Att.	Cmp.	Int.	Pct.	Yds.	TD	Plays	Yds.	TDR
43	2	5	0	68	206	3.0	36	16	4	.444	118	2	104	324	3
45	7	1	0	93	388	4.2	103	59	5	.573	1040	6	196	1428	15
46	6	2	0	104	625	6.0	100	34	9	.340	595	7	204	1220	12
47	3	7	0	111	398	3.6	109	47	14	.431	691	5	220	1089	10
Totals	18	15	0	376	1617	4.3	348	156	32	.448	2444	20	724	4061	40
Avg.							7.0 per Att.			15.7 per Cmp.			5.6		

Yr.	Receiving			Int.		Punting		Punt Ret.		K.O. Ret.		Scoring		
	No.	Yds.	Avg.	No.	Yds.	No.	Avg.	No.	Yds.	No.	Yds.	TD	XP	Pts.
43	4	53	13.3	6	135	28	35.7	14	207	9	184	1	2	8
45	3	54	18.0	*9	120	24	40.1	14	193	8	147	9	17	71
46	2	29	14.5	2	36	42	38.0	26	397	11	217	5	12	42
47	4	63	15.8	1	20	21	35.1	13	158	*20	361	5	10	40
Totals	13	199	15.3	18	311	115	35.8	67	955	48	909	20	41	161
Avg.			17.3						14.3		18.9			

* This figure led the nation.

ART WEINER
NORTH CAROLINA   E, 6-3, 212   Newark, N.J. (West Side HS)

All-America 48 and 49.

Bowls: Sugar 47—did not play (Georgia won, 20-10). Sugar 49—Oklahoma won, 14-6. Cotton 50—Rice won, 27-13. 2 bowls combined: 9 catches for 74 yards.

Yr.	Team			Rushing			Receiving				Scoring	
	W	L	T	Car.	Yds.	Avg.	No.	Yds.	TD	Avg.	TD	Pts.
46	8	1	1	5	52	10.4	3	94	3	31.3	4	24
47	8	2	0	10	86	8.6	19	386	2	20.3	2	12
48	9	0	1	7	47	6.7	31	481	6	15.5	6	36
49	7	3	0	2	6	3.0	*52	*762	7	14.7	7	42
Totals	32	6	2	24	191	8.0	105	1723	18	16.4	19	114

Other career figures—1 int. by for 5 yds., 3 kickoff ret. for 8 yds.

* This figure led the nation.

GIBBY WELCH
PITTSBURGH
HB, 5-11, 178
Parkersburg, W.Va. (Parkersburg HS)

Unanimous all-America 27.
Bowl: Rose 28 (Stanford won, 7-6).

Yr.	Team W	L	T	Rushing Car.	Yds.	Avg.	Passing Att.	Cmp.	Int.	Pct.	Yds.	TD	Total Offense Plays	Yds.	TDR
25	8	1	0	—	589	—	26	11	—	.423	182	—	—	771	—
26	5	2	2	—	815	—	56	25	—	.446	357	—	—	1172	—
27	8	0	1	—	476	—	55	27	—	.491	439	—	—	915	—
Totals	21	3	3	—	1880	—	137	63	—	.460	978	—	—	2858	—
Avg.							7.1 per Att.				14.4 per Cmp.				

Yr.	Receiving No.	Yds.	Avg.	Int. No.	Yds.	Punt Ret. No.	Yds.	K.O. Ret. No.	Yds.	Scoring TD	XP	Pts.
25	—	77	—	—	—	—	—	—	37	1	0	6
26	—	118	—	—	9	—	212	—	71	10	0	60
27	—	163	—	—	25	—	261	—	277	10	0	60
Totals	—	358	—	—	34	—	473	—	385	21	0	126

Other career figures: 3130 all-purpose yds.

GEORGE WELSH
NAVY QB, 5-10, 164 Coaldale, Pa. (Coaldale HS)

Heisman 3rd in 55.
Bowl: Sugar 55—threw 15-yard TD pass (Beat Mississippi, 21-0).

Yr.	Team W	L	T	Rushing Car.	Yds.	Avg.	Passing Att.	Cmp.	Int.	Pct.	Yds.	TD
53	4	3	2	30	20	0.7	82	39	8	.476	489	5
54	7	2	0	52	213	4.1	81	39	9	.481	527	7
55+	6	2	1	53	29	0.5	150	*94	6	*.627	*1319	8
Totals	17	7	3	135	262	1.9	313	172	23	.550	2335	20
Avg.							7.5 per Att.				13.6 per Cmp.	

Yr.	Total Offense Plays	Yds.	TDR	Scoring TD	Pts.
53	112	509	5	0	0
54	133	740	10	3	18
55	203	*1348	10	2	12
Totals	448	2597	25	5	30
Avg.		5.8			

Other career figures—6 int. by for 68 yds., 1 punt ret. for 0 yds., 5 kickoff ret. for 74 yds.

+ National champion in passing efficiency in 1955 (min. 15 att. per game) at 146.1.

* This figure led the nation.

BOB WHITE
OHIO STATE   FB, 6-2, 212   Covington, Ky. (Covington HS)

Consensus all-America 58. Heisman 4th in 58. Academic all-America 58.
Bowl: Rose 58—rushed for 93 yards, 49 during FG drive (Beat Oregon, 10-7).

Yr.	Team W	L	T	Rushing Car.	Yds.	Avg.	Int. No.	Yds.	Punting No.	Avg.	K.O. Ret. No.	Yds.	Scoring TD	Pts.
57	#8	1	0	89	552	6.2	1	21	0	0.0	2	26	1	6
58	6	1	2	218	859	3.9	3	42	11	34.8	1	15	12	72
59	3	5	1	96	312	3.3	1	4	25	40.7	0	0	0	0
Totals	17	7	3	403	1723	4.3	5	67	36	38.9	3	41	13	78
Avg.								13.4				13.7		

Other career figures—1 catch for 30 yds.
National champions.

BYRON "WHIZZER" WHITE
COLORADO
HB, 6-1, 185
Wellington, Colo. (Wellington HS)

Consensus all-America 37. Heisman 2nd in 37. Hall of Fame. Rhodes Scholar 37. Theodore Roosevelt Award, NCAA Honors Luncheon 69. Hall of Fame Gold Medal Award 62.
Bowl: Cotton 38—47-yard interception-return TD, threw 8-yard TD pass (Rice won, 28-14).

Yr.	Team W	L	T	Rushing Car.	Yds.	Avg.	Passing Att.	Cmp.	Int.	Pct.	Yds.	TD	Total Offense Plays	Yds.	TDR
35	5	4	0	34	100	2.9	20	9	4	.450	79	0	54	179	0
36	4	3	0	127	643	5.1	33	9	5	.273	120	1	160	763	9
37	8	0	0	181	*1121	6.2	43	21	7	.488	475	2	224	*1596	18
Totals	17	7	0	342	1864	5.5	96	39	16	.406	674	3	438	2538	27
Avg.							7.0 per Att.			17.3 per Cmp.			5.8		

Yr.	Int. No.	Yds.	Punting No.	Yds.	Avg.	Punt Ret. No.	Yds.	K.O. Ret. No.	Yds.	Scoring TD	XP	FG	Pts.
35	0	0	8	301	37.6	6	67	1	20	0	0	0	0
36	4	50	53	2124	40.1	29	319	7	327	8	7	0	55
37	4	103	63	2679	42.5	47	587	4	159	16	23	1	*122
Totals	8	153	124	5104	41.2	82	973	12	506	24	30	1	177
Avg.		19.1					11.9		42.2				

* This figure led the nation (also led the nation in all-purpose yards with 1,970; thus, was not an official category in 1937).

WILFORD WHITE
ARIZONA STATE   HB, 5-9, 161   Mesa, Ariz. (Mesa HS)

Bowls: Salad 50—Xavier (Ohio) won, 33-21. Salad 51—rushed 106 yards on 17 carries, 1 a 15-yard TD; 4 catches for 87 yards, one a 28-yard TD; completed 22-yard pass; 54 yards on 3 kickoff returns; 33.2 punting avg. (Miami, Ohio, won, 34-21).

	Team			Rushing			Passing					Total Offense		
Yr.	W	L	T	Car.	Yds.	Avg.	Att.	Cmp.	Int.	Pct.	Yds.	TD	Plays	Yds.	TDR
47	4	7	0	41	197	4.8	5	1	0	.200	4	0	46	201	4
48	5	5	0	120	539	4.5	9	2	1	.222	21	0	129	560	11
49	7	2	0	145	935	6.4	2	0	1	.000	0	0	147	935	11
50	9	1	0	199	*1502	*7.5	8	4	1	.500	87	3	207	1589	25
Totals	25	15	0	505	3173	6.3	24	7	3	.292	112	3	529	3285	51
Avg.														6.2	

	Receiving			Int.		Punting		Punt Ret.		K.O. Ret.		Scoring			
Yr.	No.	Yds.	TD	Avg.	No.	Yds.	No.	Avg.	No.	Yds.	No.	Yds.	TD	XP	FG	Pts.
47	7	61	0	8.7	1	75	2	42.5	10	184	7	137	4	6	0	30
48	14	272	3	19.4	3	105	29	32.4	16	354	8	287	11	20	3	95
49	17	334	2	19.6	2	32	4	38.5	14	196	4	93	11	0	0	66
50	13	225	4	17.3	1	0	25	36.2	5	64	9	274	*22	1	1	136
Totals	51	892	9	17.5	7	212	60	34.7	45	798	28	791	48	27	4	327
Avg.							30.3			17.7		28.3				

* This figure led the nation.

BOB WILLIAMS
NOTRE DAME
QB, 6-1, 185
Baltimore, Md. (Loyola HS)

Consensus all-America 49, all-America 50. Heisman 5th in 49, 6th in 50. Hall of Fame.

	Team			Rushing			Passing					Total Offense		
Yr.	W	L	T	Car.	Yds.	Avg.	Att.	Cmp.	Int.	Pct.	Yds.	TD	Plays	Yds.	TDR
48	9	0	1	6	11	1.8	17	8	2	.471	110	0	23	121	0
49+	#10	0	0	34	63	1.9	147	83	7	.565	1374	15	181	1437	16
50	4	4	1	40	115	2.9	210	99	15	.471	1035	10	250	1150	12
Totals	23	4	2	80	189	2.4	374	190	24	.508	2519	25	454	2708	28
Avg.							6.7 per Att.			13.3 per Cmp.				6.0	

Other career figures: 18 pts. scored; 120 punts for 38.0 avg.; 1 punt ret., 5 yds.; 1 K.O. ret., 15 yds.

+ National leader in pass efficiency in 1949 (min. 11 att. per game) at 159.1.

National champions.

JAMES "FROGGIE" WILLIAMS
RICE
E, 6-0, 197
Waco, Texas (Waco HS)

Consensus all-America 49. Hall of Fame.

Bowls: Orange 47—Beat Tennessee, 8-0. Cotton 50—17-yard TD catch, kicked three extra points (Beat North Caro., 27-13).

Yr.	Team W	L	T	No.	Receiving Yds.	TD	Avg.	Int. No.	Yds.	K.O. Ret. No.	Yds.	TD	Scoring XP	FG	Pts.
46	8	2	0	1	52	0	52.0	0	0	0	0	0	10	0	10
47	6	3	1	9	240	3	26.7	1	11	0	0	3	19	0	37
48	5	4	1	14	194	4	13.9	0	0	1	7	4	18	0	42
49	9	1	0	20	368	6	18.4	1	11	2	12	6	28	1	67
Totals	28	10	2	44	854	13	19.4	2	22	3	19	13	75	1	156
Avg.									11.0		6.3				

BUDDY YOUNG
ILLINOIS
HB, 5-5, 163
Chicago, Ill. (Wendell Phillips HS)

All-America 44. Heisman 5th in 44. Hall of Fame.

Bowl: Rose 47—rushed 103 yards on 20 carries, 2 for TDs; 29-yard punt return (Beat UCLA, 45-14).

Yr.	Team W	L	T	Car.	Rushing Yds.	Avg.	No.	Receiving Yds.	TD
44	5	4	1	94	840	8.9	1	36	1
46	7	2	0	85	353	4.2	4	41	0
Totals	12	6	1	179	1193	6.7	5	77	1
Avg.								15.4	

Yr.	Punt Returns No.	Yds.	K.O. Returns No.	Yds.	Scoring TD	Pts.
44	4	120	7	150	13	78
46	4	39	2	20	3	18
Totals	8	159	9	170	16	96
Avg.		4.1		18.9		

Other career figures—1 int. by for 24 yds., 1 punt for 17 yds.

1970-1989

TROY AIKMAN
UCLA   QB, 6-4, 217   Henryetta, Okla. (Henryetta HS)

Consensus all-America 88. Heisman 3rd in 88.

Bowls: At Oklahoma: Orange 85—did not play (Washington won, 28-17). Orange 86—did not play (Beat Penn St., 25-10, to win national championship). At UCLA: Aloha 87—completed 19 of 30 passes for 173 yards, including 5-yard TD and 2 interceptions and rushed minus 36 yards on 6 carries; named UCLA's Most Outstanding Player (Beat Florida, 20-16). Cotton 88—completed 19 of 27 for 172 yards, including 2-yard TD and 1 interception and rushed minus 3 yards on 9 carries; named game's Most Outstanding Offensive Player (Beat Arkansas, 17-3).

	Team				Rushing		Passing				Total Offense				
Yr.	W	L	T	G	Car.	Yds.	Att.	Cmp.	Int.	Pct.	Yds.	TD	Plays	Yds.	TDR
84	9	1	1	4	12	18	20	6	3	.300	41	0	32	59	1
85	#10	1	0	4	49	93	47	27	1	.574	442	1	96	535	1
86	(Redshirted at UCLA)														
87	9	2	0	11	73	-51	243	159	6	.654	2354	16	316	2303	18
88	9	2	0	11	69	86	327	209	8	.639	2599	23	396	2685	24
Totals	37	6	1	30	203	146	637	401	18	.630	5436	40	840	5582	44

Career: 8.5 per pass att., 13.6 per comp., 149.7 efficiency; 186.1 total offense yds. per game, 6.6 per play.

Other career figures: 24 pts. scored.

(Played at Oklahoma in 1984 and 1985.)

(Suffered broken leg in Miami [Fla.] game in 1985 and out for the season.)

National champions.

CHARLES ALEXANDER
LOUISIANA STATE
RB, 6-1, 214
Galveston, Texas (Ball HS)

Consensus all-America 77 and 78. Heisman 9th in 77, 5th in 78.

Bowls: Sun 77—rushed 197 yards on 19 carries; 7-yard TD and 55-yard non-score included (Stanford won, 24-14). Liberty 78—rushed 133 yards on 24 carries; 1-yard TD (Missouri won, 20-15).

	Team				Rushing				Receiving			All-Purpose		
Yr.	W	L	T	G	Car.	Yds.	Avg.	TD	No.	Yds.	TD	Avg.	Plays	Yds.	Avg.
75	5	6	0	11	108	301	2.8	2	1	6	0	6.0	111	335	3.0
76	7	3	1	11	155	876	5.7	7	8	82	0	10.3	164	977	6.0
77	8	3	0	11	311	1686	5.4	17	12	80	0	6.7	323	1766	5.5
78	8	3	0	11	281	1172	4.2	14	28	263	2	9.4	309	1435	4.6
Totals	%28	15	1	44	855	4035	4.7	40	49	431	2	8.8	907	4513	5.0

Career: 91.7 rush yds. per game; 102.6 all-purpose yds. per game.

Other career figures: 254 pts. scored (one 2-pt. conv.); 3 K.O. ret., 47 yds., 2 passes att., 1 cmp., 17 yds.

% Later won two forfeits over Mississippi St. by order of NCAA Council under Section 10.

ERIC ALLEN
MICHIGAN STATE
RB, 5-9, 161
Georgetown, S.C. (Howard HS)

All-America 71. Heisman 10th in 71.

	Team				Rushing				Receiving				All-Purpose		
Yr.	W	L	T	G	Car.	Yds.	Avg.	TD	No.	Yds.	TD	Avg.	Plays	Yds.	Avg.
69	4	6	0	9	76	349	4.6	2	2	3	0	1.5	115	973	8.5
70	4	6	0	10	186	811	4.4	8	10	125	2	12.5	224	1511	6.7
71	6	5	0	11	259	1494	5.8	18	18	275	0	15.3	286	1962	6.9
Totals	14	17	0	30	521	2654	5.1	28	30	403	2	13.4	625	4446	7.1

Career: 84.7 rush yds. per game; 148.2 all-purpose yds. per game.

Other career figures: 182 pts. scored (one 2-pt. conv.); 62 K.O. ret., 1340 yds., 21.6 avg.; 12 punt ret., 49 yds., 2 passes att., one int.

GREG ALLEN
FLORIDA STATE   RB, 6-0, 200   Milton, Fla. (Milton HS)

Consensus all-America 83; all-America 84. Heisman 8th in 84.

Bowls: Gator 82—rushed 138 yards on 15 carries, scoring on runs of 29 and 1 yards; caught 1 pass for 15 yards; named game's Most Valuable Player (Beat West Va., 31-12). Peach 83—rushed 97 yards on 17 carries; caught 2 passes for 18 yards (Beat North Caro., 28-3). Florida Citrus 84—injured, did not play (Tied Georgia 17-17).

	Team				Rushing				Receiving				All-Purpose		
Yr.	W	L	T	G	Car.	Yds.	Avg.	TD	No.	Yds.	TD	Avg.	Plays	Yds.	Avg.
81	6	5	0	11	139	888	6.4	3	5	35	0	7.0	158	1259	8.0
82	8	3	0	11	152	776	5.1	20	16	233	1	14.6	188	1524	8.1
83	7	4	0	11	200	1134	5.7	13	11	96	0	8.7	211	1230	5.8
84	7	3	1	9	133	971	7.3	8	2	12	0	6.0	135	983	7.3
Totals %28	15	1	42	624	3769	6.0	44	34	376	1	11.1	692	4996	7.2

Career: 89.7 rush yds. per game; 119.0 all-purpose yds. per game.

Other career figures: 278+ pts. scored; 1 pass att., 0 cmp.; 34 K.O. ret., 851 yds., 25.0 avg., 1 TD.

% Later won forfeit over Tulane by order of NCAA Council under Section 10.

+ National scoring champion at 11.5 points per game in 1983.

MARCUS ALLEN

SOUTHERN CALIFORNIA RB, 6-2, 202 San Diego, Calif. (Lincoln HS)

Unanimous all-America 81. Heisman winner 81.

Bowls: Rose 79—did not play (Beat Michigan, 17-10). Rose 80—rushed 43 yards on 9 carries; caught 2 passes for 41 yards (Beat Ohio St., 17-16). Fiesta 82—rushed 85 yards on 30 carries; caught 5 passes for 39 yards; his 2 fumbles led to 10 points (Penn St. won, 26-10).

Yr.	Team W	L	T	G	Rushing Car.	Yds.	Avg.	TD	Receiving No.	Yds.	TD	Avg.	All-Purpose Plays	Yds.	Avg.
78	#11	1	0	12	31	171	5.5	1	—	—	—	—	31	171	5.5
79	10	0	1	11	105	606	5.8	8	20	273	0	13.7	128	925	7.2
80	8	2	1	10	*354	1563	4.4	14	30	231	0	7.7	384	1794	4.7
81	9	2	0	11	*403	+*2342	5.8	+*22	29	217	1	7.5	*432	+*2259	5.9
Totals	38	5	2	44	893	4682	5.2	5.2	79	721	1	9.1	975	5449	5.6

Career: 106.4 rush yds. per game; 123.8 all-purpose yds. per game.

Other career figures: 276+ pts. scored; 3 K.O. ret., 46 yds; 3 passes att., 2 cmp., 57 yds., 1 TD.

* This figure led the nation. # National champions. + National champion in rushing at 212.9 yds. per game, in scoring at 12.5 pts. per game and in all-purpose running at 232.6 yds. per game in 1981.

CARLOS ALVAREZ

FLORIDA
WR, 6-0, 161
Miami, Fla. (Norland HS)

Consensus all-America 69. Academic all-America 69 and 71. NCAA Postgraduate Scholarship 72. Academic All-America Hall of Fame.

Bowls: Gator 69—caught 4 passes for 51 yards, including game-winning, 9-yard TD pass from John Reaves (beat Tennessee, 14-13).

Yr.	Team W	L	T	G	Rushing Car.	Yds.	Receiving No.	Yds.	TD	Avg.	Punt Returns No.	Yds.	Avg.	Scoring TD	XP	Pts.
69	8	1	1	10	—	—	88	1329	12	15.1	—	—	—	12	4	76
70	7	4	0	11	2	11	44	717	5	16.3	9	161	17.9	6	0	36
71	4	7	0	10	3	-6	40	517	2	12.9	7	29	4.1	2	0	12
Totals	19	12	1	31	5	5	172	2563	19	14.9	16	190	11.8	20	4	124

Other career figures: 2 passes att., 2 cmp., 44 yds.; 1.0 yds. per carry.

RICKY ANDERSON
VANDERBILT
P-PK, 6-2, 190
St. Petersburg, Fla. (Lakewood HS)

Unanimous all-America 84.

Bowls: Hall of Fame 82—kicked 4 of 4 PATs; missed 49-yard FG (Air Force won, 36-28).

| | Team | | | | Punting | | | | | Field Goals | | | | |
| | | | | | | | | | | | Under | 40 | | |
Yr.	W	L	T	G	No.	Yds.	Avg.	XPA	-XP	FGA-FG	Pct.	40 yds.	Plus	Long	Pts.
81*	4	7	0	11	—	—	—	—	—	— —	—	—	—	—	—
82	8	3	0	11	—	—	—	31	31	22 14	.636	8-13	6-9	49	73
83	2	9	0	11	53	2274	42.9	20	19	16 10	.625	6-9	4-7	52	49
84	5	6	0	11	58	2793	+48.2	24	22	19 16	.842	10-13	6-6	53	70
Totals	19	25	0	44	111	5067	45.6	75	72	57 40	.702	24-35	16-22	53	192

Career accuracy percentages: .960   .686   .727

+ National punting champion in 1984.   * Kicked off only.

His FGs provided winning margin: 82—Tulane, Florida; 83—Iowa St.; 84—Maryland, Alabama.

OTIS ARMSTRONG
PURDUE   RB, 5-11, 197   Chicago, Ill. (Farragut High School)

Consensus all-America 72. Heisman 8th in 72.

| | Team | | | | Rushing | | | | Receiving | | | | All-Purpose | | |
Yr.	W	L	T	G	Car.	Yds.	Avg.	TD	No.	Yds.	TD	Avg.	Plays	Yds.	Avg.
70	4	6	0	10	213	1009	4.7	2	13	148	1	11.4	227	1174	5.2
71	3	7	0	10	214	945	4.4	6	17	186	4	10.9	251	1559	6.2
72	6	5	0	11	243	1361	5.6	9	6	55	0	9.2	264	1868	7.1
Totals	13	18	0	31	670	3315	4.9	17	36	389	5	10.8	742	4601	6.2

Career: 106.9 rush yds. per game; 148.4 all-purpose yds. per game.

Other career figures: 144 pts. scored; 1 pass att., 1 int.; 36 K.O. ret., 897 yds, 24.9 avg., 2 TD.

JIM ARNOLD
VANDERBILT
P, 6-3, 205
Dalton, Ga. (Dalton HS)

Unanimous all-America 82.

Bowls: Hall of Fame 82—2 punts for 65 yards, longest 54 (Air Force won, 36-28).

Yr.	W	Team L	T	G	No.	Punting Yds.	Avg.
79	1	10	0	11	60	2516	41.9
80	2	9	0	11	72	3180	44.2
81	4	7	0	11	71	3089	43.5
82	8	3	0	11	74	3386	45.8
Totals	15	29	0	44	277	12,171	43.9

Other career figures: 2 passes att., 1 cmp., 9 yds.

STEVE BARTKOWSKI
CALIFORNIA   QB, 6-4, 215   Santa Clara, Calif. (Buchser HS)

Consensus all-America 74. Heisman 10th in 74.

Yr.	W	Team L	T	G	Rushing Car.	Yds.	Att.	Cmp.	Passing Int.	Pct.	Yds.	TD	Total Offense Plays	Yds.	TDR
72	3	8	0	9	48	-189	165	70	13	.424	944	4	213	755	4
73	4	7	0	11	45	-114	129	61	7	.473	910	3	174	796	4
74	7	3	1	11	73	-193	325	+182	7	.560	*2580	12	398	2387	13
Totals	14	18	1	31	166	-496	619	313	27	.506	4434	19	785	3938	21

Career: 7.2 per pass att., 14.2 per cmp., 112.2 efficiency; 127.0 total offense yds. per game, 5.0 per play.

Other career figures: 14 pts. scored (one 2-pt. conv.) 13 punts, 30.2 avg.

+ National passing champion with 16.5 completions per game in 1974.   * This figure led the nation.

TERRY BEASLEY
AUBURN   WR, 5-11, 186   Montgomery, Ala. (Robert E. Lee HS)

Unanimous all-America 71. Heisman 13th in 71.

Bowls: Bluebonnet 69—caught 6 passes for 76 yards and returned 1 kickoff for 19 yards (Houston won, 36-7). Gator 71—caught 8 passes (longest 42) for 143 yards and a 13-yard TD from 71 Heisman winner Pat Sullivan (beat Mississippi, 35-28). Sugar 72—caught 6 passes for 117 yards (Oklahoma won, 40-22).

	Team				Rushing		Receiving			Scoring		
Yr.	W	L	T	G	Car.	Yds.	No.	Yds.	TD	Avg.	TD	XP	Pts.
69	8	2	0	10	5	25	34	610	6	17.9	6	0	36
70	8	2	0	10	6	95	52	1051	11	20.2	12	0	72
71	9	1	0	10	3	13	55	846	12	15.4	12	0	72
Totals	25	5	0	30	14	133	141	2507	29	17.8	30	0	180

Career: 9.5 yds. per carry.

Other career figures: 2 punt ret., 14 yds.; 1 K.O. ret, 9 yds.

RICKY BELL
SOUTHERN CALIFORNIA
RB, 6-2, 218
Los Angeles, Calif. (Fremont HS)

Unanimous all-America 75 and 76. Heisman 3rd in 75, 2nd in 76.

Bowls: Rose 75—rushed for 38 yards on 6 carries (Beat Ohio St., 18-17). Liberty 75—rushed for 82 yards on 28 carries; caught 1 pass, a 76-yard TD screen pass from Vince Evans (Beat Texas A&M, 20-0). Rose 77—rushed for 16 yards on 4 carries; suffered a head injury on USC's fifth play of the game and doctors advised against playing him for the rest of the game (Beat Michigan, 14-6).

	Team				Rushing				Receiving				All-Purpose		
Yr.	W	L	T	#G	Car.	Yds.	Avg.	TD	No.	Yds.	TD	Avg.	Plays	Yds.	Avg.
73	9	1	1	9	—	—	—	—	—	—	—	—	1	17	17.0
74	9	1	1	11	39	261	6.7	1	—	—	—	—	43	307	6.7
75	7	4	0	11	*357	+1875	5.3	13	3	24	0	8.0	360	1899	5.3
76	10	1	0	10	276	1417	5.1	14	14	85	0	6.1	290	1502	5.2
Totals	35	7	2	41	672	3553	5.3	28	17	109	0	6.4	694	3725	5.4

Career: 110.0 rush yds. per game; 116.4 all-purpose yds. per game as a running back.

Other career figures: 174 pts. scored (three 2-pt. conv.); 5 K.O. ret. 63 yds.

(Played linebacker in 1973, fullback in 1974, running back in 1975-76.)

+ National rushing champion at 170.5 yds. per game in 1975.

GUY BENJAMIN
STANFORD
QB, 6-4, 202
Sepulveda, Calif. (James Monroe HS)

Consensus all-America 77. Academic all-America 77. Heisman 6th in 77.

Bowl: Sun 77—completed 23 of 36 passes for 269 yards with no interceptions and 3 touchdowns (49 and 2 yards to James Lofton and 35 yards to Darrin Nelson); attempts, completions and yardage were Sun Bowl records (Beat Louisiana St., 24-14).

Yr.	Team W	L	T	G	Rushing Car.	Yds.	Att.	Cmp.	Passing Int.	Pct.	Yds.	TD	Total Offense Plays	Yds.	TDR
74	5	4	2	5	6	-23	48	31	3	.646	397	4	54	374	4
75	6	4	1	9	22	2	135	79	8	.585	1046	10	157	1048	12
76	6	5	0	9	38	-48	295	170	17	.576	1982	12	333	1934	15
77	8	3	0	10	43	-112	330	+208	15	*.630	2521	19	373	2409	21
Totals	35	16	3	33	109	-181	808	488	43	.604	5946	45	917	5765	52

Career: 7.4 per pass att., 12.2 per cmp., 130.0 efficiency; 174.7 total offense yds. per game, 6.3 per play.

Other career figures: 42 pts. scored.

* This figure led the nation.   + National passing champion with 20.8 completions per game in 1977.

TODD BLACKLEDGE
PENN STATE   QB, 6-4, 222   North Canton, Ohio (Hoover HS)

Heisman 6th in 82. Academic all-America 82.

Bowls: Fiesta 80—completed 8 of 22 passes for 117 yards with no interceptions and rushed 12 yards on 10 carries, scoring 1 TD (Beat Ohio St., 31-19). Fiesta 82—completed 11 of 24 passes for 175 yards and 52-yard scoring pass with 2 interceptions (Beat Southern Cal, 26-10). Sugar 83—completed 13 of 23 passes for 228 yards with no interceptions and 47-yard game-winning TD pass in the fourth quarter; named game's Most Outstanding Player (Beat Georgia, 27-23, to win the national championship).

Yr.	Team W	L	T	G	Rushing Car.	Yds.	Att.	Cmp.	Passing Int.	Pct.	Yds.	TD	Total Offense Plays	Yds.	TDR
80	9	2	0	11	77	107	159	76	13	.478	1037	7	236	1144	9
81	9	2	0	11	45	19	207	104	14	.502	1557	12	252	1576	17
82	#10	1	0	11	42	-67	292	161	14	.551	2218	22	334	2151	25
Totals	28	5	0	33	164	59	658	341	41	.518	4812	41	822	4871	51

Career: 7.3 per pass att., 14.1 per cmp., 121.4 efficiency; 147.6 total offense yds. per game; 5.9 per play.

Other career figures: 60 pts. scored.

National champions.

ROBBIE BOSCO
BRIGHAM YOUNG   QB, 6-2, 188   Roseville, Calif. (Roseville HS)

Heisman 3rd in 84, 3rd in 85.

Bowls: Holiday 83—(did not play) (Beat Missouri, 21-17). Holiday 84—as game's Most Valuable Player, completed 30 of 42 passes for 343 yards and 2 TDs with 3 interceptions; directed drives of 80, 80 and 83 yards, the second tied score at 17, third came with 1:23 left, a 13-yard game-winning TD to Kelly Smith; Bosco was forced out of action in the first quarter with severely sprained left ankle—his plant foot—but returned in the second quarter, hobbling (Beat Michigan, 24-17, to clinch national championship). Florida Citrus 85—completed 26 of 50 passes for 261 yards and team's only TD, but had four interceptions (Ohio St. won, 10-7).

	Team				Rushing		Passing						Total Offense		
Yr.	W	L	T	G	Car.	Yds.	Att.	Cmp.	Int.	Pct.	Yds.	TD	Plays	Yds.	TDR
82	Redshirted														
83	10	1	0	10	10	-26	28	17	1	.607	252	3	38	226	3
84	#12	0	0	12	85	57	*458	*283	11	.618	*3875	*33	*543	+*3932	*35
85	11	2	0	13	67	-132	*511	*338	24	.661	*4273	*30	578	*4141	*32
Totals	33	3	0	35	162	-101	997	638	36	.640	8400	66	1159	8299	70

Career: 6.4 per pass att., 13.2 per cmp., 149.4 efficiency; 237.1 total offense yds. per game, 7.2 per play.

Other career figures: 26 pts. scored (one 2-pt. conv.)

National champions. + National total offense champion at 327.7 yds. per game in 1984.
* This figure led the nation.

EDDIE BROWN
MIAMI (Fla.)   WR, 6-0, 185   Miami, Fla. (Miami HS)

Consensus all-America 84.

Bowls: Orange 84—caught 6 passes for 115, longest 34 yards (Beat Nebraska, 31-30, for national championship). Fiesta 84—returned one punt for a 68-yard TD and caught 4 passes for 54 yards (UCLA won, 39-37).

	Team				Rushing		Receiving			Punt Returns			Scoring		
Yr.	W	L	T	G	Car.	Yds.	No.	Yds.	TD	Avg.	No.	Yds.	Avg.	TD	XP	Pts.
83	#10	1	0	11	5	15	30	640	5	21.3	31	143	4.6	6	0	36
84	8	4	0	12	5	36	59	1114	9	18.9	4	17	4.3	9	0	54
Totals	18	5	0	23	10	51	89	1754	14	19.7	35	160	4.6	15	0	90

Other career figures: 5.1 yds. per carry; 3 K.O. ret., 51 yds.

National champions.

TED BROWN
NORTH CAROLINA STATE
RB, 5-10, 195
High Point, N.C. (T.W. Andrews HS)

Consensus all-America 78. Heisman 6th in 78.

Bowls: Peach 75—rushed 159 yards on 21 carries, longest 54, and caught 2 passes for 19 yards (West Va. won, 13-10). Peach 77—rushed 114 yards on 25 carries, completed 2 of 2 passes for 47 yards, longest 28, and caught 7 passes for 66 yards, including a 5-yard TD (Beat Iowa St., 24-14). Tangerine 78—rushed 126 yards on 28 carries, including 1-yard TD and named game's Most Valuable Player (Beat Pittsburgh, 30-17).

	Team				Rushing				Receiving				All-Purpose		
Yr.	W	L	T	G	Car.	Yds.	Avg.	TD	No.	Yds.	TD	Avg.	Plays	Yds.	Avg.
75	7	3	1	10	142	913	6.4	12	16	160	1	10.0	165	1241	7.5
76	3	7	1	11	198	1088	5.5	13	25	239	0	9.6	223	1327	6.0
77	7	4	0	11	218	1251	5.7	13	24	164	1	6.8	242	1415	5.8
78	8	3	0	11	302	1350	4.5	11	17	197	0	11.6	321	1582	4.9
Totals	25	17	2	43	860	4602	5.4	49	82	760	2	9.3	951	5565	5.8

Career: 107.0 rush yds. per game, 129.4 all-purpose yds. per game.

Other career figures: 312 pts. scored (three 2-pt. conv.), 22 passes att., 10 cmp., 1 int., 202 yds., 1 TD.; 9 K.O. ret., 203 yds., 22.6 avg.

TIM BROWN
NOTRE DAME   FL, 6-0, 195   Dallas, Texas (Woodrow Wilson HS)

Unanimous all-America 87, all-America 86. Heisman winner 87.

Bowls: Aloha 84—caught 1 pass for 16 yards; returned 2 kickoffs for 88 yards (Southern Methodist won, 27-20). Cotton 88—caught 6 passes (longest 29) for 105 yards and a 17-yard TD; returned 6 kickoffs (longest 37) for 129 yards; returned 1 punt for 4 yards (Texas A&M won, 35-10).

	Team				Rushing				Receiving				All-Purpose		
Yr.	W	L	T	G	Car.	Yds.	Avg.	TD	No.	Yds.	TD	Avg.	Plays	Yds.	Avg.
84	7	4	0	11	1	14	14.0	0	28	340	1	12.1	36	475	13.2
85	5	6	0	10	4	30	7.5	1	25	397	3	15.9	43	765	17.8
86	5	6	0	11	59	254	4.3	2	45	910	5	20.2	131	1937	14.8
87	8	3	0	11	34	144	4.2	1	39	846	3	21.7	130	1847	14.2
Totals	25	19	0	43	98	442	4.5	4	137	2493	12	18.2	340	5024	14.8

	Scoring			Punt Returns			K.O. Returns			Comb. Kick Returns			
Yr.	TD	XP	Pts.	No.	Yds.	Avg.	No.	Yds.	Avg.	No.	Yds.	TD	Avg.
84	1	0	6	—	—	—	7	121	17.3	7	121	0	17.3
85	5	0	30	—	—	—	14	338	24.1	14	338	1	24.1
86	9	0	54	2	75	37.5	25	698	27.9	27	773	2	28.6
87	7	2	44	34	401	11.8	23	456	19.8	57	857	3	15.0
Totals	22	2	134	36	476	13.2	69	1613	23.4	105	2089	6	19.9

Other career figures: 2 passes att., 0 cmp.

KEVIN BUTLER
GEORGIA   PK, 6-1, 190   Stone Mountain, Ga. (Redan HS)

Consensus all-America 84.

Bowls: Sugar 82—2 PAT kicks (Pittsburgh won, 24-20). Sugar 83—made 27-yard FG and 2 PAT kicks (Penn St. won, 27-23). Cotton 84—made 43-yard FG and 1 PAT kick (beat Texas, 10-9). Florida Citrus 84—made 36-yard FG and 2 PAT kicks (tied Florida St., 17-17).

	Team			Punting							Field Goals			
												Under	40		
Yr.	W	L	T	G	No.	Yds.	Avg.	XPA	-XP	FGA	-FG	Pct.	40 yds.	Plus	Long	Pts.
81	10	1	0	11	—	—	—	38	37	26	+19	.731	11-14	8-12	52	*94
82	11	0	0	11	—	—	—	36	34	21	17	.810	13-13	4-8	50	85
83	9	1	1	11	—	—	—	28	28	23	18	.783	14-15	4-8	52	82
84	7	4	0	11	—	—	—	23	23	28	23	.821	12-14	11-14	60	92
Totals	37	6	1	44	—	—	—	125	122	98	77	.786	50-56	27-42	60	353

Career accuracy percentages: .976   .893   .643

+ Tied for national field-goal championship at 1.73 per game.

* Led nation in kick-scoring.

His FGs provided winning margin over: 82—Clemson, Brigham Young, Auburn; 83— Florida, Georgia Tech; 84—Southern Miss., Clemson.

KEITH BYARS
OHIO STATE
RB, 6-2, 233
Dayton, Ohio (Dayton Roth HS)

Unanimous all-America 84. Heisman 2nd in 84.

Bowls: Holiday 82—rushed 2 yards on 2 carries (Beat Brigham Young, 47-17). Fiesta 84—rushed 73 yards on 15 carries, scoring on a 1-yard run; caught 2 passes for 21 yards and returned one kickoff for a 99-yard TD (Beat Pittsburgh, 28-23). Rose 85—rushed 109 yards on 23 carries and caught 5 passes for 26 yards (Southern Cal won, 20-17). Florida Citrus 85—rushed 5 yards on 2 carries (Beat Brigham Young, 10-7).

	Team				Rushing				Receiving			All-Purpose		
Yr.	W	L	T	G	Car.	Yds.	Avg.	TD	No.	Yds.	TD	Avg.	Plays	Yds.	Avg.
82	8	3	0	8	4	17	4.3	0	1	20	0	20.0	6	65	10.8
83	8	3	0	11	207	1126	5.4	19	21	338	1	16.1	229	1501	6.6
84	9	2	0	11	*313	+*1655	5.3	*22	37	453	2	12.2	357	+2284	6.4
85	8	3	0	3	53	208	3.9	4	7	44	0	6.3	60	252	4.2
Totals	33	11	0	33	577	3006	5.2	45	66	855	3	13.0	652	4102	6.3

Career: 91.1 rush yds. per game; 124.3 all-purpose yds. per game.

Other career figures: +288 pts. scored; 9 K.O. ret. 241 yds., 26.8 avg.; 1 pass att., 1 cmp., 35 yds., 1 TD.

+ National champion in rushing at 150.5 yds. per game, in scoring at 13.1 pts. per game and in all-purpose running at 207.6 yds. per game in 1984.

* This figure led the nation.

EARL CAMPBELL
TEXAS
RB, 6-1, 220
Tyler, Texas (Tyler HS)

Unanimous all-America 77, all-America 75. Heisman winner in 77.

Bowls: Gator 74—rushed 91 yards on 23 carries (Auburn won, 27-3). Bluebonnet 75—rushed 95 yards on 19 carries and named game's Most Valuable Back (Beat Colorado, 38-21). Cotton 78—rushed 116 yards on 29 carries (Notre Dame won, 38-10).

	Team				Rushing				Receiving				All-Purpose		
Yr.	W	L	T	G	Car.	Yds.	Avg.	TD	No.	Yds.	TD	Avg.	Plays	Yds.	Avg.
74	8	3	0	11	162	928	5.7	6	—	—	—	—	163	951	5.8
75	9	2	0	11	198	1118	5.6	13	—	—	—	—	198	1118	5.6
76	5	5	1	8	138	653	4.7	3	1	17	0	17.0	139	670	4.8
77	11	0	0	11	267	+*1744	6.5	18	5	111	1	22.2	273	+1878	6.9
Totals	33	10	1	41	765	4443	5.8	40	6	128	1	21.3	773	4617	6.0

Career: 108.4 rush yds. per game; 112.6 all-purpose yds. per game.

Other career figures: 246+ pts. scored; 2 punt ret., 46 yds.; 1 pass att., 1 int.

+ National champion in rushing at 158.5 yds. per game, in scoring at 10.4 pts. per game and in all-purpose running at 107.7 yds. per game in 1977.

* This figure led the nation.

JOHN CAPPELLETTI
PENN STATE   RB, 6-1, 206   Upper Darby, Pa. (Monsignor Bonner HS)

Unanimous all-America 73. Heisman winner 73.

Bowls: Cotton 72—no statistics (Beat Texas, 30-6). Sugar 72—did not play; ill with 103-degree temperature (Oklahoma won, 14-0). Orange 74—played with a slight sprain of his right ankle suffered in practice four days earlier and used mostly as a decoy early in the game; rushed 50 yards on 26 carries, scoring the clinching TD on a 1-yard run and caught one pass for 40 yards (Beat Louisiana St., 16-9).

	Team				Rushing				Receiving				All-Purpose		
Yr.	W	L	T	G	Car.	Yds.	Avg.	TD	No.	Yds.	TD	Avg.	Plays	Yds.	Avg.
71	10	1	0	11	—	—	—	—	—	—	—	—	44	654	14.9
72	10	1	0	11	233	1117	4.8	12	16	138	1	8.6	257	1474	5.7
73	11	0	0	11	286	1522	5.3	17	6	69	0	11.5	295	1607	5.4
Totals	31	2	0	33	519	2639	5.1	29	22	207	1	9.4	596	3735	6.3

Career: 120.0 rush yds. per game as running back; 113.2 all-purpose yds. per game all three years.

Other career figures: 180 pts. scored; 31 punt ret., 333 yds., 10.7 avg; 23 K.O. ret., 531 yds., 23.1 avg.; 2 pass att., 1 cmp., 17 yds.; 1 pass int. as DB, ret. 25 yds.

(Played defensive back in 1971, running back in 1972-73).

ANTHONY CARTER

MICHIGAN WR, 5-11, 161 Riviera Beach, Fla. (Sun Coast HS)

Consensus all-America 81 and 82. All-America 80. Heisman 4th in 82, 7th in 81, 10th in 80.

Bowls: Gator 79—caught 4 passes for 141 yards, including TDs of 53 and 30 yards, returned 1 punt for 11 yards and 2 kickoffs for 28 yards (North Caro. won, 17-15). Rose 81—caught 5 passes for 68 yards and a 7-yard TD, returned 1 punt for 6 yards and 1 kickoff for 16 yards (Beat Washington, 23-6). Bluebonnet 81—caught 6 passes for 127 yards and a 50-yard TD and returned 7 punts for 46 yards (Beat UCLA, 33-14). Rose 83—caught 5 passes for 59 yards, returned 2 punts for 5 yards and 2 kickoffs for 58 yards (UCLA won, 24-14).

	Team				Rushing				Receiving			All-Purpose		
Yr.	W	L	T	G	Car.	Yds.	Avg.	TD	No.	Yds.	TD	Avg.	Plays	Yds.	Avg.
79	8	3	0	11	4	17	4.3	0	13	321	5	24.7	54	988	18.3
80	9	2	0	11	6	35	5.8	0	46	750	13	16.3	89	1355	15.2
81	8	3	0	11	11	57	5.2	1	44	825	7	18.8	80	1438	18.0
82	8	3	0	11	8	64	8.0	0	38	785	8	20.7	75	1416	18.9
Totals	33	11	0	44	29	173	6.0	1	141	2681| 33	19.0	298	5197	17.4

	Scoring			Punt Returns			K.O. Returns			Comb. Kick Returns			
Yr.	TD	XP	Pts.	No.	Yds.	Avg.	No.	Yds.	Avg.	No.	Yds.	TD	Avg.
79	6	0	36	20	265	13.3	17	385	22.6	37	650	1	17.6
80	13	0	78	23	159	6.9	14	411	29.4	37	570	0	15.4
81	8	2	50	10	150	15.0	15	406	27.1	25	556	0	22.4
82	9	2	56	17	265	15.6	12	302	25.2	29	567	1	19.6
Totals	36	4	220	70	839	12.0	58	1504	25.9	128	2343	2	18.3

Other career figures: 2 passes att., 0 cmp.

CRIS CARTER

OHIO STATE
WR, 6-3, 194
Middletown, Ohio (Middletown HS)

Consensus all-America 86.

Bowls: Rose 85—caught 9 passes for 172 yards, including an 18-yard TD (Southern Cal won, 20-17). Florida Citrus 85—caught 5 passes for 71 yards (Beat Brigham Young, 10-7). Cotton 87—caught 4 passes for 61 yards (Beat Texas A&M, 28-12).

	Team				Rushing		Receiving				Scoring		
Yr.	W	L	T	G	Car.	Yds.	No.	Yds.	TD	Avg.	TD	XP	Pts.
84	9	2	0	11	—	—	32	476	7	14.8	7	0	42
85	8	3	0	11	1	1	53	879	8	16.6	8	0	48
86	9	3	0	12	1	6	65	1066	11	16.4	11	0	66
Totals	26	8	0	34	2	7	150	2421	26	16.1	26	0	156

Other career figures: 2 passes att., 1 cmp., 26 yds., 1 TD; 3 K.O. ret., 23 yds.

DAVE CASPER
NOTRE DAME   TE, 6-3, 252   Chilton, Wis. (Chilton HS)

Consensus all-America 73. Academic all-America 73. NCAA Postgraduate Scholarship 74. Hall of Fame Scholar-Athlete 73.

Bowls: Orange 73—played offensive tackle (Nebraska won, 40-6). Sugar 73—caught 3 passes for 75 yards (Beat Alabama, 24-23, for the national championship).

Yr.	Team				Rushing		Receiving				Scoring		
	W	L	T	G	Car.	Yds.	No.	Yds.	TD	Avg.	TD	XP	Pts.
71	8	2	0	10	—	—	1	12	0	12.0	—	—	—
72	8	2	0	10	—	—	1	6	0	6.0	—	—	—
73	#10	0	0	10	—	—	19	317	4	16.7	4	0	24
Totals	26	4	0	30	—	—	21	335	4	16.0	4	0	24

(Played mostly at offensive tackle in 1971-72.)
National champions.

DALE CASTRO
MARYLAND   P-PK, 6-1, 170   Shady Side, Md. (Southern HS)

Consensus all-America 79.

Bowls: Sun 78—punted 8 times for 37.4 average, longest 58; missed 52-yard FG (Texas won, 42-0). Florida Citrus 80—made 4 FGs (34-27-26-42 yards) and punted 4 times for 39.0 average, longest 57 (Florida won, 35-20).

Yr.	Team				Punting			XPA	-XP	FGA	-FG	Field Goals				
	W	L	T	G	No.	Yds.	Avg.					Pct.	Under 40 yds.	40 Plus	Long	Pts.
78	9	2	0	11	66	2372	35.9	—	—	—	—	—	—	—	—	—
79	7	4	0	11	83	3110	37.5	20	19	21	17	.810	10-10	7-11	46	70
80	8	3	0	11	75	3066	40.9	22	21	18	10	.556	8-11	2-7	50	51
Totals	24	9	0	33	224	8548	38.2	42	40	39	27	.692	18-21	9-18	50	121

Career accuracy percentages: .952   .857 .500
Other career figures: 1 pass att., 1 cmp., 16 yds.
His FGs provided winning margin over: 79-North Caro.; 80-Wake Forest, Duke.

MARV COOK
IOWA
TE, 6-4, 243
West Branch, Iowa (West Branch HS)

Consensus all-America 88.

Bowls: Holiday 86—caught 2 passes for 51 yards, including 29-yard TD (Beat San Diego St., 39-38). Holiday 87—caught 6 passes for 43 yards and punted 8 times for 42-yard average, longest 53 (Beat Wyoming, 20-19). Peach 88—caught 9 passes for 122 yards (North Caro. St. won, 28-23).

Yr.	Team				Rushing		Receiving				Scoring		
	W	L	T	G	Car.	Yds.	No.	Yds.	TD	Avg.	TD	XP	Pts.
86	8	3	0	11	11	51	2	27	0	13.5	—	—	—
87	9	3	0	12	—	—	43	760	2	17.7	2	—	12
88	6	3	3	9	—	—	55	645	3	11.7	3	4	22
Totals	23	9	3	32	11	51	100	1432	5	14.3	5	4	34

Other career figures: 20 punts, 37.8 avg.

BENNIE CUNNINGHAM
CLEMSON
TE, 6-5, 252
Seneca, S.C. (Seneca HS)

Consensus all-America 74.

Yr.	Team				Rushing		Receiving				Scoring		
	W	L	T	G	Car.	Yds.	No.	Yds.	TD	Avg.	TD	XP	Pts.
73	5	6	0	11	11	73	22	341	1	15.5	1	0	6
74	7	4	0	11	3	4	24	391	7	16.3	7	2	44
75	2	9	0	11	3	4	18	312	2	17.3	2	0	12
Totals	14	19	0	33	17	81	64	1044	10	16.3	10	2	62

Other career figures: 4.8 yds. per carry.

ANTHONY DAVIS
SOUTHERN CALIFORNIA RB, 5-9, 183 San Fernando, Calif. (San Fernando HS)

Consensus all-America 74. Heisman 2nd in 74, 13th in 73.

Bowls: Rose 73—rushed 157 yards on 23 carries, including 20-yard TD, caught 3 passes for 17 yards (Beat Ohio St., 42-17). Rose 74—rushed 74 yards on 16 carries, scoring on a 1-yard run; caught 1 pass for 8 yards, returned 1 punt for 8 yards and 2 kickoffs for 45 yards (Ohio St. won, 42-21). Rose 75—rushed 67 yards on 13 carries, caught 1 pass for 9 yards, returned 1 kickoff for 17 yards (Beat Ohio St., 18-17).

Yr.	Team				Rushing				Receiving			All-Purpose		
	W	L	T	G	Car.	Yds.	Avg.	TD	No.	Yds.	TD	Avg.	Plays	Yds.	Avg.
72	#11	0	0	11	184	1034	5.6	16	15	115	—	7.7	217	1661	7.7
73	9	1	1	11	260	1038	4.0	13	13	39	—	3.0	287	1441	5.0
74	9	1	1	11	288	1354	4.7	13	14	87	2	6.2	313	1908	6.1
Totals	29	2	2	33	732	3426	4.7	42	42	241	2	5.7	817	5010	6.1

Career: 103.8 rush yds. per game; 151.8 all-purpose yds. per game.

Other career figures: 302 pts. scored (one 2 pt. conv.); 37 K.O. ret., +1299 yds., 35.1 avg., 6 TDs; 6 punt ret., 44 yds.; 1 pass att., 1 cmp., 9 yds, 1 TD.

National champions. + National champion in K.O. ret. in 1974 on 42.5 avg.

KENNETH DAVIS
TEXAS CHRISTIAN
RB, 5-11, 205
Temple, Texas (Temple HS)

Unanimous all-America 84. Heisman 5th in 84.

Bowl: Bluebonnet 84—rushed 19 yards on 6 carries, caught 1 pass for 3 yards; injured on the last play of the first quarter and never returned (West Va. won, 31-14).

Yr.	Team				Rushing				Receiving			All-Purpose		
	W	L	T	G	Car.	Yds.	Avg.	TD	No.	Yds.	TD	Avg.	Plays	Yds.	Avg.
82	3	8	0	11	113	549	4.9	5	15	68	0	4.5	137	778	5.7
83	1	8	2	11	145	682	4.7	3	15	142	0	9.5	160	824	5.2
84	8	3	0	11	211	1611	7.6	15	13	200	2	15.4	224	1811	8.1
Totals	12	19	2	33	469	2842	6.1	23	43	410	2	9.5	521	3413	6.6

Career: 86.1 rush yds. per game; 103.4 all-purpose yds. per game.

Other career figures: 150 pts. scored; 9 K.O. ret., 161 yds.

ANTHONY DAVIS

STEVE DAVIS
OKLAHOMA   QB, 5-10, 190   Salisaw, Okla. (Salisaw HS)

Bowl: Orange 76—completed 3 of 5 passes for 63 yards with no interceptions and rushed 55 yards on 19 carries, scoring on a 10-yard run in the fourth quarter to seal the victory; named game's Most Valuable Offensive Player (Beat Michigan 14-6, to win the national championship).

	Team			Rushing		Passing					Total Offense		
Yr.	W	L	T	G	Car.	Yds.	Att.	Cmp.	Int.	Pct.	Yds.	TD	Plays	Yds.	TDR
73	10	0	1	11	179	887	91	38	6	.418	934	9	270	1821	27
74	#11	0	0	11	165	659	63	26	4	.413	601	11	228	1260	20
75	#10	1	0	11	171	523	55	19	7	.345	438	1	226	961	7
Totals	31	1	1	33	515	2069	209	83	17	.397	1973	21	724	4042	54

Career: 9.4 per pass att., 23.8 per cmp., 135.9 efficiency; 122.5 total offense yds. per game; 5.6 per play.

Other career figures: 198 pts. scored; 4.0 yds. per rush.

National champions.

WENDELL DAVIS
LOUISIANA STATE
WR, 6-0, 186
Shreveport, La. (Fair Park HS)

Consensus all-America 87.

Bowls: Sugar 85—did not play (Nebraska won, 28-20). Liberty 85—caught 1 pass for 15 yards (Baylor won, 21-7). Sugar 87—caught 6 passes for 63 yards (Nebraska won, 30-15). Gator 87—caught 9 passes for 132 yards, including TDs of 39-12-25 yards; named winning team's Most Outstanding Player (Beat South Caro., 30-13).

	Team				Rushing		Receiving				Scoring		
Yr.	W	L	T	G	Car.	Yds.	No.	Yds.	TD	Avg.	TD	XP	Pts.
84	8	2	1	11	—	—	—	—	—	—	—	—	—
85	9	1	1	10	—	—	31	471	1	15.2	1	0	6
86	9	2	0	11	—	—	80	1244	11	15.6	11	0	66
87	9	1	1	11	—	—	72	993	7	13.8	7	0	42
Totals	35	6	3	43	—	—	183	2708	19	14.8	19	0	114

PETE DEMMERLE
NOTRE DAME
WR, 6-1, 190
New Canaan, Conn. (New Canaan HS)

Consensus all-America 74. Academic all-America 74. NCAA Postgraduate Scholarship 75. Hall of Fame Scholar-Athlete 74.

Bowls: Orange 73—caught 1 pass for a 5-yard TD (Nebraska won, 40-6). Sugar 73—caught 3 passes for 59 yards and scored on a 2-point conversion pass from Tom Clements (Beat Alabama, 24-23, for the national championship). Orange 75—caught 2 passes for 12 yards (Beat Alabama, 13-11).

	Team				Rushing		Receiving				Scoring		
Yr.	W	L	T	G	Car.	Yds.	No.	Yds.	TD	Avg.	TD	XP	Pts.
72	8	2	0	10	1	23	—	—	—	—	—	—	—
73	#10	0	0	10	—	—	26	404	5	15.5	5	0	30
74	9	2	0	10	—	—	43	667	6	15.5	6	0	36
Totals	27	4	0	30	1	23	69	1071	11	15.5	11	0	66

National champions.

ERIC DICKERSON
SOUTHERN METHODIST
RB, 6-2, 215
Sealy, Texas (Sealy HS)

Unanimous all-America 82. Heisman 3rd in 82.

Bowls: Holiday 80—rushed 110 yards on 23 carries, scoring on 15-yard and 1-yard runs; caught 1 pass for 5 yards (Brigham Young won, 46-45). Cotton 83—rushed 124 yards on 27 carries (Beat Pittsburgh, 7-3).

	Team				Rushing				Receiving			All-Purpose		
Yr.	W	L	T	G	Car.	Yds.	Avg.	TD	No.	Yds.	TD	Avg.	Plays	Yds.	Avg.
79	5	6	0	9	115	477	4.1	6	6	35	0	5.8	121	512	4.2
80	8	3	0	11	188	928	4.9	5	6	93	1	15.5	194	1021	5.3
81	10	1	0	11	255	1428	5.6	19	1	2	0	2.0	256	1430	5.6
82	10	0	1	11	232	1617	7.0	17	6	60	0	10.0	238	1677	7.0
Totals	33	10	1	42	790	4450	5.6	47	19	190	1	10.0	809	4640	5.7

Career: 106.0 rush yds. per game; 110.5 all-purpose yds. per game.
Other career figures: 288 pts. scored.

LYNN DICKEY
KANSAS STATE QB, 6-4, 213 Osawatomie, Kan. (Osawatomie HS)

Heisman 10th in 70, 12th in 69.

	Team				Rushing		Passing					Total Offense		
Yr.	W	L	T	G	Car.	Yds.	Att.	Cmp.	Int.	Pct.	Yds.	TD	Plays	Yds.	TDR
68	4	6	0	10	30	-154	258	125	18	.484	1569	8	288	1415	8
69	5	5	0	10	51	-120	372	196	19	.527	2476	14	424	2356	16
70	6	5	0	11	28	-155	364	180	28	.495	2163	7	392	2008	9
Totals	15	16	0	31	110	-429	994	501	65	.504	6208	29	1104	5779	33

Career: 6.2 per pass att., 12.4 per cmp., 99.41 efficiency; 186.4 total offense yds. per game; 5.2 per play.

Other career figures: 24 pts. scored; 1 pass caught, 11 yds.

TONY DORSETT
PITTSBURGH
RB, 5-11, 192
Aliquippa, Pa. (Hopewell HS)

Unanimous all-America 76, all-America 75 and 73. Heisman winner in 76, 4th in 75, 13th in 74, 11th in 73.

Bowls: Fiesta 73—rushed 100 yards on 30 carries, scoring on a 3-yard run, caught 2 passes for 7 yards and returned 3 kickoffs 50 yards (Arizona St. won, 28-7). Sun 75—rushed 142 yards on 27 carries, scoring on 8- and 2-yard runs (Beat Kansas, 33-19). Sugar 77—rushed 202 yards on 32 carries, scoring on an 11-yard run, and caught 1 pass for minus 6 yards (Beat Georgia, 27-3, to win national championship).

	Team				Rushing				Receiving				All-Purpose		
Yr.	W	L	T	G	Car.	Yds.	Avg.	TD	No.	Yds.	TD	Avg.	Plays	Yds.	Avg.
73	6	4	1	11	288	1586	5.5	12	12	84	0	7.0	301	1692	5.6
74	7	4	0	10	220	1004	4.6	11	9	58	0	6.4	229	1062	4.6
75	7	4	0	11	228	1544	6.8	11	11	191	3	17.4	245	1840	7.5
76	#11	0	0	11	*338	+*1948	5.8	*21	7	73	1	10.4	*345	+*2021	5.9
Totals	31	12	1	43	1074	6082	5.7	55	39	406	4	10.4	1120	6615	5.9

Career: 141.4 rush yds. per game; 153.8 all-purpose yds. per game.

Other career: 356+ pts. scored (one 2-pt. conv.); 7 K.O. ret., 127 yds.; 3 passes att., 0 cmp.

\# National champions. + National champion in rushing at 177.1 yds. per game, in scoring at 12.2 pts. per game and in all-purpose running at 183.7 yds. per game in 1976.

* This figure led the nation.

D.J. DOZIER
PENN STATE   RB, 6-1, 204   Virginia Beach, Va. (Kempsville HS)

Consensus all-America 86. Heisman 8th in 86.

Bowls: Aloha 83—rushed 37 yards on 15 carries, scoring winning TD with 3:00 remaining on 2-yard run; caught 3 passes for 22 yds.; returned 1 kickoff 22 yards (Beat Washington, 13-10). Orange 86—rushed 39 yards on 12 carries and caught 3 passes for 0 yards (Oklahoma won, 25-10, for national championship). Fiesta 87—rushed 99 yards on 20 carries, scoring winning TD with 6:47 remaining on 6-yard run and caught 2 passes for 12 yards; named game's Most Outstanding Offensive Player (Beat Miami [Fla.], 14-10, to win national championship).

	Team				Rushing				Receiving				All-Purpose		
Yr.	W	L	T	G	Car.	Yds.	Avg.	TD	No.	Yds.	TD	Avg.	Plays	Yds.	Avg.
83	7	4	1	12	174	1002	5.8	7	19	189	1	9.9	193	1191	6.2
84	6	5	0	8	125	691	5.5	4	7	50	0	7.1	135	796	5.9
85	11	0	0	9	154	723	4.7	4	14	87	1	6.2	168	810	4.8
86	#11	0	0	11	171	811	4.7	10	26	287	2	11.0	197	1098	5.6
Totals	35	9	1	40	624	3227	5.2	25	66	613	4	9.3	693	3895	5.6

Career: 80.7 rush yds. per game; 97.4 all-purpose yds. per game.

Other career figures: 174 pts. scored; 3 K.O. ret.; 55 yds.; 2 passes att., 0 cmp.

National champions.

REGGIE DUPARD
SOUTHERN METHODIST   RB, 6-0, 201   New Orleans, La. (Curtis HS)

Consensus all America 85.

Bowls: Cotton 83—returned 1 kickoff 17 yards (Beat Pittsburgh, 7-3). Sun 83—rushed 51 yards on 13 carries, caught 4 passes for 10 yards and returned 1 punt for 6 yards (Alabama won, 28-7). Aloha 84—rushed 103 yards on 23 carries, scoring the game-winning TD at 6:13 on a 12-yard run and caught 1 pass for 39 yards (Beat Notre Dame, 27-20).

	Team				Rushing				Receiving				All-Purpose		
Yr.	W	L	T	G	Car.	Yds.	Avg.	TD	No.	Yds.	TD	Avg.	Plays	Yds.	Avg.
82	10	0	1	11	13	85	6.5	2	1	2	0	2.0	35	377	10.8
83	10	1	0	11	197	1249	6.3	9	4	22	0	5.5	211	1322	6.3
84	9	2	0	11	196	1157	5.4	16	10	114	0	11.4	209	1305	6.2
85	6	5	0	11	235	1278	5.9	14	11	180	2	16.4	246	1458	5.9
Totals	35	8	1	44	641	3769	5.9	41	26	318	2	12.2	701	4462	6.4

Career: 85.7 rush yds. per game; 101.4 all-purpose yds. per game.

Other career figures: 258 pts. scored; 16 K.O. ret., 282 yds.; 18 punt ret., 93 yds.; 1 pass att., 0 cmp.

HART LEE DYKES
OKLAHOMA STATE   WR, 6-4, 220   Bay City, Texas (Bay City HS)

Consensus all-America 88.

Bowls: Gator 85—caught 8 passes for 104 yards, including 31-yard TD (Florida St. won, 34-23). Sun 87—caught 3 passes for 72 yards (Beat West Va., 35-33). Holiday 88—caught 10 passes for 163 yards, including 25-yard TD (Beat Wyoming, 62-14).

Yr.	Team W	L	T	G	Rushing Car.	Yds.	No.	Receiving Yds.	TD	Avg.	Scoring TD	XP	Pts.
85	8	3	0	8	2	4	8	101	0	12.6	—	—	—
86	6	5	0	11	1	2	60	814	7	13.6	7	0	42
87	9	2	0	11	—	—	61	978	8	16.0	8	0	48
88	9	2	0	11	—	—	74	1278	14	17.3	15	0	90
Totals	32	12	0	41	3	6	203	3171	29	15.6	30	0	180

Other career figures: 6 passes att., 1 cmp., 1 int., 36 yds; 2 K.O. ret., 23 yds.

JOHN ELWAY
STANFORD
QB, 6-4, 202
Northridge, Calif. (Grenada Hills HS)

Unanimous all-America 82. Heisman 2nd in 82. Today's Top Five, NCAA Honors Luncheon 83.

Yr.	Team W	L	T	G	Rushing Car.	Yds.	Att.	Passing Cmp.	Int.	Pct.	Yds.	TD	Total Offense Plays	Yds.	TDR
79	5	5	1	10	26	-33	96	50	3	.521	544	6	122	511	6
80	6	5	0	11	100	50	379	248	11	.654	2889	27	479	2939	31
81	4	7	0	11	74	-158	366	214	13	.585	2674	20	440	2516	21
82	5	6	0	11	59	-138	405	262	12	.647	3242	*24	464	3104	24
Totals	20	23	1	43	259	-279	1246	774	39	.621	9349	77	1505	9070	82

Career: 7.5 per pass att., 12.1 per cmp., 139.3 efficiency; 210.9 total offense yds. per game; 6.0 per play.

Other career figures: 30 pts. scored.

* This figure led the nation.

BOOMER ESIASON
MARYLAND QB, 6-4, 190   East Islip, N.Y. (East Islip HS)

Heisman 10th in 83.

Bowls: Aloha 82—completed 19 of 32 passes for 251 yards and 2 TDs (Washington won, 21-20). Florida Citrus 83—completed 4 of 6 passes for 61 yards; had to leave the game early in the second quarter with a shoulder seperation (Tennessee won, 30-23).

Yr.	Team				Rushing		Passing						Total Offense		
	W	L	T	G	Car.	Yds.	Att.	Cmp.	Int.	Pct.	Yds.	TD	Plays	Yds.	TDR
81	4	6	1	10	54	-75	242	122	9	.504	1635	9	296	1560	9
82	8	3	0	11	55	-71	314	176	10	.561	2302	18	369	2231	20
83	8	3	0	10	47	-32	294	163	8	.554	2322	15	341	2290	17
Totals	20	12	1	31	156	-178	850	461	27	.542	6259	42	1006	6081	46

Career: 7.4 per pass att; 13.6 per cmp; 126.1 efficiency, 196.2 total offense yds. per game; 6.0 per play.

Other career figures: 24 pts. scored.

JIM EVERETT
PURDUE QB, 6-5, 212   Albuquerque, N.M. (El Dorado HS)

Heisman 6th in 85.

Bowl: Peach 84—completed 22 of 42 passes for 3 TDs for 253 yards with 3 interceptions (Virginia won, 27-24).

Yr.	Team				Rushing		Passing						Total Offense		
	W	L	T	G	Car.	Yds.	Att.	Cmp.	Int.	Pct.	Yds.	TD	Plays	Yds.	TDR
81	5	6	0	3	2	-1	5	1	1	.200	7	0	7	6	0
82	3	8	0	2	5	11	13	6	0	.462	64	0	18	75	1
83	3	7	1	5	9	-26	66	31	5	.470	433	2	75	407	2
84	7	4	0	11	50	-52	389	227	13	.584	3003	15	439	2951	16
85	5	6	0	11	68	-62	450	285	11	.633	3651	23	518	+3589	24
Totals	23	31	1	32	134	-130	923	550	30	.596	7158	40	1057	7028	43

Career: 7.8 per pass cmp., 13.0 per cmp., 132.5 efficiency; 219.6 total offense yds. per game; 6.6 per play. (Redshirted in 1982.)

+ National total offense champion at 326.3 yds. per game in 1985.

VAGAS FERGUSON
NOTRE DAME   RB, 6-1, 194   Richmond, Ind. (Richmond HS)

Consensus all-America 79. Heisman 5th in 79.

Bowls: Gator 76—rushed 22 yards on 10 carries (Beat Penn St., 20-9). Cotton 78—rushed 100 yards on 21 carries; 33- and 26-yard TDs; caught 3 passes for 23 yards and 17-yard TD; named game's Outstanding Offensive Player (Beat Texas, 38-10, to win national championship). Cotton 79—rushed 19 yards on 10 carries and caught 2-point pass from Joe Montana (Beat Houston, 35-34).

	Team			Rushing				Receiving			All-Purpose		
Yr.	W	L	T	G	Car.	Yds.	Avg.	TD	No.	Yds.	TD	Avg.	Plays	Yds.	Avg.
76	8	3	0	10	81	350	4.3	2	3	27	1	9.0	84	377	4.5
77	#10	1	0	9	80	493	6.2	6	6	93	1	15.5	86	586	6.8
78	8	3	0	11	211	1192	5.6	7	20	171	1	8.6	231	1363	5.9
79	7	4	0	11	*301	1437	4.8	17	14	72	0	5.1	315	1509	4.8
Totals	33	11	0	41	673	3472	5.2	32	43	363	3	8.4	716	3835	5.4

Career: 84.7 rush yds. per game; 93.5 all-purpose yds. per game.
Other career figures: 210 pts. scored; 1 pass att., 0 comp.
National champions. * This figure led the nation.

DOUG FLUTIE
BOSTON COLLEGE
QB, 5-9, 177
Natick, Mass. (Natick HS)

Unanimous all-America 84. Heisman winner in 84, 3rd in 83. Today's Top Five, NCAA Honors Luncheon 85. Hall of Fame Scholar-Athlete 84.

Bowls: Florida Citrus 82—completed 22 of 38 passes for 299 yards and 2 TDs with 2 interceptions, rushed 12 yards on 14 carries, scoring on a 5-yard run and scored on a 2-point run; named Offensive Player of the Game (Auburn won, 33-26). Liberty 83—completed 16 of 37 passes for 287 yards and 2 TDs with 1 interception and rushed 32 yards on 5 carries; named game's Most Valuable Player (Notre Dame won, 19-18). Cotton 85—completed 13 of 37 passes for 180 yards and 2 TDs with 2 interceptions, rushed 51 yards on 4 carries (Beat Houston, 45-28).

	Team			Rushing		Passing						Total Offense		
Yr.	W	L	T	G	Car.	Yds.	Att.	Cmp.	Int.	Pct.	Yds.	TD	Plays	Yds.	TDR
81	5	6	0	9	67	79	192	105	8	.547	1652	10	269	1731	12
82	8	2	1	11	90	265	347	162	20	.467	2749	13	437	3014	15
83	9	2	0	11	69	245	345	177	15	.513	2724	17	414	2969	17
84	9	2	0	11	62	149	386	233	11	.604	3454	27	448	3603	30
Totals	31	12	1	42	288	738	1270	677	54	.533	10,579	67	1558	11,317	74

Career: 8.3 per pass att., 15.6 per cmp., 132.2 efficiency; 269.5 total offense yds. per game; 7.3 per play.
Other career figures: 44 pts. scored (one 2-pt. conv.)

TONY FRANKLIN
TEXAS A&M
PK, 5-9, 171
Fort Worth, Texas (Arlington Heights HS)

Consensus all-America 76.

Bowls: Liberty 75—did not score (Southern Cal won, 20-0). Sun 77—kicked FGs of 39-33-62 (Sun Bowl record) and 1 of 2 PATs; named game's Most Valuable Offensive Player (Beat Florida, 37-14). Bluebonnet 77—made 4 of 4 PATs (Southern Cal won, 47-28). Hall of Fame 78—made 4 of 4 PATs (Beat Iowa St., 28-12).

	Team				Punting					Field Goals				
											Under	40		
Yr.	W	L	T	G	No.	Yds.	Avg.	XPA-XP	FGA-FG	Pct.	40 yds.	Plus	Long	Pts.
75	10	1	0	11	—	—	—	31 27	28 12	.428	7-14	5-14	59	63
76	9	2	0	11	—	—	—	33 30	26 *17	.654	9-12	†8-14	†65	81
77	8	3	0	11	—	—	—	38 38	28 16	.571	8-9	8-19	57	86
78	7	4	0	11	3	143	47.7	31 28	19 11	.579	6-8	5-11	52	61
Totals	34	10	0	44	3	143	47.7	133 123	101 56	.554	30-43	26-58	65	291
Career accuracy percentages:								.925			.698	.448		

Other career figures: Kicked 65- and 64-yard FGs vs. Baylor in 76. His FGs provided winning margin over: 78-Southern Methodist.

* This figure led the nation. † Tied for first in the nation.

IRVING FRYAR
NEBRASKA   WR, 6-0, 200   Mount Holly, N.J. (Rancocas Valley HS)

Unanimous all-Amercia 83.

Bowls: Sun 80—(did not play) (Beat Mississippi St., 31-17). Orange 82—attempted 1 incomplete pass (Clemson won, 22-15). Orange 83—caught 5 passes for 51 yards, rushed 12 yards on 2 carries and returned 1 kickoff 18 yards (Beat Louisiana St., 21-20). Orange 84—caught 5 passes for 61 yards, rushed 4 yards on 2 carries, returned 3 punts 21 yards and 2 kickoffs 44 yards (Miami [Fla.] won, 31-30, for national championship).

	Team				Rushing				Receiving				All-Purpose		
Yr.	W	L	T	G	Car.	Yds.	Avg.	TD	No.	Yds.	TD	Avg.	Plays	Yds.	Avg.
80	9	2	0	4	2	14	7.0	0	—	—	—	—	3	40	13.3
81	9	2	0	11	7	26	3.7	1	3	70	1	23.3	37	469	12.7
82	11	1	0	10	20	245	12.3	2	24	346	2	14.4	66	993	15.0
83	12	0	0	12	23	318	13.8	2	40	780	8	19.5	83	1267	15.3
Totals	41	5	0	37	52	603	11.6	5	67	1196	11	17.9	189	2769	14.7

	Scoring			Punt Returns			K.O. Returns			Comb. Kick Returns			
Yr.	TD	XP	Pts.	No.	Yds.	Avg.	No.	Yds.	Avg.	No.	Yds.	TD	Avg.
80	—	—	—	—	—	—	1	26	26.0	1	26	0	26.0
81	4	0	24	24	318	13.3	3	55	18.3	27	373	2	13.8
82	5	0	30	18	277	15.4	4	125	31.3	22	402	1	18.3
83	10	4	64	18	113	6.3	2	56	28.0	20	169	0	8.5
Totals	19	4	118	60	708	11.8	10	262	26.2	60	970	3	16.2

BRENT FULLWOOD
AUBURN   RB, 5-11, 209   St. Cloud, Fla. (St. Cloud HS)

Unanimous all-America 86. Heisman 6th in 86.

Bowls: Sugar 84—returned 1 kickoff 19 yards (Beat Michigan, 9-7). Liberty 84—rushed 4 yards on 11 carries (Beat Arkansas, 21-15). Cotton 86—rushed 25 yards on 5 carries, returned 1 kickoff 28 yards (Texas A&M won, 36-16). Florida Citrus 86—rushed 152 yards on 28 carries, scoring on a 4-yard run, and caught 2 passes for 15 yards. Named Co-Offensive Player of the Game. (Beat Southern Cal, 16-7).

Yr.	Team W	L	T	G	Rushing Car.	Yds.	Avg.	TD	Receiving No.	Yds.	TD	Avg.	All-Purpose Plays	Yds.	Avg.
83	10	1	0	5	14	86	6.1	1	0	0	0	0.0	20	197	9.9
84	8	4	0	12	117	628	5.4	7	3	30	0	10.0	142	1167	8.2
85	8	3	0	10	100	684	6.8	6	1	1	0	1.0	111	882	7.9
86	9	2	0	11	167	1391	8.3	10	5	46	0	9.2	176	1512	8.6
Totals	35	10	0	38	398	2789	7.0	24	9	77	0	8.6	449	3758	8.4

Career: 73.4 rush yds. per game; 98.9 all-purpose yards per game.

Other career figures: 150 pts. scored; 42 K.O. ret., 892 yds., 1 TD, 21.2 avg.; 1 pass att., 1 cmp., 31 yds., 1 TD.

CHUCK FUSINA
PENN STATE
QB, 6-1, 195
McKees Rocks, Pa. (Sto-Rox HS)

Unanimous all-America 78. Heisman 2nd in 78.

Bowls: Sugar 75—(did not play) (Alabama won, 13-6). Gator 76—completed 14 of 33 passes for 118 yards with 2 interceptions and rushed 1 yard on 2 carries (Notre Dame won, 20-9). Fiesta 77—completed 9 of 23 passes for 83 yards and rushed minus 26 yards on 2 carries with 1 TD (Beat Arizona St., 42-30). Sugar 79—completed 15 of 30 passes for 163 yards and 1 TD with 4 interceptions (Alabama won, 14-7).

Yr.	Team W	L	T	G	Rushing Car.	Yds.	Passing Att.	Cmp.	Int.	Pct.	Yds.	TD	Total Offense Plays	Yds.	TDR
75	9	2	0	3	8	37	9	4	1	.444	42	0	17	79	0
76	7	4	0	11	31	-88	167	88	10	.527	1260	11	198	1172	14
77	10	1	0	11	29	-53	246	142	9	.577	2221	15	275	2168	16
78	11	0	0	11	51	-116	242	137	12	.566	1859	11	293	1743	13
Totals	37	7	0	36	119	-220	664	371	32	.559	5382	37	783	5162	43

Career: 5.6 per pass att., 14.5 per cmp., 132.7 efficiency; 143.4 total offense yds. per game, 6.6 per play.

Other career figures: 36 pts. scored.

TOM GATEWOOD
NOTRE DAME   SE, 6-2, 208   Baltimore, Md. (City College HS)

Consensus all-America 70. Heisman 12th in 70. Academic all-America 71. NCAA Postgraduate Scholarship 72. Hall of Fame Scholar-Athlete 71.

Bowls: Cotton 70—caught 6 passes for 112 yards, including a 54-yard TD from Joe Theismann (Texas won, 21-17). Cotton 71—caught 2 passes for 43 yards, including a 26-yard TD from Joe Theismann (Beat Texas, 24-11).

	Team				Rushing		Receiving			Scoring		
Yr.	W	L	T	G	Car.	Yds.	No.	Yds.	TD	Avg.	TD	XP	Pts.
69	9	1	0	10	1	4	77	1123	7	14.6	7	2	44
70	8	2	0	10	2	-7	33	417	4	12.6	4	0	24
71	8	1	0	10	1	0	47	743	8	15.8	8	0	48
Totals	25	4	1	30	4	-3	157	2283	19	14.5	19	2	116

WOODY GREEN
ARIZONA STATE
RB, 6-1, 202
Portland, Ore. (Jefferson HS)

Consensus all-America 72 and 73. Heisman 8th in 73.

Bowls: Fiesta 71—rushed 101 yards on 24 carries, scoring on runs of 1, 2 and 2 yards; caught 2 passes for 46 yards; returned 1 punt 1 yard and 1 kickoff 29 yards (Beat Florida St., 45-38). Fiesta 72—rushed 202 yards on 25 carries, scoring on runs of 2, 12, 17 and 21 yards; named game's Most Valuable Offensive Player (Beat Missouri, 49-35). Fiesta 73—rushed 131 yards on 25 carries, scoring on runs of 3, 23 and 1 yards; caught 2 passes for 13 yards; returned 1 punt minus 6 yards and 1 kickoff 26 yards (Beat Pittsburgh, 28-7).

	Team				Rushing				Receiving			All-Purpose		
Yr.	W	L	T	G	Car.	Yds.	Avg.	TD	No.	Yds.	TD	Avg.	Plays	Yds.	Avg.
71	10	1	0	10	208	1209	5.8	9	4	94	2	23.5	238	1620	6.8
72	9	2	0	10	209	1363	6.5	15	9	115	0	12.8	229	1607	7.0
73	10	1	0	10	184	1182	6.4	9	22	328	5	14.9	214	1589	7.4
Totals	29	4	0	30	601	3754	6.2	33	35	537	7	15.3	681	4816	7.1

Career: 125.1 rush yds. per game; 160.5 all-purpose yds. per game.

Other career figures: 246 pts. scored; 24 punt ret., 202 yds., 8.4 avg.; 21 K.O. ret., 323 yds., 15.4 avg.; 3 passes att., 1 cmp., 1 int., 10 yds.

ARCHIE GRIFFIN
OHIO STATE
RB, 5-9, 182
Columbus, Ohio (Eastmoor HS)

Unanimous all-America 74 and 75, all-America 73. Heisman winner 74 and 75, 5th in 73. Today's Top Five, NCAA Honors Luncheon 75.

Bowls: Rose 73—rushed 95 yards on 20 carries and caught 2 passes for 27 yards (Southern Cal won, 42-17). Rose 74—rushed 149 yards on 22 carries, one a 45-yard TD, and returned 2 kickoffs 39 yards (Beat Southern Cal, 42-21). Rose 75—rushed 75 yards on 20 carries and caught 2 passes for 25 yards (Southern Cal won, 18-17). Rose 76—rushed 93 yards on 17 carries, caught 1 pass for 12 yards and returned 2 kickoffs 41 yards (UCLA won, 23-10).

	Team				Rushing			Receiving			All-Purpose		
Yr.	W	L	T	G	Car.	Yds.	Avg.	TD	No.	Yds.	TD	Avg.	Plays	Yds.	Avg.
72	9	1	0	10	139	772	5.6	3	4	44	0	11.0	153	1012	6.6
73	9	0	1	10	225	1428	6.3	6	5	32	1	6.4	235	1642	7.0
74	10	1	0	11	236	*1620	6.9	12	3	52	0	17.3	243	1743	7.2
75	11	0	0	11	245	1357	5.5	4	13	158	0	12.2	263	1606	6.1
Totals	39	2	1	42	845	5177	6.1	25	25	286	1	11.4	894	6003	6.7

Career: 123.3 rush yds. per game; 142.9 all-purpose yds. per game.

Other career figures: 162 pts. scored; 24 K.O. ret., 540 yds., 22.5 avg., 1 TD.

* This figure led the nation.

CHUCK HARTLIEB
IOWA QB, 6-3, 205 Woodstock, Ill. (Marian Central Catholic HS)

Academic all-America 87. Heisman 8th in 88.

Bowls: Rose 86—no statistics (UCLA won, 45-28). Holiday 86—no statistics (Beat San Diego St., 39-38). Holiday 87—completed 21 of 35 passes for 237 yards with no interceptions (Beat Wyoming, 20-19). Peach 88—completed 30 of 51 passes for 428 yards and 3 TDs, 2 to Deven Herberts, with 4 interceptions (North Caro. St. won, 28-23).

	Team				Rushing		Passing						Total Offense			
Yr.	W	L	T	G	Car.	Yds.	Att.	Cmp.	Int.	Pct.	Yds.	TD	Plays	Yds.	Avg.	TDR
85	10	1	0	11	5	-12	—	—	—	—	—	—	5	-12	—	—
86	8	3	0	11	3	3	8	7	0	.875	104	1	11	107	9.7	1
87	9	3	0	12	41	-138	299	196	8	.656	2855	19	340	2717	*8.0	20
88	6	3	3	12	54	-240	409	258	+9	.631	3310	14	463	3070	6.6	15
Totals	33	10	3	46	103	-387	716	461	17	.643	6269	34	819	5882	7.2	36

Career avg.: 8.8 pass yds. per att.; 13.6 per cmp.; 148.9 efficiency.

Career per game: 256.9 yds. passing, 241.1 total offense last two seasons.

Other career figures: 12 pts. scored.

+ Led nation in int. avoidance at 2.20 pct. (min 15 att. pg and 130 rating pts.)

* This figure led the nation (min. 200 yds. pg total offense).

CHUCK HARTLIEB

BARRY HELTON
COLORADO P, 6-4, 200 Simla, Colo. (Big Sandy HS)

Consensus all-America 86 and 85.

Bowls: Freedom 85—punted 5 times for 39-yard average, longest 54 (Washington won, 20-17). Bluebonnet 86—punted 5 times for 37.6-yard average (Baylor won, 21-9).

Yr.	Team W	L	T	G	Punting No.	Yds.	Avg.
84	1	10	0	9	4	126	31.5
85	7	4	0	11	52	2390	46.0
86	6	5	0	11	57	2599	45.6
87	7	4	0	11	40	1758	44.0
Totals	21	23	0	42	153	6873	44.9

MARK HERRMANN
PURDUE
QB, 6-4, 187
Carmel, Ind. (Carmel HS)

Unanimous all-America 80. Heisman 8th in 79, 4th in 80. Today's Top Five, NCAA Honors Luncheon 81.

Bowls: Peach 78—completed 12 of 24 passes for 166 yards and 2 TDs with 2 interceptions; rushed 3 yards on 5 carries, including 2-yard TD; named game's Most Valuable Player (Beat Georgia Tech, 41-21). Bluebonnet 79—completed 21 of 39 passes for 303 yards and 3 TDs with no interceptions; rushed minus 38 yards on 3 carries; named game's Most Valuable Offensive Player (Beat Tennessee, 27-22). Liberty 80—completed 22 of 28 passes for 289 yards and 4 TDs; rushed minus 33 yards on 6 carries; named game's Most Valuable Player (Beat Missouri, 28-25).

Yr.	Team W	L	T	G	Rushing Car.	Yds.	Passing Att.	Cmp.	Int.	Pct.	Yds.	TD	Total Offense Plays	Yds.	TDR
77	5	6	0	11	35	-263	319	175	27	.548	2453	18	354	2190	18
78	8	2	1	11	30	-83	250	140	10	.560	1738	12	280	1655	12
79	9	2	0	11	44	-245	309	182	19	.589	2074	13	353	1829	14
80	8	3	0	10	27	-153	340	220	17	.647	2923	19	367	2770	19
Totals	30	13	1	43	136	-744	1218	717	73	.589	9188	62	1354	8444	63

Career: 7.5 per pass att., 12.8 per comp., 127.1 efficiency; 196.4 total offense yds. per game, 6.2 per play.
Other career figures: 6 pts. scored.

CRAIG HEYWARD
PITTSBURGH
RB, 6-0, 260
Passaic, N.J. (Passaic HS)

Consensus all-America 87. Heisman 5th in 87.

Bowl: Bluebonnet 87—136 yards on 30 carries, scoring on a 4-yard run, and caught 11 passes for 9 yards (Texas won, 32-27).

	Team				Rushing				Receiving			All-Purpose		
Yr.	W	L	T	G	Car.	Yds.	Avg.	TD	No.	Yds.	TD	Avg.	Plays	Yds.	Avg.
84	3	7	1	11	123	539	4.4	4	10	70	0	7.0	142	763	5.4
85	Did Not Play														
86	5	5	1	11	171	756	4.4	8	29	361	1	12.4	200	1117	5.6
87	8	3	0	11	*357	1655	4.6	11	21	198	1	9.4	378	1853	4.9
Totals	16	15	2	33	651	2950	4.5	23	60	629	2	10.5	720	3733	5.2

Career: 89.4 rush yds. per game; 113.1 all-purpose yds. per game.

Other career figures: 152 pts. scored (one 2-pt. conv.); 9 K.O. ret., 154 yds.; 2 passes att., 2 cmp., 57 yds., 1 TD.

* This figure led the nation.

CLARKSTON HINES
DUKE
WR, 6-1, 170
Chapel Hill, N.C. (Chapel Hill HS two years, then Bolles School, Jacksonville, Fla.)

Unanimous all-America 89, all-America 88.

Bowl: 89 All-American—Caught 6 passes for 112 yards (Texas Tech won, 49-21).

	Team				Rushing		Receiving				Scoring		
Yr.	W	L	T	G	Car.	Yds.	No.	Yds.	TD	Avg.	TD	XP	Pts.
86	4	7	0	11	1	-5	3	9	0	3.0	—	—	—
87	5	6	0	11	2	-6	57	1093	11	19.2	11	0	66
88	7	3	1	11	—	—	68	1067	10	15.7	10	4	64
89	8	3	0	11	1	-5	61	1149	17	18.8	17	2	104
Totals	24	19	1	44	4	-16	189	3318	38	17.6	38	6	234

GORDON HUDSON
BRIGHAM YOUNG   TE, 6-4, 231   Kennewick, Wash. (Kennewick HS)

Unanimous all-America 82 and 83.

Bowls: Holiday 80—(did not play) (Beat Southern Methodist, 46-45). Holiday 81—caught 7 passes for 126 yards, including 7-yard TD (Beat Washington St., 38-36). Holiday 82—caught 7 passes for 81 yards, including 13-yard TD (Ohio St. won, 47-17). Holiday 83—(did not play) (Beat Missouri, 21-17).

Yr.	Team				Rushing		Receiving				Scoring		
	W	L	T	G	Car.	Yds.	No.	Yds.	TD	Avg.	TD	XP	Pts.
80	11	1	0	2	—	—	—	—	—	—	—	—	—
81	10	2	0	12	0	0	67	960	10	14.3	10	0	60
82	8	3	0	11	2	22	67	928	6	13.9	6	0	36
83	10	1	0	8	—	—	44	596	6	13.5	6	0	36
Totals	39	7	0	33	2	22	178	2484	22	14.0	22	0	132

BO JACKSON
AUBURN
RB, 6-1, 222
Bessemer, Ala. (McAdory HS, McCalla, Ala.)

Consensus all-America 83. Unanimous all-America 85. Heisman winner 85.

Bowls: Florida Citrus 82—rushed 64 yards on 14 carries, scoring on 1- and 6-yard runs; caught 1 pass for 11 yards (Beat Boston College, 33-26). Sugar 84—rushed 130 yards on 22 carries, caught 1 pass for 6 yards; named game's Most Outstanding Player (Beat Michigan, 9-7). Liberty 84—rushed 88 yards on 18 carries, scoring on 2- and 39-yard runs and caught 1 pass for 25 yards; named game's Most Valuable Player (Beat Arkansas, 21-15). Cotton 86— rushed 129 yards on 31 carries, scoring on a 5-yard run and caught 2 passes for 73 yards, scoring on a 73-yard play; named game's Most Outstanding Offensive Player (Texas A&M won, 36-16).

Yr.	Team				Rushing				Receiving			All-Purpose		
	W	L	T	G	Car.	Yds.	Avg.	TD	No.	Yds.	TD	Avg.	Plays	Yds.	Avg.
82	8	3	0	10	127	829	6.5	9	5	64	0	12.8	139	1047	7.5
83	10	1	0	11	158	1213	7.7	12	13	73	2	5.6	178	1449	8.1
84	8	4	0	6	87	475	5.5	5	4	62	0	15.5	91	537	5.9
85	8	3	0	11	278	1786	6.4	17	4	73	0	18.3	282	1859	6.6
Totals	34	11	0	38	650	4303	6.6	43	26	272	2	10.5	690	4892	7.1

Career: 113.2 rush yds. per game; 128.7 all-purpose yds. per game.

Other career figures: 274 pts. scored (two 2-pt. conv.); 1 pass att., 0 cmp.; 14 K.O. ret., 317 yds., 22.6 avg.

KEITH JACKSON
OKLAHOMA
TE, 6-3, 248
Little Rock, Ark. (Parkview HS)

Unanimous all-America 86 and 87. Today's Top Six Award; NCAA Honors Luncheon 88.

Bowls: Orange 85—no statistics (Washington won, 28-17). Orange 86—caught 2 passes for 83 yards, including 71-yard TD pass (Beat Penn St., 25-10, to win national championship). Orange 87—caught 1 pass for 11 yards (Beat Arkansas, 42-8). Orange 88—caught 3 passes for 45 yards (Miami [Fla.] won, 20-14).

| | Team | | | | Rushing | | Receiving | | | Scoring | | |
Yr.	W	L	T	G	Car.	Yds.	No.	Yds.	TD	Avg.	TD	XP	Pts.
84	9	1	1	11	—	—	15	223	3	14.9	3	0	18
85	#10	1	0	11	7	153	20	486	2	24.3	3	0	18
86	10	1	0	11	6	98	14	403	5	28.8	8	0	48
87	11	0	0	10	7	38	13	358	4	27.5	4	0	24
Totals	40	3	1	43	20	289	62	1470	14	23.7	18	0	108

Other career figures: 14.5 yds. per carry.
\# National champions.

JEFF JAEGER
WASHINGTON
PK, 5-11, 191
Kent, Wash. (Kent Meridian HS)

Consensus all-America 86.

Bowls: Aloha 83—kicked 39-yard FG and made 1 of 1 PATs (Penn St. won, 13-10). Orange 85—made 4 of 4 PATs (Beat Oklahoma, 28-17). Freedom 85—kicked 30- and 18-yard FGs, including the game-winning FG with 14:57 remaining, and 2 of 2 PATs (Beat Colorado, 20-17). Sun 86—kicked 31- and 34-yard FGs (Alabama won, 28-6).

| | Team | | | | Punting | | | | | | Field Goals | | Under 40 | 40 Plus | | |
Yr.	W	L	T	G	No.	Yds.	Avg.	XPA	-XP	FGA	-FG	Pct.	40 yds.	Plus	Long	Pts.
83	8	3	0	11	—	—	—	28	27	26	20	.769	11-14	9-12	52	87
84	10	1	0	11	—	—	—	33	30	28	22	.789	20-22	2-6	47	96
85	6	5	0	11	—	—	—	19	19	24	21	.875	17-18	4-6	49	82
86	8	2	1	11	—	—	—	43	42	21	17	.810	11-14	6-7	45	93
Totals	32	11	1	44	—	—	—	123	118	99	80	.808	59-68	21-31	52	358

Career accuracy percentages: .959 .868 .677

His FGs provided winning margin over: 83—Michigan, Arizona; 84—Washington St.; 85—Oregon, Southern Cal.

DAVE JAYNES
KANSAS
QB, 6-2, 212
Bonner Springs, Kan. (Bonner Springs HS)

Consensus all-America 73. Heisman 4th in 73.

Bowl: Liberty 73—completed 24 of 38 passes with 2 interceptions for 218 yards, a 12-yard scoring pass and a 2-point conversion pass (North Caro. St. won, 31-18).

Yr.	Team W	L	T	G	Rushing Car.	Yds.	Att.	Cmp.	Passing Int.	Pct.	Yds.	TD	Total Offense Plays	Yds.	TDR
71	4	7	0	11	66	-124	137	64	8	.467	748	7	203	624	7
72	4	7	0	11	70	-171	287	153	21	.533	2253	15	357	2082	16
73	7	3	1	11	96	-198	330	172	9	.521	2131	13	426	1933	17
Totals	15	17	1	33	232	-493	754	389	38	.516	5132	35	986	4639	40

Career: 6.8 per pass att., 13.2 per cmp., 114.0 efficiency; 140.6 total offense yds. per game, 4.7 per play.

Other career figures: 36 pts. scored (three 2-pt. conv.)

JOHN JEFFERSON
ARIZONA STATE
WR, 6-1, 184
Dallas, Texas (Roosevelt HS)

Consensus all-America 77.

Bowls: Fiesta 75—caught 8 passes for 113 yards, including 10-yard TD; named game's Most Outstanding Offensive Player (Beat Nebraska, 17-14). Fiesta 77—caught 5 passes for 56 yards (Penn St. won, 42-30).

Yr.	Team W	L	T	G	Rushing Car.	Yds.	No.	Receiving Yds.	TD	Avg.	Scoring TD	XP	Pts.
74	7	5	0	11	4	36	30	423	1	14.1	1	0	6
75	11	0	0	11	—	—	44	805	5	18.3	5	0	30
76	4	7	0	11	—	—	48	681	5	14.2	5	0	30
77	9	2	0	11	2	11	53	912	8	17.2	9	0	54
Totals	31	14	0	44	6	47	175	2821	19	16.1	20	0	120

ERNIE JENNINGS
AIR FORCE FL, 6-0, 172 Kansas City, Mo. (Central HS)

Consensus all-America 70. Heisman 8th in 70. Academic all-America 70. NCAA Postgraduate Scholarship 71.
Bowl: Sugar 71—caught 2 passes for 31 yards and returned 2 kickoffs 18 yards (Tennessee won, 34-13).

	Team				Rushing				Receiving			All-Purpose		
Yr.	W	L	T	G	Car.	Yds.	Avg.	TD	No.	Yds.	TD	Avg.	Plays	Yds.	Avg.
68	7	3	0	10	50	300	6.0	2	23	375	2	16.3	91	1026	11.3
69	6	4	0	10	27	72	2.7	0	51	729	9	14.3	94	1270	13.5
70	9	2	0	11	14	24	1.7	2	74	1289	*17	17.4	98	1545	15.8
Totals	22	9	0	31	91	396	4.4	4	148	2393	28	16.2	283	3841	13.6

	Scoring			Punt Returns			K.O. Returns			Comb. Kick Returns			
Yr.	TD	XP	Pts.	No.	Yds.	Avg.	No.	Yds.	Avg.	No.	Yds.	TD	Avg.
68	4	0	24	1	-1	-1.0	17	352	20.7	18	351	0	19.5
69	10	0	60	—	—	—	16	469	29.3	16	469	1	29.3
70	19	0	114	—	—	—	10	232	23.2	10	232	0	23.2
Totals	33	0	198	1	-1	-1.0	43	1053	24.5	44	1052	1	23.9

* This figure led the nation.

KERMIT JOHNSON
UCLA RB, 6-0, 185 Los Angeles, Calif. (Blair HS)

Consensus all-America 73. Heisman 10th in 73.

	Team				Rushing				Receiving			All-Purpose		
Yr.	W	L	T	G	Car.	Yds.	Avg.	TD	No.	Yds.	TD	Avg.	Plays	Yds.	Avg.
71	2	7	1	9	80	414	5.2	2	2	11	0	5.5	93	642	6.9
72	8	3	0	11	140	952	6.8	7	2	36	0	18.0	144	1027	7.1
73	9	2	0	11	150	1129	7.5	16	—	—	—	—	161	1446	9.0
Totals	19	12	1	31	370	2495	6.7	25	4	47	0	11.8	398	3115	7.8

Career: 80.5 rush yds. per game; 100.5 all-purpose yds. per game.
Other career figures: 150 pts. scored; 24 K.O. ret., 573 yds., 23.9 avg.

BERT JONES
LOUISIANA STATE   QB, 6-3, 205   Ruston, La. (Ruston HS)

Consensus all-America 72. Heisman 4th in 72.

Bowls: Orange 71—completed 12 of 23 passes with no interceptions for 182 yards and a 31-yard TD pass (Nebraska won, 17-12). Sun 71—completed 12 of 18 passes with no interceptions for 227 yards, including TD passes of 37, 21 and 6 yards and a non-scoring pass of 77 yards (Beat Iowa St., 33-15). Bluebonnet 72—rushed 7 yards on 10 carries, scoring on a 2-yard run, and completed 7 of 19 passes with no interceptions for 90 yards (Tennessee won, 24-17).

Yr.	Team				Rushing		Passing						Total Offense		
	W	L	T	G	Car.	Yds.	Att.	Cmp.	Int.	Pct.	Yds.	TD	Plays	Yds.	TDR
70	9	2	0	11	56	-64	100	52	5	.520	864	5	156	800	5
71	8	3	0	11	67	-7	119	66	4	.555	945	9	186	938	13
72	9	1	1	11	90	18	199	103	7	.518	1446	14	289	1464	18
Totals	26	6	1	33	213	-53	418	221	16	.529	3255	28	631	3202	36

Career: 7.8 per pass att., 14.7 per cmp., 132.7 efficiency; 97.0 total offense yds. per game, 5.1 per play.

Other career figures: 48 pts. scored.

JIM KELLY
MIAMI (FLA.)
QB, 6-3, 215
East Brady, PA. (East Brady HS)

Bowl: Peach 81—completed 11 of 22 passes for 179 yards and 1 TD. Named game's Most Valuable Player (Beat Virginia Tech, 20-10).

Yr.	Team				Rushing		Passing						Total Offense		
	W	L	T	G	Car.	Yds.	Att.	Cmp.	Int.	Pct.	Yds.	TD	Plays	Yds.	TDR
79	5	6	0	10	37	53	104	48	6	.462	721	5	141	774	7
80	8	3	0	11	61	36	206	109	7	.529	1519	11	267	1555	13
81	9	2	0	11	79	5	285	168	14	.589	2403	13	364	2408	16
82	7	4	0	3	15	30	81	51	1	.630	585	3	96	615	3
Totals	29	15	0	35	192	124	676	376	28	.556	5228	32	868	5352	39

Career: 7.7 per pass att., 13.9 per cmp., 127.9 efficiency; 152.9 total offense yds. per game; 6.2 per play.

Other career figures: 42 pts. scored; 1 pass caught, minus 2 yds.

BERNIE KOSAR
MIAMI (FLA.)
QB, 6-5, 207
Boardman, Ohio (Boardman HS)

Heisman 4th in 84. Academic all-America 84.

Bowls: Orange 84—completed 19 of 35 attempts for 300 yards and 2 TDs with 1 interception; named game's Most Outstanding Offensive Player (Beat Nebraska, 31-30, to win national championship). Fiesta 85—completed 31 of 44 passes for 294 yards and 2 TDs with 1 interception (UCLA won, 39-37).

	Team				Rushing		Passing						Total Offense		
Yr.	W	L	T	G	Car.	Yds.	Att.	Cmp.	Int.	Pct.	Yds.	TD	Plays	Yds.	TDR
82	Redshirted														
83	#10	1	0	11	52	-156	327	201	13	.615	2329	15	379	2173	19
84	8	4	0	12	52	-230	416	262	16	.630	3642	25	468	3412	29
Totals	18	5	0	23	104	-386	743	463	29	.623	5971	40	847	5585	48

Career: 8.0 per pass att., 12.9 per cmp., 139.8 efficiency 242.8 total offense yds. per game; 6.6 per play.

Other career figures: 48 pts. scored; 1 pass caught, minus 4 yds.

National champions.

TOMMY KRAMER
RICE
QB, 6-2, 190
San Antonio, Texas (Lee HS)

Consensus all-America 76. Heisman 5th in 76.

	Team				Rushing		Passing						Total Offense		
Yr.	W	L	T	G	Car.	Yds.	Att.	Cmp.	Int.	Pct.	Yds.	TD	Plays	Yds.	TDR
73	5	6	0	9	56	4	139	58	7	.417	705	2	195	709	4
74	2	8	1	10	73	-37	170	67	10	.394	847	6	243	810	7
75	2	9	0	11	131	217	226	113	16	.500	1328	8	357	1545	12
76	3	8	0	11	61	-45	*501	+269	19	.537	*3317	21	*562	+3272	25
Totals	12	31	1	41	321	139	1036	507	52	.489	6197	37	1357	6336	48

Career: 6.0 per pass att., 12.2 per cmp., 100.9 efficiency; 154.5 total offense yds per game, 4.7 per play.

Other career figures: 68 pts. scored (one 2 pt. conv.); one pass caught for 20 yds.

+ National champion in passing with 24.5 completions per game and in total offense with 297.5 yds. per game in 1976. * This figure led the nation.

ROOSEVELT LEAKS
TEXAS
RB, 5-11, 209
Brenham, Texas (Brenham HS)

Consensus all-America 73. Heisman 3rd in 73.

Bowls: Cotton 73—rushed 120 yards on 25 carries (Beat Alabama, 17-13). Cotton 74—rushed 48 yards on 13 carries (Nebraska won, 19-3). Gator 74—Did not play (Auburn won, 27-3).

	Team				Rushing				Receiving			All-Purpose		
Yr.	W	L	T	G	Car.	Yds.	Avg.	TD	No.	Yds.	TD	Avg.	Plays	Yds.	Avg.
72	9	1	0	10	230	1099	4.8	8	2	17	0	8.5	233	1127	4.8
73	8	2	0	10	229	1415	6.2	14	—	—	—	—	229	1415	6.2
74	8	3	0	10	96	409	4.3	4	—	—	—	—	96	409	4.3
Totals	25	6	0	30	555	2923	5.3	26	2	17	—	8.5	558	2951	5.3

Career: 97.4 rush yds. per game; 98.4 all-purpose yds. per game.
Other career figures: 158 pts. scored (one 2-pt. conv.); 1 K.O. ret., 11 yds.

JOHN LEE
UCLA   PK, 5-11, 187   Downey, Calif. (Downey HS)

Unanimous all-America 85, all-America 84.

Bowls: Rose 83—kicked 39-yard FG and 3 extra points (Beat Michigan, 24-14). Rose 84—kicked 29-yard FG and 6 extra points (Beat Illinois, 45-9). Fiesta 85—kicked FGs of 51-33-22 yards and 4 extra points (Beat Miami [Fla.], 39-37). Rose 86—kicked 42-yard FG and 6 extra points (Beat Iowa, 45-28).

	Team				Punting						Field Goals				
												Under	40		
Yr.	W	L	T	G	No.	Yds.	Avg.	XPA	-XP	FGA	-FG	Pct.	40 yds.	Plus	Long	Pts.
82	9	1	1	10	—	—	—	40	39	17	14	.824	10-10	4-7	50	81
83	6	4	1	11	—	—	—	27	27	18	15	.833	12-13	3-5	52	72
84	8	3	0	11	—	—	—	17	17	*33	+*29	.879	16-16	13-17	51	104
85	8	2	1	11	—	—	—	33	33	24	21	.875	16-17	5-7	47	96
Totals	31	10	3	43	—	—	—	117	116	92	79	.859	54-56	25-36	52	353

Career accuracy percentages: .991   .964   .694

His FGs provided winning margin over: 82—Stanford, Southern Cal; 83—Washington; 84—San Diego St., Long Beach St., Washington St., California, Oregon St.; 85—Brigham Young, Washington St.

+ National field-goal champion at 2.64 per game in 1984. * This figure led the nation.

STEVE LITTLE

ARKANSAS PK, 6-0, 179 Overland Park, Kan. (Shawnee Mission South HS)

Consensus all-America 77, all-America 76.

Bowls: Cotton 76—made 39-yard FG and 4 of 4 PATs (Beat Georgia, 31-10). Orange 78—made 32-yard FG, 4 of 4 PATs and punted 4 times for 40.5-yard average (Beat Oklahoma, 31-6).

	Team				Punting			XPA	-XP	FGA	-FG	Pct.	Field Goals Under 40 yds.	40 Plus	Long	Pts.
Yr.	W	L	T	G	No.	Yds.	Avg.									
74	6	4	1	11	—	—	—	33	29	16	12	.750	10-12	2-4	47	65
75	9	2	0	11	—	—	—	34	32	20	11	.550	11-15	0-5	37	65
76	5	5	1	11	63	2797	44.4	26	23	23	11	.478	4-6	7-17	61	56
77	10	1	0	11	48	2127	44.3	38	37	*30	†19	.633	13-15	6-15	†67	*94
Totals	30	12	2	44	111	4924	44.4	131	121	89	53	.596	38-48	15-41	67	280

Career accuracy percentages: .924 .792 .366

Other career figures: Kicked record-tying 67-yard FG vs. Texas in 77; also kicked 61-yard FG vs. Tulsa in 76.

His FGs provided winning margin over: 75-Rice; 76-Oklahoma St.; 77-Texas A&M and Texas Tech.

* This figure led the nation. † This figure tied for first in the nation.

CHUCK LONG

IOWA QB, 6-4, 213 Wheaton, Ill. (North HS)

Unanimous all-America 85. Heisman 2nd in 85, 7th in 84.

Bowls: Rose 82—rushed 11 yards on 2 carries (Washington won, 28-0). Peach 82—completed 19 of 26 passes for 304 yards and 3 TDs with 1 interception, rushed 2 yards on 12 carries and named game's Most Valuable Offensive Player (Beat Tennessee, 28-22). Gator 83—completed 13 of 29 passes for 167 yards with 4 interceptions and rushed minus 30 yards on 7 carries (Florida won, 14-6). Freedom 83—completed 29 of 39 passes for 461 yards and 6 TDs with no interceptions, rushed minus 20 yards on 7 carries and named game's Most Valuable Offensive Player (Beat Texas, 55-17). Rose 86—completed 29 of 37 passes for 319 yards and 1 TD with 1 interception and rushed for minus 34 yards on 6 carries, scoring on a 4-yard run (UCLA won, 45-28).

	Team				Rushing		Passing							Total Offense		
Yr.	W	L	T	G	Car.	Yds.	Att.	Cmp.	Int.	Pct.	Yds.	TD	Plays	Yds.	TDR	
81	8	3	0	1	0	0	1	1	0	1000	14	0	1	14	0	
82	7	4	0	11	129	119	201	129	10	.642	1374	8	330	1493	12	
83	9	2	0	10	85	-30	236	144	8	.610	2434	14	321	2404	19	
84	7	4	1	12	84	-174	283	187	12	*.661	2410	16	367	2236	20	
85	10	1	0	11	40	-91	351	231	15	.658	2978	26	391	2887	27	
Totals	41	14	1	45	338	-176	1072	692	46	.646	9210	64	1410	9034	78	

Career: 8.6 per pass att., 13.3 per comp., 147.8 efficiency. 200.8 total offense yds. per game; 6.4 per play.

Other career figures: 84 pts. scored.

(Granted another year of competition because of freshman redshirt.)

* This figure led the nation.

ROB LYTLE
MICHIGAN
RB, 6-1, 195
Fremont, Ohio (Fremont-Ross HS)

Consensus all-America 76. Heisman 3rd in 76.

Bowls: Orange 76—rushed 32 yards on 10 carries; returned 1 kickoff 25 yards (Oklahoma won, 14-6). Rose 77—rushed 67 yards on 18 carries; 1-yard TD (Southern Cal won, 14-6).

	Team				Rushing				Receiving			All-Purpose		
Yr.	W	L	T	G	Car.	Yds.	Avg.	TD	No.	Yds.	TD	Avg.	Plays	Yds.	Avg.
73	10	0	1	2	3	6	2.0	0	—	—	—	—	3	6	2.0
74	10	1	0	11	140	802	5.7	2	4	65	1	16.3	146	897	6.1
75	8	1	2	11	183	1008	5.5	10	4	82	0	20.5	191	1149	6.0
76	10	1	0	11	203	1402	6.9	13	9	81	2	9.0	213	1509	7.1
Totals	38	3	3	35	529	3218	6.1	25	17	228	3	13.4	553	3561	6.4

Career: 91.9 rush yds. per game; 101.7 all-purpose yds. per game.
Other career figures: 170 pts. scored (one 2-pt. conv.); 7 K.O. ret., 115 yds.

KEN MacAFEE
NOTRE DAME
TE, 6-4, 250
Brockton, Mass. (Brockton HS)

Unanimous all-America 77, consensus all-America 76. Heisman 3rd in 77. Academic all-America 77.

Bowls: Orange 75—(no statistics) (Beat Alabama, 13-11). Gator 76—caught 5 passes for 78 yards (Beat Penn St., 20-9). Cotton 78—caught 4 passes for 45 yards (Beat Texas, 38-10, for the national championship).

	Team				Rushing		Receiving				Scoring		
Yr.	W	L	T	G	Car.	Yds.	No.	Yds.	TD	Avg.	TD	XP	Pts.
74	9	2	0	10	—	—	14	146	1	10.4	1	0	6
75	8	3	0	11	—	—	26	333	5	12.8	5	0	30
76	8	3	0	11	—	—	34	482	3	14.2	3	0	18
77	#10	1	0	11	—	—	54	797	6	14.8	6	0	36
Totals	35	9	0	43	—	—	128	1758	15	13.7	15	0	90

Other career figures: 4 K.O. ret., 34 yds.
National champions.

ARCHIE MANNING
MISSISSIPPI
QB, 6-4, 204
Drew, Miss. (Drew HS)

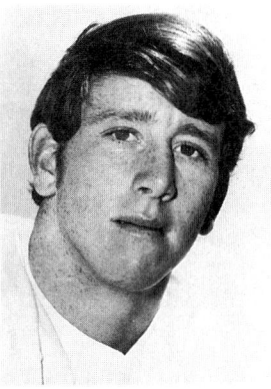

Heisman 3rd in 70, 4th in 69.

Bowls: Liberty 68—completed 12 of 28 passes for 141 yards and 2 TDs with 1 interception and rushed 21 yards on 11 carries (Beat Virginia Tech, 34-17). Sugar 70—completed 21 of 35 passes for 273 yards and 1 TD with 2 interceptions and rushed 39 yards on 13 carries; named game's Most Outstanding Player (Beat Arkansas, 27-22). Gator 71—completed 19 of 28 passes for 180 yards and 1 TD with 1 interception and rushed 95 yards on 11 carries and 1 TD (Auburn won, 35-28).

	Team				Rushing		Passing						Total Offense		
Yr.	W	L	T	G	Car.	Yds.	Att.	Cmp.	Int.	Pct.	Yds.	TD	Plays	Yds.	TDR
68	6	3	1	8	110	208	263	127	17	.483	1510	8	373	1718	13
69	7	3	0	10	124	502	265	154	9	.581	1762	9	389	2264	23
70	7	3	0	8	82	113	233	121	14	.519	1481	14	315	1594	20
Totals	20	9	1	26	316	823	761	402	40	.528	4753	31	1077	5576	56

Career: 6.2 per pass att., 11.8 per cmp., 108.2 efficiency; 214.5 total offense yds. per game; 5.2 per play.
Other career figures: 154 pts. scored (two 2-pt. conv.); 1 pass caught, minus 2 yds.

KEN MARGERUM
STANFORD WR, 6-1, 175 Fountain Valley, Calif. (Fountain Valley HS)

Unanimous all-America 80. Consensus all-America 79.

Bowls: Sun 77—(no statistics) (Beat Louisiana St., 24-14). Bluebonnet 78—caught 5 passes for 87 yards, including 32- and 14-yard TDs (Beat Georgia, 25-22).

	Team				Rushing		Receiving				Scoring		
Yr.	W	L	T	G	Car.	Yds.	No.	Yds.	TD	Avg.	TD	XP	Pts.
77	8	3	0	11	—	—	3	64	0	21.3	—	—	—
78	7	4	0	11	3	21	53	942	9	17.8	9	0	54
79	5	5	1	10	1	11	41	733	10	17.9	10	0	60
80	6	5	0	11	3	33	44	691	11	15.7	11	0	66
Totals	26	17	1	43	7	65	141	2430	30	17.2	30	0	180

Other career figures: 9.3 yds. per carry.

ED MARINARO
CORNELL
RB, 6-3, 210
New Milford, N.J. (New Milford HS)

Unanimous all-America 71, all-America 70. Heisman 2nd in 71, 11th in 70.

Yr.	Team W	L	T	G	Rushing Car.	Yds.	Avg.	TD	Receiving No.	Yds.	TD	Avg.	All-Purpose Plays	Yds.	Avg.
69	4	5	0	9	277	1409	5.1	14	6	52	0	8.7	283	1461	5.2
70	6	3	0	9	285	+1425	5.0	12	11	129	2	11.7	296	1554	5.3
71	8	1	0	9	*356	+1881	5.3	24	6	51	0	8.5	362	1932	5.3
Totals	18	9	0	27	918	4715	5.1	50	23	232	2	10.1	941	4947	5.3

Career: 174.6 rush yds. per game, 183.2 all-purpose yds. per game.

Other career figures: +318 pts. scored (three 2-pt. conv.); 1 pass att., 1 int.

+ National rushing champion at 158.3 yds. per game in 1970; national champion rushing at 209.0 yds. per game and in scoring at 16.9 pts. per game in 1971. * This figure led the nation.

DAN MARINO
PITTSBURGH
QB, 6-4, 215
Pittsburgh, Pa. (Central Catholic HS)

All-America 81. Heisman 4th in 81, 9th in 82.

Bowls: Fiesta 79—completed 15 of 29 passes for 172 yards and 1 TD (Beat Arizona, 16-10). Gator 80—completed 7 of 10 passes for 78 yards and 1 TD (Beat South Caro., 37-9). Sugar 82—completed 26 of 41 passes for 261 yards and 3 TDs, rushed 11 yards on 4 carries; named game's Most Outstanding Player (Beat Georgia, 24-20). Cotton 83—completed 17 of 37 passes for 181 yards (Southern Methodist won, 7-3).

Yr.	Team W	L	T	G	Rushing Car.	Yds.	Passing Att.	Cmp.	Int.	Pct.	Yds.	TD	Total Offense Plays	Yds.	TDR
79	10	1	0	9	27	-62	193	115	7	.596	1508	9	220	1446	10
80	10	1	0	10	13	-55	211	109	14	.517	1531	14	224	1476	14
81	10	1	0	10	20	-106	339	200	21	.590	2615	*34	359	2509	36
82	9	2	0	11	41	-47	341	202	22	.592	2251	17	382	2204	17
Totals	39	5	0	40	101	-270	1084	626	64	.577	7905	74	1185	7635	77

Career: 7.3 per pass att., 12.6 per cmp., 129.7 efficiency; 190.0 total offense yds. per game; 6.4 per play.

Other career figures: 18 pts. scored.

* This figure led the nation.

TERANCE MATHIS
NEW MEXICO
WR, 5-9, 162
Stone Mountain, Ga. (Redan HS)

Consensus all-America 89.

Yr.	Team				Rushing				Receiving				All-Purpose		
	W	L	T	G	Car.	Yds.	Avg.	TD	No.	Yds.	TD	Avg.	Plays	Yds.	Avg.
85	3	8	0	11	32	150	4.7	0	49	852	5	17.4	114	1470	12.9
86	4	8	0	10	27	105	3.9	0	53	955	10	18.0	93	1222	13.1
87	0	11	0	11	4	36	9.0	0	73	1132	8	15.5	114	1861	16.3
89	2	10	0	12	17	38	2.2	0	88	1315	13	14.9	136	2138	15.7
Totals	9	37	0	44	80	329	4.1	0	263	4254	36	16.2	457	6691	14.6

Yr.	Scoring			Punt Returns			K.O. Returns			Comb. Kick Returns			
	TD	XP	Pts.	No.	Yds.	Avg.	No.	Yds.	Avg.	No.	Yds.	TD	Avg.
85	5	0	30	7	46	6.6	26	422	16.2	33	468	0	14.2
86	10	0	60	8	53	6.6	5	109	21.8	13	162	0	12.5
87	8	2	50	8	16	2.0	29	677	23.3	37	693	0	18.7
89	16	2	98	—	—	—	31	785	25.3	31	785	3	25.3
Totals	39	4	238	23	115	5.0	91	1993	21.9	114	2108	3	18.5

Other career figures: 6 passes att., 2 cmp., 0 int., 32 yds., 1 TD.

RUEBEN MAYES
WASHINGTON STATE RB, 6-0, 220 North Battleford, Saskatchewan, Can. (North Battleford Comprehensive HS)

Consensus all-America 84. Heisman 10th in 84.

Yr.	Team				Rushing				Receiving				All-Purpose		
	W	L	T	G	Car.	Yds.	Avg.	TD	No.	Yds.	TD	Avg.	Plays	Yds.	Avg.
82	3	7	1	11	89	425	4.8	1	5	31	0	6.2	113	832	7.4
83	7	4	0	6	61	221	3.6	1	11	109	1	9.9	72	330	4.6
84	6	5	0	11	258	1637	6.3	11	13	113	1	8.7	272	1768	6.5
85	4	7	0	11	228	1236	5.4	10	24	252	1	10.5	252	1488	5.9
Totals	20	23	1	39	636	3519	5.5	23	53	505	3	9.5	709	4418	6.2

Career: 90.2 rush yds. per game; 113.3 all-purpose yds. per game.

Other career figures: 158 pts. scored (one 2-pt. conv.); 20 K.O. ret., 394 yds.

NAPOLEON McCALLUM
NAVY
RB, 6-2, 214
Milford, Ohio (Milford HS)

Consensus all-America 83. All-America 85. Heisman 6th in 83, 8th in 85.

Bowl: Liberty 81—rushed 0 yards on 1 carry and caught 2 passes for 45 yards, longest 34 (Ohio St. won, 31-28).

Yr.	Team W	L	T	G	Car.	Rushing Yds.	Avg.	TD	No.	Receiving Yds.	TD	Avg.	All-Purpose Plays	Yds.	Avg.
81	7	3	1	11	85	335	3.9	2	4	47	0	11.8	92	473	5.1
82	6	5	0	10	165	739	4.5	5	20	196	0	9.8	233	1646	7.1
83	3	8	0	11	331	1587	4.8	10	24	166	1	6.9	393	*+2385	6.1
84	4	6	1	2	40	191	4.8	0	4	29	0	7.3	50	338	6.8
85	4	7	0	11	287	1327	4.6	14	44	358	1	8.1	369	+2330	6.3
Totals	24	29	2	45	908	4179	4.6	31	96	796	2	8.3	1137	7172	6.3

Yr.	Scoring TD	XP	Pts.	Punt Returns No.	Yds.	Avg.	K.O. Returns No.	Yds.	Avg.	Comb. Kick Returns No.	Yds.	TD	Avg.
81	2	0	12	—	—	—	3	91	30.0	3	91	0	30.3
82	5	0	30	32	379	11.8	16	332	20.8	48	711	0	14.8
83	11	0	66	21	272	13.0	17	360	21.1	38	632	0	16.6
84	0	2	2	2	50	25.0	4	68	17.0	6	118	0	19.7
85	15	0	90	18	157	8.7	20	488	24.4	38	645	0	17.0
Totals	33	2	200	73	858	11.8	60	1339	22.3	133	2197	0	16.5

Other career figures: 3 passes att., 2 cmp., 1 int., 17 yds., 1 TD.

(Granted another year of competition because of injury hardship in 1984.)

* This figure led the nation.   + National all-purpose champion in 1983 at 216.8 yds. per game and in 1985 at 211.8 yds. per game.

DON McCAULEY
NORTH CAROLINA   RB, 6-0, 211   Garden City, N.Y. (Garden City HS)

Consensus all-America 70. Heisman 9th in 70.

Bowl: Peach 70—rushed 143 yards on 36 carries, scoring on runs of 1, 17 and 4 yards, punted 6 times for 27-yard average and returned 1 kickoff 23 yards (Arizona St. won, 48-26).

Yr.	Team W	L	T	G	Car.	Rushing Yds.	Avg.	TD	No.	Receiving Yds.	TD	Avg.	All-Purpose Plays	Yds.	Avg.
68	3	7	0	10	75	360	4.8	2	23	313	1	13.6	124	1238	10.0
69	5	5	0	10	204	1092	5.4	8	14	238	2	17.0	235	1770	7.5
70	8	3	0	11	*324	*1720	5.3	†19	15	235	2	15.7	342	2021	5.9
Totals	16	15	0	31	603	3172	5.3	29	52	786	5	15.1	701	5029	7.2

Career: 102.3 rush yds. per game; 162.2 all-purpose yds. per game.

Other career figures: 210+ pts. scored; 4 passes att., 1 cmp., 2 int., 9 yds.; 1 punt ret., 12 yds.; 45 K.O. ret., 1059 yds., 23.5 avg., 1 TD; 48 punts, 38.5 avg.

+ Led nation in pts. scored at 126 and TDs at 21 in 1970.   * This figure led the nation.
† This figure tied for first in nation.

TIM McGEE
TENNESSEE   WR, 5-10, 181   Cleveland, Ohio (John Hay HS)

Consensus all-America 85.

Bowls: Florida Citrus 83—caught 1 pass for 7 yards (Beat Maryland, 30-23). Sun 84—caught 6 passes for 66 yards and 6-yard TD (Maryland won, 28-27). Sugar 86—caught 7 passes for 94 yards; recovered offensive fumble in end zone for a TD (Beat Miami [Fla.], 35-7).

	Team				Rushing		Receiving				Punt Returns			Scoring		
Yr.	W	L	T	G	Car.	Yds.	No.	Yds.	TD	Avg.	No.	Yds.	Avg.	TD	XP	Pts.
83	8	3	0	11	1	-9	19	286	2	15.1	21	192	9.1	2	0	12
84	7	3	1	11	2	-4	54	809	6	15.0	1	6	6.0	6	0	36
85	8	1	2	11	0	0	50	947	7	18.9	7	18	2.6	7	0	42
Totals	23	7	3	33	3	-13	123	2042	15	16.6	29	216	7.4	15	0	90

Other career figures: 3 K.O. ret., 23 yds.

JIM McMAHON
BRIGHAM YOUNG
QB, 6-0, 185
Roy, Utah (Roy HS)

Unanimous all-America 81, all-America 80. Heisman 3rd in 81, 5th in 80.

Bowls: Holiday 78—completed 9 of 18 passes for 133 yards, 1 TD and 1 interception; rushed 17 yards on 12 carries including 2-yard TD (Navy won, 23-16). Holiday 80—completed 32 of 49 passes for 446 yards, 1 interception and 4 TDs—64, 13, 15 and game-winning 41-yard "Hail Mary" pass on the final play to Clay Brown; rushed 0 yards on 10 carries; named game's Most Valuable Player (Beat Southern Methodist, 46-45). Holiday 81—completed 27 of 43 passes for 342 yards with no interceptions, 3 TDs; rushed minus 23 yards on 12 carries; named game's Most Valuable Offensive Player (Beat Washington St., 38-36).

	Team				Rushing		Passing						Total Offense		
Yr.	W	L	T	G	Car.	Yds.	Att.	Cmp.	Int.	Pct.	Yds.	TD	Plays	Yds.	TDR
77	9	2	0	11	7	-20	16	10	1	.625	103	1	23	83	1
78	9	3	0	11	99	248	176	87	8	.494	1307	6	275	1555	10
79	Redshirted														
80	11	1	0	12	95	56	*445	*284	18	.638	*+4571	*47	*540	*+4627	*53
81	10	2	0	10	64	-97	423	*272	7	*.643	+3555	30	487	+3458	30
Totals	39	8	0	44	265	187	1060	653	34	.616	9536	84	1325	9723	94

Career: 9.0 per pass att., 14.6 per cmp., 156.9 efficiency; 221.0 total offense yds. per game, 7.3 per play.

Other career figures: 62 pts. scored (one 2-pt. conv.); 38.4 punting avg. on 105 punts.

+ National champion in passing efficiency at 176.9 and in total offense at 385.6 yds. per game in 1980; national champion in passing efficiency at 155.0 and in total offense at 345.8 yds. per game in 1981.

* This figure led the nation.

DON McPHERSON
SYRACUSE
QB, 6-0, 182
West Hempstead, N.Y. (West Hempstead HS)

Unanimous all-America 87. Heisman 2nd in 87.

Bowls: Cherry 85—completed 18 of 30 passes for 204 yards with 3 interceptions and rushed 111 yards on 21 carries, scoring on a 17-yard run (Maryland won, 35-18). Sugar 88—completed 11 of 21 passes for 140 yards and 1 TD with no interceptions and rushed 31 yards on 20 carries; named game's Most Outstanding Player (Tied Auburn, 16-16).

	Team				Rushing			Passing					Total Offense		
Yr.	W	L	T	G	Car.	Yds.	Att.	Cmp.	Int.	Pct.	Yds.	TD	Plays	Yds.	TDR
83	6	5	0	1	2	-2	1	0	0	.000	0	0	3	-2	0
84	6	5	0	5	34	42	29	11	2	.279	175	0	63	217	0
85	7	4	0	11	157	489	159	85	5	.535	1469	12	316	1958	19
86	5	6	0	11	191	523	269	142	7	.529	1827	12	460	2350	18
87	11	0	0	11	110	199	229	129	11	.563	2341	22	339	2540	27
Totals	35	20	0	38	494	1251	687	367	26	.534	5812	46	1181	7063	64

Career: 8.5 per pass att., 15.8 per cmp., 139.0 efficiency; 185.9 total offense yds. per game; 6.0 per play.

Other career figures: 114 pts. scored; 1 pass caught, 7 yds., 1 TD.

(Granted another year of competition due to injury in 1983.)

JACK MILDREN
OKLAHOMA
QB, 6-0, 200
Abilene, Texas (Cooper HS)

Heisman 6th in 71. Academic all-America 71. NCAA Postgraduate Scholarship 72. Hall of Fame Scholar-Athlete 71.

Bowls: Bluebonnet 70—completed 6 of 7 passes for 66 yards with no interceptions and rushed 73 yards on 16 carries (Tied Alabama, 24-24). Sugar 72—completed 1 of 4 passes for 11 yards with no interceptions and rushed 149 yards on 30 carries, scoring 3 TDs; named game's Most Outstanding Player (Beat Auburn, 40-22).

	Team				Rushing			Passing					Total Offense		
Yr.	W	L	T	G	Car.	Yds.	Att.	Cmp.	Int.	Pct.	Yds.	TD	Plays	Yds.	TDR
69	6	4	0	10	127	345	173	79	12	.457	1319	7	300	1664	14
70	7	4	0	11	175	318	110	54	11	.491	818	6	285	1136	11
71	10	1	0	11	193	1140	64	31	2	.484	878	10	257	2018	27
Totals	23	9	0	32	495	1803	347	164	25	.473	3015	23	842	4818	52

Career: 8.7 per pass att., 18.4 per cmp., 127.7 efficiency; 150.6 total offense yds. per game; 6.5 per play.

Other career figures: 182 pts. scored (four 2-pt conv.); 3.6 yds. per rush.

JIM MILLER
MISSISSIPPI
P, 5-11, 183
Ripley, Miss. (Ripley HS)

Consensus all-America 79.

		Team				Punting	
Yr.	W	L	T	G	No.	Yds.	Avg.
76	6	5	0	11	71	2875	40.5
77	6	5	0	11	66	3029	+45.9
78	5	6	0	11	76	3283	43.2
79	4	7	0	11	53	2362	44.6
Totals	%21	23	0	44	266	11,549	43.4

+ National punting champion in 1977.
% Later won two forfeits over Mississippi State by order of NCAA Council under Section 10.

JUNIOR MILLER
NEBRASKA TE, 6-4, 222 Midland, Texas (Robert E. Lee HS)

Unanimous all-America 79.

Bowls: Liberty 77—caught 1 pass for 3 yards (Beat North Caro., 21-17). Orange 79—caught 3 passes for 49 yards and 2-yard TD (Oklahoma won, 31-24). Cotton 80—caught 2 passes for 26 yards (Houston won, 17-14).

	Team				Rushing		Receiving				Scoring		
Yr.	W	L	T	G	Car.	Yds.	No.	Yds.	TD	Avg.	TD	XP	Pts.
77	8	3	0	10	—	—	4	76	0	19.0	—	—	—
78	9	2	0	11	—	—	30	560	5	18.7	5	0	30
79	10	1	0	11	7	79	21	409	7	19.5	7	0	42
Totals	27	6	0	32	7	79	55	1045	12	19.0	12	0	72

TERRY MILLER
OKLAHOMA STATE
RB, 6-0, 196
Colorado Springs, Colo. (Mitchell HS)

Consensus all-America 77, all-America 76. Heisman 2nd in 77, 4th in 76.

Bowls: Fiesta 74—rushed minus 1 yard on 1 carry (Beat Brigham Young, 16-6). Florida Citrus 76—rushed 173 yards on 23 carries; scored TDs on runs of 3, 78, 6 and 1; returned 3 kickoffs 30 yards; named game's Most Outstanding Back (Beat Brigham Young, 49-21).

	Team				Rushing				Receiving				All-Purpose		
Yr.	W	L	T	G	Car.	Yds.	Avg.	TD	No.	Yds.	TD	Avg.	Plays	Yds.	Avg.
74	6	5	0	10	86	335	3.9	1	3	10	0	3.3	89	345	3.9
75	7	4	0	11	179	1026	5.7	11	1	-3	0	-3.0	185	1125	6.1
76	8	3	0	11	268	1541	5.8	19	—	—	—	—	274	1633	6.0
77	4	7	0	11	*314	1680	5.4	14	1	2	0	2.0	320	1786	5.6
Totals	25	19	0	43	847	4582	5.4	45	5	9	0	1.8	868	4889	5.6

Career: 106.6 rush yds. per game; 113.7 all-purpose yds. per game.

Other career figures: 270 pts. scored; 10 passes att., 3 cmp., 1 int., 68 yds.; 16 K.O. ret., 298 yds., 18.6 avg.

* This figure led the nation.

JOE MONTANA
NOTRE DAME   QB, 6-3, 191   Monongahela, Pa. (Ringgold HS)

Bowls: Cotton 78—completed 10 of 25 passes for 111 yards and 1 TD with 1 interception and rushed 3 yards on 1 carry (Beat Texas, 38-10, to win national championship). Cotton 79—completed 13 of 34 passes for 163 yards with no interceptions and 2 TDs, including game-winning 8-yard TD pass to Kris Haines on the final play; rushed 26 yards on 7 carries, scoring on 3- and 2-yard runs; named game's Most Valuable Offensive Player (Beat Houston, 35-34).

	Team				Rushing		Passing						Total Offense		
Yr.	W	L	T	G	Car.	Yds.	Att.	Cmp.	Int.	Pct.	Yds.	TD	Plays	Yds.	TDR
75	8	3	0	7	25	-5	66	28	8	.424	507	4	91	502	6
76	Injury Redshirt														
77	#10	1	0	9	32	5	189	99	8	.524	1604	11	221	1609	17
78	8	3	0	11	72	104	260	141	9	.542	2010	10	332	2114	16
Totals	26	7	0	27	129	104	515	268	25	.520	4121	25	644	4225	39

Career: 8.0 per pass att., 15.4 per cmp., 127.3 efficiency; 156.5 total offense yds. per game; 6.6 per play.

Other career figures: 86 pts. scored (one 2-pt. conv.).

National champions.

CHUCK MUNCIE

CALIFORNIA   RB, 6-3, 220   Uniontown, Pa. (Uniontown, HS)

Consensus all-America 75. Heisman 2nd in 75.

Yr.	Team				Rushing				Receiving			All-Purpose		
	W	L	T	G	Car.	Yds.	Avg.	TD	No.	Yds.	TD	Avg.	Plays	Yds.	Avg.
73	4	7	0	11	157	801	5.1	11	27	283	1	10.5	187	1122	6.0
74	7	3	1	11	164	791	4.8	8	31	410	3	13.2	195	1201	6.2
75	8	3	0	11	228	1460	6.4	13	39	392	2	10.1	268	1871	7.0
Totals	19	13	1	33	549	3052	5.6	32	97	1085	6	11.2	650	4194	6.5

Career: 92.5 rush yds. per game; 127.1 all-purpose yds. per game.

Other career figures: 230 pts. scored (one 2 pt. conv.); 4 passes att., 4 cmp., 153 yds., 3 TDs; 1 punt ret., 6 yds.; 3 K.O. ret., 51 yds.

JOHNNY MUSSO
ALABAMA
RB, 5-11, 194
Birmingham, Ala. (Banks HS)

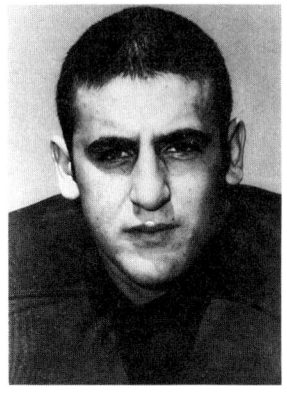

Consensus all-America 71. Heisman 4th in 71. Academic all-America 70 and 71. NCAA Postgraduate Scholarship 72. Hall of Fame Scholar-Athlete 71.

Bowls: Liberty 69—rushed 107 yards on 23 carries and 2-yard TD; caught 3 passes for 22 yards and a 10-yard TD; returned 2 kickoffs 23 yards (Colorado won, 47-33). Bluebonnet 70—rushed 138 yards on 27 carries and completed only pass attempt for 25 yards (Tied Oklahoma, 24-24). Orange 72—rushed 79 yards on 15 carries and caught 1 pass for 22 yards (Nebraska won, 38-6).

Yr.	Team				Rushing				Receiving				All-Purpose		
	W	L	T	G	Car.	Yds.	Avg.	TD	No.	Yds.	TD	Avg.	Plays	Yds.	Avg.
69	6	4	0	9	157	516	3.3	10	26	321	3	12.3	188	939	4.9
70	6	5	0	11	226	1137	5.0	8	30	160	1	5.3	256	1297	5.1
71	11	0	0	10	191	1088	5.7	16	5	14	0	2.8	196	1102	5.6
Totals	23	9	0	30	574	2741	4.8	34	61	495	4	8.1	640	3338	5.2

Career: 91.4 rush yds. per game; 111.3 all-purpose yds. per game.

Other career figures: 232 pts. scored (two 2-pt. conv.); 6 passes att.; 5 cmp, 88 yds., 2 TDs; 5 K.O. ret., 102 yds.

BRAD MUSTER
STANFORD   RB, 6-3, 226   Novato, Calif. (San Marin HS)

Consensus all-America 86. Academic all-America 87.

Bowl: Gator 86—rushed 70 yards on 17 carries, scoring on a 1-yard run; caught 4 passes for 53 yards, scoring on 13- and 36-yard passes (Clemson won, 27-21).

Yr.	Team				Rushing				Receiving			All-Purpose		
	W	L	T	G	Car.	Yds.	Avg.	TD	No.	Yds.	TD	Avg.	Plays	Yds.	Avg.
84	5	6	0	9	184	823	4.5	2	33	228	0	6.9	218	1066	4.9
85	4	7	0	9	140	521	3.7	6	78	654	4	8.4	218	1175	5.4
86	8	3	0	11	243	1053	4.3	12	61	565	1	9.3	304	1618	5.3
87	5	6	0	9	119	543	4.6	7	24	222	1	9.3	143	765	5.3
Totals	22	22	0	38	686	2940	4.3	27	196	1669	6	8.5	883	4624	5.2

Career: 77.4 rush yds. per game; 121.7 all-purpose yds. per game.

Other career figures: 200 pts. scored (one 2-pt. conv.); 1 K.O. ret., 15 yds.; 1 pass att., 1 cmp., 18 yds.

CHUCK NELSON
WASHINGTON
PK, 5-11, 178
Everett, Wash. (Everett HS)

Unanimous all-America 82. Academic all-America 81 and 82. NCAA Postgraduate Scholarship 83.

Bowls: Rose 81—kicked 53- and 25-yard FGs (Michigan won, 23-6). Rose 82—made 2 of 2 PATs (Beat Iowa, 28-0). Aloha 82—made 3 of 3 PATs (Beat Maryland, 21-20).

Yr.	Team				Punting			XPA	-XP	FGA	-FG	Field Goals				
													Under 40 yds.	Plus	Long	Pts.
	W	L	T	G	No.	Yds.	Avg.					Pct.				
80	9	2	0	11	—	—	—	34	31	26	18	.692	12-16	6-10	47	85
81	9	2	0	11	—	—	—	29	29	20	16	.800	13-14	3-6	51	77
82	9	2	0	11	—	—	—	34	34	26	25	*.962	22-23	3-3	49	109
Totals	27	6	0	33	—	—	—	97	94	72	59	.819	47-53	12-19	51	271

Career accuracy percentages: .969   .887   .632

His FGs provided winning margin over: 80-Oklahoma St. and Stanford; 81-California and Texas Tech; 82-UCLA.

* This figure led the nation.

DARRIN NELSON
STANFORD
RB, 5-9, 180
Los Angeles, Calif. (Pius X HS)

Heisman 6th in 81.

Bowls: Sun 77—Caught 5 passes for 77 yards, including 35-yard TD from Guy Benjamin in last quarter; rushed 36 yards on 11 carries (Beat Louisiana St., 24-14). Bluebonnet 78—Rushed 100 yards on 16 carries; caught 3 passes for 24 yards, including 19-yard TD from Steve Dils (Beat Georgia, 25-22).

	Team				Rushing				Receiving			All-Purpose		
Yr.	W	L	T	G	Car.	Yds.	Avg.	TD	No.	Yds.	TD	Avg.	Plays	Yds.	Avg.
77	8	3	0	11	183	1069	5.8	3	50	524	3	10.5	241	1672	6.9
78	7	4	0	11	167	1061	6.4	6	50	446	4	8.9	238	1774	7.5
80	6	5	0	10	161	889	5.5	4	47	552	4	11.7	228	1579	6.9
81	4	7	0	11	192	1014	5.3	11	67	846	5	12.6	259	1860	7.2
Totals	25	19	0	43	703	4033	5.7	24	214	2368	16	11.1	966	6885	7.1

Other career figures: 242 pts. scored (one 2-pt. conv.); 48 punt ret., 471 yds., 9.8 avg.; 1 K.O. ret., 13 yds.; 1 pass att., 1 int.
(Missed 1979 season with injury.)

OZZIE NEWSOME
ALABAMA
SE, 6-4, 210
Leighton, Ala. (Colbert County HS)

Consensus all-America 77.

Bowls: Orange 75—caught 6 passes for 68 yards (Notre Dame won, 13-11). Sugar 75—caught 4 passes for 97 yards (Beat Penn St., 13-6). Liberty 76—caught 2 passes for 13 yards (Beat UCLA, 36-6). Sugar 78—caught 2 passes for 45 yards (Beat Ohio St., 35-6).

	Team				Rushing		Receiving			Punt Returns			Scoring		
Yr.	W	L	T	G	Car.	Yds.	No.	Yds.	TD	Avg.	No.	Yds.	Avg.	TD	XP	Pts.
74	11	0	0	11	—	—	20	374	1	18.7	—	—	—	1	0	6
75	10	1	0	11	—	—	21	363	5	17.3	—	—	—	5	0	30
76	8	3	0	11	2	15	25	529	5	21.2	23	187	8.1	6	2	38
77	10	1	0	11	—	—	36	804	4	22.3	17	114	6.7	4	0	24
Totals	39	5	0	44	2	15	102	2070	16	20.3	40	301	7.5	16	2	98

Other career figures: 2 K.O. ret., 40 yds.

GIFFORD NIELSEN
BRIGHAM YOUNG   QB, 6-5, 203   Provo, Utah (Provo HS)

All-America 76. Heisman 6th in 76.

Bowl: Tangerine 76—completed 23 of 34 passes for 209 yards with a 27-yard TD and 4 interceptions (Oklahoma St. won, 49-21).

Yr.	Team W L T G				Rushing Car. Yds.		Passing Att. Cmp. Int. Pct. Yds. TD						Total Offense Plays Yds. Avg.			TDR
75	6	5	0	9	57	-144	180	110	7	.611	1474	10	237	1330	5.6	12
76	9	2	0	11	77	-273	372	207	19	.556	3192	*29	449	2919	6.5	*30
77	9	2	0	4	29	-25	156	98	3	.628	1167	16	185	1142	6.2	16
Totals	24	9	0	24	163	-442	708	415	29	.586	5833	55	871	5391	6.2	58

Career avg: 8.2 pass yds. per att.; 14.1 per cmp.; 145.3 efficiency.

Career per game: 243.0 yds. passing; 224.6 total offense.

Other career figures: 18 pts. scored.

* This figure led the nation.

(Missed last seven games of 1977 season with injury.)

JAY NOVACEK
WYOMING   TE, 6-4, 211   Gothenburg, Neb. (Gothenburg HS)

Consensus all-America 84.

Yr.	Team W L T G				Rushing Car. Yds.		Receiving No. Yds. TD Avg.				Scoring TD XP Pts.		
82	5	7	0	12	—	—	16	288	3	18.0	3	0	18
83	7	5	0	11	2	42	34	503	3	14.8	4	0	24
84	6	6	0	12	1	15	33	745	4	22.6	4	2	26
Totals	18	18	0	35	3	57	83	1536	10	18.5	11	2	68

PAUL PALMER
TEMPLE   RB, 5-10, 180   Potomac, Md. (Churchill HS)

Unanimous all-America 86. Heisman 2nd in 86.

Yr.	Team				Rushing				Receiving				All-Purpose		
	W	L	T	G	Car.	Yds.	Avg.	TD	No.	Yds.	TD	Avg.	Plays	Yds.	Avg.
83	4	7	0	11	141	628	4.5	6	33	271	2	8.2	181	1024	5.7
84	6	5	0	11	182	885	4.9	9	29	193	1	6.7	218	1209	5.5
85	4	7	0	9	279	1516	5.4	9	13	131	1	10.1	298	1743	5.8
86	6	5	0	11	346	+*1866	5.4	15	12	110	0	9.2	386	+*2633	6.8
Totals	20	24	0	42	948	4895	5.2	39	87	705	4	8.1	1083	6609	6.1

Career: 116.5 rush yds. per game; 157.4 all-purpose yds. per game.

Other career figures: 264 pts. scored (three 2-pt. conv.), 47 K.O. ret., 997 yds, 21.2 avg.; 1 punt ret., 12 yds.; 11 passes att., 4 cmp., 3 int., 146 yds., 2 TD.

* This figure led the nation.   + National champion in rushing at 169.6 yards per game and in all-purpose running at 239.4 yards per game in 1986.

RODNEY PEETE
SOUTHERN CALIFORNIA
QB, 6-2, 195
Mesa, Ariz. (Sahuaro HS three years, then Shawnee Mission South HS, Overland Park, Kan.)

All-America 88. Heisman 2nd in 88.

Bowls: Aloha 85—completed 10 of 17 passes for 65 yards with 1 interception and rushed 13 yards on 6 carries (Alabama won, 24-3). Florida Citrus 87—completed 12 of 30 passes for 113 yards with 4 interceptions (Auburn won, 16-7). Rose 88—completed 22 of 41 passes for 249 yards and 2 TDs with 3 interceptions and rushed 54 yards on 11 carries (Michigan St. won, 20-17). Rose 89—completed 15 of 21 for 158 yards and rushed 42 yards on 9 carries (Michigan won, 22-14).

Yr.	Team				Rushing		Passing						Total Offense		
	W	L	T	G	Car.	Yds.	Att.	Cmp.	Int.	Pct.	Yds.	TD	Plays	Yds.	TDR
85	6	5	0	7	43	65	68	40	2	.588	501	5	111	566	6
86	7	4	0	11	93	127	275	148	11	.538	2025	10	368	2152	13
87	8	3	0	11	59	91	291	175	9	.601	2460	19	350	2551	22
88	10	1	0	11	59	26	338	208	10	.615	2654	18	397	2680	21
Totals	31	13	0	40	254	309	972	571	32	.587	7640	52	1226	7949	62

Career: 7.9 per pass att., 13.4 per cmp., 135.8 efficiency; 198.7 total offense yds. per game; 6.5 per play.

Other career figures: 60 pts. scored; 1 pass caught, minus 4 yds.; 1 punt, 32 yds.

JASON PHILLIPS
HOUSTON
WR, 5-9, 175
Houston, Texas (Sterling HS)

Consensus all-America 88.

Bowl: Aloha 88—caught 2 passes for 14 yards (Washington St. won, 24-22).

Yr.	Team W	L	T	G	Rushing Car.	Yds.	No.	Receiving Yds.	TD	Avg.	Punt Returns No.	Yds.	Avg.	Scoring TD	XP	Pts.
87	4	6	1	11	—	—	+*99	875	3	8.8	15	156	10.4	3	0	18
88	9	2	0	11	2	15	+*108	*1444	15	13.4	—	—	—	15	0	90
Totals	13	8	1	22	2	15	207	2319	18	11.2	15	156	10.4	18	0	108

* This figure led the nation.   + National pass receiving champion in 1987 at 9.0 per game and in 1988 at 9.8 per game.

JIM PLUNKETT
STANFORD
QB, 6-3, 204
San Jose, Calif. (James Lick HS)

Consensus all-America 70. Heisman winner in 70, 8th in 69.

Bowl: Rose 71—completed 20 of 30 passes for 265 yards with 1 interception and 10-yard TD pass to Randy Vataha; rushed 26 yards on 9 carries (Beat Ohio St., 27-17).

Yr.	Team W	L	T	G	Rushing Car.	Yds.	Att.	Cmp.	Passing Int.	Pct.	Yds.	TD	Total Offense Plays	Yds.	TDR
68	6	3	1	10	81	47	268	142	14	.530	2156	14	349	2203	20
69	7	2	1	10	53	113	336	197	15	.586	2673	20	389	2786	21
70	8	3	0	11	78	183	358	191	18	.534	2715	18	436	*2898	21
Totals	21	8	2	31	212	343	962	530	47	.551	7544	52	1174	7887	62

Career: 7.8 per pass att., 14.2 per comp., 129.0 efficiency; 254.4 total offense yds. per game, 6.7 per play.

Other career figures: 60 pts. scored; one pass caught for minus 16 yds.

* This figure led the nation.

GREG PRUITT
OKLAHOMA
RB, 5-9, 177
Houston, Texas (Elmore HS)

Unanimous all-America 72 and 71. Heisman 2nd in 72, 3rd in 71.

Bowls: Bluebonnet 70—rushed 97 yards on 8 carries, scoring on runs of 58 and 25 yards, caught 2 passes for minus 2 yards and returned 3 kickoffs 71 yards; game's Most Valuable Player (tied Alabama, 24-24). Sugar 72 (1-1)—rushed 95 yards on 18 carries, scoring on a 2-yard run, and returned 1 kickoff 25 yards (Beat Auburn, 40-22). Sugar 72 (12-31)—rushed 86 yards on 21 carries, caught 2 passes for 43 yards and threw an incomplete pass (Beat Penn St., 14-0).

	Team				Rushing				Receiving			All-Purpose		
Yr.	W	L	T	G	Car.	Yds.	Avg.	TD	No.	Yds.	TD	Avg.	Plays	Yds.	Avg.
70	7	4	0	11	45	241	5.4	5	19	240	2	12.6	88	940	10.7
71	10	1	0	11	178	1665	*9.4	17	4	108	0	27.0	191	1946	10.2
72	10	1	0	11	152	938	6.2	13	7	102	1	15.0	164	1104	6.7
Totals	27	6	0	33	375	2844	7.6	35	30	450	3	15.0	443	3990	9.0

Career: 86.2 rush yds. per game; 120.9 all-purpose yds. per game.

Other career figures: 232 pts. scored (two 2-pt. conv.); 10 punt ret., 139 yds., 13.9 avg., 28 K.O. ret., 557 yds., 19.9 avg.

* This figure led the nation.

JARVIS REDWINE
NEBRASKA   RB, 5-11, 204   Inglewood, Calif. (Inglewood HS)

Consensus all-America 80. Heisman 8th in 80.

Bowls: Cotton 80—rushed 58 yards on 17 carries, 9-yard TD; completed 1 pass for 13 yards; caught 1 pass for 6 yards (Houston won, 17-14). Sun 80—rushed 42 yards on 13 carries (Beat Mississippi St., 31-17).

	Team				Rushing				Receiving			All-Purpose		
Yr.	W	L	T	G	Car.	Yds.	Avg.	TD	No.	Yds.	TD	Avg.	Plays	Yds.	Avg.
76	2	10	0	8	53	216	4.1	2	1	0	0	0	54	216	4.1
77	2	9	0	4	16	94	5.9	1	0	0	0	0	16	94	5.9
78	Did Not Play														
79	10	1	0	11	148	1042	7.0	8	6	29	1	4.8	155	1097	7.1
80	9	2	0	9	156	1119	7.2	9	7	67	0	9.6	163	1186	7.3
Totals	23	22	0	32	373	2471	6.6	20	14	96	1	6.9	388	2593	6.7

Career: 77.2 rush yds. per game; 81.0 all-purpose yds. per game.

Other career figures: 126 pts. scored; 1 K.O. ret., 26 yds. (Played at Oregon St. in 1976 and 1977.)

STEVE RIVERA
CALIFORNIA
WR, 6-0, 185
Wilmington, Calif. (Banning HS)

Consensus all-America 75.

Yr.	Team W	L	T	G	Rushing Car.	Yds.	No.	Receiving Yds.	TD	Avg.	Punt Returns No.	Yds.	Avg.	Scoring TD	XP	Pts.
73	4	7	0	11	—	—	25	357	1	14.3	—	—	—	1	0	6
74	7	3	1	11	—	—	56	938	4	16.8	26	183	7.0	4	0	24
75	8	3	0	10	—	—	57	790	4	13.9	11	62	5.6	4	0	24
Totals	19	13	1	32	—	—	138	2085	9	15.1	37	245	6.6	9	0	54

REGGIE ROBY
IOWA   P, 6-3, 215   Waterloo, Iowa (East HS)

Consensus all-America 81.

Bowls: Rose 82—punted 4 times for 51.0-yard average, longest 56 (Washington won, 28-0). Peach 82—punted 4 times for 35.8-yard average, longest 52 (Beat Tennessee, 28-22).

Yr.	Team W	L	T	G	Punting No.	Yds.	Avg.	XPA	-XP	FGA	-FG	Pct.	Field Goals Under 40 yds.	40 Plus	Long	Pts.
79	5	6	0	11	35	1492	42.6	25	22	10	5	.500	4-5	1-5	44	37
80	4	7	0	11	41	1663	40.6	9	6	15	6	.400	4-8	2-7	48	24
81	8	3	0	11	44	2193	+49.8	0	0	3	0	.000	0-0	0-3	0	0
82	7	4	0	11	52	2501	+48.1	0	0	1	0	.000	0-0	0-1	0	0
Totals	24	20	0	44	172	7849	45.6	34	28	29	11	.379	8-13	3-16	48	61

Career accuracy percentages: .824   .616   .188

His FGs provided margin over: Illinois in 79.

+ National punting champion in 1981 and 1982.

JOHNNY RODGERS
NEBRASKA   WB, 5-9, 173   Omaha, Neb. (Omaha Tech HS)

Unanimous all-America 72. Consensus all-America 71. Heisman winner in 72.

Bowls: Orange 71—rushed 0 yards on 3 carries, caught 4 passes for 45 yards, returned 1 punt 3 yards and 2 kickoffs 34 yards (Beat Louisiana St., 17-12, for national championship). Orange 72—rushed 10 yards on 4 carries, caught 4 passes for 84 yards and returned 6 punts 136 yards, including a 77-yard TD (Beat Alabama, 38-6, for national championship). Orange 73—rushed 81 yards on 15 carries, scoring on runs of 8, 4 and 5 yards, caught 3 passes for 71 yards, scoring on a 52-yard pass, returned 1 punt minus 3 yards and 1 kickoff 11 yards; game's Most Valuable Player (Beat Notre Dame, 40-6).

	Team				Rushing				Receiving				All-Purpose		
Yr.	W	L	T	G	Car.	Yds.	Avg.	TD	No.	Yds.	TD	Avg.	Plays	Yds.	Avg.
70	#10	0	1	11	36	219	6.1	2	35	665	7	19.0	114	1592	14.0
71	#12	0	0	12	36	259	7.2	2	53	872	11	16.5	132	1983	15.0
72	8	2	1	11	58	267	4.6	7	55	942	8	17.1	160	2011	*12.6
Totals	30	2	2	34	130	745	5.7	11	143	2479	26	17.3	406	5586	13.8

	Scoring			Punt Returns			K.O. Returns			Comb. Kick Returns			
Yr.	TD	XP	Pts.	No.	Yds.	Avg.	No.	Yds.	Avg.	No.	Yds.	TD	Avg.
70	11	0	66	26	349	13.4	17	359	21.1	43	708	2	16.5
71	17	0	102	33	548	16.6	10	304	30.4	43	852	4	19.8
72	17	0	102	39	*618	15.8	35	847	23.0	47	802	2	17.8
Totals	45	0	270	98	1515	15.5	35	847	24.2	133	2362	8	17.8

Other career figures: 2 passes att., 0 cmp.

National champions. * This figure led the nation.

GEORGE ROGERS
SOUTH CAROLINA
RB, 6-2, 220
Duluth, Ga. (Duluth HS)

Unanimous all-America 80, all-America 79. Heisman winner in 80, 7th in 79.

Bowls: Hall of Fame 79—rushed 133 yards on 25 carries; caught 3 passes for 18 yards; named game's co-Most Valuable Player (Missouri won, 24-14). Gator 80—rushed 113 yards on 27 carries (Pittsburgh won, 37-9).

	Team				Rushing				Receiving				All-Purpose		
Yr.	W	L	T	G	Car.	Yds.	Avg.	TD	No.	Yds.	TD	Avg.	Plays	Yds.	Avg.
77	5	7	0	12	143	623	4.4	3	14	185	1	13.2	163	954	5.9
78	5	5	1	10	176	1006	5.7	6	8	41	0	5.1	190	1240	6.5
79	8	3	0	11	286	1548	5.4	8	11	122	1	11.1	297	1670	5.6
80	8	3	0	11	297	1781	6.0	14	7	23	0	3.3	304	1804	5.9
Totals	26	18	1	44	902	4958	5.5	31	40	371	2	9.3	954	5668	5.9

Career: 112.7 rush yds. per game; 128.8 all-purpose yds. per game.

Other career figures: 202 pts. scored (two 2-pt. conv.); 12 K.O. ret., 339 yds., 28.3 avg.

MIKE ROZIER
NEBRASKA
RB, 5-11, 210
Camden, N.J. (Wilson HS)

Unanimous all-America 83, consensus all-America 82. Heisman winner in 83, 10th in 82.

Bowls: Orange 82—rushed 75 yards on 15 carries, completed 1 pass for 25 yards and a TD, and returned 3 kickoffs 78 yards (Clemson won, 22-15). Orange 83—rushed 118 yards on 26 carries and caught 3 passes for 28 yards and 1 TD (Beat Louisiana St., 21-20). Orange 84—rushed 147 yards on 25 carries, caught 2 passes for 4 yards and returned 1 kickoff 31 yards (Miami [Fla.] won, 31-30, for national championship).

	Team				Rushing				Receiving			All-Purpose		
Yr.	W	L	T	G	Car.	Yds.	Avg.	TD	No.	Yds.	TD	Avg.	Plays	Yds.	Avg.
81	9	2	0	11	151	943	6.2	5	4	64	0	16.0	160	1169	7.3
82	11	1	0	12	242	1689	7.0	15	6	46	2	7.7	252	1790	7.1
83	12	0	0	12	275	+*2148	*7.8	29	10	106	0	10.6	296	*2486	8.4
Totals	32	3	0	35	668	4780	7.2	49	20	26	2	10.8	708	5445	7.7

Career: 136.6 rush yds. per game; 155.6 all-purpose yds. per game.
Other career figures: 312 pts. scored; 20 K.O. ret., 449 yds., 1 T.D., 22.5 avg.

+ National rushing champion at 179.0 yards per game and scoring champion at 14.5 points per game in 1983.   * This figure led the nation.

BARRY SANDERS
OKLAHOMA STATE   RB, 5-8, 197   Wichita, Kan. (Wichita North HS)

Unanimous all-America 88. Heisman winner in 88.

Bowls: Sun 87—rushed 19 yards on 6 carries (Beat West Va., 35-33). Holiday 88—rushed 222 yards on 29 carries, scoring 5 TDs on runs of 33, 2, 67, 1 and 10 yards and caught 2 passes for 36 yards; named Offensive Player of the Game (Beat Wyoming, 62-14).

	Team				Rushing				Receiving				All-Purpose		
Yr.	W	L	T	G	Car.	Yds.	Avg.	TD	No.	Yds.	TD	Avg.	Plays	Yds.	Avg.
86	6	5	0	8	74	325	4.4	2	—	—	—	—	89	534	6.0
87	9	2	0	11	205	603	5.7	8	4	59	1	14.8	138	1348	9.8
88	9	2	0	11	*344	*+2628	*7.6	*37	19	106	0	5.6	*393	*+3250	8.3
Totals	24	9	0	30	523	3556	6.8	47	23	165	1	7.2	620	5132	8.3

	Scoring			Punt Returns			K.O. Returns			Comb. Kick Returns			
Yr.	TD	XP	Pts.	No.	Yds.	Avg.	No.	Yds.	Avg.	No.	Yds.	TD	Avg.
86	2	0	12	8	43	5.4	7	166	23.7	15	209	0	13.9
87	13	0	78	15	244	16.3	14	442	+*31.6	29	686	4	23.7
88	*39	0	*+234	9	95	10.6	21	421	20.0	30	516	2	17.2
Totals	54	0	324	32	382	11.9	42	1029	24.5	74	1411	6	19.1

Career: 118.5 rush yds. per game; 171.0 all purpose yds. per game.

* This figure led the nation.   + National champion in rushing at 238.9 yards per game, in scoring at 21.3 points per game and in all-purpose running at 295.5 yds. per game in 1988; national champion in kickoff return avg. at 31.6 in 1987.

BARRY SANDERS

JOHN SCIARRA
UCLA   QB, 5-10, 178   Alhambra, Calif. (Bishop Amat HS)

Consensus all-America 75. Heisman 7th in 75. Academic all-America 75. Today's Top Five, NCAA Honors Luncheon 75. NCAA Postgraduate Scholarship 76.

Bowl: Rose 76—completed 13 of 19 passes with 2 interceptions, 212 yards and TD passes of 16 and 67 yards; rushed minus 19 yards on 11 carries; named Player of the Game (Beat Ohio St., 23-10).

	Team				Rushing		Passing						Total Offense		
Yr.	W	L	T	G	Car.	Yds.	Att.	Cmp.	Int.	Pct.	Yds.	TD	Plays	Yds.	TDR
72	8	3	0	11	10	130	0	0	0	.000	0	0	10	130	0
73	9	2	0	11	72	496	62	27	3	.435	503	3	134	999	8
74	6	3	2	7	91	400	92	47	5	.511	835	4	183	1235	8
75	8	2	1	11	187	806	126	61	12	.484	1101	6	313	1907	20
Totals	31	10	3	40	360	1832	280	135	20	.482	2439	13	640	4271	36

Career: 8.7 per pass att., 18.1 per cmp., 122.4 efficiency; 106.8 total offense yds. per game (142.8 as a QB), 6.7 per play (6.6 as a QB).

Other career figures: 138 pts. scored, 5.1 yds. per rush; 1 pass caught, 9 yds.; 35 punt ret., 431 yds., 12.3 avg.; 15 K.O. ret., 339 yds., 22.6 avg.; 2,611 all-purpose yds., 411 plays; 6.4 per play. (Was receiver-kick returner in 1972.)

LARRY SEIVERS
TENNESSEE
WR, 6-4, 200
Clinton, Tenn. (Clinton HS)

Consensus all-America 75 and 76. Heisman 12th in 76.

Bowl: Liberty 74—caught 4 passes for 38 yards and 11-yard TD (beat Maryland, 7-3).

	Team				Rushing		Receiving				Scoring		
Yr.	W	L	T	G	Car.	Yds.	No.	Yds.	TD	Avg.	TD	XP	Pts.
74	6	3	2	11	—	—	25	347	2	13.9	2	2	14
75	7	5	0	11	—	—	41	840	4	20.5	4	0	24
76	6	5	0	11	—	—	51	737	2	14.5	2	0	12
Totals	19	13	2	33	—	—	117	1924	8	16.4	8	2	50

BILLY SIMS
OKLAHOMA RB, 6-0, 205 Hooks, Texas (Hooks HS)

Unanimous all-America 78 and 79. Heisman winner in 78, 2nd in 79.

Bowls: Orange 76—did not play (Beat Michigan, 14-6). Fiesta 76—did not play (Beat Wyoming, 41-7). Orange 78—rushed 7 yards on 6 carries (Arkansas won, 31-6). Orange 79—rushed 134 yards on 25 carries; 3- and 11-yard TDs; named game's Most Valuable Back (Beat Nebraska, 31-24). Orange 80—rushed 164 yards on 24 carries; 22-yard TD (Beat Florida St., 24-7).

Yr.	Team W	L	T	G	Car.	Rushing Yds.	Avg.	TD	No.	Receiving Yds.	TD	Avg.	All-Purpose Plays	Yds.	Avg.
75	#10	1	0	9	15	95	6.3	2	—	—	—	—	16	108	6.8
76	8	2	1	1	3	44	14.7	0	—	—	—	—	3	44	14.7
77	10	1	0	10	65	406	6.2	6	—	—	—	—	66	447	6.8
78	10	1	0	11	231	+1762	*7.6	*20	1	35	0	35.0	232	1797	7.7
79	10	1	0	11	224	*1506	6.7	*22	1	42	0	42.0	225	1548	6.9
Totals	48	6	1	42	538	3813	7.1	50	2	77	0	38.5	542	3944	7.3

Career: 90.8 rush yds. per game; 93.9 all-purpose yds. per game. Other career figures: +300 pts. scored; 2 K.O. ret., 54 yds.

(Granted an additional year of competition due to injury in 1976.)

\# National champions. + National champion in rushing at 160.2 yds. per game and in scoring at 10.9 pts. per game in 1978; national scoring champion with 12.0 pts. per game in 1979. * This figure led the nation.

EMMITT SMITH
FLORIDA
RB, 5-10, 201
Pensacola, Fla. (Escambia HS)

Unanimous all-America 89. Heisman 9th in 87, 7th in 89.

Bowls: Aloha 87—rushed 128 yards on 17 carries, caught 4 passes for 19 yards (UCLA won, 20-16). All-American 88—rushed 159 yards on 28 carries, including TD runs of 55 (on Florida's first offensive play from scrimmage) and 2 yards; named Most Valuable Player (Beat Illinois, 14-10). Freedom 89-rushed 17 yards on 7 carries, caught 2 passes for 12 yards (Washington won, 34-7).

Yr.	Team W	L	T	G	Car.	Rushing Yds.	Avg.	TD	No.	Receiving Yds.	TD	Avg.	All-Purpose Plays	Yds.	Avg.
87	6	5	0	11	229	1341	5.9	13	25	184	0	7.4	254	1525	6.0
88	6	5	0	9	187	988	5.3	9	10	72	0	7.2	197	1060	5.4
89	7	4	0	11	284	1599	5.6	14	21	207	0	9.9	305	1806	5.9
Totals	19	14	0	31	700	3928	5.6	36	56	463	0	8.3	756	4391	5.8

Career: 126.7 rush yds. per game; 141.6 all-purpose yds. per game.
Other career figures: 222 pts. scored; 1 pass att., 0 cmp.

WILLIE SMITH
MIAMI (FLA.)   TE, 6-2, 230   Jacksonville, Fla. (Englewood HS)

Consensus all-America 85.

Bowl: Fiesta 85—caught 8 passes for 61 yards (UCLA won, 39-37). Sugar 86—caught 4 passes for 26 yards (Tennessee won, 35-7).

Yr.	Team W	L	T	G	Rushing Car.	Yds.	Receiving No.	Yds.	TD	Avg.	Scoring TD	XP	Pts.
84	8	4	0	12	—	—	66	852	5	12.9	5	0	30
85	10	1	0	11	—	—	48	669	1	13.9	1	0	6
Totals	18	5	0	23	—	—	114	1521	6	13.3	6	0	36

PAT SULLIVAN
AUBURN
QB, 6-0, 191
Birmingham, Ala. (John Caroll HS)

Consensus all-America 71. Heisman winner in 71, 6th in 70.

Bowls: Bluebonnet 69—completed 10 of 30 passes for 132 yards with 1 interception (Houston won, 36-7). Gator 71—completed 27 of 43 passes for 351 yards with 1 interception and TD passes of 13 and 8 yards; rushed 35 yards on 10 carries, scoring on a 37-yard run; game's Co-Most Valuable Player (Beat Mississippi, 35-28). Sugar 72—completed 20 of 44 passes for 250 yards with 1 interception and an 11-yard TD pass (Oklahoma won, 40-22).

Yr.	Team W	L	T	G	Rushing Car.	Yds.	Passing Att.	Cmp.	Int.	Pct.	Yds.	TD	Total Offense Plays	Yds.	TDR
69	8	2	0	10	52	206	257	123	16	.479	1686	16	309	1892	23
70	8	2	0	10	52	270	281	167	12	.594	2586	17	333	+2856	*26
71	9	1	0	10	47	84	281	162	11	.577	2012	20	328	2096	22
Totals	25	5	0	30	151	560	819	452	39	.552	6284	53	970	6844	71

Career: 7.7 per pass att., 13.9 per cmp., 131.5 efficiency; 228.1 total offense yds. per game, 7.1 per play.

Other career figures: 108 pts. scored; 3.7 yds. per rush.

+ National total offense champion at 285.6 yds. per game in 1970. * This figure led the nation.

LYNN SWANN
SOUTHERN CALIFORNIA
FL, 6-0, 180
Foster City, Calif. (Serra HS)

Consensus all-America 73. Heisman 12th in 73.

Bowls: Rose 73—caught 6 passes for 108 yards, including 10-yard TD pass and rushed 2 yards on 1 carry (Beat Ohio St., 42-17). Rose 74—caught 5 passes for 47 yards (Ohio St. won, 42-21).

Yr.	Team				Rushing		Receiving				Punt Returns			Scoring		
	W	L	T	G	Car.	Yds.	No.	Yds.	TD	Avg.	No.	Yds.	Avg.	TD	XP	Pts.
71	6	4	1	11	1	-16	27	306	2	11.3	11	157	14.3	2	0	12
72	#11	0	0	10	10	115	21	435	2	20.7	18	253	14.1	3	0	18
73	9	1	1	11	14	99	37	667	6	18.0	19	191	10.1	7	0	42
Totals	26	5	2	32	25	198	85	1408	10	16.6	48	601	12.5	12	0	72

Other career figures: 9 passes att., 4 cmp., 52 yds., 1 TD; 3 K.O. ret., 66 yds.

National champions.

JERRY TAGGE
NEBRASKA
QB, 6-2, 215
Green Bay, Wis. (Green Bay HS)

Heisman 7th in 71.

Bowls: Sun 69—completed 6 of 12 passes for 53 yards and rushed 37 yards on 4 carries and 1 TD (Beat Georgia, 45-6). Orange 71—completed 12 of 25 passes for 153 yards with 1 interception and rushed 40 yards on 16 carries and 1 TD; named game's Most Valuable Offensive Player (Beat Louisiana St., 17-12, to win national championship). Orange 72—completed 11 of 19 passes for 159 yards and 1 TD with 1 interception and rushed 2 yards on 5 carries for 1 TD. Named game's Most Outstanding Offensive Player (Beat Alabama, 38-6, to win national championship).

Yr.	Team				Rushing		Passing						Total Offense		
	W	L	T	G	Car.	Yds.	Att.	Cmp.	Int.	Pct.	Yds.	TD	Plays	Yds.	TDR
69	8	2	0	10	79	152	177	101	8	.571	1302	4	256	1454	7
70+	#11	0	1	11	69	113	165	104	7	.630	1383	12	234	1496	16
71*	#12	0	0	12	107	314	239	143	4	.598	2019	17	346	2333	25
Totals	31	2	1	33	255	579	581	348	19	.599	4704	33	836	5283	48

Career: 8.1 per pass att., 13.5 per cmp., 140.1 efficiency; 160.1 total offense yds. per game, 6.3 per play.

Other career figures: 90 pts. scored.

+ National leader in passing efficiency in 1970 (min. 15 att. per game) at 149.0.

* National leader in passing efficiency in 1971 (min. 15 att. per game) at 150.9.

National champions.

VINNY TESTAVERDE
MIAMI (FLA.)
QB, 6-5, 218
Elmont, N.Y. (Sewanhaka HS)

Unanimous all-America 86. Heisman winner in 86, 5th in 85.

Bowls: Fiesta 85—did not play (UCLA won, 39-37). Sugar 86—completed 20 of 36 passes for 217 yards and 1 TD with 3 interceptions and rushed minus 78 yards on 10 carries (Tennessee won, 35-7). Fiesta 87—completed 26 of 50 passes for 285 yards with 5 interceptions and rushed minus 10 yards on 9 carries (Penn St. won, 14-10, for national championship).

	Team				Rushing		Passing						Total Offense		
Yr.	W	L	T	G	Car.	Yds.	Att.	Cmp.	Int.	Pct.	Yds.	TD	Plays	Yds.	TDR
82	7	4	0	4	3	-10	12	5	0	.417	79	1	15	69	1
83	Redshirted														
84	8	4	0	6	8	-49	34	17	1	.500	184	0	42	135	0
85	10	1	0	11	68	-158	352	216	15	.614	3238	21	420	3080	25
86	11	0	0	10	46	-103	276	175	9	.634	2557	26	322	2454	30
Totals	36	9	0	31	125	-320	674	413	25	.613	6058	48	799	5738	56

Career: 9.0 per pass att., 14.7 per cmp., 152.9 efficiency; 185.1 total offense yds. per game, 7.2 per play.

Other career figures: 48 pts. scored; 1 pass caught, 13 yds.

JOE THEISMANN
NOTRE DAME   QB, 6-0, 170   South River, N.J. (South River HS)

All-America 70. Heisman 2nd in 70. Academic all-America 70.

Bowls: Cotton 70—completed 17 of 27 passes for 231 yards and 2 TDs with 1 interception and rushed 48 yards on 11 carries (Texas won, 21-17). Cotton 71—completed 9 of 16 passes for 176 yards and 1 TD with 1 interception and rushed 22 yards on 18 carries for 2 TDs (Beat Texas, 24-11).

	Team				Rushing		Passing						Total Offense		
Yr.	W	L	T	G	Car.	Yds.	Att.	Cmp.	Int.	Pct.	Yds.	TD	Plays	Yds.	TDR
68	7	2	1	9	59	259	49	27	5	.551	451	2	108	710	6
69	8	1	1	10	116	378	192	108	16	.563	1531	13	308	1909	19
70	9	1	0	10	123	384	268	155	14	.578	2429	16	391	2813	20
Totals	24	4	2	10	298	1021	509	290	35	.570	4411	31	807	5432	45

Career: 8.7 per pass att., 15.2 per cmp., 136.1 efficiency; 187.3 total offense yds. per game; 6.7 per play.

Other career figures: 92 pts. scored (one 2-pt. conv.); 2 passes caught, 20 yds, 1 TD; 14 punt ret., 99 yds.

THURMAN THOMAS

OKLAHOMA STATE   RB, 5-11, 186   Missouri City, Texas (Willow Ridge HS)

Consensus all-America 85. Heisman tied for 10th in 85, 6th in 87.

Bowls: Gator 84—rushed 155 yards on 32 carries, scoring on a 1-yard run, caught 3 passes for 3 yards and was named the game's Most Valuable Player (Beat South Caro., 21-14). Gator 85—rushed 97 yards on 26 carries and caught 3 passes for 44 yards, including a 29-yard TD (Florida St. won, 34-23). Sun 87—rushed 157 yards on 33 carries, scoring 4 TDs on runs of 5, 9, 4 and 4 yards, caught 3 passes for 20 yards and was named the game's Most Valuable Player (Beat West Va., 35-33).

Yr.	Team W	L	T	G	Rushing Car.	Yds.	Avg.	TD	Receiving No.	Yds.	TD	Avg.	All-Purpose Plays	Yds.	Avg.
84	9	2	0	11	173	688	4.0	6	19	119	0	6.3	197	888	4.5
85	8	3	0	11	302	1553	5.1	15	19	98	0	5.2	335	1781	5.3
86	6	5	0	11	173	741	4.3	4	18	150	1	8.3	194	919	4.7
87	9	2	0	11	250	1613	6.5	18	19	184	0	9.7	278	1938	7.0
Totals	32	12	0	44	898	4595	5.1	43	75	551	1	7.3	1004	5526	5.5

Career: 104.4 rush yds. per game; 125.6 all-purpose yds. per game.

Other career figures: 272 pts. scored (one 2-pt. conv); 15 punt ret., 143 yds., 1 TD; 16 K.O. ret., 237 yds; 3 pass att., 2 cmp., 15 yds., 2 TD.

ANTHONY THOMPSON

INDIANA
RB, 6-0, 209
Terre Haute, Ind. (North HS)

Unanimous all-America 89. Consensus all-America 88. Heisman 2nd in 89, 9th in 88.

Bowls: All-American 86—rushed 127 yards on 28 carries (Florida St. won, 27-13). Peach 88—rushed 67 yards on 18 carries, scoring on a 12-yard run, and caught 6 passes for 28 yards (Tennessee won, 27-22). Liberty 88—rushed 140 yards on 26 carries, scoring on a 7- and 8-yard run, and caught 2 passes for 14 yards (Beat South Caro., 34-10).

Yr.	Team W	L	T	G	Rushing Car.	Yds.	Avg.	TD	Receiving No.	Yds.	TD	Avg.	All-Purpose Plays	Yds.	Avg.
86	6	5	0	8	163	679	4.2	5	10	79	0	7.9	174	776	4.5
87	8	3	0	11	239	947	4.0	11	20	214	0	10.7	259	1161	4.5
88	7	3	1	11	329	1546	4.7	24	29	219	0	7.6	358	1765	4.9
89+#	5	6	0	11	*358	*1793	5.0	24	35	201	1	5.7	411	2388	5.8
Totals	26	17	1	41	1089	4965	4.6	64	94	713	1	7.6	1202	6090	5.1

Career: 121.1 rush yds. per game; 148.5 all-purpose yds. per game.

Other career figures: 394 pts. scored (two 2-pt. conv.); 19 K.O. ret., 412 yds., 21.7 avg.

+ National scoring champion in 1989 at 14.0 pts. per game (154 in 11 games).

National rushing champion in 1989 at 163.0 yards per game.

* This figure led the nation.

EMANUEL TOLBERT
SOUTHERN METHODIST
WR, 5-10, 180
Little Rock, Ark. (Central HS)

Consensus all-America 78.

Yr.	Team W	L	T	G	Rushing Car.	Yds.	No.	Receiving Yds.	TD	Avg.	K.O. Returns No.	Yds.	Avg.	Scoring TD	XP	Pts.
76	3	8	0	11	17	108	17	371	4	21.8	6	86	14.3	5	0	30
77	4	7	0	11	23	70	64	996	6	15.6	—	—	—	6	2	38
78	4	6	1	11	4	12	62	1040	11	16.8	2	46	23.0	11	0	66
79	5	6	0	11	0	0	28	376	4	13.4	—	—	—	4	0	24
Totals	16	27	1	44	44	190	171	2783	25	16.3	8	132	16.5	26	2	158

Other career figures: 4.3 yds. per carry; 4 punt ret., 6 yds.

KENDALL TRAINOR
ARKANSAS   PK, 6-2, 205   Fredonia, Kan. (Fredonia HS)

Consensus all-America 88.

Bowls: Holiday 85—kicked game-winning 37-yard FG with 0:21 remaining and 1 of 1 PAT (Beat Arizona St., 18-17). Orange 87—no statistics (Oklahoma won, 42-8). Liberty 87—kicked 43-yard FG and 2 of 2 PATs (Georgia won, 20-17). Cotton 89—kicked 49-yard FG (UCLA won, 17-3).

Yr.	Team W	L	T	G	Punting No.	Yds.	Avg.	XPA	-XP	FGA	-FG	Pct.	Field Goals Under 40 yds.	40 Plus	Long	Pts.
85	9	2	0	11	—	—	—	12	10	9	4	.444	1-2	3-7	47	22
86	9	2	0	11	—	—	—	39	39	13	10	.769	5-6	5-7	55	69
87	9	3	0	12	58	2285	39.4	33	32	20	13	.650	10-11	3-9	48	71
88	10	1	0	11	—	—	—	32	30	27	+24	.889	14-15	10-12	58	102
Totals	37	8	0	45	58	2285	39.4	116	111	69	51	.739	30-34	21-35	38	264

Career accuracy percentages: .957   .882   .600

His FGs provided winning margin over: 87—Baylor; 88—Mississippi, Texas, Houston and Texas A&M.

(Trainor was a walk-on.)

+ National field goal champion at 2.18 per game in 1988 and finished career by making 23 consecutive field goals.

DAVID TREADWELL
CLEMSON PK, 6-1, 165 Jacksonville, Fla. (Bolles HS)

Consensus all-America 87.

Bowls: Independence 85—made 39- and 21-yard FGs and 1 of 1 PATs (Minnesota won, 20-13). Gator 86—made 21- and 46-yard FGs and 3 of 3 PATs (Beat Stanford, 27-21). Florida Citrus 88—made 5 of 5 PATs (Beat Penn St., 35-10).

	Team				Punting						Field Goals			
												Under	40		
Yr.	W	L	T	G	No.	Yds.	Avg.	XPA	-XP	FGA	-FG	Pct.	40 yds.	Plus	Long	Pts.
85	6	5	0	11	—	—	—	24	24	22	15	.682	10-12	5-10	49	69
86	7	2	2	11	—	—	—	31	31	18	10	.556	9-12	1-6	46	61
87	9	2	0	10	—	—	—	29	28	21	18	.857	14-15	4-6	43	82
Totals	22	9	2	32	—	—	—	84	83	61	43	.705	33-39	10-22	49	212

Career accuracy percentages: .988 .846 .455

His FGs provided winning margin over: 85—Virginia Tech, Virginia; 86—Georgia; 87—Georgia.

TOM TUPA
OHIO STATE
P-QB, 6-5, 215
Brecksville, Ohio (Brecksville, Ohio)

Unanimous all-America punter 87.

Bowls: Rose 85—punted 4 times for 47.8-yard average, longest 66 (Southern Cal won, 20-17). Florida Citrus 85—punted 6 times for 41.0-yard average, longest 51 (Beat Brigham Young, 10-7). Cotton 87—punted 6 times for 35.2-yard average, longest 58, and completed 3 of 8 passes for 23 yards with one interception (Beat Texas A&M, 28-12).

	Team				Punting			Passing						Total Off.	
Yr.	W	L	T	G	No.	Yds.	Avg.	Att.	Cmp.	Int.	Pct.	Yds.	TD	Plays	Yds.
84	9	2	0	11	41	1927	47.0	—	—	—	—	—	—	3	-23
85	8	3	0	11	42	1784	42.5	13	7	0	.538	68	0	17	79
86	9	3	0	12	50	2180	43.6	41	27	1	.659	375	3	62	398
87	6	4	1	11	63	2963	+47.0	242	134	10	.554	1786	12	314	1831
Totals	32	12	1	45	196	8854	45.2	296	168	11	.568	2229	15	396	2285

Career: 7.5 per pass att., 13.3 per cmp., 129.3 efficiency; 5.8 total-offense yds. per play; 19 TDs-responsible-for.

Other career figures: 24 pts. scored; 100 net rushing yds on 56 carries.

+ National punting champion in 1987.

HERSCHEL WALKER
GEORGIA
RB, 6-2, 222
Wrightsville, Ga. (Johnson County HS)

Unanimous all-America 80, 81, 82. Heisman 3rd in 80, 2nd in 81, winner in 82.

Bowls: Sugar 81—rushed 150 yards on 36 carries, including 1- and 3-yard TDs; 1 incomplete pass; named game's Most Outstanding Player (Beat Notre Dame, 17-10, to win national championship). Sugar 82—rushed 84 yards on 25 carries, including 8- and 10-yard TDs; caught 3 passes for 53 yards, longest 31 (Pittsburgh won, 24-20). Sugar 83—rushed 103 yards on 28 carries, including 1-yard TD; caught 1 pass for 15 yards; returned 1 kickoff 23 yards (Penn St. won, 27-23, for national championship).

	Team				Rushing				Receiving				All-Purpose		
Yr.	W	L	T	G	Car.	Yds.	Avg.	TD	No.	Yds.	TD	Avg.	Plays	Yds.	Avg.
80	#11	0	0	11	274	1616	5.9	15	7	70	0	10.0	287	1805	6.3
81	10	1	0	11	385	1891	4.9	18	14	84	2	6.0	405	2067	5.1
82	11	0	0	11	335	1752	5.2	16	5	89	1	17.8	342	1877	5.5
Totals	32	1	0	33	994	5259	5.3	49	26	243	3	9.2	1034	5749	5.6

Career: 159.4 rush yds. per game; 174.2 all-purpose yds. per game.

Other career figures: 314 pts. scored (one 2-pt. conv.) 14 K.O. ret., 247 yds.; 1 pass att., 1 int.

National champions.

STEVE WALSH
MIAMI (FLA.)   QB, 6-3, 195   St. Paul, Minn. (Cretin HS)

Consensus all-America 88. Heisman 4th in 88.

Bowls: Fiesta 87—did not play (Penn St. won, 14-10, for national championship). Orange 88—completed 18 of 30 passes for 209 yards, including 30- and 23-yard TD passes with 1 interception (Beat Oklahoma, 20-14, to win national championship). Orange 89—completed 21 of 44 passes for 277 yards, including 22- and 42-yard TD passes with 3 interceptions; named Miami's Most Valuable Player (Beat Nebraska, 23-3).

	Team				Rushing		Passing						Total Offense		
Yr.	W	L	T	G	Car.	Yds.	Att.	Cmp.	Int.	Pct.	Yds.	TD	Plays	Yds.	TDR
85	Redshirted														
86	11	0	0	2	—	—	2	1	0	.500	5	0	2	5	0
87	#11	0	0	11	33	-8	298	176	7	.591	2249	19	331	2241	20
88	10	1	0	11	15	-33	390	233	12	.597	3115	29	405	3082	29
Totals	32	1	0	24	48	-41	690	410	19	.594	5369	48	738	5328	49

Career: 7.8 per pass att., 13.1 per cmp., 142.2 efficiency; 222.0 total offense yds. per game, 7.2 per play.

Other career figures. 6 pts. scored.

National champions.

ANDRE WARE
HOUSTON
QB, 6-2. 205
Dickinson, Texas (Dickinson HS)

Consensus all-America 89. Heisman winner 89.

Bowl: Aloha 88—completed 8 of 28 passes for 44 yards with 2 interceptions and rushed 3 times for minus 1 (Washington State won, 24-22).

Yr.	Team W	L	T	G	Rushing Car.	Yds.	Att.	Cmp.	Passing Int.	Pct.	Yds.	TD	Total Offense Plays	Yds.	TDR
87	4	6	1	7	35	-58	140	83	5	.593	996	4	175	938	5
88	9	2	0	11	35	-48	356	212	8	.596	2507	25	391	2459	27
89	9	2	0	11	50	-38	*578	*365	15	.631	*4699	*46	*628+	*4661	*49
Totals	22	10	1	29	120	-144	1074	660	28	.615	8202	75	1194	8058	81

Career: 7.6 yds. per pass att., 12.4 per cmp.; 143.4 efficiency; 277.9 total offense yds. per game, 6.7 per play.

Other career figures: 18 pts. scored; 2-pt. conv. passes: 4 att., 1 cmp.; 1 pass caught, 37 yds.

+ National champion in total offense at 423.7 yds. per game in 1989.

* This figure led the nation.

CURT WARNER
PENN STATE RB, 6-1, 198 Wyoming, W. Va. (Pineville HS)

All-America 81. Heisman tied for 10th in 82.

Bowls: Liberty 79—rushed for 57 yards on 14 carries (Beat Tulane, 9-6). Fiesta 80—rushed for 155 yards on 18 carries, scoring on a 64-yard run, caught 1 pass for 0 yards and returned 3 kickoffs 69 yards; named game's Most Outstanding Offensive Player (Beat Ohio St., 31-19). Fiesta 82—rushed 145 yards on 26 carries, scoring on 21- and 17-yard runs and caught 3 passes for 10 yards; named game's Most Outstanding Offensive Player (Beat Southern Cal, 26-10). Sugar 83—rushed 117 yards on 18 carries, scoring 2 TDs and caught 2 passes for 23 yards (Beat Georgia, 27-23, to win the national championship).

Yr.	Team W	L	T	G	Rushing Car.	Yds.	Avg.	TD	Receiving No.	Yds.	TD	Avg.	All-Purpose Plays	Yds.	Avg.
79	7	4	0	8	84	391	4.7	2	10	129	1	12.9	111	1013	9.1
80	9	2	0	11	196	922	4.7	6	13	92	0	7.1	219	1364	6.2
81	9	2	0	9	171	1044	6.1	8	9	106	0	11.8	185	1229	6.6
82	#10	1	0	11	198	1041	5.3	8	24	335	5	14.0	222	1376	6.2
Totals	35	9	0	39	649	3398	5.2	24	56	662	6	11.8	737	4982	6.8

Career: 85.8 rush yds. per game; 127.7 all-purpose yds. per game.

Other career figures: 198 pts. scored; 32 K.O. ret., 922 yds. 28.8 yds., 3 TD.

National champions.

JOE WASHINGTON
OKLAHOMA
RB, 5-10, 178
Port Arthur, Texas (Lincoln HS)

Unanimous all-America 74. All-America 75. Heisman 3rd in 74, 5th in 75.

Bowls: Sugar 72—rushed 3 yards on 2 carries; returned 3 punts 21 yards (Beat Penn St., 14-0). Orange 76—rushed 73 yards on 17 carries; returned 2 punts 1 yard (Beat Michigan, 14-6).

Yr.	Team W	L	T	G	Rushing Car.	Yds.	Avg.	TD	Receiving No.	Yds.	TD	Avg.	All-Purpose Plays	Yds.	Avg.
72	10	1	0	11	115	630	5.5	7	2	37	0	18.5	135	786	5.8
73	10	0	1	11	176	1173	6.7	9	5	89	0	17.8	218	1744	8.0
74	#11	0	0	11	194	1321	6.8	12	2	71	1	35.5	228	1904	8.4
75	#10	1	0	11	171	871	5.1	11	4	56	0	14.0	215	1347	6.3
Totals	41	2	1	44	656	3995	6.1	39	13	253	1	19.5	796	5781	7.3

Yr.	Scoring TD	XP	Pts.	Punt Returns No.	Yds.	Avg.	K.O. Returns No.	Yds.	Avg.	Comb. Kick Returns No.	Yds.	TD	Avg.
72	7	2	44	14	68	4.9	4	51	12.8	18	119	0	6.6
73	10	0	60	25	260	10.4	12	222	18.5	37	482	1	13.0
74	14	0	84	24	332	13.8	8	180	22.5	32	512	1	16.0
75	12	2	74	25	147	5.7	15	273	18.2	40	420	1	10.5
Totals	43	4	262	88	807	9.2	39	726	18.6	127	1533	3	12.1

Other career figures: 5 passes att., 1 cmp., 3 int., 40 yds., 1 TD; 10 punts, 50.2 avg.

National champions.

JACK WEIL
WYOMING   P, 5-11, 171   Northglenn, Colo. (Northglenn HS)

Consensus all-America 83.

Yr.	Team W	L	T	G	Punting No.	Yds.	Avg.
80	6	5	0	11	43	1892	44.0
81	8	3	0	11	65	2693	41.4
82	5	7	0	12	71	2886	40.6
83	7	5	0	12	52	2369	+45.6
Totals	26	20	0	46	231	9840	42.6

Other career figures: 1 carry, 17 yds. rushing.

+ National punting champion in 1983.

CHARLES WHITE
SOUTHERN CALIFORNIA
RB, 6-0, 185
San Fernando, Calif. (San Fernando HS)

Unanimous all-America 78 and 79. Heisman winner 79, 4th in 78.

Bowls: Rose 77—rushed 114 yards on 32 carries; 7-yard TD (Beat Michigan, 14-6). Bluebonnet 77—rushed 187 yards on 21 carries and caught 1 pass for 25 yards and a TD (Beat Texas A&M, 47-28). Rose 79—rushed 99 yards on 32 carries and a 3-yard TD and caught 2 passes for 2 yards; named Co-Player of the Game (Beat Michigan, 17-10). Rose 80—rushed 247 yards on 39 carries and a game-winning 1-yard run with 1:32 remaining; caught 2 passes for 7 yards; named Player of the Game (Beat Ohio St., 17-16).

	Team					Rushing				Receiving			All-Purpose		
Yr.	W	L	T	G	Car.	Yds.	Avg.	TD	No.	Yds.	TD	Avg.	Plays	Yds.	Avg.
76	10	1	0	11	124	744	6.0	9	6	65	1	10.8	144	1104	7.7
77	7	4	0	11	264	1291	4.9	7	8	113	1	14.1	272	1404	5.2
78	#11	1	0	12	*342	1760	5.1	12	20	191	1	9.6	369	+2096	5.7
79	10	0	1	10	293	+1803	6.2	18	20	138	0	6.9	313	+1941	6.2
Totals	38	6	1	44	1023	5598	5.5	46	54	507	3	9.4	1098	6545	6.0

Career: 127.2 rush yds. per game; 148.8 all-purpose yds. per game.

Other career figures: 296 pts. scored (one 2-pt. conv.); 21 K.O. ret., 440 yds., 21.0 avg; 2 pass att., 1 cmp. minus 5 yds.

National champions.   + National champion in all-purpose running at 174.7 yds. per game in 1978; national champion in rushing at 180.3 yds. per game and in all-purpose running at 194.1 yds. per game in 1979.   * This figure led the nation.

DANNY WHITE
ARIZONA STATE   QB, 6-3, 175   Mesa, Ariz. (Westwood HS)

All-America 73. Heisman 9th in 73.

Bowls: Fiesta 71—completed 15 of 30 passes for 250 yards and 2 TDs, rushed 16 yards on 11 carries, punted 6 times for a 37-yard average (Beat Florida St., 45-38). Fiesta 72—completed 13 of 23 passes for 266 yards and 2 TDs with 3 interceptions, rushed 25 yards on 4 carries and punted 3 times for 43.7-yard average (Beat Missouri, 49-35). Fiesta 73—completed 14 of 19 passes for 269 yards and 1 TD with 3 interceptions and punted 5 times for 46-yard average (Beat Pittsburgh, 28-7).

	Team				Rushing		Passing						Total Offense		
Yr.	W	L	T	G	Car.	Yds.	Att.	Cmp.	Int.	Pct.	Yds.	TD	Plays	Yds.	TDR
71	10	1	0	11	39	46	165	86	9	.521	1393	15	204	1439	17
72	9	2	0	11	65	222	219	113	15	.516	1930	21	284	2151	28
73+	10	1	0	11	60	253	265	146	12	.551	2609	23	325	2862	28
Totals	29	4	0	33	164	521	649	345	36	.532	5932	59	813	6453	73

Career: 9.1 per pass att., 17.2 per cmp., 148.9 efficiency; 195.5 total offense yds. per game, 7.9 per play.

Other career figures: 150 punts, 41.7 avg.; 94 pts. scored (five 2-pt. conv.); 2 passes caught, 3 yds.

+ National leader in passing efficiency in 1973 (min. 15 att. per game) at 157.4.

LORENZO WHITE
MICHIGAN STATE
RB, 5-11, 211
Fort Lauderdale, Fla. (Dillard HS)

Unanimous all-America 85, consensus all-America 87. Heisman 4th in 87, 4th in 85.

Bowls: Cherry 84—rushed 103 yards on 23 carries and caught 1 pass for minus 3 yards (Army won, 10-6). All-American 85—rushed 158 yards on 33 carries (Georgia Tech won, 17-14). Rose 88—rushed 113 yards on 35 carries, scoring on 3- and 5-yard runs (Beat Southern Cal, 20-7).

Yr.	Team W	L	T	G	Rushing Car.	Yds.	Avg.	TD	Receiving No.	Yds.	TD	Avg.	All-Purpose Plays	Yds.	Avg.
84	6	5	0	11	119	513	4.3	4	7	47	0	6.7	126	560	4.4
85	7	4	0	11	*386	*+1908	4.9	†17	6	28	0	4.6	392	1936	4.9
86	6	5	0	9	164	633	3.9	6	11	78	0	7.1	175	711	4.1
87	8	2	1	11	322	1459	4.5	14	12	115	0	9.6	334	1574	4.7
Totals	27	16	1	42	991	4513	4.6	41	36	268	0	7.4	1027	4781	4.7

Career: 107.4 rush yds. per game; 113.8 all-purpose yds. per game.
Other career figures: 246 pts. scored.

+ National rushing champion at 173.5 yards per game in 1985.   * This figure led the nation.
† This figure tied for first in the nation.

DAVID WILLIAMS
ILLINOIS   WR, 6-3, 195   Los Angeles, Calif. (Serra HS)

Unanimous all-America 84 and 85.

Bowls: Rose 84—caught 10 passes for 88 yards (UCLA won, 45-9). Peach 85—caught 7 passes for 109 yards, including 15- and 54-yard TDs (Army won, 31-29).

Yr.	Team W	L	T	G	Rushing Car.	Yds.	Receiving No.	Yds.	TD	Avg.	Scoring TD	XP	Pts.
83	10	1	0	11	—	—	59	870	6	14.8	6	0	36
84	7	4	0	11	2	-4	+*101	*1278	8	12.7	8	0	48
85	6	4	1	11	2	-1	85	1047	8	12.3	8	2	50
Totals	23	9	1	33	4	-5	245	3195	22	13.0	22	2	134

* This figure led the nation. + National pass receiving champion at 9.2 catches per game in 1984.

DAVID WILLIAMS

MARC WILSON
BRIGHAM YOUNG
QB, 6-5, 204
Seattle, Wash. (Shorecrest HS)

Unanimous all-America 79. Heisman 3rd in 79. NCAA Postgraduate Scholarship 80.

Bowls: Holiday 78—completed 7 of 16 passes with 1 interception for 48 yards; rushed 10 yards on 7 carries (Navy won, 23-16). Holiday 79—completed 28 of 43 passes with 3 interceptions for 380 yards and TD passes of 13 and 15 yards; rushed 28 yards on 9 carries and 3-yard TD; named game's Most Valuable Offensive Player (Indiana won, 38-37).

	Team				Rushing		Passing						Total Offense		
Yr.	W	L	T	G	Car.	Yds.	Att.	Cmp.	Int.	Pct.	Yds.	TD	Plays	Yds.	TDR
77	9	2	0	11	81	20	277	164	18	.592	2418	24	358	2438	26
78	9	3	0	11	104	85	233	121	13	.519	1499	8	337	1584	10
79	11	0	0	11	61	-140	427	250	15	.585	3720	29	488	3580	32
Totals	29	5	0	33	246	-35	937	535	46	.571	7637	61	1183	7602	68

Career: 8.2 per pass att., 14.3 per cmp., 137.2 efficiency; 230.4 total offense yds. per game, 6.4 per play.

Other career figures: 42 pts. scored; 1 pass caught, minus 5 yds.

KELLEN WINSLOW
MISSOURI
TE, 6-6, 235
East St. Louis, Ill. (East St. Louis HS)

Consensus all-America 78.

Bowl: Liberty 78—caught 2 passes for 17 yards; 16-yard TD (Beat Louisiana St., 20-15).

	Team				Rushing		Receiving			Scoring		
Yr.	W	L	T	G	Car.	Yds.	No.	Yds.	TD	Avg.	TD	XP	Pts.
75	6	5	0	3	—	—	1	12	0	12.0	—	—	—
76	6	5	0	11	—	—	16	240	1	15.0	1	0	6
77	4	7	0	10	—	—	25	358	3	14.3	3	0	18
78	7	4	0	11	—	—	29	479	6	16.5	6	0	36
Totals	23	21	0	35	—	—	71	1089	10	15.3	10	0	60

STEVE WORSTER
TEXAS RB, 6-0, 210 Bridge City, Texas (Bridge City HS)

Consensus all-America 70. All-America 69. Heisman 4th in 70.

Bowls: Cotton 69—rushed 85 yards on 10 carries, scoring on a 14-yard run and caught 1 pass for 25 yards (Beat Tennessee, 36-13). Cotton 70—rushed 155 yards on 20 carries, including a long of 43 (Beat Notre Dame, 21-17). Cotton 71—rushed 42 yards on 16 carries (Notre Dame won, 24-11).

Yr.	Team				Rushing				Receiving				All-Purpose		
	W	L	T	G	Car.	Yds.	Avg.	TD	No.	Yds.	TD	Avg.	Plays	Yds.	Avg.
68	8	1	1	10	161	806	5.0	13	8	64	0	8.0	171	884	5.2
69	#10	0	0	9	136	649	4.8	9	2	38	0	19.0	138	687	5.0
70	#10	0	0	10	160	898	5.6	14	1	11	0	11.0	161	909	5.6
Totals	28	1	1	29	457	2353	5.1	36	11	113	0	10.3	470	2480	5.3

Career: 81.1 rush yds. per game; 85.5 all-purpose yds. per game.
Other career figures: 216 pts. scored; 2 K.O. ret., 14 yds.
National champions.

ELMO WRIGHT
HOUSTON WR, 6-0, 195 Brazoria, Texas (Sweeny HS)

Consensus all-America 70.

Bowl: Bluebonnet 69—caught 4 passes for 62 yards and rushed 10 yards on 1 carry (Beat Auburn, 36-7).

Yr.	Team			Rushing		Receiving			Scoring		
	W	L	T	Car.	Yds.	No.	Yds.	TD	Avg.	TD	XP	Pts.
68	6	2	2	10	5	113	43	1198	11	*27.9	12	0	72
69	8	2	0	10	5	28	63	1275	14	*20.2	14	6	90
70	8	3	0	11	3	-6	47	874	9	18.6	9	2	56
Totals	22	7	2	31	13	135	153	3347	34	21.9	35	8	218

Other career figures: 10.4 yds. per carry.
* This figure led the nation.

TIM WRIGHTMAN
UCLA TE, 6-3, 237 San Pedro, Calif. (Mary Star of the Sea HS)

Consensus all-America 81.

Bowls: Fiesta 78—(no statistics) (Tied Arkansas, 10-10). Bluebonnet 81—caught 2 passes for 14 yards; 9-yard TD (Michigan won, 33-14).

Yr.	Team				Rushing		Receiving			Scoring		
	W	L	T	G	Car.	Yds.	No.	Yds.	TD	Avg.	TD	XP	Pts.
78	8	3	0	11	—	—	7	82	0	11.7	—	—	—
79	5	6	0	11	—	—	22	321	2	14.6	2	0	12
80	9	2	0	11	—	—	17	236	2	13.9	2	0	12
81	7	3	1	11	—	—	26	294	5	11.3	5	0	30
Totals	29	14	1	44	—	—	72	933	9	13.0	9	0	54

CHARLES YOUNG
SOUTHERN CALIFORNIA TE, 6-4, 228 Fresno, Calif. (Edison HS)

Unanimous all-America 72.

Bowl: Rose 73—caught 6 passes for 82 yards (Beat Ohio St., 42-17).

Yr.	Team				Rushing		Receiving			Scoring		
	W	L	T	G	Car.	Yds.	No.	Yds.	TD	Avg.	TD	XP	Pts.
70	6	4	1	11	—	—	16	322	1	20.1	1	0	6
71	6	4	1	11	1	-2	23	308	6	13.4	6	0	36
72	#11	0	0	11	—	—	23	378	3	16.4	3	0	18
Totals	23	8	1	33	1	-2	62	1008	10	16.3	10	0	60

National champions.

DAVE YOUNG
PURDUE   TE, 6-6, 242   Akron, Ohio (East HS)

Unanimous all-America 80.

Bowls: Peach 78—caught 1 pass for 28 yards (Beat Georgia Tech, 41-21). Bluebonnet 79—caught 4 passes for 72 yards; 12- and 17-yard TDs (Beat Tennessee, 27-22). Liberty 80—caught 3 passes for 42 yards and 5-yard TD (Beat Missouri, 28-25).

	Team				Rushing		Receiving				Scoring		
Yr.	W	L	T	G	Car.	Yds.	No.	Yds.	TD	Avg.	TD	XP	Pts.
77	5	6	0	11	—	—	28	373	5	13.3	5	0	30
78	8	2	1	11	—	—	26	372	3	14.3	3	0	18
79	9	2	0	11	—	—	51	512	8	10.0	8	0	48
80	8	3	0	11	—	—	67	917	8	13.7	8	0	48
Totals	30	13	1	44	—	—	172	2174	24	12.6	24	0	144

STEVE YOUNG
BRIGHAM YOUNG
QB, 6-1, 198
Greenwich, Conn. (Greenwich HS)

Unanimous all-America 83. Heisman 2nd in 83. Today's Top Five, NCAA Honors Luncheon 84. NCAA Postgraduate Scholarship 84. Hall of Fame Scholar-Athlete 83.

Bowls: Holiday 81—completed 1 of 1 passes for 26 yards (Beat Washington St., 38-36). Holiday 82—completed 27 of 45 passes for 341 yards and 2 TDs with 1 interception and rushed for minus 4 yards on 9 carries (Ohio St. won, 47-17). Holiday 83—completed 24 of 36 passes for 314 yards with 3 interceptions; rushed for minus 7 yards on 12 carries; caught 14-yard flea-flicker pass from Eddie Stinnett for game-winning score with 23 seconds remaining; named game's Most Valuable Offensive Player (Beat Missouri, 21-17).

	Team				Rushing		Passing						Total Offense		
Yr.	W	L	T	G	Car.	Yds.	Att.	Cmp.	Int.	Pct.	Yds.	TD	Plays	Yds.	TDR
81	10	2	0	9	53	233	112	56	5	.500	731	5	165	964	5
82	8	3	0	11	114	407	367	230	18	.627	3100	18	481	3507	28
83	10	1	0	11	102	444	429	*306	10	*.713	+*3802	*33	531	+*4346	41
Totals	28	6	0	31	269	1084	908	592	33	.652	7733	56	1177	8817	74

Career: 8.5 per pass att., 13.1 per cmp., 149.8 efficiency; 284.4 total offense yards per game; 7.5 per play.

* This figure led the nation.   + National passing efficiency champion at 168.5 and total offense champion at 395.1 yards per game in 1983.

LUIS ZENDEJAS

ARIZONA STATE PK, 5-9, 186 Chino, Calif. (Don Antonio Lugo HS)

Consensus all-America 83.

Bowl: Fiesta 83—made three FGs (32-22-54 yards) and 3 of 3 PATs (Beat Oklahoma, 32-21).

	Team				Punting					Field Goals				
Yr.	W	L	T	G	No.	Yds.	Avg.	XPA	-XP	FGA	-FG	Pct.	Under 40 yds.	40 Plus	Long	Pts.
81	9	2	0	11	—	—	—	45	45	20	16	.800	12-13	4-7	51	93
82	9	2	0	11	—	—	—	27	27	28	21	.750	13-13	8-15	55	90
83	6	4	1	11	—	—	—	29	28	+*37	†28	.757	19-22	9-15	*52	+112
84	5	6	0	11	—	—	—	34	34	20	13	.650	9-11	4-9	52	73
Totals	29	14	1	44	—	—	—	135	134	105	78	.743	53-59	25-46	55	368

Career accuracy percentages: .992   .898   .543

His FGs provided winning margin over: 83-San Jose St.

+ National champion in field goals at 2.55 per game and kick scoring-leader at 10.2 pts. per game in 1983.   * This figure led the nation.   † Tied for first in the nation.

ALL-AMERICA ROSTER

SYMBOLS USED FOR TEAMS USED IN COMPILING NCAA CONSENSUS TEAMS

AA—All-America Board
AP—Associated Press
C—Walter Camp (published in Harper's Weekly 1897; in Collier's magazine, 1898-1924)
COL—Collier's magazine (selections by Grantland Rice 1925-47; it published American Football Coaches Association teams 1948-56, listed under FC)
FBW—Football World magazine
CP—Central Press
FC—American Football Coaches Association (published by Saturday Evening Post magazine 1945-47, by Collier's 1948-56.)
FN—Football News
FW—Football Writers Association of America (published by Look magazine 1946-70)
INS—International News Service (merged with United Press in 1958 to form UPI)
L—Look magazine (published FWAA teams, 1946-70, listed under FW).
LIB—Liberty magazine
M—Frank Menke Syndicate
N—Newsweek magazine
NANA—North American Newspaper Alliance
NEA—Newspaper Enterprise Association
SN—Sporting News
UP—United Press (merged with INS in 1958 to form UPI)
UPI—United Press International
W—Caspar Whitney (published in The Week's Sport in association with Walter Camp 1889-90; published in Harper's Weekly 1891-96 and in Outing magazine, which he owned, 1898-1908. Walter Camp substituted for Whitney, who was on a world tour, and selected the Harper's Weekly team for 1897)
WCF—Walter Camp Foundation

YEAR-BY-YEAR SELECTIONS USED

1889-1912

Yr.	W	C
89	X	
90	X	
91	X	
92	X	
93	X	
94	X	
95	X	
96	X	
97	X	
98	X	X
99	X	X
00	X	X
01	X	X
02	X	X
03	X	X
04	X	X
05	X	X
06	X	X
07	X	X
08	X	X
09		X
10		X
11		X
12		X

1913-23

Yr.	C	INS	M	NEA	FBW
13	X	X			
14	X	X			
15	X	X			
16	X	X	X		
17	**	X	X	X	
18	X		X		
19	X		X		
20	X	X	X		
21	X				X
22	X				
23	X				X

** See footnote next page.

1924-30

Yr.	C	INS	NEA	FWB	AA	LIB	AP	COL	UP	NANA
24	X	X	X	X	X	X				
25		X	X	X	X	X	X	X	X	
26		X	X		X		X	X	X	
27		X	X		X		X	X	X	X
28		X	X		X		X	X	X	X
29		X	X		X		X	X	X	X
30		X	X		X		X	X	X	X

1931-41

Yr.	INS	NEA	AA	LIB	AP	COL	UP	NANA	SN	N
31	X	X	X	X	X	X	X			
32	X	X	X	X	X	X	X	X		
33	X	X	X	X	X	X	X	X		
34	X	X	X	X	X	X	X	X	X	
35	X	X	X	X	X	X	X	X	X	
36	X	X	X	X	X	X	X	X	X	
37	X	X	X	X	X	X	X	X	X	X
38	X	X	X	X	X	X	X		X	X
39	X	X	X	X	X	X	X		X	X
40	X	X	X	X	X	X	X		X	X
41	X	X	X	X	X	X	X		X	X

1942-57

Yr.	INS	NEA	AA	AP	COL	UP	SN	N	L	FBN	FW	FC
42	X	X	X	X	X	X	X	X	X			
43	X		X	X	X	X	X		X	X		
44	X	X	X	X	X	X	X		X	X	X	
45	X	X	X	X	X	X	X		X		X	X
46	X	X	X	X	X	X	X		##		X	X
47	X	X		X	X	X	X				X	X
48@	X	X		X	++	X	X				X	X
49	X	X	X	X		X	X				X	X
50	X	X	X	X		X	X				X	X
51	X	X	X	X		X	X				X	X
52	X	X	X	X		X	X				X	X
53	X	X	X	X		X	X				X	X
54	X	X	X	X		X	X				X	X
55	X	X	X	X		X	X				X	X
56	X	X		X		X	X				X	X
57	X	X		X		X	X				X	X

1958-70

Yr.	NEA	AP	UPI	SN	FW	FC	CP
58	X	X	X	X	X	X	
59	X	X	X	X	X	X	
60	X	X	X	X	X	X	
61	X	X	X	X	X	X	
62	X	X	X	X	X	X	
63	X	X	X	X	X	X	X
64	X	X	X		X	X	X
65	X	X	X		X	X	X
66	X	X	X		X	X	X
67	X	X	X		X	X	X
68	X	X	X		X	X	X
69	X	X	X		X	X	X
70	X	X	X		X	X	X

1971-89

Yr.	NEA	AP	UPI	FW	FC	WCF
71	X	X	X	X	X	
72	X	X	X	X	X	X
73	X	X	X	X	X	X
74		X	X	X	X	X
75		X	X	X	X	
76		X	X	X	X	
77		X	X	X	X	
78		X	X	X	X	
79		X	X	X	X	
80		X	X	X	X	
81		X	X	X	X	
82		X	X	X	X	
83		X	X	X	X	X
84		X	X	X	X	X
85		X	X	X	X	X
86		X	X	X	X	X
87		X	X	X	X	X
88		X	X	X	X	X
89		X	X	X	X	X

** In 1917, Walter Camp selected an all-Service, all-America team composed of military personnel.

During 1946-70, Look Magazine published the Football Writers Association of America selections, listed under FW.

++ During 1948-56, Collier's magazine published the American Football Coaches Association selections, listed under FC.

@ INS was the first to select offensive and defensive teams in 1948 (Iron-man football returned in 1953 through 1963, two-platoon resumed in 1964; but the first NCAA two-platoon Consensus all-America was not until 1965).

ALL-TIME ALL-AMERICA ROSTER

In the following pages, college by college, are the 2,390 players from 148 colleges over 101 years who made at least one first team on the all-America teams used by the NCAA to compile its major-college consensus all-America teams. Those who also made consensus are in **bold face** with an asterisk (*) on that consensus year; unanimous choices are noted with a plus sign (+).

Every name on this all-time list was cross-checked against his college's AA list, which often included teams <u>not</u> used in determining the consensus (only teams with national input and national distribution are used). All first-team claims were checked against NCAA files and just one player was added.

In some cases, players (particularly defensive players) were placed by the selectors under a general category like "DL," for defensive line or "OL," for offensive line. For this reason, every player in this list is placed at the position he actually played, according to his college. For the positions designated by the selectors, see the NCAA record book.

AIR FORCE

Brock Strom, T..........*58
Ernie Jennings, E.......*70
Dave Lawson, PK-LB......74
Johnnie Jackson, DB........81
Scott Thomas, DB,......*85
Terry Maki, LB..............86
Chad Hennings, DT,...+*87

ALABAMA

Hoyt Winslett, E............26
Tony Holm, FB..............29
Fred Sington, T.......+*30
Johnny Cain, FB............31
Don Hutson, E..........*34
Bill Lee, T...............*34
Dixie Howell, B.........*34
Riley Smith, B..........*35
Arthur White, G............36
Leroy Monsky, G........*37
Jim Ryba, T..................37
Joe Kilgrow, HB............37
Carey Cox, G................39
Holt Rast, E...............*41
Joe Domnanovich, C....*42
Don Whitmire, T............42
Vaughn Mancha, C......*45
Harry Gilmer, HB..........45
Ed Salem, HB................50
Billy Neighbors, T......*61
Lee Roy Jordan, C......+*62
Dan Kearley, OT............64
Wayne Freeman, OG......64
Paul Crane, C...........*65
Ray Perkins, SE.........*66

Cecil Dowdy, OT.......+*66
Dennis Homan, SE........67
Bobby Johns, DB.....66, *67
Mike Hall, LB................68
Johnny Musso, TB.......*71
John Hannah, OT..........71
      OG......+*72
Jim Krapf, C.................72
John Mitchell, DE............72
Wayne Wheeler, SE.........73
Buddy Brown, OT......*73
Woodrow Lowe, LB.......73, *74, 75
Leroy Cook, DE...*74, +*75
Sylvester Croom, C.........74
Ozzie Newsome, WR....*77
Marty Lyons, DT........*78
Jim Bunch, OT..........*79
E.J. Junior, DE...........+*80
Tommy Wilcox, DB......*81
Mike Pitts, DE...........*82
Jeremiah Castille, DB.......82
Cornelius Bennett, LB....85, +*86
Bobby Humphrey, RB.......87
Derrick Thomas, LB...+*88
Keith McCants, LB.....+*89

AMHERST

John Hubbard, B........*05

ARIZONA

Ricky Hunley, LB.......*82, +*83

Allan Durden, DB..........85
Chuck Cecil, DB........*87

ARIZONA STATE

Ron Pritchard, LB..........68
Woody Green, B....*72, *73
Steve Holden, WR..........72
Danny White, QB...........73
Bob Breunig, LB............74
Mike Haynes, DB..........75
John Jefferson, WR......*77
Al Harris, DE...........+*78
Mike Richardson, DB..*81, *82
Vernon Maxwell, LB....*82
Luis Zendejas, PK.......*83
David Fulcher, DB......*84, *85
Danny Villa, OT........*86
Randall McDaniel, OG...86, *87

ARKANSAS

Wear Schoonover, E........29
Jim Benton, E...............37
Clyde Scott, TB..........*48
Bud Brooks, T..........*54
Jim Mooty, HB..............59
Wayne Harris, G-LB........60
Lance Alworth, B..........61
Bill Moore, QB..............62
Ronnie Caveness, C........64
Glen Ray Hines, OT.....*65

Loyd Phillips, DT......*65,
+*66
Bobby Crockett, E..........65
Martine Bercher, DB.........66
Jim Barnes, OG.........*68
Rodney Brand, C.......*69
Chuck Dicus, SE.........69, 70
Cliff Powell, LB..............69
Dick Bumpas, DT.......*70
Bruce James, DT............70
Bill McClard, K.............70
Chuck Dicus, OE............70
Steve Little, PK........76, *77
Leotis Harris, G.........*77
Dan Hampton, DT...........78
Jimmy Walker, DL..........78
Greg Kolenda, OT......+*79
Billy Ray Smith, DL..+*81,
+*82
Bruce Lahay, PK............81
Steve Korte, OG........+*82
Ron Faurot, DE.............83
Greg Horne, P.............86
Tony Cherico, MG..........87
Kendall Trainor, PK.....*88
Wayne Martin, DT......*88
Jim Mabry, OT..........+89

ARKANSAS STATE

Ken Jones, OG..............75
T.J. Humphreys, OG..........76

ARMY

Charles Romeyn, B......*98
William Smith, E........*00
Paul Bunker, T..........*01
T-HB.......*02
Charles Daly, QB........*01
Robert Boyers, C........*02
Arthur Tipton, C........*04
Henry Torney, B....*04, *05
William Erwin, G........*07
Leland Devore, T........*11
Louis Merillat, E........*13
John McEwan, C........*14
Elmer Oliphant, HB...*16,
*17
Edgar Garbisch, C......*22
G.......24
Gus Farwick, G............24
Charles Born, E.............25
Harry Wilson, HB...........26
Bud Sprague, T......*26, 27
Red Cagle, HB....*27, +*28,
*29
Jack Price, T.............30, 31
Milt Summerfelt, G.....*32
Jack Buckler, B..............33
Bill Shuler, E................35
Harry Stella, T..............39

Robin Olds, T...............42
Frank Merritt, T.........42, 43
Casimir Myslinski, C..+*43
Glenn Davis, HB........*44,
+*45, +*46
Doc Blanchard, FB.....*44,
+*45, +*46
Tex Coulter, T............*45
John Green, G......44, *45
Barney Poole, E.............44
Joe Stanowicz, G............44
Doug Kenna, QB............44
Hank Foldberg, E....45, *46
Albert Nemetz, T...........45
Arnold Tucker, QB..........46
Joe Steffy, G.............*47
Joe Henry, G................48
Bobby Stuart, HB...........48
Arnold Galiffa, QB......*49
Dan Foldberg, E....49, +*50
J.D. Kimmel, T..............50
Charles Shira, T............50
Elmer Stout, C..............50
Don Holleder, E.............54
Ralph Chesnauskas, G......54
Tommy Bell, HB............54
Bob Anderson, HB...*57, 58
Pete Dawkins, HB......+*58
Bob Novogratz, G..........58
Bill Carpenter, E........*59
Townsend Clarke, LB.......66
Ken Johnson, LB............68
Don Smith, OG.............85

AUBURN

Jimmy Hitchcock, B.....*32
Roy Gafford, HB............42
Tex Warrington, C..........44
Frank D'Agostino, T........55
Joe Childress, FB............55
Jimmy Phillips, E......+*57
Zeke Smith, G.......*58, 59
Jackie Burkett, C............58
Ken Rice, T............59, *60
Ed Dyas, FB................60
Jimmy Sidle, QB............63
Tucker Frederickson, B *64
Jack Thornton, T...........65
David Campbell, DT........68
Buddy McClinton, DB...*69
Larry Willingham, DB..*70
Pat Sullivan, QB.......+*71
Terry Beasley, WR.....+*71
Ken Bernich, LB........*74
Bo Jackson, TB....*83, +*85
Gregg Carr, LB.........*84
Lewis Colbert, P............85
Ben Tamburello, C.....+*86
Brent Fullwood, TB....+*86
Tracy Rocker, DT.......*87,
+*88
Aundray Bruce, LB......*87

Stacy Searles, OT...........87
Kurt Crain, LB..............87
Ed King, OG................89

BAYLOR

Barton Koch, G.........*30
Stan Williams, E............51
Larry Isbell, QB.............51
Jim Ray Smith, T...........53
Bill Glass, G...........+*56
Don Trull, QB...............63
Lawrence Elkins, E.....*63
B.....*64
Greg Pipes, DT..............67
Roger Goree, DE...........72
Aubrey Schulz, C...........74
Gary Green, DB.........*76
Mike Singletary, LB...*79,
+*80
Frank Ditta, OG............80
Gerald McNeil, WR.........83
Thomas Everett, DB......85,
+*86
James Francis, LB..........89

BOSTON COLLEGE

Luke Urban, E..........*20
Charles Darling, B.........24
Charles O'Rourke, HB.........40
Gene Goodreault, E.....*40
Chet Gladchuck, C.........40
Mike Holovak, FB.......*42
Fred Naumetz, C............42
Dan Currivan, E............42
Laurent Bouley, T..........42
Al Krevis, OT...............74
Steve Schindler, OG........76
Doug Flutie, QB........+*84
Tony Thurman, DB......*84
Mike Ruth, MG.........*85

BOSTON U.

Harry Agganis, HB.........51

BRIGHAM YOUNG

Eldon Forte, TB.............62
Gifford Nielsen, QB.........76
Marc Wilson, QB......+*79
Nick Eyre, OT..........*80
Jim McMahon, QB......80,
+*82
Gordon Hudson, TE...+*82,
+*83

Steve Young, QB......+*83
Kyle Morrell, DB...........84
Jason Buck, DE.........*86
Pat Thompson, P...........88
**Mohammed Elewonibi,
OG**........*89

BROWN

Thomas Barry, HB......*02
John Mayhew, HB......*06
Adrian Regnier, E......*09
Earl Sprackling, QB.....*10
George Crowther, QB...*12
Fritz Pollard, HB........*16
Hal Broda, E................26
Orland Smith, T.............26
Roy Randall, QB............26

BUCKNELL

John Dempsey, T............33

CALIFORNIA

Brick Muller, E.....*21, *22
Dan McMillan, T........*21
Edwin Horrell, C........*24
H. Dana Carey, G...........25
Irv Phillips, E...........*28
Roy Riegles, C..............29
Bert Schwarz, G.............29
Ted Beckett, G..........*30
Rusty Gill, HB...............31
Arleigh Williams, HB.......34
Larry Lutz, T............*35
Bob Herwig, C..........36, 37
Sam Chapman, HB......*37
Vard Stockton, G............37
Perry Schwartz, E...........37
Vic Bottari, HB..........*38
Bob Reinhard, T.........40, 41
Bill Hachten, G..............44
Jackie Jensen, FB.......*48
Rod Franz, G...47, 48, +*49
Jim Turner, T............48, 49
Forrest Klein, G.............49
Les Richter, G......*50, *51
John Olszewski, HB.........52
Matt Hazeltine, C........53, 54
Paul Larson, QB.............54
Joe Kapp, QB................58
Craig Morton, B.............64
Ed White, MG...........*68
Sherman White, DT.....*71
Steve Bartkowski, QB...*74
Chris Mackie, OG...........74
Chuck Muncie, RB......*75
Steve Rivera, WR........*75
Ted Albrecht, OT............76
Ron Rivera, LB..........*83

Robbie Keen, P.............89

CARLISLE

Isaac Seneca, B.........*99
James Johnson, B.......*05
Albert Exendine, E......*07
Peter Hauser, B.........*07
Jim Thorpe, HB.....*11, *12

CARNEGIE-
MELLON

Lloyd Yoder, T..............26
Theodore Rosenzweig, E....28
Howard Harpster, B.....*28

CENTENARY

Paul Geisler, E..........*33

CENTRE

James Weaver, C.......*19
Bo McMillin, QB...*19, *21
James Roberts, E............21

CHICAGO

**Clarence Herschberger,
B**..........*98
Fred Speik, E............*04
Walter Eckersall, QB..*04,
*05, *06
Mark Catlin, E..........*05
Walter Steffen, B.......*08
Paul Des Jardien, C.....*13
C. G. Higgins, G............17
Charles McGuire, T.....20, 21
John Thomas, B.........*22
Joe Pondelik, G..........*24
Franklin Gowdy, T..........24
Ellmore Patterson, C........34
Jay Berwanger, HB...34, *35

CINCINNATI

Mike Woods, LB............77

CITADEL

John Small, LB..............69
Brian Ruff, LB...............76

CLEMSON

Banks McFadden, HB.......39
Joe Blaylock, E..............41
Bobby Gage, DB............48
Jackie Calvert, DB..........50
Wayne Mass, OT............66
Harry Olszewski, OG...*67
**Bennie Cunningham,
TE**.........*74
Joe Bostic, OG..............77
Jerry Butler, SE..............78
Jim Stuckey, DT.........*79
Jeff Davis, LB............*81
Terry Kinard, DB.......*81,
+*82
William Perry, MG..*83, 84
John Phillips, OL............86
Terrence Flagler, RB....*86
John Phillips, OG............86
David Treadwell, PK....*87
Michael Dean Perry, DT....87
Donnell Woolford, DB....87,
*88

COLGATE

Ellery Huntington, QB..*13
Earl Abell, T.................15
Clarence Horning, T....*16
D. Belford West, T..*16, *19
Oscar Anderson, QB....*16
J. Edward Tryon, HB........25
Leonard Macaluso, FB..*30
John Orsi, E.................31
Robert Smith, G.............32
Joe Bogdanski, E............34
Charles Wasicek, T.........35
Macel Chesbro, T...........36

COLORADO

**Byron "Whizzer" White,
HB**........*37
Don Branby, E..............52
Bob Stransky, HB...........57
John Wooten, G.............58
Joe Romig, G......*60, *61
Jerry Hillebrand, E..........61
Dick Anderson, DB......*67
Mike Montler, OT.......*68
Bob Anderson, TB.......*69
Bill Brundige, DE............69
Don Popplewell, C......*70
Herb Orvis, DE..............71
Bud Magrum, LB...........72
Cullen Bryant, DB......*72
Mark Koncar, OT............75
Matt Miller, OT..............78
Mark Haynes, DB...........79
Barry Helton, P.....*85, *86
Keith English, P.........*88
Joe Garten, OT..........*89

Alfred Williams, LB.....*89
Tom Rouen, P............*89
Kanavis McGhee, LB........89

COLORADO COLLEGE

Earl Clark, QB..............28

COLORADO STATE

Thurman McGraw, T.....48, 49
Harvey Achziger, T.........52
Mike Bell, DL...........*78

COLUMBIA

Bill Morley, B......*00, *01
Harold Weekes, B.......*01
Richard Smith, B........*03
Walter Koppisch, B.........24
Tony Matal, E...............33
Sid Luckman, QB............38
Paul Governali, QB.....*42
Bill Swiacki, E..........*47

CORNELL

Clinton Wyckoff, B......*95
Raymond Starbuck, B...*00
William Warner, G.....*01, *02
Sanford Hunt, G.........*01
Elmer Thompson, G.....*06
William Newman, C....*06
Bernard O'Rourke, G...*08
John O'Hearn, E.........*14
Charles Barrett, B..*14, *15
Murray Shelton, E.......*15
Edgar Kaw, B.......*21, *22
George Pfann, B........*23
Frank Sundstrom, T.........23
Jose Martinez-Zorilla, E.....32
Brud Holland, E......37, *38
Sid Roth, G..................38
William McKeever, T.......38
Nick Drahos, T.....*39, *40
Ed Marinaro, RB....70, +*71

DARTMOUTH

Henry Hooper, C........*03
Myron Witham, QB.....*03
Joseph Gilman, G.......*04
Ralph Glaze, E..........*05
George Schildmiller, E..*08

Clarke Tobin, G.........*08
Wesley Englehorn, T....*12
Robert Hogsett, E........*13
Clarence Spears, G.....*14, *15
Milton Ghee, QB............14
Eugene Neely, G.........*17
Adolph Youngstrom, G..*19
Clark Diehl, G.....*24, *25
Henry Bjorkman, E.........24
Edwin Dooley, B............24
Nathan Parker, T...........25
George Tully, E..........*25
Andy Oberlander, HB..+*25
Alton Marsters, HB.........29
Bob MacLeod, HB.......*38
Dale Armstrong, E..........48
Donald McKinnon, C........62
E. Winters Mabry, DB......66
Murry Bowden, DB.........70
Reggie Williams, LB........75

DAYTON

Fred Dugan, E..............62

DETROIT

Vince Banonis, C...........41

DRAKE

Ted Sloane, E...............25
Johnny Bright, B............50

DUKE

Fred Crawford, T........*33
Ace Parker, HB..........*36
Dan Hill, C...................38
Eric Tipton, TB..............38
Steve Lach, HB..............41
Pat Preston, T...............43
Bob Gantt, E................43
Ed Meadows, T........52, 53
Tom Topping, T............57
Mike McGee, T.............59
Claude Moorman, E.........60
Jean Berry, G................62
Jay Wilkinson, HB..........63
Bob Matheson, C...........66
Ernie Jackson, DB.......*71
Billy Bryan, C................76
Clarkston Hines, WR....88, +*89
Chris Port, OT..............89

DUQUESNE

Mike Basrak, C.........*36
John Rokisky, E............41

EAST CAROLINA

Terry Long, OL..........*83

FLORIDA

Dale Vansickle, E...........28
Charles LaPradd, T.........52
John Barrow, G.............56
Vel Heckman, T............58
Larry Dupree. FB..........64
Chuck Casey, E.............65
Lynn Matthews, E..........65
Bruce Bennett, DB.........65
Steve Spurrier, QB..65, +*66
Guy Dennis, G..............68
Carlos Alvarez, FL......*69
Jack Youngblood, DE.......70
Sammy Green, LB.......*75
Wes Chandler, SE...........77
David Little, LB.........*80
David Galloway, DT.........81
Wilber Marshall, LB...*82, *83
Lomas Brown, OT......*84
Jeff Zimmerman, OT.....85, 86
Jarvis Williams, DB.........87
Louis Oliver, DB.........*88
Emmitt Smith, RB......+*89

FLORIDA STATE

Fred Biletnikoff, SE.....*64
Ron Sellers, FL......*67, 68
Dale McCullers, LB.........68
Barry Smith, WR...........72
Gary Huff, QB..............72
Ron Simmons, MG *79, *80
Rohn Stark, P............80, 81
Greg Allen, RB......*83, 84
Jamie Dukes, OG........*85
Paul McGowan, LB..........87
Pat Tomberlin, OT...........88
Deion Sanders, DB....+*87, +*88
LeRoy Butler, DB.........*89
Michael Tanks, C...........89
Odell Haggins, MG.........89

FORDHAM

Henry Wisniewski, G.......30
Jim Murphy, B..............30
Alex Wojciechowicz, C.....*36, *37

Ed Franco, T............*37
Jim Lansing, E...............41

FRESNO STATE

Jackie Fellows, B............42
Steve Cordle, DB...........81

GEORGETOWN (D.C.)

Harry Connaughton, G..*26
Augie Lio, G................40

GEORGIA

Tom Nash, E.............*27
Ivey Shiver, E................27
Ralph Maddox, G..........30
Vernon Smith, E........*31
Frank Sinkwich, HB....*41, +*42
Mike Castonis, T.............45
Charley Trippi, HB.....+*46
John Rauch, QB.............48
John Carson, E..............53
Pat Dye, G...................59
Ray Rissmiller, E............64
Jim Wilson, T...............64
George Patton, DT.......65, 66
Ed Chandler, OG.....66, *67
Bill Stanfill, DT.........*68
Jake Scott, DB..........*68
Royce Smith, OG.......+*71
Craig Hertwig, OT..........74
Randy Johnson, OG.....*75
Joel Parrish, OG.........*76
Mike Wilson, OT............76
Rex Robinson, PK...........80
Scott Woerner, DB..........80
Herschel Walker, TB..+*80, +*81, +*82
Terry Hoage, DB...*82, *83
Freddie Gilbert, DE.........83
Kevin Butler, PK........*84
Jeff Sanchez, DB........*84
Pete Anderson, C........*85
John Little, DB..............86
Troy Sadowski, TE...........88
Tim Worley, RB........*88

GEORGIA TECH

Everett Strupper, B......*17
Walker Carpenter, T.........17
Bill Fincher, T......*18, *20
Joe Guyon, T-HB.........*18
Ashel Day, C.............*18
Pete Pund, C............*28
Warner Mizell, B............28
Frank Speer, T...............28
Harvey Hardy, G........*42
John Steber, G..............43
Phil Tinsley, E..........*44
Paul Duke, C............*46
Bob Davis, T............*47
George Brodnax, E..........48
William Healy, DG..........48
Lamar Wheat, T..............51
Ray Beck, G.................51
Hal Miller, OT...........*52
Buck Martin, E..............52
Pete Brown, C...............52
George Morris, LB..........52
Bobby Moorhead, DB.......52
Leon Hardeman, HB........52
Larry Morris, C.........*53
Don Stephenson, C......56, 57
Maxie Baughan, C......*59
Rufus Guthrie, G............62
Billy Lothridge, QB.........63
Billy Martin, E..............63
Gerry Bussell, DB..........64
Jim Breland, C..........66
Lenny Snow, TB.............66
Rock Perdoni, DT......*70
Smylie Gebhart, DE.........71
Randy Rhino, DB....72, *73, 74
Lucius Sanford, LB..........77
Pat Swilling, DE.............85

GONZAGA

George Karamatic, TB......37

GRAMBLING

Alphonse Dotson, E.........64
Doug Williams, QB.........77

HARVARD

Arthur Cumnock, E.....*89
John Cranston, G.......*89
          C........*90
James Lee, HB..........*89
Frank Hallowell, E.....*90, *92
Marshall Newell, T.....*90, *91, *92, *93
Dudley Dean, QB........*90
John Corbett, HB........*90
Everett Lake, HB........*91
Bertram Waters, G......*92
          T........*94
William Lewis, C..*92, *93
Charles Brewer, HB....*92, *93, *95
Norman Cabot, E...*95, *96
Edgar Wrightington, HB........*96
Alan Doucette, C........*97
Benjamin Dibblee, B...*97, *98
John Hallowell, E...*98, *00
Walter Boal, G...........*98
Charles Daly, QB......*98, *99, *00
David Campbell, E.....*99, *00, *01
Edward Bowditch, E...*01, *02
Oliver Cutts, T..........*01
Crawford Blagden, T....*01
William Lee, G..........*01
Charles Barnard, G.....*01
Robert Kernan, HB......*01
Thomas Graydon, FB...*01, *02
Daniel Knowlton, T......*03
Andrew Marshall, G....*03
Daniel Hurley, HB......*04, *05
Beaton Squires, T.......*05
Karl Brill, T.............*05
Francis Burr, G.....*05, *06
Charles Osborne, T......*06
Patrick Grant, C.........*07
John Wendell, HB.......*07
Hamilton Fish, T...*08, *09
Charles Nourse, C........*08
Hamilton Corbett, HB...*08
Wayland Minot, HB....*09
Robert McKay, T........*10
Robert Fisher, G...*10, *11
Percy Wendell, HB.....*10, *11
Samuel Felton, E........*12
Stanley Pennock, G.....*12, *13, *14
Charles Brickley, HB..*12, *13
Harvey Hitchcock, T....*13
Edward Mahan, FB....*13, *14, *15
Huntington Hardwick, E........*14
Frederick Bradlee, HB.......14
Walter Trumbull, T.....*14
Joseph Gilman, T........*15
Richard King, HB.......*15
Harrie Dadmun, G......*16
Edward Casey, HB......*19
Tom Woods, G..........*20
James Tolbert, G..........20
Arnold Horween, FB.......20
John Brown, G..........*21
Charles Hubbard, G....*22, *23
Ben Ticknor, C....*29, +*30

Barry Wood, QB........*31
Endicott Peabody, G...+*41
Pat McInally, TE............74

HASKELL
John Levi, HB..............23

HAWAII
Al Noga, DT...............86

HOLY CROSS
Hilary Mahaney, E..........24
Chet Millett, G.............51
John Provost, DB-RB.....*74
Gordon Lockbaum, DB-RB..86

HOUSTON
J.D. Kimmel, DT.............52
Hogan Wharton, T..........58
Rich Stotter, OG.........*67
Ken Hebert, SE.............67
Paul Gipson, FB.............68
Bill Bridges, OG........*69
Elmo Wright, WR.......*70
Mack Mitchell, DE...........74
Robert Giblin, DB...........74
Wilson Whitley, DT.....*76
Melvin Jones, OT...........79
David Hodge, LB...........79
Leonard Mitchell, DT...*80
Hosea Taylor, MG...........80
Jason Phillips, WR......*88
Andre Ware, QB.........*89
Emmanuel Hazard, WR.....89

IDAHO
John Yarno, C...............76

ILLINOIS
Perry Graves, E.........*14
Ralph Chapman, G......*14
Bart Macomber, HB.....*15
John Depler, C...........*18
Charles Carney, E.......*20
James McMillen, G.....*23
Red Grange, HB........*23,
+*24, *25
Bernie Shively, G........*26
Russ Crane, G..............27
Robert Reitsch, C...........27
Albert Nowack, T...........28
Leroy Wietz, G.............28

Lou Gordon, T..............29
Jim Reeder, T...............39
Alex Agase, G........42, *46
Buddy Young, HB...........44
Ralph Serpico, G............44
Bill Vohaska, C.............50
Al Tate, T...................50
Johnny Karras, HB......*51
Al Brosky, DB...............51
Charles Ulrich, T...........51
Charles Boerio, LB..........51
J. C. Caroline, HB.......*53
Bill Burrell, G...........*59
Dick Butkus, C....+*63, *64
George Donnelly, DB.......64
Jim Grabowski, FB.......64,
+*65
Don Thorpe, DT............83
David Williams, WR..+*84,
+*85
Moe Gardner, DT......+*89

INDIANA
Corby Davis, FB............37
Billy Hillenbrand, HB...*42
Pete Pihos, E................43
John Tavener, C.........*44
Bob Ravensberg, E......*45
George Taliaferro, HB.......48
Tom Nowatzke, FB..........64
Don Croftcheck, G..........64
Garry Cassells, G..........67
Ernie Jones, WR............87
Anthony Thompson,
RB....*88, +*89

IOWA
Lester Belding, E........*19
Aubrey Devine, QB......*21
Gordon Locke, FB.........22
Dick Romney, E.............25
Willis Glassgow, HB........29
Francis Schammel, G........33
Ozzie Simmons, HB........35
Nile Kinnick, HB........*39
Mike Enich, T...............40
Jerry Hilgenberg, C.........53
Calvin Jones, G.....*54, *55
Alex Karras, T.......56, *57
Jim Gibbons, E..............57
Curt Merz, E................58
Randy Duncan, QB.....+*58
Don Norton, E...............59
Mark Manders, G...........60
Larry Ferguson, HB.........60
Bill Van Buren, G...........61
Mike Reilly, G..............63
Karl Noonan, E..............64
Craig Clemons, DB.........71
Andre Tippett, DE.......*81

Reggie Roby, P..........*81
Larry Station, LB.......*84,
+*85
Chuck Long, QB.......+*85
Dave Croston, OT...........86
Dave Haight, MG...........88
Marv Cook, TE..........*88

IOWA STATE
Ed Bock, G...............*38
Jim Doran, WR...............50
Dwight Nichols, RB.........59
Dave Hoppmann, TB........62
Tom Vaughn, FB............63
John Van Sicklen, OT........64
Matt Blair, LB...............73
Luther Blue, SE..............76
Mike Busch, TE.........*89

KANSAS
Ray Evans, HB..............47
George Mrkonic, DT........51
Oliver Spencer, T...........52
Gil Reich, QB...............52
John Hadl, HB..............60
QB..............61
Gale Sayers, HB....*63, *64
Bob Douglass, QB..........68
John Zook, DE..........*68
Dave Jaynes, QB........*73
Bruce Kallmeyer, PK........83

KANSAS STATE
Henry Cronkite, E..........31
George Maddox, T.........34
Clarence Scott, DB..........70
Gary Spani, LB..........*77

KENT
Jim Corrigall, LB............69

KENTUCKY
Clyde Johnson, T...........42
Bob Gain, G...............49
T............*50
Babe Parilli, QB....*50, *51
Doug Moseley, C..........51
Steve Meilinger, E.......52, 53
Ray Correll, G..............53
Howard Schnellenberger,
E............55
Lou Michaels, T....*56, *57
Herschel Turner, T..........63

Sam Ball, OT............*65
Warren Bryant, OT..........76
Art Still, DE............+*77

LAFAYETTE

Walter Bachman, C....*00,
*01
Frank Schwab, G...*21, *22
Charles Berry, E............24
George Wilson, HB.........26

LEHIGH

Bill Ciaravino, G............50

LONG BEACH STATE

Leon Burns, FB.............70

LOUISIANA STATE

Gaynell Tinsley, E......*35,
+*36
Ken Kavanaugh, E......*39
George Tarasovic, C........51
Sid Fournet, T...........*54
Jimmy Taylor, FB...........57
Max Fugler, C..............58
Billy Cannon, HB......+*58,
*59
Roy Winston, G........+*61
Jerry Stovall, HB.......+*62
Fred Miller, T...............62
Remi Prudhomme, T........64
John Garlington, E..........67
George Bevan, LB..........69
Mike Anderson, LB....*70
Tommy Casanova, DB..*70,
*71
Ronnie Estay, DT............71
Bert Jones, QB...........*72
Warren Capone, LB...72, 73
Tyler Lafauci, OG........73
Mike Williams, DB......74
Charles Alexander,
RB....*77, *78
Lance Smith, OT............84
Michael Brooks, LB.........85
Wendell Davis, SE...86, *87
Nacho Albergamo, C..+*87

LOUISIANA TECH

Mike Barber, TE............75

LOUISVILLE

Ken Kortas, E..............63
Tom Jackson, LB............72

MARQUETTE

Arthur Krueger, C..........32
Ray Buivid, B............*36

MARYLAND

Bob Ward, G........50, +*51
Ed Modzelewski, FB........51
Dick Modzelewski, DT..*52
Jack Scarbath, QB.....+*52
Stan Jones, T...........+*53
Bernie Faloney, QB.........53
Mike Sandusky, T...........55
Bob Pellegrini, C......+*55
Gary Collins, E..........*61
Paul Vellano, DG...........73
Randy White, DT...73, +*74
Joe Campbell, DT.......*76
Dale Castro, PK.........*79
J.D. Maarleveld, OT.....*85

MEMPHIS STATE

Harry Schuh, T..........63, 64
Eric Harris, DB..............76

MIAMI (Fla.)

Al Carapella, T..............50
Frank McDonald, E.........54
Don Bosseler, FB............56
Bill Miller, E........60, *61
George Mira, QB...........62
Ed Weisacosky, E..........65
Tom Beier, DB............*66
Ted Hendricks, DE....+*67,
+*68
Tony Cristiani, MG.....*73
Rubin Carter, MG.......*74
Eddie Edwards, DT.........76
Don Smith, DT..............78
Lester Williams, DT.........81
Fred Marion, DB........*81
Eddie Brown, WR......*84
Willie Smith, TE........*85
Vinny Testaverde,
QB.......+*86
Jerome Brown, DT.....+*86

Bennie Blades, DB......*86,
+*87
Daniel Stubbs, DE......+*87
Bill Hawkins, DE........*88
Steve Walsh, QB.........*88
Greg Mark, DL..........*89

MIAMI (Ohio)

Bob Babich, LB.............68
Brad Cousino, LB...........74

MICHIGAN

William Cunningham,
C.........*98
Neil Snow, E.............*01
Willie Heston, HB..*03, *04
Adolph Schulz, C........*07
Albert Benbrook, G.....*09,
*10
Stanfield Wells, E.......*10
Miller Pontius, T........*13
Jim Craig, HB...........*13
John Maulbetsch, HB...*14
Frank Culver, G.............17
Frank Steketee, FB..........18
Henry Vick, C..............21
Harry Kipke, HB........*22
Jack Blott, C............*23
Edliff Slaughter, G...........24
Robert Brown, C...........25
Bennie Oosterbaan,
E......*25, *26, +*27
Benny Friedman, QB...*25,
*26
Otto Pommerening, T...*28
Maynard Morrison, C......31
Harry Newman, QB....+*32
Ted Petoskey, E.........32, 33
Francis Wistert, T......*33
Chuck Bernard, C..32, +*33
Ralph Heikkinen, G....+*38
Tom Harmon, HB......*39,
+*40
Ed Frutig, E.................40
Bob Westfall, FB........*41
Albert Wistert, T........*42
Julie Franks, G.........*42
Bill Daley, FB..........+*43
Merv Pregulman, T.........43
Elmer Madar, E.............46
Bob Chappuis, HB.....+*47
Bump Elliott, HB...........47
Pete Elliott, QB..............48
Dick Rifenburg, E.......*48
Alvin Wistert, T....*48, *49
Allen Wahl, T..........49, 50
Lowell Perry, E..............51
Art Walker, T...............54
Ron Kramer, E....*55, +*56
Jim Pace, HB...............57

Bob Timberlake, QB........64
Bill Yearby, DT......64, ***65**
Jack Clancy, E........+***66**
Ron Johnson, HB...........68
Jim Mandich, TE.....+***69**
Tom Curtis, DB.........***69**
Henry Hill, MG..............70
Marty Huff, LB..............70
Dan Dierdorf, OT.......***70**
Reggie McKenzie, OG..***71**
Mike Taylor, LB.......+***71**
Tom Darden, DB............71
Paul Seymour, OT......***72**
Randy Logan, DB.......***72**
Dave Gallagher, DT....***73**
Dave Brown, DB...***73**, +***74**
Don Dufek, DB..............75
Jim Smith, WR..............76
Calvin O'Neal, LB..........76
Rob Lytle, RB...........***76**
Mark Donahue, OG....***76**,
+***77**
Walt Downing, C...........77
John Anderson, LB.........77
Rick Leach, QB.............78
Ron Simpkins, LB......***79**
Curtis Greer, DT............79
Anthony Carter, WR.....80,
+***81**, +***82**
Ed Muransky, OT.......***81**
Kurt Becker, OG........***81**
Stefan Humphries, OG......83
Tom Dixon, C...............83
**Mike Hammerstein,
DT**........***85**
Brad Cochran, DB......***85**
John Elliott, OT.......86, ***87**
Garland Rivers, DB.....***86**
John Vitale, C..........***88**
Mark Messner, DT.....+***88**
Tripp Williams, DB....+***89**

MICHIGAN STATE

**Neno Jerry DaPrato,
HB**........***15**
Sidney Wagner, G......***35**
Johnny Pingel, HB..........38
Lynn Chandnois, HB........49
Ed Bagdon, G...........***49**
Dorne Dibble, E............50
Sonny Grandelius, HB......50
Al Dorow, QB..............51
Bob Carey, E...........***51**
Don Coleman, T.......+***51**
Frank Kush, G..............52
Dick Tamburo, C...........52
Don McAuliffe, HB.........52
Don Dohoney, E........***53**
Norman Masters, T.....***55**
Earl Morrall, QB.......***55**

Dan Currie, C..........***57**
Walt Kowalczyk, HB....***57**
Sam Williams, E........***58**
Dean Look, QB.............59
Dave Behrman, G...........61
George Saimes, FB.....***62**
Sherman Lewis, HB.....***63**
Bubba Smith, DE.......***65**,
+***66**
George Webster, DB..+***65**,
+***66**
Gene Washington, E.....65, 66
Harold Lucas, MG..........65
Ron Goovert, LB............65
Steve Juday, QB.............65
Clint Jones, HB.......65, ***66**
Jerry West, T................66
Al Brenner, DB..............68
Ron Saul, OG...............69
Eric Allen, RB...............71
Ron Curl, DT................71
Brad Van Pelt, DB..71, +***72**
Kirk Gibson, FL..............78
Mark Brammer, TE..........78
Morten Andersen, PK.......81
Carl Banks, LB..............83
Greg Montgomery, P.......86
Lorenzo White, TB....+***85**,
*87
Tony Mandarich, OT....***88**
Bob Kula, OT............***89**
Percy Snow, LB........+***89**

MINNESOTA

Fred Schacht, T.........***03**
John McGovern, QB.....***09**
James Walker, T........***10**
Bert Baston, E.......15, ***16**
Claire Long, QB..............16
George Hauser, T......16, ***17**
Ray Ecklund, E.........***23**
Earl Martineau, HB..........23
Herb Joesting, FB..***26**, ***27**
Harold Hanson, G...........27
George Gibson, G...........28
Kenneth Haycraft, E........28
Bronko Nagurski, T.....***29**
Robert Tanner, E............29
Biggie Munn, G.........***31**
Frank Larson, E......33, ***34**
Bill Bevan, G............***34**
Pug Lund, HB........33, ***34**
Ed Widseth, T......34, ***35**,
+***36**
Dick Smith, T................35
Sheldon Beise, FB..........35
Andy Uram, FB.............36
Ray King, T..................37
Francis Twedell, G..........38
Helge Pukema, G...........40
Urban Odson, T.........***40**
George Franck, HB.....***40**

Dick Wildung, T...***41**, ***42**
Bruce Smith, HB........***41**
Leo Nomellini, T-G.....***48**,
*49
**Clayton Tonnemaker,
C**........+***49**
Paul Giel, HB......52, +***53**
Bob McNamara, FB-HB.....54
Bob Hobert, T..............56
Tom Brown, G.........+***60**
Sandy Stephens, QB.....***61**
Bobby Bell, T........61, ***62**
Carl Eller, T.............***63**
Aaron Brown, DE........***65**
Bob Stein, E.................67
Doug Kingsriter, TE.........70

MISSISSIPPI

Frank Kinard, T.........36, 37
Parker Hall, HB.............38
Charley Conerly, TB....***47**
Barney Poole, E.........47, 48
Kline Gilbert, T.............52
Crawford Mims, G......***53**
Rex Boggan, T..............54
Jack Simpson, G............57
Charlie Flowers, FB.....***59**
Marvin Terrell, G............59
Jake Gibbs, QB.........+***60**
Billy Ray Adams, FB........61
Jim Dunaway, T.........***62**
Glynn Griffing, QB..........62
Kenny Dill, C................63
Allen Brown, E..............64
Glenn Cannon, DB..........69
Harry Harrison, DB.........73
Jim Miller, P.............***79**
Fred Nunn, DE..............84
Bill Smith, P.............85, 86
Wesley Walls, TE............88

MISSISSIPPI STATE

Buddy Elrod, E..............40
Jackie Parker, QB...........53
Hal Easterwood, C..........54
Scott Suber, G...............55
Art Davis, HB................55
D.D. Lewis, LB..............67
Jimmy Webb, DT........***74**
Glen Collins, DT.............81
Johnnie Cooks, LB..........81

MISSISSIPPI VALLEY STATE

Jerry Rice, WR..............84

MISSOURI

Edgar Lindenmeyer, T......25
Paul Christman, TB.........39
Darold Jenkins, C......*41
Bob Steuber, HB............42
Harold Burnine, E..........55
Danny LaRose, E.......+*60
Ed Blaine, T...............61
Conrad Hitchler, E..........62
Johnny Roland, DB.....*65
Roger Wehrli, DB......*68
Mike Carroll, OG...........69
John Moseley, DB...........73
Henry Marshall, SE.........75
Kellen Winslow, TE....*78
Jeff Gaylord, DT...........81
Conrad Goode, OT...........83
John Clay, OL..........*86

MONTANA STATE

Bill Kollar, DL...............73

NAVY

Bill Dague, E...........*07
Percy Northcroft, T....*08
Ed Lange, QB...........*08
Jack Dalton, FB.........*11
John Brown, G...........*13
Ernest Von Heimberg, E.....17
Lyman Perry, G.........*18
Wolcott Roberts, HB....*18
Wendell Taylor, E......*22
Frank Wickhorst, T....+*26
Tom Hamilton, B............26
Ed Burke, G............*28
Slade Cutter, T............34
Fred Borries, HB.......*34
Don Whitmire, T.*43, +*44
George Brown, G............43
Ben Chase, G...........*44
Bob Jenkins, HB........*44
Dick Duden, E..........*45
Dick Scott, C............45, 47
Steve Eisenhauer, G....52, 53
Ron Beagle, E....*54, +*55
Bob Reifsnyder, T..........57
Tom Forrestal, QB..........57
Joe Bellino, HB........+*60
Greg Mather, E.............61
Roger Staubach, QB...+*63
Chet Moeller, DB......+*75
**Napoleon McCallum,
   TB**....*83, *85

NEBRASKA

Vic Halligan, T.............14
Guy Chamberlin, E.....*15
Ed Weir, T.........*24, +*25
Lonnie Stiner, T.............26
Dan McMullen, G..........28
Ray Richards, T............29
Hugh Rhea, T..............30
Lawrence Ely, C...........32
George Sauer, FB......*33
Sam Francis, FB.......*36
Fred Shirey, T.............37
Charles Brock, C..........37
Warren Alfson, G..........40
Forrest Behm, T............40
Tom Novak, C.............49
Bob Reynolds, HB.........50
Jerry Minnick, T...........52
Bob Brown, G.........+*63
Larry Kramer, OT.....+*64
Freeman White, SE....*65
Walt Barnes, DT......*65
Tony Jeter, TE..............65
Larry Wachholtz, DB.......66
LaVerne Allers, OG....*66
Wayne Meylan, MG...*66, *67
Joe Armstrong, OG.........68
Jerry Murtaugh, LB........70
Bob Newton, OT.......*70
Johnny Rodgers, WB..*71, +*72
Willie Harper, DE..*71, *72
Rich Glover, MG...71, +*72
Larry Jacobson, DT....*71
Daryl White, OT........72, 73
John Dutton, DT......+*73
Marvin Crenshaw, OT..*74
Rik Bonness, C......74, *75
David Humm, QB...........74
Wonder Monds, DB........75
Mike Fultz, DT..............76
Dave Butterfield, DB..*76
Tom Davis, C...............77
Kelvin Clark, OT.......*78
Junior Miller, TE.....+*79
Randy Schleusener, OG.......*80
Jarvis Redwine, RB....*80
Derrie Nelson, DE..........80
Jimmy Williams, DE........81
Dave Rimington, C...+*81, +*82
Mike Rozier, RB...*82, +*83
Irving Fryar, WB.....+*83
Dean Steinkuhler, OG..*83
Mark Traynowicz, C...+*84
Bret Clark, DB..............84
Bill Lewis, C................85
Jim Skow, DT...............85
Danny Noonan, DL....+*86
John McCormick, OL.......87
Jake Young, C......*88, *89
Broderick Thomas, DE..87, +*88
Doug Glaser, OT...........89

NEVADA-LAS VEGAS

Randall Cunningham,
   P (QB)......83

NEVADA-RENO

Stan Heath, QB.............48
Marty Zendejas, PK......86, 87

NEW MEXICO

Bob Berg, PK...............75
Terance Mathis, WR....*89

NEW MEXICO STATE

Pervis Atkins, HB...........60

NEW YORK U.

Al Lassman, T..............26
Ken Strong, B..........*28

NORTH CAROLINA

George Barclay, G..........34
Andy Bershak, E.......*37
Paul Severin, E..........39, 40
Art Weiner, E............48, 49
Charlie Justice, B...*48, *49
Irvin Holdash, C............50
Al Goldstein, E.............58
Bob Lacey, E...............63
Don McCauley, HB.....*70
Ron Rusnak, G.........*72
Ken Huff, G............*74
Dee Hardison, DT......*77
Lawrence Taylor, LB..+*80
David Drechsler, OG.....81, 82
Brian Blados, OT...........83
William Fuller, DT...82, *83
Harris Barton, OT..........86

NORTH CAROLINA STATE

Dick Christy, HB............57
Roman Gabriel, QB......60, 61
Dennis Byrd, DT.....66, *67
Fred Combs, DB............67
Ron Carpenter, DT.........68
Bill Yoest, G...........*73
Don Buckey, SE............75

Jim Ritcher, C.....*78, +*79
Ted Brown, RB..........*78

NORTH TEXAS

Joe Greene, DT..........*68

NORTHWESTERN

Tim Lowry, C...............25
Ralph Baker, HB........*26
Bob Johnson, T..............26
Harry Anderson, G.........29
Frank Baker, E..........*30
Fayette Russell, FB.........30
Wade Woodworth, G.......30
Jack Riley, T.............*31
Dallas Marvil, T.........*31
Pug Rentner, HB........*31
Edgar Manske, E...........33
Paul Tangora, G.............35
Steve Reid, G............*36
Bob Voigts, T...............38
John Haman, C..............39
Alf Bauman, T.......*40, 41
Otto Graham, HB...........43
Herb Hein, E................43
Max Morris, E...........*45
Alex Sarkisian, C............48
Art Murakowski, FB........48
Don Stonesifer, E............50
Joe Collier, E............52, 53
Andy Cvercko, T...........58
Ron Burton, HB..........*59
Jim Andreotti, C.............59
Jack Cvercko, G.........*62
Tom Myers, QB..............62
Eric Hutchinson, DB........71

NOTRE DAME

Gus Dorais, QB..........*13
Stan Cofall, HB..............16
Frank Rydzewski, C.....*17
Roger Kiley, E............20, 21
George Gipp, HB........*20
Eddie Anderson, E......*21
Hunk Anderson, G..........21
Don Miller, HB...............23
Harry Stuhldreher, QB..*24
Jimmy Crowley, HB.....*24
Elmer Layden, FB.......*24
Bud Boeringer, C........*26
John Smith, G............*27
Christy Flanagan, HB.......27
Fred Miller, T................28
Jack Cannon, G..........*29
Frank Carideo, QB....+*29, +*30
Marchy Schwartz, HB..*30, *31

Bert Metzger, G..............30
Marty Brill, HB...............30
Tommy Yarr, C..........*31
Joe Kurth, T........31, +*32
Nordy Hoffman, G..........31
Jack Robinson, C.......*34
Wayne Millner, E........*35
Bill Shakespeare, HB........35
John Lautar, G...............36
Chuck Sweeney, E......*37
Ed Beinor, T.........37, +*38
Earl Brown, E...............38
Bud Kerr, E...................39
Bob Dove, E........*41, *42
Bernie Crimmins, G.........41
Angelo Bertelli, QB..42, *43
John Yonakor, E.........*43
Jim White, T.............*43
Pat Filley, G..............*43
Creighton Miller, HB...*43
John Mastrangelo, G.....45, 46
George Strohmeyer, C......46
George Connor, T..*46, *47
John Lujack, QB.......+*46, +*47
Leon Hart, E...47, *48, +*49
Bill Fischer, G........*47, *48
Ziggy Czarobski, T........47
Marty Wendell, G..........48
Emil Sitko, E......*48, +*49
Bob Williams, QB...*49, 50
Jim Martin, T................49
Jerry Groom, C..........*50
Bob Toneff, T................51
Johnny Lattner, HB....+*52, +*53
Art Hunter, T............*53
Ralph Guglielmi, B....+*54
Frank Varrichione, T........54
Pat Bisceglia, G..............55
Don Schaefer, FB...........55
Paul Hornung, HB......*55
QB.........56
Al Ecuyer, G........*57, 58
Nick Pietrosante, FB........58
Monty Stickles, E....58, *59
Jim Kelly, E.................63
Jim Carroll, LB..............64
Jack Snow, E.............*64
John Huarte, QB........*64
Dick Arrington, G......+*65
Nick Rassas, DB..........*65
Tom Regner, G...........*66
Nick Eddy, HB.........+*66
Alan Page, DE............*66
Jim Lynch, LB...........+*66
Pete Duranko, DT..........66
Tom Schoen, DB.........*67
Jim Seymour, E..........67, 68
Kevin Hardy, DE............67
George Kunz, T..........*68
Terry Hanratty, QB......*68
Mike McCoy, DT......+*69
Jim Reilly, OT................69

Larry DiNardo, OG..69, *70
Tom Gatewood, SE......*70
Joe Theismann, QB.........70
Clarence Ellis, DB...70, *71
Walt Patulski, DE......+*71
Greg Marx, DT.........+*72
Dave Casper, TE.........*73
Mike Townsend, DB.....*73
Pete Demmerle, SE......*74
Gerry DiNardo, G.......*74
Tom Clements, QB..........74
Mike Fanning, DT..........74
Greg Collins, LB............74
Steve Niehaus, DT.....+*75
Ken MacAfee, TE...75, *76, +*77
Ross Browner, DE.....+*76, +*77
Luther Bradley, DB......*77
Dave Huffman, C........*78
Bob Golic, LB..........+*78
Vagas Ferguson, RB.....*79
Tim Foley, OT...............79
Scott Zettek, DL............80
John Scully, C..........+*80
Bob Crable, LB.....*80, *81
Dave Duerson, DB..........82
Mark Bavaro, TE............84
Tim Brown, FL......86, +*87
Andy Heck, OT..............88
Mike Stonebreaker, LB..*88
Frank Stams, DE..........*88
Chris Zorich, DT........*89
Todd Lyght, DB........+*89
Raghib Ismail, K-RET.......89

OHIO STATE

Robert Karch, T.............16
Charles Harley, B.......*16, *17, *19
Charles Bolen, E........*17
Iolas Huffman, G........*20
T.......*21
Gaylord Stinchcomb, B..........*20
Ed Hess, G................*25
Edwin Hayes, G............26
Marty Karow, B.............26
Leo Raskowski, T...........27
Wes Fesler, E......*28, *29, +*30
Joe Gailus, G...............32
Regis Monahan, G..........34
Merle Wendt, E........34, 35
Gomer Jones, C..........*35
Inwood Smith, G............35
Gus Zarnas, G...............37
Esco Sarkkinen, E.......*39
Donald Scott, B.............39
Bob Shaw, E................42
Charles Csuri, T............42

Lindell Houston, G..........42
Jack Dugger, E.........*44
Bill Hackett, G.........*44
Les Horvath, QB.......+*44
Bill Willis, T................44
Warren Amling, G....+*45
T......*46
Vic Janowicz, HB......+*50
Bob Momsen, G............50
Bob McCullough, C........50
Mike Takacs, G.............52
Howard Cassady, HB..+*54,
+*55
Dean Dugger, E.............54
Jim Parker, G......55, +*56
Aurelius Thomas, G.........57
Jim Houston, E..............58
Jim Marshall, T.............58
Bob White, B...........*58
Bob Ferguson, FB.....+*60,
+*61
Dwight Kelley, LB........64, 65
Arnold Chonko, DB.........64
Jim Davidson, T.............64
Doug Van Horn, OT.........65
Ray Pryor, C................66
Dave Foley, OT.........+*68
Jim Otis, FB.............*69
Jim Stillwagon, MG....*69,
+*70
Jack Tatum, DB...*69, +*70
Rex Kern, QB...............69
John Brockington, FB........70
Mike Sensibaugh, DB.......70
Jan White, T................70
Tom DeLeone, C............71
John Hicks, OT......72, +*73
Randy Gradishar, LB...*72,
+*73
Van DeCree, DE........73, 74
Archie Griffin, TB.......73,
+*74, +*75
Kurt Schumacher, OT...*74
Steve Myers, C..........*74
Neal Colzie, DB.............74
Tom Skladany, P.........74, 75
Ted Smith, OG..........*75
Tim Fox, DB............*75
Chris Ward, OT...*76, +*77
Bob Brudzinski, DE.....*76
Tom Cousineau, LB.....*77,
***78**
Aaron Brown, MG..........77
Ken Fritz, OG...........*79
Marcus Marek, LB......*82
Jim Lachey, OG.........*84
Keith Byars, TB........+*84
Pepper Johnson, LB........85
Cris Carter, SE..........*86
Chris Spielman, LB....*86,
+*87
Tom Tupa, P (QB)......+*87

OKLAHOMA
Cash Gentry, T..............34
Dub Wheeler, G............35
Waddy Young, E........*38
Frank Ivy, E.................39
Buddy Burris, G........*48
Jim Owens, E...............49
Wade Walker, E.............49
Stan West, G................49
Darrell Royal, QB...........49
George Thomas, HB........49
Jim Weatherall, T......*50,
+*51
Leon Heath, FB.........*50
Frank Anderson, E..........50
Buddy Jones, DB............50
Billy Vessels, HB........*52
Tom Catlin, C...............52
Buck McPhail, FB...........52
J. D. Roberts, G.........*53
Max Boydston, E.......*54
Kurt Burris, C..........*54
Bo Bolinger, G..........*55
Tommy McDonald, HB...55,
***56**
Jerry Tubbs, C.........+*56
Ed Gray, T..................56
Bill Krisher, G..........*57
Clendon Thomas, HB....*57
Bob Harrison, C........*58
Leon Cross, G...............62
Jim Grisham, FB........*63
Ralph Neely, T..........*64
Carl McAdams, LB..64, *65
Granville Liggins,
MG......+*67
Bob Kalsu, OT...............67
Steve Owens, TB........+*69
Greg Pruitt, RB..+*71, +*72
Tom Brahaney, C...*71, *72
Derland Moore, DT.........72
Eddie Foster, OT............73
Lucious Selmon, MG...+*73
Ron Shoate, LB....*73, +*74
John Roush, G..........*74
Joe Washington, RB....+*74
KRB.....75
Randy Hughes, DB..........74
Terry Webb, OG.............75
Lee Roy Selmon, DT....+*75
Dewey Selmon, MG.....*75
Jimbo Elrod, DE.........*75
Mike Vaughan, OT.....+*76
Zac Henderson, DB.....+*77
Reggie Kinlaw, MG......77, 78
George Cumby, LB......77,
+*79
Greg Roberts, OG......+*78
Billy Sims, RB...+*78, +*79
Louis Oubre, OT.........*80
Terry Crouch, OG.......*81
Rick Bryan, DT...*82, +*83

Tony Casillas, MG.....*84,
***85**
Brian Bosworth, LB...+*85,
+*86
Keith Jackson, TE.....+*86,
+*87
Mark Hutson, OG...86, +*87
Dante Jones, LB.........*87
Rickey Dixon, DB......*87
Darrell Reed, DE............87
Anthony Phillips, OG..+*88

OKLAHOMA
STATE
Bob Fenimore, HB...44, *45
Jim Wood, E.................58
Harry Cheatwood, DB.......67
John Ward, OT..........*69
Cleveland Vann, LB.........73
Terry Miller, RB....76, +*77
Derrel Gofourth, C......*76
John Corker, LB.............78
Gary Lewis, DL..............82
Leslie O'Neal, DT...84, +*85
Rod Brown, DB..........*84
Mark Moore, DB.........85, 86
Thurman Thomas, RB..*85,
87
Hart Lee Dykes, WR.....*88
Barry Sanders, RB.....+*88

OREGON
Norm Van Brocklin, QB.....48
Steve Barnett, T.............62
Mel Renfro, HB......*62, 63
Bob Berry, QB...............64
Jim Smith, DB...............67
Bobby Moore, RB...........71
Lew Barnes, WR............85
Chris Oldham, DB..........89

OREGON STATE
Gap Powell, FB..............21
Norman Franklin, HB.......33
Ade Schwammel, T.........33
John Witte, T.........55, *56
Ted Bates, T............*58
Terry Baker, QB........+*62
Vern Burke, E...........*63
Jack O'Billovich, G..........64
Jon Sandstrom, T...........67
Jess Lewis, T................67
John Didion, C.........+*68
Bill Enyart, FB...............68
Steve Brown, LB............72

PACIFIC

Art McCaffray, T............43
John Podesto, B.............43
Eddie LeBaron, QB.........49
Ken Buck, WR..............53

PENNSYLVANIA

John Adams, C..........*91
Harry Thayer, B.........*92
Charles Gelbert, E.....*94,
                    *95, *96
Arthur Knipe, B.........*94
George Brooke, B..*94, *95
Charles Wharton, G....*95,
                        *96
Alfred Bull, C............*95
Wylie Woodruff, G......*96
John Outland, T.........*97
          B...........*98
T. Truxtun Hare, G......*97,
               *98, *99, *00
John Minds, B...........*97
Pete Overfield, C...*98, *99
Josiah McCracken, B...*99
Frank Piekarski, G.....*04
Vincent Stevenson, B....*04
Andrew Smith, B........*04
Otis Lamson, T...........*05
Robert Torrey, C.........*05
August Ziegler, G..*06, *07
William Hollenback,
          B....*06, *08
Dexter Draper, T........*07
Hunter Scarlett, E.......*08
Ernest Cozens, C........*10
E. LeRoy Mercer, B.....*10,
                        *12
J. Howard Berry, B............17
Henry Miller, E.....*17, *19
Robert Hopper, E.............18
John Thurman, T........*22
Ed McGinley, T.........*24
Alton Papworth, G..........24
George Thayer, C............25
John Butler, C................26
Charles Rodgers, B.........26
Ed Hake, T................*27
John Smith, T................27
Paul Scull, B..............*28
Harlan Gustafson, E.........39
Francis Reagan, B..........40
Ray Frick, C..................40
Bernard Kuczynski, E.......42
Bob Odell, HB...........*43
George Savitsky, T.....*45,
                   46, 47
Tony Minisi, B................47
Chuck Bednarik, C.....*47,
                        *48
John Schweder, G...........49
Bernard Lemonick, G.......50

Francis Bagnell, B..........50
Ed Bell, E.................51, 52
Jack Shanefalt, T............53

PENN STATE

William Dunn, C........*06
Bob Higgins, E.......15, *19
Charles Way, HB........*20
Glenn Killinger, HB....*21
Harry Wilson, HB.......*23
Joe Bedenk, G...............23
Leon Gajecki, C.............40
Steve Suhey, G..............47
Sam Tamburo, E............48
Sam Valentine, G...........56
Richie Lucas, QB.......*59
Bob Mitinger, E..............61
Roger Kochman, HB........62
Dave Robinson, E...........62
Glenn Ressler, C-MG....*64
Ted Kwalick, TE....67, +*68
Dennis Onkotz, LB.....*68,
                        *69
Mike Reid, DT..........+*69
Charlie Pittman, HB.........69
Neal Smith, DB..............69
Jack Ham, LB............*70
Dave Joyner, OT........*71
Lydell Mitchell, HB..........71
Charlie Zapiec, LB...........71
John Hufnagel, QB..........72
Bruce Bannon, DE......*72
John Skorupan, LB......*72
John Cappelletti, HB...+*73
Ed O'Neil, LB.................73
Randy Crowder, DT.........73
John Nessel, DT..............74
Mike Hartenstine, DE...*74
Greg Buttle, LB..........*75
Tom Rafferty, OG............75
Chris Bahr, PK...........75, 78
Kurt Allerman, LB..........76
Randy Sidler, MG............77
Matt Millen, DT..............78
Pete Harris, DB..............78
Keith Dorney, OT...77, +*78
Chuck Fusina, QB.....+*78
Bruce Clark, DT..+*78, *79
Bill Dugan, OT...............80
Curt Warner, TB.............81
Sean Farrell, OG.......+*81
Kenny Jackson, FL..........82
Mark Robinson, DB.........82
Michael Zordich, DB........85
Chris Conlin, OT.............86
Tim Johnson, DT............86
D.J. Dozier, HB..........*86
Shane Conlan, LB......*86
Steve Wisniewaki, OG......88
Blair Thomas, RB............89
Andre Collins, LB............89

PITTSBURGH

Robert Peck, C..14, *15, *16
James Herron, E.........*16
Claude Thornhill, G.........16
Dale Seis, G...............*17
Jock Sutherland, G......*17
George McLaren, B..17, *18
Leonard Hilty, T.........*18
Tom Davies, B.......*18, 20
Herb Stein, C.......*20, *21
Ralph Chase, T..........*25
Bill Kern, T....................27
Gibby Welch, B........+*27
Mike Getto, T............*28
Joe Donchess, E........+*29
Ray Montgomery, G....*29
Toby Uansa, B................29
Tom Parkinson, B...........29
Jesse Quatse, T..........*31
Joe Skladany, E....*32, *33
Warren Heller, B......+*32
Charles Hartwig, G.....*34
Ken Ormiston, G............34
George Shotwell, C.........34
Art Detzel, T..................35
Bill Glassford, G..............36
Averell Daniell, T.......*36
Art Souchak, E...............37
Tony Matisi, T............*37
Marshall Goldberg,
          HB.....*37, +*38
Bill Daddio, E............37, 38
Ralph Fife, G..................41
Bernie Barkouskie, G.......49
Eldred Kraemer, T..........52
Joe Schmidt, LB..............52
Joe Walton, E.............*56
John Guzik, G............*58
Mike Ditka, E...........+*60
Paul Martha, HB........*63
Ernie Borghetti, T............63
Gary Burley, MG............74
Tony Dorsett, RB......73, 75,
                      +*76
Al Romano, MG.........*76
Tom Brzoza, C..........*77
Randy Holloway, DT.....*77
Bob Jury, DB..............*77
Matt Cavanaugh, QB........77
Gordon Jones, WR...........78
Hugh Green, DE........*78,
              +*79, +*80
Mark May, OT..........+*80
Sal Sunseri, LB...........*81
Julius Dawkins, SE..........81
Dan Marino, QB.............81
Bill Fralic, OT......82, +*83,
                      +*84
Jimbo Covert, OT......+*83
Randy Dixon, OT........*86
Tony Woods, DE........*86
Ezekial Gadson, LB..........87
Craig Heyward, RB.....*87

Jerry Olsavky, LB..........88
Mark Stepnoski, OG....*88

PRINCETON

Hector Cowan, T........*89
William George, C.....*89
Edgar Allan Poe, B.....*89
Roscoe Channing, B....*89
Knowlton Ames, B......*89
Ralph Warren, E........*90
Jesse Riggs, G......*90, *91
Sheppard Homans, B...*90,
*91
Philip King, QB...*91, *92,
*93
Arthur Wheeler, G......*92,
*93, *94
Langdon Lea, T....*93, *94,
*95
Thomas Trenchard, E...*93
Franklin Morse, B......*93
Dudley Riggs, G........*95
William Church, T.....*96
Robert Gailey, C........*96
Addison Kelly, B...*96, *97
John Baird, B...........*96
Garrett Cochran, E.....*97
Lew Palmer, E..........*98
Arthur Hillebrand, T...*98,
*99
Arthur Poe, E...........*99
Howard Reiter, B.......*99
Ralph Davis, E..........*01
John DeWitt, G.....*02, *03
Howard Henry, E........*03
J. Dana Kafer, B........*03
James Cooney, T...*04, *06
James McCormick,
FB....*05, *07
L. Casper Wister, E.....*06,
*07
Edward Dillon, B........*06
Edwin Harlan, B........*07
Frederick Tibbott, B...*08
Talbot Pendleton, B....*10
Sanford White, E.......*11
Edward Hart, T.........*11
Joseph Duff, G..........*11
John Logan, G..........*12
Harold Ballin, T....*13, *14
Frank Hogg, G..........*16
Frank Murrey, B.......*18
Stan Keck, T............*20
G............*21
Donold Lourie, B........*20
Armant Legendre, E........20
C. Herbert Treat, T......*22
Edmund Stout, E............24
Charles Beattie, T..........24
Ed McMillan, C.........*25
Jacob Slagle, B..............25
Mike Miles, T..............27

Charles Howe, C...........28
Charles Ceppi, T...........33
John Weller, G..........*35
George Salla, B.............49
Dick Kazmaier, HB......50,
+*51
Holland Donan, T..........50
Ray Finney, C..............50
Frank McPhee, E.....51, *52
Cosmo Iacavazzi, B.........64
Stas Maliszewski, G-LB...64
OG...*65

PURDUE

Elmer Sleight, T........*29
Ralph Welch, HB........*29
Charles Miller, C............31
Roy Horstmann, FB.........32
Paul Moss, E........31, +*32
Duane Purvis, HB...*33, 34
Dave Rankin, E......39, *40
Alex Agase, G...........*43
Tony Butkovich, FB.........43
Boris Dimancheff, HB......44
Tom Hughes, T.............45
Bernie Flowers, E.....*52
Tom Bettis, G...............54
Gene Selawski, T...........58
Jerry Beabout, T............60
Don Brumm, T.............62
Harold Wells, DE...........64
Bob Griese, QB......*65, 66
Karl Singer, OT.............65
Jerry Shay, DT..............65
Jim Bierne, E................66
Leroy Keyes, HB-DB...+*67,
+*68
Chuck Kyle, MG........*68
Mike Phipps, QB......+*69
Otis Armstrong, HB.....*72
Dave Butz, DT..........*72
Larry Burton, WR...........74
Ken Novak, DT..............75
Dave Young, TE........+*80
Mark Herrmann, QB...+*80
Rod Woodson, DB.......*86

RICE

Bill Wallace, B..............34
Hamilton Nichols, G........44
Weldon Humble, G......*46
James Williams, E......*49
Joe Watson, C...............49
Bill Howton, E...............51
John Hudson, T.............53
Kosse Johnson, B...........53
Dicky Maegle, HB.......*54
King Hill, QB................57
Buddy Dial, E..........*58

Malcolm Walker, C.........64
Tommy Kramer, QB.....*76

RICHMOND

Walker Gillette, WR.....*69
Jeff Nixon, DB..........*78

RUTGERS

Paul Robeson.......*17, *18
Homer Hazel, E.............23
B.............24
Billy Austin, RB.............58
Alex Kroll, C.............*61

ST. MARY'S (Calif.)

Larry Bettencourt, C....*27
Ike Frankian, E..............28
George Ackerman, T.......29
Angel Brovelli, B............32
John Vezerski, T............33
Herman Wedemeyer,
HB.......+*45

SAN DIEGO STATE

Henry Allison, OG..........70
Henry Williams, DB........78

SAN FRANCISCO

Ollie Matson, B.............51

SAN JOSE STATE

Dave Chaney, LB...........71

SANTA CLARA

Nello Falaschi, B...........36
Alvord Wolff, T.........*38
John Schiechl, C.......*39
Phil Daugherty, G..........37

SOUTH CAROLINA

Frank Mincevich, G........54
Warren Muir, FB............69
Jimmy Poston, DT..........70
Dick Harris, DB.............70

John LeHeup, DT............72
George Rogers, RB.......79,
+*80
Del Wilkes, OG..........*84
James Seawright, LB.........84
Sterling Sharpe, WB........87

SOUTHERN CALIFORNIA

Brice Taylor, G..............25
Mort Kaer, QB..........*26
Jesse Hibbs, T..........*27
Morley Drury, B........*27
Don Williams, B............28
Francis Tappaan, E.........29
Garrett Arbelbide, E........30
Erny Pinckert, B.....*30, 31
John Baker, G...........*31
Gus Shaver, HB..........*31
Ernie Smith, T.........+*32
Aaron Rosenberg, G......32, *33
Cotton Warburton, QB.......+*33
Larry Stevens, G.............33
Harry Smith, G.....38, +*39
Ralph Heywood, E......*43
John Ferraro, T......*44, 47
Paul Cleary, E...........*47
Pat Cannamela, LB..........51
Frank Gifford, HB...........51
Elmer Willhoite, G....*52
Jim Sears, DB...........*52
Jon Arnett, B................55
Marlin McKeever, E.........59
Mike McKeever, G..........59
Hal Bledsole, E..........*62
Damon Bame, LB........62, 63
Bill Fisk, OG................64
Mike Garrett, TB...64, +*65
Ron Yary, OT.......*66, +*67
Nate Shaw, DB..........*66
O. J. Simpson, TB.....+*67, +*68
Tim Rossovich, DE......*67
Adrian Young, LB......*67
Mike Battle, B..............68
Jim Gunn, DE...........*69
Al Cowlings, DT............69
Sid Smith, OT..............69
Charlie Weaver, DE....*70
John Vella, OT..............71
Pete Adams, OT............72
Sam Cunningham, RB.......72
John Grant, DT.............72
Charles Young, TE.....+*72
Richard Wood, LB...72, +*73, *74
Lynn Swann, WR.......*73
Booker Brown, OT.......*73
Artimus Parker, DB.....*73

Anthony Davis.........+*74
Charles Phillips, DB........74
Marvin Powell, OT.......75, 76
Ricky Bell, TB...+*75, +*76
Gary Jeter, DT...........*76
Dennis Thurman, DB...*76, +*77
Pat Howell, G..........+*78
Charles White, TB...+*78, +*79
Brad Budde, OG.......+*79
Dennis Johnson, LB.........79
Roy Foster, OG......80, *81
Keith Van Horne, OT....*80
Ronnie Lott, DB.......+*80
Marcus Allen, RB......+*81
Chip Banks, LB.............81
Don Mosebar, OT......+*82
Bruce Matthews, OG....*82
George Achica, MG.....*82
Tony Slaton, C...........*83
Jack Del Rio, LB.........*84
Duane Bickett, LB..........84
Jeff Bregel, OG.....*85, *86
Tim McDonald, DB......*86
Dave Cadigan, OT.......*87
Erik Affholter, SE............88
Tim Ryan, DT..............88
Rodney Peete, QB..........88
Mark Carrier, DB...88, +*89
Tim Ryan, DT...........*89

SOUTHERN METHODIST

Marion Hammon, T.........29
Clyde Carter, T..............34
J. C. Wetsel, G..........*35
Bobby Wilson, HB...34, *35
Truman Spain, T............35
Doak Walker, HB......*47, +*48, *49
Kyle Rote, HB............*50
Dick Hightower, C......*51
Don Meredith, QB........58, 59
John LaGrone, MG......*66
Jerry LeVias, FL.........*68
Robert Popelka, DB.....*72
Louie Kelcher, MG......*74
Emanuel Tolbert, WR...*78
John Simmons, DB......*80
Harvey Armstrong, DT......81
Eric Dickerson, TB.....+*82
Russell Carter, DB.....+*83
Reggie Dupard, TB......*85

SOUTHERN MISSISSIPPI

Ray Guy, P..................72

SOUTHWESTERN (Texas)

Harold Fischer, G...........43

STANFORD

Jim Lawson, E..........*24
Ernie Nevers, FB........*25
Ted Shipkey, B..............26
Seraphim Post, G......*28
Don Robesky, G........*28
Phil Moffatt, HB............30
Bill Corbus, G......*32, *33
Bob Reynolds, T........*34
Bobby Grayson, B..*34, *35
Monk Moscrip, E....34, *35
Bones Hamilton, HB........34
Hugh Gallarneau, HB.......40
Frank Albert, QB...*40, *41
Chuck Taylor, G........*42
Ken Rose, E.................49
Bill McColl, E......*50, *51
Gary Kerkorian, QB..........51
Sam Morley, E..............53
Bob Garrett, QB............53
Paul Wiggin, T..........55, 56
John Brodie, B..........*56
Chris Burford, E.............59
Don Parish, LB..............69
Jim Plunkett, QB.......*70
Jeff Siemon, LB..........*71
Pat Donovan, T.....73, *74
Roger Stillwell, DL...........73
Duncan McColl, DE.........76
Guy Benjamin, QB......*77
Ken Margerum, FL....*79, +*80
John Elway, QB........+*82
Brad Muster, RB........*86

SYRACUSE

Frank Horr, T...........*08
Harold White, G........*15
Christopher Schlachter, G...15
Alfred Cobb, T..........*17
Lou Usher, T.............*18
Joe Alexander, G....*18, *19
C............20
Bertrand Gulick, T..........20
Pete McRae, E..........*23
Vic Hanson, E...........*26
James Steen, T..............34
Bob Fleck, G............52, 53
Jim Brown, HB.........+*56
Ron Luciano, T.............58
Robert Yates, T.............59
Roger Davis, G.........+*59
Fred Mautino, E.............59
Ernie Davis, HB...*60, +*61
Pat Killorin, C...............64

Floyd Little, HB......64, 65, 66
Gary Bugenhagen, T........66
Larry Csonka, FB...66, +***67**
Joe Ehrmann, DT...........70
Tom Myers, DB.............71
Ray Preston, LB............75
Art Monk, WR..............79
Gary Anderson, PK.........81
Mike Charles, DT...........82
Tim Green, DT........+***85**
Don McPherson, QB...+***87**
Ted Gregory, MG.......***87**
Markus Paul, DB............88

TEMPLE

Bill Singletary, OG...........72
Steve Joachim, QB..........74
John Rienstra, OL......***85**
Paul Palmer, RB........+***86**

TENNESSEE

Gene McEver, B.........***29**
Bobby Dodd, B.............30
Herman Hickman, G........31
Beattie Feathers, HB....***33**
Bowden Wyatt, E........***38**
Bob Suffridge, G......38, 39,
+***40**
Ed Molinski, G......***39**, 40
George Cafego, HB..38, ***39**
Dick Huffman, T........***46**
Bud Sherrod, E.............50
Ted Daffer, G............50, 51
Bill Pearman, T..............51
Hank Lauricella, HB...+***51**
John Michels, G..........**52**
Doug Atkins, T..............52
Darris McCord, T............54
John Majors, HB........+***56**
Buddy Cruze, E.............56
Bill Johnson, G..............57
Steve DeLong, G........63, 64
Frank Emmanuel, LB...***65**
Paul Naumoff, LB.......***66**
Austin Denney, E............66
Al Dorsey, B.................67
Bob Johnson, C........+***67**
**Charles Rosenfelder,
OG**......+***68**
Steve Kiner, LB....***68**, +***69**
Jim Weatherford, DB........68
Chip Kell, OG.....***69**, +***70**
Bobby Majors, DB......+***71**
Jackie Walker, LB........70, 71
Jamie Rotella, LB.............72
Conrad Graham, DB........72
Ricky Townsend, K......72, 73
Larry Seivers, WR......***75**,
*76
Roland James, DB.......***79**

Willie Gault, KRB (WR).....82
Jimmy Colquitt, P...........83
Reggie White, DT......+***83**
Bill Mayo, OG...........***84**
Tim McGee, WR.......***85**
Keith DeLong, LB...........88
Eric Still, OG...........+***89**

TENNESSEE STATE

Ed Jones, DL................73

TENNESSEE TECH

Jim Youngblood, LB.........72

TEXAS

Malcolm Kutner, E..........41
Chal Daniel, G..............41
Joe Parker, E................41
Hubert Bechtol, E...44, ***45**,
*46
Bobby Layne, QB........***47**
Dick Harris, T...............47
Randall Clay, B.............49
Bud McFadin, G....49, +***50**
Don Menasco, E............50
Bobby Dillon, DB...........51
Tom Stolhandske, E.........52
Harley Sewell, G............52
Carlton Massey, E.......***53**
Herb Gray, T................55
Maurice Doke, G...........59
Jimmy Saxton HB......+***61**
Don Talbert, T..............61
Johnny Treadwell, G...+***62**
Scott Appleton, T.......+***63**
Tommy Ford, B.............63
Tommy Nobis, OG-LB....64,
*65
Corby Robertson, E.........67
Loyd Wainscott, OT........68
Chris Gilbert, HB.......***68**
Bob McKay, OT..........***69**
Charles Speyrer, E..........69
Bobby Wuensch, OT.....69,
*70
Glen Halsell, LB.............69
Steve Worster, FB....69, ***70**
Bill Atessis, DE...........***70**
Scott Henderson, LB........70
Jerry Sisemore, OT....+***71**,
+***72**
Bill Wyman, C...........***73**
Roosevelt Leaks, FB.....***73**
Bob Simmons, OT....74, ***75**
Doug English, DT...........74

Marty Akins, QB............75
Earl Campbell, RB......75,
+***77**
Russell Erxleben, PK-P.....76,
77, 78
Brad Shearer, DT.......+***77**
Johnnie Johnson, DB..+***78**,
+***79**
Steve McMichael, DT..+***79**
Kenneth Sims, DT......***80**,
+***81**
Terry Tausch, OT........***81**
Doug Dawson, OG......***83**
Jeff Leiding, LB.........***83**
Jerry Gray, DB....***83**, +***84**
Mossy Cade, DB............83
Tony Degrate, DT.......***84**
Gene Chilton, C.............85
Jeff Ward, PK...............86
Britt Hager, LB..............88

TEXAS A&I

Johnny Bailey, RB...........89

TEXAS A&M

Joe Routt, G..........36, ***37**
John Kimbrough, FB...***39**,
+***40**
Joe Boyd, T.................39
Marshall Robnett, G....***40**
Bob Smith, FB..............50
Jack Little, T................51
Charles Krueger, T......56, 57
John David Crow, HB..+***57**
Jack Pardee, FB.............56
Maurice Moorman, OT......66
Bill Hobbs, LB...........67, 68
Dave Elmendorf, DB....***70**
Pat Thomas, DB....***74**, ***75**
Ed Simonini, LB.........***75**
Tony Franklin, PK..***76**, 78
Robert Jackson, LB.....+***76**
Jacob Green, DE............79
Ray Childress, DE..........84
Johnny Holland, LB....***85**
John Roper, LB.........***87**
Darren Lewis, RB...........88

TEXAS CHRISTIAN

Rags Matthews, E...........27
John Vaught, G..............32
Darrell Lester, C....34, ***35**,
36
Sammy Baugh, QB...35, ***36**
J.B. Hale, T.............37, 38
Ki Aldrich, C............***38**

Davey O'Brien, QB.....+*38
Derrell Palmer, T............42
Clyde Flowers, T.............44
Lindy Berry, QB..............49
Doug Conaway, T............51
Keith Flowers, C.............51
Jim Swink, HB......+*55, 56
Hugh Pitts, C................55
Norman Hamilton, T........56
Don Floyd, T.........58, *59
Jack Spikes, FB..............59
Bob Lilly, T.............+*60
Tommy Crutcher, FB........63
Stanley Washington, SE.....81
Kenneth Davis, RB.....+*84

TEXAS TECH

E. J. Holub, C........59, *60
David Parks, E..............63
Donny Anderson, B..64, *65
Phil Tucker, OG..............67
Dick Campbell, DE..........69
Denton Fox, DB..............69
Andre Tillman, TE...........73
Thomas Howard, LB........76
Dan Irons, OT...........*77
**Gabriel Rivera,
               MG-DT**....*82
Tyrone Thurman,
            KRT (WB)...88

TOLEDO

Tom Beutler, MG.............67
Curtis Johnson, DB..........69
Mel Long, DT........70, *71
Gene Swick, QB..............75

TULANE

Charles Flourney, B.........25
Willis Banker, B..............29
Jerry Dalrymple, E......30,
                      +*31
Don Zimmerman, B......31,
                       *32
Harley McCollum, T....*39
Ernie Blandin, T........*41
Paul Lea, T...................48
Eddie Price, FB..............49
Jerome Helluin, G...........50
Tony Sardisco, G............55
Charles Hall, DT.............73
Marc Zeno, WR..............87

TULSA

Glenn Dobbs, HB............42
Felto Prewitt, C..............44

Ellis Jones, G................44
Marv Matuszak, T......51, 52
Jerry Rhome, QB............64
Howard Twilley, SE....+*65
Drane Scrivener, DB........72

UCLA

Kenny Washington, HB......39
Al Sparlis, G.................45
Burr Baldwin..........+*46
Donn Moomaw, C....50, *52
Paul Cameron, TB...52, *53
Jack Ellena, T...........*54
Jim Salisbury, G..............54
Bob Davenport, FB......54, 55
Hardiman Cureton, G...*55
Rommie Loudd, E...........55
James Brown, G..............55
Dick Wallen, E..........*57
Bill Kilmer, HB...............60
Ron Hull, C...................61
John Richardson, G.........66
Mel Farr, HB.............*66
Gary Beban, QB.......+*67
Don Manning, LB.......*67
Larry Slagle, DT..............67
Floyd Reese, E................69
Mike Ballou, LB.........*69
Al Oliver, OT..................73
Jimmy Allen, DB..............73
Kermit Johnson, RB.....*73
John Sciarra, QB........*75
Randy Cross, OG............75
Oscar Edwards, DB.........76
Jerry Robinson, LB.....*76,
                 +*77, +*78
Kenny Easley, DB......*78,
                 +*79, +*80
Freeman McNeil, TB........80
Tim Wrightman, TE...+*81
Don Rogers, DB.........*83
John Lee, PK........84, +*85
Gaston Green, TB............87
Ken Norton, LB...............87
Carnell Lake, LB..............88
Darryl Henley, DB.......*88
Troy Aikman, QB........*88

UTAH

Earl Pomeroy, FB............29
Frank Christensen, FB......32
Lee Grosscup, QB............57
Roy Jefferson, SE............64
Marv Bateman, P............70
Steve Odom, KRB (FL)......73
Steve Clark, DT..............81
Carlton Walker, OG.........84
Erroll Tucker, KRB (DB)......85

UTAH STATE

Elmer Ward, C...............34
Kent Ryan, B.................36
Merlin Olsen, T......60, *61
Bill Staley, T..................67
Phil Olsen, DE..........*69

UTEP

Fred Carr, B..................67
Chris Jacke, PK..............88

VANDERBILT

Lynn Bomar, E..........*23
Henry Wakefield, E......23,
                        *24
Bill Spears, QB...............27
John Brown, G................29
Pete Gracey, C..........*32
Carl Hinkle, C.................37
Bucky Curtis, E...............50
George Deiderich, G....*58
Chip Healy, LB...............68
Bob Asher, OT................69
Jim Arnold, P..........+*82
Ricky Anderson, P.....+*84
Chris Gaines, LB..............87

VILLANOVA

Ed Michaels, G...............35
John Wysocki, E.........37, 38
Nick Liotta, G................51
Gene Filipski, HB............52
Al Atkinson, E................64

VIRGINIA

Eugene Mayer, HB......*15
Bill Dudley, HB.........*41
Joe Palumbo, MG............51
Tom Scott, DE................52
Jim Bakhtiar, FB.............57
Jim Dombrowski, OT..+*85
Ray Savage, DE..............89

VIRGINIA TECH

Carroll Dale, SE..............59
Bob Schweickert, QB........64
Frank Loria, DB......66, *67
Mike Widger, LB.............68
Bruce Smith, DT.....83, *84

WAKE FOREST
Bill Barnes, FB.............56
Win Headley, DT...........70
Chuck Ramsey, K..........73
Bill Armstrong, DB....+*76
Paul Kiser, OG.............86

WASHINGTON
George Wilson, HB.....*25
Charles Carroll, HB.....*28
Merle Hufford, HB..........29
Paul Schwegler, T...........31
Dave Nisbet, E..............32
Bill Smith, E.................33
Max Starcevich, G.....*36
Jim Cain, HB.................36
Vic Markov, T..............37
Rudy Mucha, C........*40
Jay MacDowell, E...........40
Ray Frankowski, G..40, *41
Don Heinrich, QB........50, 52
Richard Sprague, DB......50
Hugh McElhenny, FB......51
Milt Bohart, G...............53
Bob Schloredt, QB.........59
Roy McKasson, C..........60
Rick Redman, G-LB....*63,
*64
Tom Greenlee, DE......*66
Al Worley, DB...........*68
Calvin Jones, DB............72
Mark Stewart, LB...........82
Chuck Nelson, PK.....+*82
Ron Holmes, DT.........*84
Jeff Jaeger, PK.........*86
Reggie Rogers, DT.....*86

WASHINGTON & JEFFERSON
John Spiegel, B..........*14
M. M. Witherspoon, T.......15
Wilbur Henry, T.....17, *18,
*19
Russell Stein, T..............21
Forrest Douds, G...........28

WASHINGTON STATE
A. G. Edwards, T.............30
Mel Hein, C.................30
Ed Goddard, QB.....34, 35, 36
Bob Kennedy, B............42
Lauri Niemi, T...............48
Bill Steiger, E................56
Clarence Williams, DB......64
Wayne Foster, T............65
Geoff Reece, C.............74

Dan Lynch, OG.............84
Rueben Mayes, RB.....*84
Mark Utley, OL.........*88
Jason Hanson, PK.....+*89

WEST VIRGINIA
Russell Bailey, C............17
Ira Rodgers, FB.........*19
Bob Orders, C...............53
Sam Huff, T.................55
Bruce Bosley, T.........*55
Jim Braxton, TE..............70
Danny Buggs, WR..........73
Darryl Talley, LB......+*82
Rob Bennett, TE............84
Brian Jozwiak, OT......*85
Major Harris, QB............89

WILLIAM & MARY
Gerrard Ramsey, G.........42
Jack Cloud, HB.............48

WILLIAMS
Ben Boynton. B.....*17, *19,
20

WISCONSIN
Robert Butler, T.........*12
Ray Keeler, G...........*13
Arlie Mucks, G..............14
Howard Buck, T.........*15
Charles Carpenter, C...*19
Ralph Scott, T...........*20
Frank Weston, E............20
Marty Below, T.........*23
Milo Lubratovich, T.....*30
Howard Weiss, FB..........38
Dave Schreiner, E......41,
+*42
Pat Harder, FB..............42
Earl Girard, QB..............44
Ed Withers, DB.............50
Pat O'Donahue, E...........51
Hal Faverty, G-LB...........51
Don Voss, E.................52
David Suminski, OT.........52
Alan Ameche, FB...53, +*54
Dan Lanphear, T.......+*59
Pat Richter, E.......61, *62
Dennis Lick, OT........*75
Tim Krumrie, MG......*81
Matt Vanden Boom, DB.....81
Richard Johnson, DB........84

WYOMING
Eddie Talboom, HB.........50
Dewey McConnell, E........51
Jim Crawford, HB...........56
Mike Dirks, T................67
Bob Jacobs, K...............69
Dennis Baker, OT...........77
Ken Fantetti, LB.............78
Jack Weil, P.............*83
Jay Novacek, TE........*84

XAVIER (Ohio)
John Shinners, OG..........68

YALE
Amos Alonzo Stagg, E...*89
Charles Gill, T..........*89
Pudge Heffelfinger, G..*89,
*90, *91
Thomas McClung,
HB...*90, *91
William Rhodes, T......*90
John Hartwell, E.........*91
Frank Hinkey, E...*91, *92,
*93, *94
Wallace Winter, T.......*91
A. Hamilton Wallis, T...*92
Vance McCormick,
QB........*92
William Hickok, G.....*93,
*94
Frank Butterworth,
FB....*93, *94
Philip Stillman, C........*94
George Adee, QB........*94
Fred Murphy, T....*95, *96
Samuel Thorne, HB......*95
Clarence Fincke, QB....*96
John Hall, E..............*97
Burr Chamberlin, T....*97,
*98
Gordon Brown, G......*97,
*98, *99, *00
Charles DeSaulles, B...*97
Malcolm McBride, B..*98,
*99
George Stillman, T.....*99,
*00
Albert Sharpe, HB......*99
James Bloomer, T........*00
G........*03
Herman Olcott, G........*00
George Chadwick,
HB...*00, *02
Perry Hale, FB...........*00
William Fincke, QB......*00
Henry Holt, C.......*01, *02
Thomas Shevlin, E......*02,
*04, *05

Ralph Kinney, T.........*02
G........*04
James Hogan, T....*02, *03,
*04
Edgar Glass, G.........*02
Foster Rockwell, QB...*02,
*04
Charles Rafferty, E......*03
Ledyard Mitchell, HB...*03
Roswell Tripp, G........*05
Howard Roome, HB.....*05
Guy Hutchinson, QB....*05
Robert Forbes, E........*06
Horatio Biglow, T.......*06,
*07
Hugh Knox, HB..........*06
Paul Veeder, FB.........*06
Clarence Alcott, E.......*07
Thomas A. D. Jones,
QB........*07
Edward Coy, FB...*07, *08,
*09
William Goebel, G......*08
Hamlin Andrus, G......*08,
*09
John Kilpatrick, E......*09,
*10
Henry Hobbs, T.........*09
Carroll Cooney, C.......*09
Stephen Philbin, HB.....*09
Douglass Bomeisler,
E.....*11, *12
Henry Ketcham, C......*11,
*12
Arthur Howe, QB........*11
Nelson Talbott, T........*13
Harry LeGore, HB.......*14
Clinton Black, G........*16
George Moseley, E..........16
Charles Comerford, E.......16
Tim Callahan, G........*20
Malcolm Aldrich, HB...*21
Century Milstead, T....*23
William Mallory, FB....*23
Dick Luman, E..........*24
Winslow Lovejoy, C.........24
Raymond Pond, HB.........24
John Joss, T.................25
Herbert Sturhahn, G.....25, 26
Sidney Quarrier, T..........27
Bill Webster, G..........*27
John Charlesworth, C...*27
Frederick Linehan, G.......30
Clint Frank, HB.....36, +*37
Larry Kelley, E..........*36
Spencer Moseley, C........42
Paul Walker, E..........*44
Ben Balme, G...............60
Dick Jauron, HB.............72
Rich Diana, HB..............81

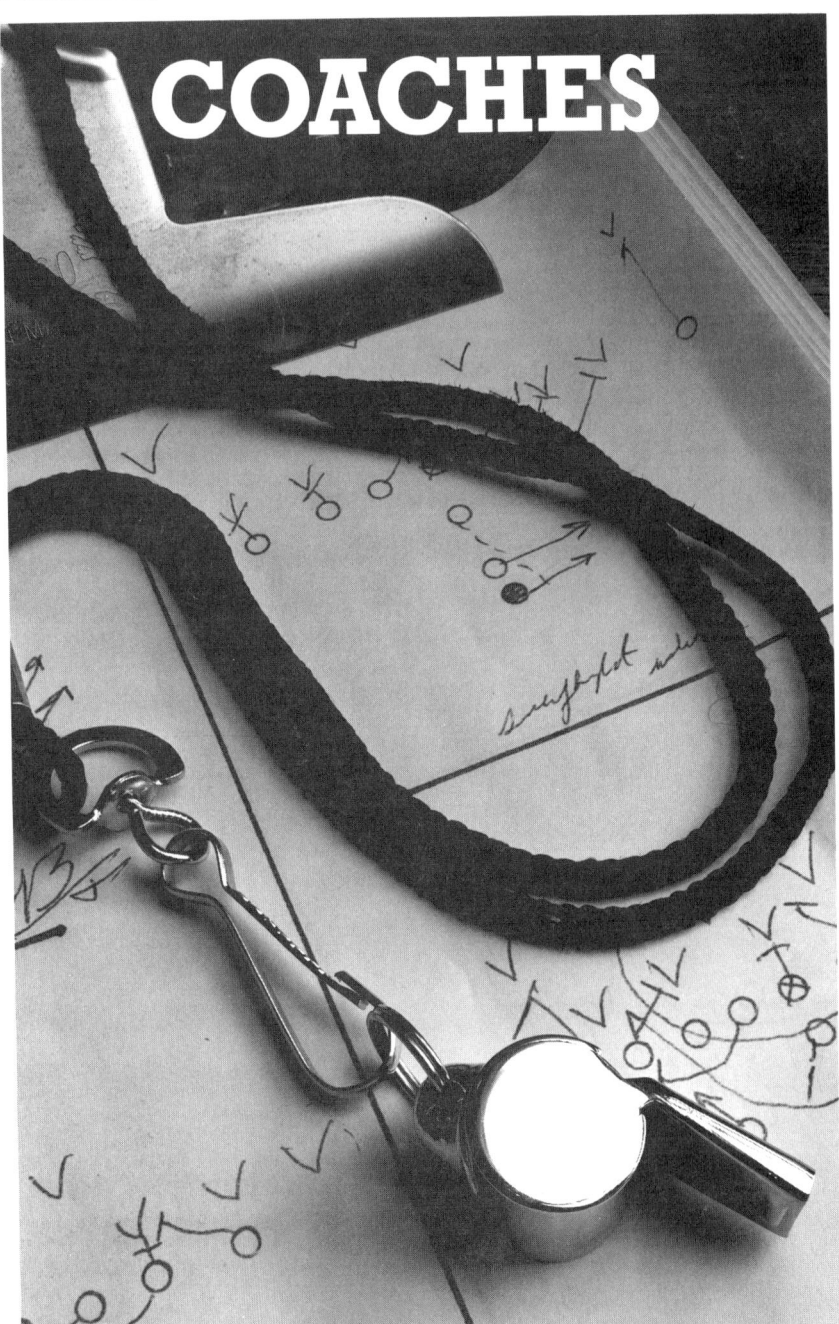

COACHES' SECTION

The year-by-year records in these pages include all 63 coaches with at least 10 head-coaching seasons at the major-college, or Division I-A, level who won at least 70 percent of their games, or won 200 games, or both.

Space limitations prevent the inclusion of many other great coaches who won at least 80 percent at the four-year level over at least 10 years but head-coached less than 10 seasons in I-A, such as Sid Gillman, Jake Gaither, Don Coryell, Doyt Perry, Dave Maurer and Bob Reade. Also excluded at the same high level—200 and over .700—are Eddie Robinson, 358 victories (first all-time) and .734; Roy Kidd, 208 and .724; John Gagliardi, 268 and .743; Ron Schipper, 224 and .794; the late John Merritt, 232 and .771; Darrell Mudra, 200 and .709; and others (see NCAA Football).

In the early years before team classification, the decision on major teams was made by researcher Steve Boda (see Foreword). At various times, the Haskell and Carlisle Indians, Centre College, Washington & Jefferson, Lafayette and many others now in other divisions or without football played major schedules in certain seasons.

In addition, early-day teams played many exhibition or practice games and some high school opponents. It was Boda's research, for instance, that established Amos Alonzo Stagg as No. 1 at 314 and Glenn "Pop" Warner next at 313, long after their retirement (and before Bryant and Robinson, of course).

Each coach's complete bowl record, game by game, is footnoted, along with his national championship teams (starting in 1883; see Foreword for details).

Listed at the top are his alma mater and year, birthplace, date of birth and/or death, inclusion in the Hall of Fame (those who made it as a player are noted) and years voted Coach of the Year by his peers in the American Football Coaches Association. Active coaches are footnoted.

James M. Van Valkenburg

The 63 coaches with at least 10 years as a Division I head coach and with a career winning percentage of at least .700 or at least 200 career victories:

EDDIE ANDERSON
(Notre Dame '22)
B 11-13-00 Mason City, Iowa
D 4-26-74
Hall of Fame
Coach of Year 39

Yr.	Team	W-L-T
22	Loras	7-0-0
23	Loras	4-4-1
24	Loras	5-2-1
25	DePaul	5-1-1
26	DePaul	3-3-0
27	DePaul	1-5-1
28	DePaul	1-4-1
29	DePaul	2-4-0
30	DePaul	3-2-0
31	DePaul	6-3-0
33	Holy Cross	7-2-0
34	Holy Cross	8-2-0
35	Holy Cross	9-0-1
36	Holy Cross	7-2-1
37	Holy Cross	8-0-2
38	Holy Cross	8-1-0
39	Iowa	6-1-1
40	Iowa	4-4-0
41	Iowa	3-5-0
42	Iowa	6-4-0
46	Iowa	5-4-0
47	Iowa	3-5-1
48	Iowa	4-5-0
49	Iowa	4-5-0
50	Holy Cross	4-5-1
51	Holy Cross	8-2-0
52	Holy Cross	8-2-0
53	Holy Cross	5-5-0
54	Holy Cross	3-7-0
55	Holy Cross	6-4-0
56	Holy Cross	5-3-1
57	Holy Cross	5-3-1
58	Holy Cross	6-3-0
59	Holy Cross	6-4-0
60	Holy Cross	6-4-0
61	Holy Cross	7-3-0
62	Holy Cross	6-4-0
63	Holy Cross	2-6-1
64	Holy Cross	5-5-0

39 yrs. .606 201-128-15

IKE ARMSTRONG
(Drake '23)
B 6-8-95 Seymour, Iowa
D 9-4-83
Hall of Fame

Yr.	Team	W-L-T	B
25	Utah	6-2-0	
26	Utah	7-0-0	
27	Utah	3-3-1	
28	Utah	5-0-2	
29	Utah	7-0-0	
30	Utah	8-0-0	
31	Utah	7-2-0	
32	Utah	5-1-1	
33	Utah	5-3-0	
34	Utah	5-3-0	
35	Utah	4-3-1	
36	Utah	6-3-0	
37	Utah	5-3-0	
38	Utah	7-1-2	1
39	Utah	6-1-2	
40	Utah	7-2-0	
41	Utah	6-0-2	
42	Utah	6-3-0	
43	Utah	0-7-0	
44	Utah	5-2-1	
45	Utah	4-4-0	
46	Utah	8-3-0	
47	Utah	8-1-1	
48	Utah	8-1-1	
49	Utah	2-7-1	

25 yrs. .702 140-55-15

Bowl game included above:
1 New Mexico 26-0 Sun W

Bowls W-L-T: 1-0-0

DANA X. BIBLE
(Carson-Newman '12)
B 10-8-91 Jefferson City, Tenn.
D 1-19-80
Hall of Fame

Yr.	Team	W-L-T	B
13	Miss. College	5-2-0	
14	Miss. College	4-2-1	
15	Miss. College	3-3-1	
16	Louisiana St.	1-0-2	
17	Texas A&M	8-0-0	
19	Texas A&M	10-0-0	
20	Texas A&M	6-1-1	
21	Texas A&M	6-1-2	1
22	Texas A&M	5-4-0	
23	Texas A&M	5-3-1	
24	Texas A&M	7-2-1	
25	Texas A&M	7-1-1	
26	Texas A&M	5-3-1	
27	Texas A&M	8-0-1	
28	Texas A&M	5-4-1	
29	Nebraska	4-1-3	
30	Nebraska	4-3-2	
31	Nebraska	8-2-0	
32	Nebraska	7-1-1	
33	Nebraska	8-1-0	
34	Nebraska	6-3-0	
35	Nebraska	6-2-1	
36	Nebraska	7-2-0	
37	Texas	2-6-1	
38	Texas	1-8-0	
39	Texas	5-4-0	
40	Texas	8-2-0	
41	Texas	8-1-1	
42	Texas	9-2-0	2
43	Texas	7-1-1	3
44	Texas	5-4-0	
45	Texas	10-1-0	4
46	Texas	8-2-0	

33 yrs. .715 198-72-23

Bowl games included above:
1 Centre 22-14 Dixie Classic W
2 Georgia Tech 14-7 Cotton W
3 Randolph Field 7-7 Cotton T
4 Missouri 40-27 Cotton W

Bowls W-L-T: 3-0-1

EARL "RED" BLAIK
(Miami [Ohio] '18, Army '20)
B 2-17-97 Detroit, Mich.
D 5-6-89
Hall of Fame
Coach of Year 46

Yr.	Team	W-L-T
34	Dartmouth	6-3-0
35	Dartmouth	8-2-0
36	Dartmouth	7-1-1
37	Dartmouth	7-0-2
38	Dartmouth	7-2-0
39	Dartmouth	5-3-1
40	Dartmouth	5-4-0
41	Army	5-3-1
42	Army	6-3-0
43	Army	7-2-1
44*	Army	9-0-0
45*	Army	9-0-0
46	Army	9-0-1
47	Army	5-2-2
48	Army	8-0-1
49	Army	9-0-0
50	Army	8-1-0
51	Army	2-7-0
52	Army	4-4-1
53	Army	7-1-1
54	Army	7-2-0
55	Army	6-3-0
56	Army	5-3-1
57	Army	7-2-0
58	Army	8-0-1

25 yrs. .759 166-48-14

* National Champions

BOBBY BOWDEN
(Samford '53)
B 11-8-29 Birmingham, Ala.

Yr.	Team	W-L-T	B
59	Samford	9-1-0	
60	Samford	8-1-0	
61	Samford	7-2-0	
62	Samford	7-2-0	
70	West Va.	8-3-0	
71	West Va.	7-4-0	
72	West Va.	8-4-0	1
73	West Va.	6-5-0	
74	West Va.	4-7-0	
75	West Va.	9-3-0	2
76	Florida St.	5-6-0	
77	Florida St.	10-2-0	3
78	Florida St.	8-3-0	
79	Florida St.	11-1-0	4
80	Florida St.	10-2-0	5
81	Florida St.	6-5-0	
82	Florida St.	9-3-0	6
83@	Florida St.	8-4-0	7
84	Florida St.	7-3-2	8
85	Florida St.	9-3-0	9
86	Florida St.	7-4-1	10
87	Florida St.	11-1-0	11
88	Florida St.	11-1-0	12
89	Florida St.	10-2-0	13

24 yrs. .728   195-72-3

Bowl games included above:
1 North Caro. St. 13-49 Peach L
2 North Caro. St. 13-10 Peach W
3 Texas Tech 40-17 Tangerine W
4 Oklahoma 7-24 Orange L
5 Oklahoma 17-18 Orange L
6 West Va. 31-12 Gator W
7 North Caro. 28-3 Peach W
8 Georgia 17-17 Florida Citrus T
9 Oklahoma St. 34-23 Gator W
10 Indiana 27-13 All-American W
11 Nebraska 31-28 Fiesta W
12 Auburn 13-7 Sugar W
13 Nebraska 41-17 Fiesta W

Bowls W-L-T: 9-3-1

@ One victory over Tulane included, by action of NCAA Council under Section 10. (Active coach in 1989)

FRANK BROYLES
(Georgia Tech '47)
B 12-26-24 Decatur, Ga.
Hall of Fame
Co-Coach of Year 64

Yr.	Team	W-L-T	B
57	Missouri	5-4-1	
58	Arkansas	4-6-0	
59	Arkansas	9-2-0	1
60	Arkansas	8-3-0	2
61	Arkansas	8-3-0	3
62	Arkansas	9-2-0	4
63	Arkansas	5-5-0	
64*	Arkansas	11-0-0	5
65	Arkansas	10-1-0	6
66	Arkansas	8-2-0	
67	Arkansas	4-5-1	
68	Arkansas	10-1-0	7
69	Arkansas	9-2-0	8
70	Arkansas	9-2-0	
71	Arkansas	8-3-1	9
72	Arkansas	6-5-0	
73	Arkansas	5-5-1	
74	Arkansas	6-4-1	
75	Arkansas	10-2-0	10
76	Arkansas	5-5-1	

20 yrs. .700   149-62-6

* National Champions

Bowl games included above:
1 Georgia Tech 14-7 Gator W
2 Duke 6-7 Cotton L
3 Alabama 3-10 Sugar L
4 Mississippi 13-17 Sugar L
5 Nebraska 10-7 Cotton W
6 Louisiana St. 7-14 Cotton L
7 Georgia 16-2 Sugar W
8 Mississippi 22-27 Sugar L
9 Tennessee 13-14 Liberty L
10 Georgia 31-10 Cotton W

Bowls W-L-T: 4-6-0

PAUL "BEAR" BRYANT
(Alabama '36)
B 9-11-13 Moro Bottoms, Ark.
D 1-26-83
Hall of Fame
Coach of Year 61, 71, 73

Yr.	Team	W-L-T	B
45	Maryland	6-2-1	
46	Kentucky	7-3-0	
47	Kentucky	8-3-0	1
48	Kentucky	5-3-2	
49	Kentucky	9-3-0	2
50	Kentucky	11-1-0	3
51	Kentucky	8-4-0	4
52	Kentucky	5-4-2	
53	Kentucky	7-2-1	
54	Texas A&M	1-9-0	
55	Texas A&M	7-2-1	
56	Texas A&M	9-0-1	
57	Texas A&M	8-3-0	5
58	Alabama	5-4-1	
59	Alabama	7-2-2	6
60	Alabama	8-1-2	7
61*	Alabama	11-0-0	8
62	Alabama	10-1-0	9
63	Alabama	9-2-0	10
64*	Alabama	10-1-0	11
65*	Alabama	9-1-1	12
66	Alabama	11-0-0	13
67	Alabama	8-2-1	14
68	Alabama	8-3-0	15
69	Alabama	6-5-0	16
70	Alabama	6-5-1	17
71	Alabama	11-1-0	18
72	Alabama	10-2-0	19
73*	Alabama	11-1-0	20
74	Alabama	11-1-0	21
75	Alabama	11-1-0	22
76	Alabama	9-3-0	23
77	Alabama	11-1-0	24
78*	Alabama	11-1-0	25
79*	Alabama	12-0-0	26
80	Alabama	10-2-0	27
81	Alabama	9-2-1	28
82	Alabama	8-4-0	29

38 yrs. .780   323-85-17

* National Champions.

Bowl games included above:
1 Villanova 24-14
2 Santa Clara 13-21   Great Lakes W
3 Oklahoma 13-7   Orange L
4 Texas Christian 10-7   Sugar W
5 Tennessee 0-3   Cotton W
6 Penn St. 0-7   Gator L
7 Texas 3-3   Liberty L
8 Arkansas 10-3   Bluebonnet T
9 Oklahoma 17-0   Sugar W
10 Mississippi 12-7   Orange W
11 Texas 17-21   Sugar W
12 Nebraska 39-28   Orange L
13 Nebraska 34-7   Orange W
14 Texas A&M 16-20   Sugar W
15 Missouri 10-35   Cotton L
16 Colorado 33-47   Gator L
17 Oklahoma 24-24   Liberty L
18 Nebraska 6-38   Bluebonnet T
19 Texas 13-17   Orange L
20 Notre Dame 23-24   Cotton L
21 Notre Dame 11-13   Sugar L
22 Penn St. 13-6   Orange L
23 UCLA 36-6   Sugar W
24 Ohio St. 35-6   Liberty W
25 Penn St. 14-7   Sugar W
26 Arkansas 24-9   Sugar W
27 Baylor 30-2   Sugar W
28 Texas 12-14   Cotton W
29 Illinois 21-15   Cotton L
                          Liberty W

Bowls W-L-T: 15-12-2

FRANK CAVANAUGH
(Dartmouth '97)
B 4-28-76 Worcester, Mass.
D 8-29-33
Hall of Fame

Yr.	Team	W-L-T
98	Cincinnati	5-1-3
03	Holy Cross	8-2-0
04	Holy Cross	2-5-2
05	Holy Cross	6-3-0
11	Dartmouth	8-2-0
12	Dartmouth	7-2-0
13	Dartmouth	7-1-0
14	Dartmouth	8-1-0
15	Dartmouth	7-1-1
16	Dartmouth	5-2-2
19	Boston College	5-3-0
20	Boston College	8-0-0
21	Boston College	4-3-1
22	Boston College	6-2-1
23	Boston College	7-1-1
24	Boston College	6-3-0
25	Boston College	6-2-0
26	Boston College	6-0-2
27	Fordham	3-5-0
28	Fordham	4-5-0
29	Fordham	7-0-2
30	Fordham	8-1-0
31	Fordham	6-1-2
32	Fordham	6-2-0

24 yrs. .731   145-48-17

HERBERT "FRITZ" CRISLER
(Chicago '22)
B 1-12-99 Earlville, Ill.
D 8-19-82
Hall of Fame
Coach of Year 47

Yr.	Team	W-L-T	B
30	Minnesota	3-4-1	
31	Minnesota	7-3-0	
32	Princeton	2-2-3	
33	Princeton	9-0-0	
34	Princeton	7-1-0	
35	Princeton	9-0-0	
36	Princeton	4-2-2	
37	Princeton	4-4-0	
38	Michigan	6-1-1	
39	Michigan	6-2-0	
40	Michigan	7-1-0	
41	Michigan	6-1-1	
42	Michigan	7-3-0	
43	Michigan	8-1-0	
44	Michigan	8-2-0	
45	Michigan	7-3-0	
46	Michigan	6-2-1	
47	Michigan	10-0-0	1

18 yrs. .768   116-32-9

Bowl game included above:
1 Southern Cal 49-0   Rose W

Bowls W-L-T: 1-0-0

JIMMY CROWLEY
(Notre Dame '25)
B 9-10-02 Chicago, Ill.
D 1-15-86
Hall of Fame (as a player)

Yr.	Team	W-L-T	B
29	Michigan St.	5-3-0	
30	Michigan St.	5-1-2	
31	Michigan St.	5-3-1	
32	Michigan St.	7-1-0	
33	Fordham	6-2-0	
34	Fordham	5-3-0	
35	Fordham	6-1-2	
36	Fordham	5-1-2	
37	Fordham	7-0-1	
38	Fordham	6-1-2	
39	Fordham	6-2-0	
40	Fordham	7-2-0	1
41	Fordham	8-1-0	2

13 yrs. .761   78-21-10

Bowl games included above:
1 Texas A&M 12-13   Cotton L
2 Missouri 2-0   Sugar W

Bowls W-L-T: 1-1-0

BOB DEVANEY
(Alma '39)
B 4-13-15 Saginaw, Mich.
Hall of Fame
Coach of Year 71

Yr.	Team	W-L-T	B
57	Wyoming	4-3-3	
58	Wyoming	8-3-0	1
59	Wyoming	9-1-0	
60	Wyoming	8-2-0	
61	Wyoming	6-1-2	
62	Nebraska	9-2-0	2
63	Nebraska	10-1-0	3
64	Nebraska	9-2-0	4
65	Nebraska	10-1-0	5
66	Nebraska	9-2-0	6
67	Nebraska	6-4-0	
68	Nebraska	6-4-0	
69	Nebraska	9-2-0	7
70*	Nebraska	11-0-1	8
71*	Nebraska	13-0-0	9
72	Nebraska	9-2-1	10

16 yrs. .806   136-30-7

* National Champions

Bowl games included above:
1 Hardin-Simmons 14-6   Sun W
2 Miami (Fla.) 36-34   Gotham W
3 Auburn 13-7   Orange W
4 Arkansas 7-10   Cotton L
5 Alabama 28-39   Orange L
6 Alabama 7-34   Sugar L
7 Georgia 45-6   Sun W
8 Louisiana St. 17-12   Orange W
9 Alabama 38-6   Orange W
10 Notre Dame 40-6   Orange W

Bowls W-L-T: 7-3-0

DAN DEVINE
(Minn.-Duluth '48)
B 12-23-24 Augusta, Wis.
Hall of Fame

Yr.	Team	W-L-T	B
55	Arizona St.	8-2-1	
56	Arizona St.	9-1-0	
57	Arizona St.	10-0-0	
58	Missouri	5-4-1	
59	Missouri	6-5-0	1
60	Missouri	10-1-0	2
61	Missouri	7-2-1	
62	Missouri	8-1-2	3
63	Missouri	7-3-0	
64	Missouri	6-3-1	
65	Missouri	8-2-1	4
66	Missouri	6-3-1	
67	Missouri	7-3-0	
68	Missouri	8-3-0	5
69	Missouri	9-2-0	6
70	Missouri	5-6-0	
75	Notre Dame	8-3-0	
76	Notre Dame	9-3-0	7
77*	Notre Dame	11-1-0	8
78	Notre Dame	9-3-0	9
79	Notre Dame	7-4-0	
80	Notre Dame	9-2-1	10

22 yrs. .742 172-57-9
* National Champions

Bowl games included above:
1 Georgia 0-14   Orange L
2 Navy 21-14   Orange W
3 Georgia Tech 14-10
                       Bluebonnet W
4 Florida 20-18   Sugar   W
5 Alabama 35-10   Gator   W
6 Penn St. 3-10   Orange L
7 Penn St. 20-9   Gator   W
8 Texas 38-10   Cotton W
9 Houston 35-34   Cotton W
10 Georgia 10-17   Sugar   L

Bowls W-L-T: 7-3-0

GIL DOBIE
(Minnesota '02)
B 1-31-79 Hastings, Minn.
D 12-24-48
Hall of Fame

Yr.	Team	W-L-T
06	North Dak. St.	4-0-0
07	North Dak. St.	3-0-0
08	Washington	6-0-1
09	Washington	7-0-0
10	Washington	6-0-0
11	Washington	7-0-0
12	Washington	6-0-0
13	Washington	7-0-0
14	Washington	6-0-1
15	Washington	7-0-0
16	Washington	6-0-1
17	Navy	7-1-0
18	Navy	4-1-0
19	Navy	6-1-0
20	Cornell	6-2-0
21*	Cornell	8-0-0
22*	Cornell	8-0-0
23	Cornell	8-0-0
24	Cornell	4-4-0
25	Cornell	6-2-0
26	Cornell	6-1-1
27	Cornell	3-3-2
28	Cornell	3-3-2
29	Cornell	6-2-0
30	Cornell	6-2-0
31	Cornell	7-1-0
32	Cornell	5-2-1
33	Cornell	4-3-0
34	Cornell	2-5-0
35	Cornell	0-6-1
36	Boston College	6-1-2
37	Boston College	4-4-1
38	Boston College	6-1-2

33 yrs. .781 180-45-15
* National Champions

BOBBY DODD
(Tennessee '31)
B 11-11-08 Galax, Va.
D 6-21-88

Yr.	Team	W-L-T	B
45	Georgia Tech	4-6-0	
46	Georgia Tech	9-2-0	1
47	Georgia Tech	10-1-0	2
48	Georgia Tech	7-3-0	
49	Georgia Tech	7-3-0	
50	Georgia Tech	5-6-0	
51	Georgia Tech	11-0-1	3
52	Georgia Tech	12-0-0	4
53	Georgia Tech	9-2-1	5
54	Georgia Tech	8-3-0	6
55	Georgia Tech	9-1-1	7
56	Georgia Tech	10-1-0	8
57	Georgia Tech	4-4-2	
58	Georgia Tech	5-4-1	
59	Georgia Tech	6-5-0	9
60	Georgia Tech	5-5-0	
61	Georgia Tech	7-4-0	10
62	Georgia Tech	7-3-1	11
63	Georgia Tech	7-3-0	
64	Georgia Tech	7-3-0	
65	Georgia Tech	7-3-1	12
66	Georgia Tech	9-2-0	13

22 yrs. .713 165-64-8

Bowl games included above:
1 St. Mary's (Cal.) 41-19   Oil   W
2 Kansas 20-14   Orange W
3 Baylor 17-14   Orange W
4 Mississippi 24-7   Sugar   W
5 West Va. 42-19   Sugar   W
6 Arkansas 14-6   Cotton W
7 Pittsburgh 7-0   Sugar   W
8 Pittsburgh 21-14   Gator   W
9 Arkansas 7-14   Gator   L
10 Pittsburgh 15-30   Gator   L
11 Missouri 10-14   Bluebonnet L
12 Texas Tech 31-21   Gator   W
13 Florida 12-27   Orange L

Bowls W-L-T: 9-4-0

TERRY DONAHUE
(UCLA '67)
B 6-24-44 Los Angeles, Calif.

Yr.	Team	W-L-T	B
76	UCLA	9-2-1	1
77	UCLA	7-4-0	
78	UCLA	8-3-1	2
79	UCLA	5-6-0	
80	UCLA	9-2-0	
81	UCLA	7-4-1	3
82	UCLA	10-1-1	4
83	UCLA	7-4-1	5
84	UCLA	9-3-0	6
85	UCLA	9-2-1	7
86	UCLA	8-3-1	8
87	UCLA	10-2-0	9
88	UCLA	10-2-0	10
89	UCLA	3-7-1	

14 yrs. .701 111-45-8

Bowl games included above:
1. Alabama 6-36 Liberty L
2. Arkansas 10-10 Fiesta T
3. Michigan 14-33 Bluebonnet L
4. Michigan 24-14 Rose W
5. Illinois 45-9 Rose W
6. Miami (Fla.) 39-37 Fiesta W
7. Iowa 45-28 Rose W
8. Brigham Young 31-10 Freedom W
9. Florida 20-16 Aloha W
10. Arkansas 17-3 Cotton W

Bowls W-L-T: 7-2-1

(Active coach in 1989)

VINCE DOOLEY
(Auburn '54)
B 9-4-32 Mobile, Ala.
Coach of Year 80

Yr.	Team	W-L-T	B
64	Georgia	7-3-1	1
65	Georgia	6-4-0	
66	Georgia	10-1-0	2
67	Georgia	7-4-0	3
68	Georgia	8-1-2	4
69	Georgia	5-5-1	5
70	Georgia	5-5-0	
71	Georgia	11-1-0	6
72	Georgia	7-4-0	
73	Georgia	7-4-1	7
74	Georgia	6-6-0	8
75	Georgia	9-3-0	9
76	Georgia	10-2-0	10
77	Georgia	5-6-0	
78	Georgia	9-2-1	11
79	Georgia	6-5-0	
80*	Georgia	12-0-0	12
81	Georgia	10-2-0	13
82	Georgia	11-1-0	14
83	Georgia	10-1-1	15
84	Georgia	7-4-1	16
85	Georgia	7-3-2	17
86	Georgia	8-4-0	18
87	Georgia	9-3-0	19
88	Georgia	9-3-0	20

25 yrs. .715 201-77-10
* National Champions

Bowl games included above:
1. Texas Tech 7-0 Sun W
2. Southern Methodist 24-9 Cotton W
3. North Caro. St. 7-14 Liberty L
4. Arkansas 2-16 Sugar L
5. Nebraska 6-45 Sun L
6. North Caro. 7-3 Gator W
7. Maryland 17-16 Peach W
8. Miami (Ohio) 10-21 Tangerine L
9. Arkansas 10-31 Cotton L
10. Pittsburgh 3-27 Sugar L
11. Stanford 22-25 Bluebonnet L
12. Notre Dame 17-10 Sugar W
13. Pittsburgh 20-24 Sugar L
14. Penn St. 23-27 Sugar L
15. Texas 10-9 Cotton W
16. Florida St. 17-17 Florida Citrus T

17. Arizona 13-13 Sun T
18. Boston College 24-27 Hall of Fame L
19. Arkansas 20-17 Liberty W
20. Michigan St. 34-27 Gator W

Bowls W-L-T: 8-10-2

(1988 last active season)

PAT DYE
(Georgia '62)
B 11-6-39 Augusta, Ga.

Yr.	Team	W-L-T	B
74	East Caro.	7-4-0	
75	East Caro.	8-3-0	
76	East Caro.	9-2-0	
77	East Caro.	8-3-0	
78	East Caro.	9-3-0	1
79	East Caro.	7-3-1	
80	Wyoming	6-5-0	
81	Auburn	5-6-0	
82	Auburn	9-3-0	2
83	Auburn	11-1-0	3
84	Auburn	9-4-0	4
85	Auburn	8-4-0	5
86	Auburn	10-2-0	6
87	Auburn	9-1-2	7
88	Auburn	10-2-0	8
89	Auburn	10-2-0	9

16 yrs. .734 135-48-3

Bowl games included above:
1. Louisiana Tech 35-13 Independence W
2. Boston College 33-26 Tangerine W
3. Michigan 9-7 Sugar W
4. Arkansas 21-15 Liberty W
5. Texas A&M 16-36 Cotton L
6. Southern Cal 16-7 Florida Citrus W
7. Syracuse 16-16 Sugar T
8. Florida St. 7-13 Sugar L
9. Ohio St. 31-14 Hall of Fame W

Bowls W-L-T: 6-2-1

(Active coach in 1989)

221

LaVELL EDWARDS
(Utah St. '52)
B 10-11-30 Orem, Utah
Coach of Year 84

Yr.	Team	W-L-T	B
72	Brigham Young	7-4-0	
73	Brigham Young	5-6-0	
74	Brigham Young	7-4-1	1
75	Brigham Young	6-5-0	
76	Brigham Young	9-3-0	2
77	Brigham Young	9-2-0	
78	Brigham Young	9-4-0	3
79	Brigham Young	11-1-0	4
80	Brigham Young	12-1-0	5
81	Brigham Young	11-2-0	6
82	Brigham Young	8-4-0	7
83	Brigham Young	11-1-0	8
84*	Brigham Young	13-0-0	9
85	Brigham Young	11-3-0	10
86	Brigham Young	8-5-0	11
87	Brigham Young	9-4-0	12
88	Brigham Young	9-4-0	13
89	Brigham Young	10-3-0	14

18 yrs.   .745   165-56-1

* National Champions
Bowl games included above:
1 Oklahoma St. 6-16   Fiesta   L
2 Oklahoma St. 21-49
                       Tangerine L
3 Navy 16-23   Holiday L
4 Indiana 37-38   Holiday L
5 Southern Methodist 46-45
                       Holiday W
6 Washington St. 38-36
                       Holiday W
7 Ohio St. 17-47   Holiday L
8 Missouri 21-17   Holiday W
9 Michigan 24-17   Holiday W
10 Ohio St. 7-10 Florida Citrus L
11 UCLA 10-31   Freedom L
12 Virginia 16-22 All-American L
13 Colorado 20-17   Freedom W
14 Penn St. 39-50   Holiday L

Bowls W-L-T: 5-9-0
(Active coach in 1989)

FRED FOLSOM
(Dartmouth '95)
B 11-9-71 Old Town, Me.
D 11-11-44

Yr.	Team	W-L-T
95	Colorado	4-1-0
96	Colorado	5-0-0
97	Colorado	7-1-0
98	Colorado	4-4-0
99	Colorado	7-2-0
01	Colorado	5-1-1
02	Colorado	5-1-0
03	Dartmouth	9-1-0
04	Dartmouth	7-0-1
05	Dartmouth	7-1-2
06	Dartmouth	6-3-1
08	Colorado	5-2-0
09	Colorado	6-0-0
10	Colorado	6-0-0
11	Colorado	6-0-0
12	Colorado	6-3-0
13	Colorado	5-1-1
14	Colorado	5-1-0
15	Colorado	1-6-0

19 yrs.   .779   106-28-6

DANNY FORD
(Alabama '70)
B 4-2-48 Gadsden, Ala.
Coach of Year 81

Yr.	Team	W-L-T	B
78	Clemson	1-0-0	1
79	Clemson	8-4-0	2
80	Clemson	6-5-0	
81*	Clemson	12-0-0	3
82	Clemson	9-1-1	
83	Clemson	9-1-1	
84	Clemson	7-4-0	
85	Clemson	6-6-0	4
86	Clemson	8-2-2	5
87	Clemson	10-2-0	6
88	Clemson	10-2-0	7
89	Clemson	10-2-0	8

11+ yrs.   .760   96-29-4

* National Champions
Bowl games included above:
1 Ohio St. 17-15   Gator   W
2 Baylor 18-24   Peach   L
3 Nebraska 22-15   Orange W
4 Minnesota 13-20
                   Independence L
5 Stanford 27-21   Gator   W
6 Penn St. 35-10
                  Florida Citrus W
7 Oklahoma 13-6
                  Florida Citrus W
8 West Va. 27-7   Gator   W

Bowls W-L-T: 6-2-0

+ Last game (Gator Bowl) 78 not counted as a season.

PERCY HAUGHTON
(Harvard '99)
B 7-11-76 Staten Island, N.Y.
D 10-27-24
Hall of Fame

Yr.	Team	W-L-T
99	Cornell	7-3-0
00	Cornell	10-2-0
08	Harvard	9-0-1
09	Harvard	8-1-0
10*	Harvard	8-0-1
11	Harvard	6-2-1
12*	Harvard	9-0-0
13*	Harvard	9-0-0
14	Harvard	7-0-2
15	Harvard	8-1-0
16	Harvard	7-3-0
23	Columbia	4-4-1
24	Columbia	4-1-0

13 yrs.   .832   96-17-6
* National Champions

WOODY HAYES
(Denison '35)
B 2-14-13 Clifton, Ohio
D 3-12-87
Hall of Fame
Coach of Year 57, 68, 75

Yr.	Team	W-L-T	B
46	Denison	2-6-0	
47	Denison	9-0-0	
48	Denison	8-0-0	
49	Miami (Ohio)	5-4-0	
50	Miami (Ohio)	9-1-0	1
51	Ohio St.	4-3-2	
52	Ohio St.	6-3-0	
53	Ohio St.	6-3-0	
54*	Ohio St.	10-0-0	2
55	Ohio St.	7-2-0	
56	Ohio St.	6-3-0	
57*	Ohio St.	9-1-0	3
58	Ohio St.	6-1-2	
59	Ohio St.	3-5-1	
60	Ohio St.	7-2-0	
61*	Ohio St.	8-0-1	
62	Ohio St.	6-3-0	
63	Ohio St.	5-3-1	
64	Ohio St.	7-2-0	
65	Ohio St.	7-2-0	
66	Ohio St.	4-5-0	
67	Ohio St.	6-3-0	
68*	Ohio St.	10-0-0	4
69	Ohio St.	8-1-0	
70*	Ohio St.	9-1-0	5
71	Ohio St.	6-4-0	
72	Ohio St.	9-2-0	6
73	Ohio St.	10-0-1	7
74	Ohio St.	10-2-0	8
75	Ohio St.	11-1-0	9
76	Ohio St.	9-2-1	10
77	Ohio St.	9-3-0	11
78	Ohio St.	7-4-1	12

33 yrs. .759   238-72-10

* National Champions

Bowl games included above:
1 Arizona St. 34-21   Salad W
2 Southern Cal 20-7   Rose W
3 Oregon 10-7   Rose W
4 Southern Cal 27-16 Rose W
5 Stanford 17-27   Rose L
6 Southern Cal 17-42 Rose L
7 Southern Cal 42-21 Rose W
8 Southern Cal 17-18 Rose L
9 UCLA 10-23   Rose L
10 Colorado 27-10   Orange W
11 Alabama 6-35   Sugar L
12 Clemson 15-17   Gator L

Bowls W-L-T: 6-6-0

JOHN HEISMAN
(Brown '90; Pennsylvania '92)
B 10-23-69 Cleveland, Ohio
D 10-3-36
Hall of Fame

Yr.	Team	W-L-T
92	Oberlin	7-0-0
93	Akron	5-2-0
94	Oberlin	4-3-1
95	Auburn	2-1-0
96	Auburn	3-1-0
97	Auburn	2-0-1
98	Auburn	2-1-0
99	Auburn	3-1-1
00	Clemson	6-0-0
01	Clemson	3-1-1
02	Clemson	6-1-0
03	Clemson	4-1-1
04	Georgia Tech	8-1-1
05	Georgia Tech	6-0-1
06	Georgia Tech	5-3-1
07	Georgia Tech	4-4-0
08	Georgia Tech	6-3-0
09	Georgia Tech	7-2-0
10	Georgia Tech	5-3-0
11	Georgia Tech	6-2-1
12	Georgia Tech	5-3-0
13	Georgia Tech	7-2-0
14	Georgia Tech	6-2-0
15	Georgia Tech	7-0-1
16	Georgia Tech	8-0-1
17*	Georgia Tech	9-0-0
18	Georgia Tech	6-1-0
19	Georgia Tech	7-3-0
20	Pennsylvania	6-4-0
21	Pennsylvania	4-3-2
22	Pennsylvania	6-3-0
23	Wash. & Jeff.	6-1-1
24	Rice	4-4-0
25	Rice	4-4-1
26	Rice	4-4-1
27	Rice	2-6-1

36 yrs. .711   185-70-17

* National Champions

ELMER "GUS" HENDERSON
(Oberlin '12)
B 3-10-89 Oberlin, Ohio
D 12-16-65

Yr.	Team	W-L-T	B
19	Southern Cal	4-1-0	
20	Southern Cal	6-0-0	
21	Southern Cal	10-1-0	
22	Southern Cal	10-1-0	1
23	Southern Cal	6-2-0	
24	Southern Cal	9-2-0	2
25	Tulsa	6-2-0	
26	Tulsa	7-2-0	
27	Tulsa	8-1-0	
28	Tulsa	7-2-1	
29	Tulsa	6-3-1	
30	Tulsa	7-2-0	
31	Tulsa	8-3-0	
32	Tulsa	7-1-1	
33	Tulsa	6-1-0	
34	Tulsa	5-2-1	
35	Tulsa	3-6-1	
40	Occidental	3-4-1	
41	Occidental	5-2-1	
42	Occidental	3-4-0	

20 yrs. .740   126-42-7

Bowl games included above:
1 Penn St. 14-3   Rose W
2 Missouri 20-7
                  Christmas Festival W

Bowls W-L-T: 2-0-0

HOWARD JONES
(Yale '08)
B 8-23-85 Excello, Ohio
D 7-27-41
Hall of Fame

Yr.	Team	W-L-T	B
08	Syrcause	6-3-1	
09*	Yale	10-0-0	
10	Ohio St.	6-1-3	
13	Yale	5-2-3	
16	Iowa	4-3-0	
17	Iowa	3-5-0	
18	Iowa	6-2-1	
19	Iowa	5-2-0	
20	Iowa	5-2-0	
21	Iowa	7-0-0	
22	Iowa	7-0-0	
23	Iowa	5-3-0	
24	Duke	4-5-0	
25	Southern Cal	11-2-0	
26	Southern Cal	8-2-0	
27	Southern Cal	8-1-1	
28*	Southern Cal	9-0-1	
29	Southern Cal	10-2-0	1
30	Southern Cal	8-2-0	
31*	Southern Cal	10-1-0	2
32	Southern Cal	10-0-0	3
33	Southern Cal	10-1-1	
34	Southern Cal	4-6-1	
35	Southern Cal	5-7-0	
36	Southern Cal	4-2-3	
37	Southern Cal	4-4-2	
38	Southern Cal	9-2-0	4
39	Southern Cal	8-0-2	5
40	Southern Cal	3-4-2	

29 yrs. .733   194-64-21

* National Champions

Bowl games included above:
1 Pittsburgh 47-14   Rose W
2 Tulane 21-12   Rose W
3 Pittsburgh 35-0   Rose W
4 Duke 7-3   Rose W
5 Tennessee 14-0   Rose W

Bowls W-L-T: 5-0-0

LAWRENCE "BIFF" JONES
(Army '17)
B 10-8-95 Washington, D.C.
D 1-12-80
Hall of Fame

Yr.	Team	W-L-T	B
26	Army	7-1-1	
27	Army	9-1-0	
28	Army	8-2-0	
29	Army	6-4-1	
32	Louisiana St.	6-3-1	
33	Louisiana St.	7-0-3	
34	Louisiana St.	7-2-2	
35	Oklahoma	6-3-0	
36	Oklahoma	3-3-3	
37	Nebraska	6-1-2	
38	Nebraska	3-5-1	
39	Nebraska	7-1-1	
40	Nebraska	8-2-0	1
41	Nebraska	4-5-0	

14 yrs. .700   87-33-15

Bowl game included above:
1 Stanford 13-21   Rose L

Bowls W-L-T: 0-1-0

TAD JONES
(Yale '08)
B 2-22-87 Excello, Ohio
D 6-19-57
Hall of Fame

Yr.	Team	W-L-T
09	Syracuse	4-5-1
10	Syracuse	5-4-1
16	Yale	8-1-0
20	Yale	5-3-0
21	Yale	8-1-0
22	Yale	6-3-1
23	Yale	8-0-0
24	Yale	6-0-2
25	Yale	5-2-1
26	Yale	4-4-0
27	Yale	7-1-0

11 yrs. .719   66-24-6

A. R. "DOC" KENNEDY
(Kansas '98)
B 10-24-76 Douglas County, Kan.
D 9-3-69

Yr.	Team	W-L-T
04	Kansas	8-1-1
05	Kansas	10-1-0
06	Kansas	7-2-2
07	Kansas	5-3-0
08	Kansas	9-0-0
09	Kansas	8-1-0
10	Kansas	6-1-1
11	Haskell	3-2-3
12	Haskell	6-4-0
13	Haskell	9-1-0
14	Haskell	6-2-0
15	Haskell	5-5-0
16	Haskell	3-6-0

13 yrs. .720   85-31-7

FRANK KUSH
(Michigan St. '53)
B 1-20-29 Windber, Pa.
Coach of Year 75

Yr.	Team	W-L-T	B
58	Arizona St.	7-3-0	
59	Arizona St.	10-1-0	
60	Arizona St.	7-3-0	
61	Arizona St.	7-3-0	
62	Arizona St.	7-2-1	
63	Arizona St.	8-1-0	
64	Arizona St.	8-2-0	
65	Arizona St.	6-4-0	
66	Arizona St.	5-5-0	
67	Arizona St.	8-2-0	
68	Arizona St.	8-2-0	
69	Arizona St.	8-2-0	
70	Arizona St.	11-0-0	1
71	Arizona St.	11-1-0	2
72	Arizona St.	10-2-0	3
73	Arizona St.	11-1-0	4
74	Arizona St.	7-5-0	
75	Arizona St.	12-0-0	5
76	Arizona St.	4-7-0	
77	Arizona St.	9-3-0	6
78	Arizona St.	9-3-0	7
79	Arizona St.	3-2-0	

22 yrs. .764   176-54-1

Bowl games included above:
1 North Caro. 48-26 Peach W
2 Florida St. 45-38 Fiesta W
3 Missouri 49-35 Fiesta W
4 Pittsburgh 28-7 Fiesta W
5 Nebraska 17-14 Fiesta W
6 Penn St. 30-42 Fiesta L
7 Rutgers 34-18 Garden State W

Bowls W-L-T: 6-1-0

ELMER LAYDEN
(Notre Dame '25)
B 5-4-03 Davenport, Iowa
D 6-30-73
Hall of Fame (as a player)

Yr.	Team	W-L-T
25	Loras	4-3-1
26	Loras	4-2-1

Yr.	Team	W-L-T
27	Duquesne	4-4-1
28	Duquesne	8-1-0
29	Duquesne	9-0-1
30	Duquesne	7-3-0
31	Duquesne	3-5-3
32	Duquesne	7-2-1
33	Duquesne	10-1-0
34	Notre Dame	6-3-0
35	Notre Dame	7-1-1
36	Notre Dame	6-2-1
37	Notre Dame	6-2-1
38	Notre Dame	8-1-0
39	Notre Dame	7-2-0
40	Notre Dame	7-2-0

16 yrs. .733   103-34-11

FRANK LEAHY
(Notre Dame '31)
B 8-27-08 O'Neill, Neb.
D 6-21-73
Hall of Fame
Coach of Year 41

Yr.	Team	W-L-T	B
39	Boston College	9-2-0	1
40	Boston College	11-0-0	2
41	Notre Dame	8-0-1	
42	Notre Dame	7-2-2	
43*	Notre Dame	9-1-0	
46*	Notre Dame	8-0-1	
47*	Notre Dame	9-0-0	
48	Notre Dame	9-0-1	
49*	Notre Dame	10-0-0	
50	Notre Dame	4-4-1	
51	Notre Dame	7-2-1	
52	Notre Dame	7-2-1	
53	Notre Dame	9-0-1	

13 yrs. .864   107-13-9

* National Champions

Bowl games included above:
1 Clemson 3-6 Cotton L
2 Tennessee 19-13 Sugar W

Bowls W-L-T: 1-1-0

JOHN McEWAN
(Army '17)
B 2-18-93 Alexandria, Minn.
D 8-9-70
Hall of Fame (as a player)

Yr.	Team	W-L-T
23	Army	6-2-1
24	Army	5-1-2
25	Army	7-2-0
26	Oregon	2-4-1
27	Oregon	2-4-1
28	Oregon	9-2-0
29	Oregon	7-3-0
30	Holy Cross	8-2-0
31	Holy Cross	7-2-1
32	Holy Cross	6-1-0
10 yrs. .705		59-23-6

DAN McGUGIN
(Michigan '04)
B 7-29-79 Tingley, Iowa
D 1-19-36
Hall of Fame

Yr.	Team	W-L-T
04	Vanderbilt	9-0-0
05	Vanderbilt	7-1-0
06	Vanderbilt	8-1-0
07	Vanderbilt	5-1-1
08	Vanderbilt	7-2-1
09	Vanderbilt	7-3-0
10	Vanderbilt	8-0-1
11	Vanderbilt	8-1-0
12	Vanderbilt	8-1-1
13	Vanderbilt	5-3-0
14	Vanderbilt	2-6-0
15	Vanderbilt	9-1-0
16	Vanderbilt	7-1-1
17	Vanderbilt	5-3-0
19	Vanderbilt	5-1-2
20	Vanderbilt	5-3-1
21	Vanderbilt	7-0-1
22	Vanderbilt	8-0-1
23	Vanderbilt	5-2-1
24	Vanderbilt	6-3-1
25	Vanderbilt	6-3-0
26	Vanderbilt	8-1-0
27	Vanderbilt	8-1-2
28	Vanderbilt	8-2-0
29	Vanderbilt	7-2-0
30	Vanderbilt	8-2-0
31	Vanderbilt	5-4-0
32	Vanderbilt	6-1-2
33	Vanderbilt	4-3-3
34	Vanderbilt	6-3-0
30 yrs. .762		197-55-19

JOHN McKAY
(Oregon '50)
B 7-5-23 Everettsville, W. Va.
Hall of Fame
Coach of Year 62, 72

Yr.	Team	W-L-T	B
60	Southern Cal	4-6-0	
61	Southern Cal	4-5-1	
62*	Southern Cal	11-0-0	1
63	Southern Cal	7-3-0	
64	Southern Cal	7-3-0	
65	Southern Cal	7-2-1	
66	Southern Cal	7-4-0	2
67*	Southern Cal	10-1-0	3
68	Southern Cal	9-1-1	4
69	Southern Cal	10-0-1	5
70	Southern Cal	6-4-1	
71	Southern Cal	6-4-1	
72*	Southern Cal	12-0-0	6
73	Southern Cal	9-2-1	7
74*	Southern Cal	10-1-1	8
75	Southern Cal	8-4-0	9
16 yrs. .749		127-40-8	

* National Champions

Bowl games included above:
1	Wisconsin 42-37	Rose W
2	Purdue 13-14	Rose L
3	Indiana 14-3	Rose W
4	Ohio St. 16-27	Rose L
5	Michigan 10-3	Rose W
6	Ohio St. 42-17	Rose W
7	Ohio St. 21-42	Rose L
8	Ohio St. 18-17	Rose W
9	Texas A&M 20-0	Liberty W

Bowls W-L-T: 6-3-0

JOHN "CHICK" MEEHAN
(Syracuse '18)
B 9-5-93 Shelbourne Falls, Mass.
D 11-9-72

Yr.	Team	W-L-T
20	Syracuse	6-2-1
21	Syracuse	7-2-0
22	Syracuse	6-1-2
23	Syracuse	8-1-0
24	Syracuse	8-2-1
25	New York U.	6-2-1
26	New York U.	8-1-0
27	New York U.	7-1-2
28	New York U.	8-2-0
29	New York U.	7-3-0
30	New York U.	7-3-0
31	New York U.	6-3-1
32	Manhattan	5-3-2
33	Manhattan	6-3-1
34	Manhattan	3-5-1
35	Manhattan	5-3-1
36	Manhattan	6-4-0
37	Manhattan	6-3-1
18 yrs. .705		115-44-14

CHARLEY MORAN
(Tennessee '18)
B 2-22-78 Nashville, Tenn.
D 6-14-49

Yr.	Team	W-L-T	B
09	Texas A&M	7-0-1	
10	Texas A&M	8-1-0	
11	Texas A&M	6-1-0	
12	Texas A&M	8-1-0	
13	Texas A&M	3-4-2	
14	Texas A&M	6-1-1	
19	Centre	9-0-0	
20	Centre	8-2-0	1
21	Centre	10-1-0	2
22	Centre	8-2-0	
23	Centre	7-1-1	
24	Bucknell	8-2-0	
25	Bucknell	7-3-1	
26	Bucknell	4-5-1	
30	Catawba	8-0-1	
31	Catawba	7-2-1	
32	Catawba	6-2-1	
33	Catawba	2-5-2	

18 yrs. .766 122-33-12

Bowl games included above:
1 Texas Christian 63-7
    Fort Worth Classic W
2 Texas A&M 14-22
    Dixie Classic L

Bowls W-L-T: 1-1-0

JESS NEELY
(Vanderbilt '24)
B 1-4-98 Smyrna, Tenn.
D 4-9-83
Hall of Fame

Yr.	Team	W-L-T	B
24	Rhodes	3-6-0	
25	Rhodes	7-2-0	
26	Rhodes	5-4-1	
27	Rhodes	5-5-1	
31	Clemson	1-6-2	
32	Clemson	3-5-1	
33	Clemson	3-6-2	
34	Clemson	5-4-0	
35	Clemson	6-3-0	
36	Clemson	5-5-0	
37	Clemson	4-4-1	
38	Clemson	7-1-1	
39	Clemson	9-1-0	1
40	Rice	7-3-0	
41	Rice	6-3-1	
42	Rice	7-2-1	
43	Rice	3-7-0	
44	Rice	5-6-0	
45	Rice	5-6-0	
46	Rice	9-2-0	2
47	Rice	6-3-1	
48	Rice	5-4-1	
49	Rice	10-1-0	3
50	Rice	6-4-0	
51	Rice	5-5-0	
52	Rice	5-5-0	
53	Rice	9-2-0	4
54	Rice	7-3-0	
55	Rice	2-7-1	
56	Rice	4-6-0	
57	Rice	7-4-0	5
58	Rice	5-5-0	
59	Rice	1-7-2	
60	Rice	7-4-0	6
61	Rice	7-4-0	7
62	Rice	2-6-2	
63	Rice	6-4-0	
64	Rice	4-5-1	
65	Rice	2-8-0	
66	Rice	2-8-0	

40 yrs. .539 207-176-19

Bowl games included above:
1 Boston College 6-3 Cotton W
2 Tennessee 8-0 Orange W
3 North Caro. 27-13 Cotton W
4 Alabama 28-6 Cotton W
5 Navy 7-20 Cotton L
6 Mississippi 6-14 Sugar L
7 Kansas 7-33 Bluebonnet L

Bowls W-L-T: 4-3-0

BOB NEYLAND
(Army '16)
B 2-17-92 Greenville, Texas
D 3-28-62
Hall of Fame

Yr.	Team	W-L-T	B
26	Tennessee	8-1-0	
27	Tennessee	8-0-1	
28	Tennessee	9-0-1	
29	Tennessee	9-0-1	
30	Tennessee	9-1-0	
31	Tennessee	9-0-1	
32	Tennessee	9-0-1	
33	Tennessee	7-3-0	
34	Tennessee	8-2-0	
36	Tennessee	6-2-2	
37	Tennessee	6-3-1	
38	Tennessee	11-0-0	1
39	Tennessee	10-1-0	2
40	Tennessee	10-1-0	3
46	Tennessee	9-2-0	4
47	Tennessee	5-5-0	
48	Tennessee	4-4-2	
49	Tennessee	7-2-1	
50	Tennessee	11-1-0	5
51*	Tennessee	10-1-0	6
52	Tennessee	8-2-1	7

21 yrs. .829 173-31-12

* National Champions

Bowl games included above:
1 Oklahoma 17-0 Orange W
2 Southern Cal 0-14 Rose L
3 Boston College 13-19 Sugar L
4 Rice 0-8 Orange L
5 Texas 20-14 Cotton W
6 Maryland 13-28 Sugar L
7 Texas 0-16 Cotton L

Bowls W-L-T: 2-5-0

TOM OSBORNE
(Hastings '59)
B 2-23-37 Hastings, Neb.

Yr.	Team	W-L-T	B
73	Nebraska	9-2-1	1
74	Nebraska	9-3-0	2
75	Nebraska	10-2-0	3
76	Nebraska	9-3-1	4
77	Nebraska	9-3-0	5
78	Nebraska	9-3-0	6
79	Nebraska	10-2-0	7
80	Nebraska	10-2-0	8
81	Nebraska	9-3-0	9
82	Nebraska	12-1-0	10
83	Nebraska	12-1-0	11
84	Nebraska	10-2-0	12
85	Nebraska	9-3-0	13

86	Nebraska	10-2-0	14
87	Nebraska	10-2-0	15
88	Nebraska	11-2-0	16
89	Nebraska	10-2-0	17
17 yrs.	.813	168-38-2	

Bowl games included above:
1	Texas 19-3	Cotton	W
2	Florida 13-10	Sugar	W
3	Arizona St. 14-17	Fiesta	L
4	Texas Tech 27-24	Bluebonnet	W
5	North Caro. 21-17	Liberty	W
6	Oklahoma 24-31	Orange	L
7	Houston 14-17	Cotton	L
8	Mississippi St. 31-17	Sun	W
9	Clemson 15-22	Orange	L
10	Louisiana St. 21-20	Orange	W
11	Miami (Fla.) 30-31	Orange	L
12	Louisiana St. 28-10	Sugar	W
13	Michigan 23-27	Fiesta	L
14	Louisiana St. 30-15	Sugar	W
15	Florida St. 28-31	Fiesta	L
16	Miami (Fla.) 3-23	Orange	L
17	Florida St. 17-41	Fiesta	L

Bowls W-L-T: 8-9-0

(Active coach in 1989)

BENNIE OWEN

(Kansas '00)
B 7-24-75 Chicago, Ill.
D 2-26-70
Hall of Fame

Yr.	Team	W-L-T
00	Washburn	6-2-0
01	Bethany (Kan.)	5-2-1
02	Bethany (Kan.)	8-1-1
03	Bethany (Kan.)	7-1-1
04	Bethany (Kan.)	7-0-0
05	Oklahoma	7-2-0
06	Oklahoma	5-2-2
07	Oklahoma	4-4-0
08	Oklahoma	8-1-1
09	Oklahoma	6-4-0
10	Oklahoma	4-2-1
11	Oklahoma	8-0-0
12	Oklahoma	5-4-0
13	Oklahoma	6-2-0
14	Oklahoma	9-1-1
15	Oklahoma	10-0-0
16	Oklahoma	6-5-0
17	Oklahoma	6-4-1
18	Oklahoma	6-0-0
19	Oklahoma	5-2-3
20	Oklahoma	6-0-1
21	Oklahoma	5-3-0
22	Oklahoma	2-3-3
23	Oklahoma	3-5-0
24	Oklahoma	2-5-1
25	Oklahoma	4-3-1
26	Oklahoma	5-2-1
27 yrs.	.703	155-60-29

ARA PARSEGHIAN

(Miami, [Ohio] '49)
B 5-21-23 Akron, Ohio
Hall of Fame
Co-Coach of Year 64

Yr.	Team	W-L-T	B
51	Miami (Ohio)	7-3-0	
52	Miami (Ohio)	8-1-0	
53	Miami (Ohio)	7-1-1	
54	Miami (Ohio)	8-1-0	
55	Miami (Ohio)	9-0-0	
56	Northwestern	4-4-1	
57	Northwestern	0-9-0	
58	Northwestern	5-4-0	
59	Northwestern	6-3-0	
60	Northwestern	5-4-0	
61	Northwestern	4-5-0	
62	Northwestern	7-2-0	
63	Northwestern	5-4-0	
64*	Notre Dame	9-1-0	
65	Notre Dame	7-2-1	
66*	Notre Dame	9-0-1	
67	Notre Dame	8-2-0	
68	Notre Dame	7-2-1	
69	Notre Dame	8-2-1	1
70	Notre Dame	10-1-0	2
71	Notre Dame	8-2-0	
72	Notre Dame	8-3-0	3
73*	Notre Dame	11-0-0	4
74	Notre Dame	10-2-0	5
24 yrs.	.739	170-58-6	

* National Champions

Bowl games included above:
1	Texas 17-21	Cotton	L
2	Texas 24-11	Cotton	W
3	Nebraska 6-40	Orange	L
4	Alabama 24-23	Sugar	W
5	Alabama 13-11	Orange	W

Bowls W-L-T: 3-2-0

JOE PATERNO

B 12-21-26 Brooklyn, N.Y.
Coach of Year 68, 78, 82, 86

Yr.	Team	W-L-T	B
66	Penn St.	5-5-0	
67	Penn St.	8-2-1	1
68	Penn St.	11-0-0	2
69	Penn St.	11-0-0	3
70	Penn St.	7-3-0	
71	Penn St.	11-1-0	4
72	Penn St.	10-2-0	5
73	Penn St.	12-0-0	6
74	Penn St.	10-2-0	7
75	Penn St.	9-3-0	8
76	Penn St.	7-5-0	9
77	Penn St.	11-1-0	10
78	Penn St.	11-1-0	11
79	Penn St.	8-4-0	12
80	Penn St.	10-2-0	13
81	Penn St.	10-2-0	14
82*	Penn St.	11-1-0	15
83	Penn St.	8-4-1	16
84	Penn St.	6-5-0	
85	Penn St.	11-1-0	17
86*	Penn St.	12-0-0	18
87	Penn St.	8-4-0	19
88	Penn St.	5-6-0	
89	Penn St.	8-3-1	20
24 yrs.	.791	220-57-3	

* National Champions

Bowl games included above:
1	Flordia St. 17-17	Gator	T
2	Kansas 15-14	Orange	W
3	Missouri 10-3	Orange	W
4	Texas 30-6	Cotton	W
5	Oklahoma 0-14	Sugar	L
6	Louisiana St. 16-9	Orange	W
7	Baylor 41-20	Cotton	W
8	Alabama 6-13	Sugar	L
9	Notre Dame 9-20	Gator	L
10	Arizona St. 42-30	Fiesta	W
11	Alabama 7-14	Sugar	L
12	Tulane 9-6	Liberty	W
13	Ohio St. 31-19	Fiesta	W
14	Southern Cal 26-10	Fiesta	W
15	Georgia 27-23	Sugar	W
16	Washington 13-10	Aloha	W
17	Oklahoma 10-25	Orange	L
18	Miami (Fla.) 14-10	Fiesta	W
19	Clemson 10-35	Florida Citrus	L

20 Brigham Young 50-39
                    Holiday W
      Bowls W-L-T: 13-6-1
(Active coach in 1989)

KNUTE ROCKNE
(Notre Dame '14)
B 3-4-88 Voss, Norway
D 3-31-31
Hall of Fame

Yr.	Team	W-L-T	B
18	Notre Dame	3-1-2	
19	Notre Dame	9-0-0	
20	Notre Dame	9-0-0	
21	Notre Dame	10-1-0	
22	Notre Dame	8-1-1	
23	Notre Dame	9-1-0	
24*	Notre Dame	10-0-0	1
25	Notre Dame	7-2-1	
26	Notre Dame	9-1-0	
27	Notre Dame	7-1-1	
28	Notre Dame	5-4-0	
29*	Notre Dame	9-0-0	
30*	Notre Dame	10-0-0	

13 yrs. .881 105-12-5
* National Champions

Bowl game included above:
 1 Stanford 27-10   Rose W
      Bowls W-L-T: 1-0-0

BILL ROPER
(Princeton '03)
B 8-22-80 Philadelphia, Pa.
D 12-10-33
Hall of Fame

Yr.	Team	W-L-T
03	Va. Military	2-1-0
04	Va. Military	3-4-1
06*	Princeton	9-0-1
07	Princeton	7-2-0
08	Princeton	5-2-3
09	Missouri	7-0-1
10	Princeton	7-1-0
11*	Princeton	8-0-2
15	Swarthmore	5-3-0
16	Swarthmore	6-1-1
19	Princeton	4-2-1
20	Princeton	6-0-1
21	Princeton	4-3-0
22	Princeton	8-0-0
23	Princeton	3-3-1
24	Princeton	4-2-1
25	Princeton	5-1-1
26	Princeton	5-1-1
27	Princeton	6-1-0
28	Princeton	5-1-2
29	Princeton	2-4-1
30	Princeton	1-5-1

22 yrs. .723 112-37-19
* National Champions

DARRELL ROYAL
(Oklahoma '50)
B 7-6-24 Hollis, Okla.
Hall of Fame
Coach of Year 63, 70

Yr.	Team	W-L-T	B
54	Mississippi St.	6-4-0	
55	Mississippi St.	6-4-0	
56	Washington	5-5-0	
57	Texas	6-4-1	1
58	Texas	7-3-0	
59	Texas	9-2-0	2
60	Texas	7-3-1	3
61	Texas	10-1-0	4
62	Texas	9-1-1	5
63*	Texas	11-0-0	6
64	Texas	10-1-0	7
65	Texas	6-4-0	
66	Texas	7-4-0	8
67	Texas	6-4-0	
68	Texas	9-1-1	9
69*	Texas	11-0-0	10
70*	Texas	10-1-0	11
71	Texas	8-3-0	12
72	Texas	10-1-0	13
73	Texas	8-3-0	14
74	Texas	8-4-0	15
75	Texas	10-2-0	16
76	Texas	5-5-1	

23 yrs. .749 184-60-5
* National Champions

Bowl games included above:
 1 Mississippi 7-39   Sugar   L
 2 Syracuse 14-23   Cotton   L
 3 Alabama 3-3   Bluebonnet T
 4 Mississippi 12-7   Cotton   W
 5 Louisiana St. 0-13 Cotton   L
 6 Navy 28-6   Cotton   W
 7 Alabama 21-17   Orange   W
 8 Mississippi 19-0   Bluebonnet W
 9 Tennessee 36-13   Cotton   W
10 Notre Dame 21-17   Cotton   W
11 Notre Dame 11-24   Cotton   L
12 Penn St. 6-30   Cotton   L
13 Alabama 17-13   Cotton   W
14 Nebraska 3-19   Cotton   L
15 Auburn 3-27   Gator   L
16 Colorado 38-21   Bluebonnet W
      Bowls W-L-T: 8-7-1

HENRY "RED" SANDERS
(Vanderbilt '27)
B 3-7-05 Asheville, N.C.
D 8-14-58
Coach of Year 54

Yr.	Team	W-L-T	B
40	Vanderbilt	3-6-1	
41	Vanderbilt	8-2-0	
42	Vanderbilt	6-4-0	
46	Vanderbilt	5-4-0	
47	Vanderbilt	6-4-0	
48	Vanderbilt	8-2-1	
49	UCLA	6-3-0	
50	UCLA	6-3-0	
51	UCLA	5-3-1	
52	UCLA	8-1-0	
53	UCLA	8-2-0	1
54*	UCLA	9-0-0	
55	UCLA	9-2-0	2
56	UCLA	7-3-0	
57	UCLA	8-2-0	

15 yrs. .709 102-41-3
* National Champions

Bowl games included above:
 1 Michigan St. 20-28   Rose L
 2 Michigan St. 14-17   Rose L
      Bowls W-L-T: 0-2-0

GLENN "BO" SCHEMBECHLER
(Miami [Ohio] '51)
B 9-1-29 Barberton, Ohio
Coach of Year 69

Yr.	Team	W-L-T	B
63	Miami (Ohio)	5-3-2	
64	Miami (Ohio)	6-3-1	
65	Miami (Ohio)	7-3-0	
66	Miami (Ohio)	9-1-0	
67	Miami (Ohio)	6-4-0	
68	Miami (Ohio)	7-3-0	
69	Michigan	8-3-0	1
70	Michigan	9-1-0	
71	Michigan	11-1-0	2
72	Michigan	10-1-0	
73	Michigan	10-0-1	
74	Michigan	10-1-0	
75	Michigan	8-2-2	3
76	Michigan	10-2-0	4

Yr.	Team	W-L-T	B
77	Michigan	10-2-0	5
78	Michigan	10-2-0	6
79	Michigan	8-4-0	7
80	Michigan	10-2-0	8
81	Michigan	9-3-0	9
82	Michigan	8-4-0	10
83	Michigan	9-3-0	11
84	Michigan	6-6-0	12
85	Michigan	10-1-1	13
86	Michigan	11-2-0	14
87	Michigan	8-4-0	15
88	Michigan	9-2-1	16
89	Michigan	10-2-0	17

27 yrs. .775 234-65-8

Bowl games included above:
1 Southern Cal 3-10 Rose L
2 Stanford 12-13 Rose L
3 Oklahoma 6-14 Orange L
4 Southern Cal 6-14 Rose L
5 Washington 20-27 Rose L
6 Southern Cal 10-17 Rose L
7 North Caro. 15-17 Gator L
8 Washington 23-6 Rose W
9 UCLA 33-14 Bluebonnet W
10 UCLA 14-24 Rose L
11 Auburn 7-9 Sugar L
12 Brigham Young 17-24 Holiday L
13 Nebraska 27-23 Fiesta W
14 Arizona St. 15-22 Rose L
15 Alabama 28-24 Hall of Fame W
16 Southern Cal 22-14 Rose W
17 Southern Cal 10-17 Rose L

Bowls W-L-T: 5-12-0

FRANCIS SCHMIDT

(Nebraska '13)
B 12-3-85 Downs, Kan.
D 9-19-44
Hall of Fame

Yr.	Team	W-L-T
19	Tulsa	8-0-1
20	Tulsa	10-0-1
21	Tulsa	6-3-0
22	Arkansas	5-4-0
23	Arkansas	6-2-1
24	Arkansas	7-2-1
25	Arkansas	4-4-1
26	Arkansas	5-5-0
27	Arkansas	8-1-0
28	Arkansas	7-2-0
29	Texas Christian	9-0-1
30	Texas Christian	9-2-1
31	Texas Christian	9-2-1
32	Texas Christian	10-0-1
33	Texas Christian	9-2-1
34	Ohio St.	7-1-0
35	Ohio St.	7-1-0
36	Ohio St.	5-3-0
37	Ohio St.	6-2-0
38	Ohio St.	4-3-1
39	Ohio St.	6-2-0
40	Ohio St.	4-4-0
41	Idaho	4-5-0
42	Idaho	3-7-0

24 yrs. .723 158-57-11

ANDY SMITH

(Penn St., Pennsylvania '05)
B 9-10-83 DuBois, Pa.
D 1-8-26
Hall of Fame

Yr.	Team	W-L-T	B
09	Pennsylvania	7-1-2	
10	Pennsylvania	9-1-1	
11	Pennsylvania	7-4-0	
12	Pennsylvania	7-4-0	
13	Purdue	4-1-2	
14	Purdue	5-2-0	
15	Purdue	3-3-1	
16	California	6-4-1	
17	California	5-5-1	
18	California	7-2-0	
19	California	6-2-1	
20*	California	9-0-0	1
21	California	9-0-1	2
22	California	9-0-0	
23	California	9-0-1	
24	California	8-0-2	
25	California	6-3-0	

17 yrs. .761 116-32-13

* National Champions

Bowl games included above:
1 Ohio St. 28-0 Rose W
2 Wash. & Jeff. 0-0 Rose T

Bowls W-L-T: 1-0-1

AMOS ALONZO STAGG

(Yale '88)
B 8-16-62 West Orange, N.J.
D 3-17-65
Hall of Fame
Coach of Year 43

Yr.	Team	W-L-T	B
90	Springfield	5-3-0	
91	Springfield	5-8-1	
92	Chicago	7-4-2	
93	Chicago	6-4-2	
94	Chicago	15-7-1	
95	Chicago	11-3-0	
96	Chicago	14-2-1	
97	Chicago	11-1-0	
98	Chicago	9-2-0	
99	Chicago	12-0-2	
00	Chicago	7-5-1	
01	Chicago	5-5-2	
02	Chicago	11-1-0	
03	Chicago	10-2-1	
04	Chicago	8-1-1	
05*	Chicago	10-0-0	
06	Chicago	4-1-1	
07	Chicago	4-1-0	
08	Chicago	5-0-1	
09	Chicago	4-1-2	
10	Chicago	2-5-0	
11	Chicago	6-1-0	
12	Chicago	6-1-0	
13	Chicago	7-0-0	
14	Chicago	4-2-1	
15	Chicago	5-2-0	
16	Chicago	3-4-0	
17	Chicago	3-2-1	
18	Chicago	0-6-0	
19	Chicago	5-2-0	
20	Chicago	3-4-0	
21	Chicago	6-1-0	
22	Chicago	6-1-0	
23	Chicago	7-1-0	
24	Chicago	4-1-3	
25	Chicago	3-4-1	
26	Chicago	2-6-0	
27	Chicago	4-4-0	
28	Chicago	2-7-0	
29	Chicago	7-3-0	
30	Chicago	1-5-2	
31	Chicago	2-5-1	
32	Chicago	3-4-1	
33	Pacific	5-5-0	
34	Pacific	4-5-0	
35	Pacific	5-4-1	
36	Pacific	5-4-1	
37	Pacific	3-5-2	
38	Pacific	7-3-0	
39	Pacific	6-6-1	
40	Pacific	4-5-0	
41	Pacific	4-7-0	
42	Pacific	2-6-1	
43	Pacific	7-2-0	
44	Pacific	3-8-0	
45	Pacific	0-10-1	
46	Pacific	5-7-0	1

57 yrs. .605 314-199-35

* National Champions

Bowl game included above:
1 North Texas 13-14 Optimist L

Bowls W-L-T: 0-1-0

EWALD "JUMBO" STIEHM
(Wisconsin '09)
B 4-9-85 Johnson Creek, Wis.
D 8-18-23

Yr.	Team	W-L-T
10	Ripon	4-3-0
11	Nebraska	5-1-2
12	Nebraska	7-1-0
13	Nebraska	8-0-0
14	Nebraska	7-0-1
15	Nebraska	8-0-0
16	Indiana	2-4-1
17	Indiana	5-2-0
18	Indiana	2-2-0
19	Indiana	3-4-0
20	Indiana	5-2-0
21	Indiana	3-4-0
12 yrs.	.709	59-23-4

JOCK SUTHERLAND
(Pittsburgh '18)
B 3-21-89 Coupar Angus, Scotland
D 4-11-48
Hall of Fame

Yr.	Team	W-L-T	B
19	Lafayette	6-2-0	
20	Lafayette	5-3-0	
21	Lafayette	9-0-0	
22	Lafayette	7-2-0	
23	Lafayette	6-1-2	
24	Pittsburgh	5-3-1	
25	Pittsburgh	8-1-0	
26	Pittsburgh	5-2-2	
27	Pittsburgh	8-1-1	1
28	Pittsburgh	6-2-1	
29	Pittsburgh	9-1-0	2
30	Pittsburgh	6-2-1	
31	Pittsburgh	8-1-0	
32	Pittsburgh	8-1-2	3
33	Pittsburgh	8-1-0	
34	Pittsburgh	8-1-0	
35	Pittsburgh	7-1-2	
36	Pittsburgh	8-1-1	4
37*	Pittsburgh	9-0-1	
38	Pittsburgh	8-2-0	
20 yrs.	.812	144-28-14	

* National Champions

Bowl games included above:
1 Stanford 6-7 Rose L
2 Southern Cal 14-47 Rose L
3 Southern Cal 0-35 Rose L
4 Washington 21-0 Rose W

Bowls W-L-T: 1-3-0

BARRY SWITZER
(Arkansas '60)
B 10-5-37 Crossett, Ark.

Yr.	Team	W-L-T	B
73	Oklahoma	10-0-1	
74*	Oklahoma	11-0-0	
75*	Oklahoma	11-1-0	1
76	Oklahoma	9-2-1	2
77	Oklahoma	10-2-0	3
78	Oklahoma	11-1-0	4
79	Oklahoma	11-1-0	5
80	Oklahoma	10-2-0	6
81	Oklahoma	7-4-1	7
82	Oklahoma	8-4-1	8
83	Oklahoma	8-4-0	
84	Oklahoma	9-2-1	9
85*	Oklahoma	11-1-0	10
86	Oklahoma	11-1-0	11
87	Oklahoma	11-1-0	12
88	Oklahoma	9-3-0	13
16 yrs.	.837	157-29-4	

* National Champions

Bowl games included above:
1 Michigan 14-6 Orange W
2 Wyoming 41-7 Fiesta W
3 Arkansas 6-31 Orange L
4 Nebraska 31-24 Orange W
5 Florida St. 24-7 Orange W
6 Florida St. 18-17 Orange W
7 Houston 40-14 Sun W
8 Arizona St. 21-32 Fiesta L
9 Washington 17-28 Orange L
10 Penn St. 25-10 Orange W
11 Arkansas 42-8 Orange W
12 Miami (Fla.) 14-20 Orange L
13 Clemson 6-13 Florida Citrus L

Bowls W-L-T: 8-5-0

(1988 last active season)

JIM TATUM
(North Carolina '35)
B 8-22-13 McColl, S.C.
D 7-23-59
Hall of Fame
Coach of Year 53

Yr.	Team	W-L-T	B
42	North Caro.	5-2-2	
46	Oklahoma	8-3-0	1
47	Maryland	7-2-2	2
48	Maryland	6-4-0	
49	Maryland	9-1-0	3
50	Maryland	7-2-1	
51	Maryland	10-0-0	4
52	Maryland	7-2-0	
53*	Maryland	10-1-0	5
54	Maryland	7-2-1	
55	Maryland	10-1-0	6
56	North Caro.	2-7-1	
57	North Caro.	6-4-0	
58	North Caro.	6-4-0	
14 yrs.	.729	100-35-7	

* National Champions

Bowl games included above:
1 North Caro. St. 34-13 Gator W
2 Georgia 20-20 Gator T
3 Missouri 20-7 Gator W
4 Tennessee 28-13 Sugar W
5 Oklahoma 0-7 Orange L
6 Oklahoma 6-20 Orange L

Bowls W-L-T: 3-2-1

FRANK THOMAS
(Notre Dame '23)
B 11-15-98 Muncie, Ind.
D 5-10-54
Hall of Fame

Yr.	Team	W-L-T	B
25	Tenn.-Chatt.	4-4-0	
26	Tenn.-Chatt.	6-2-2	
27	Tenn.-Chatt.	8-1-0	
28	Tenn.-Chatt.	8-2-0	
31	Alabama	9-1-0	
32	Alabama	8-2-0	
33	Alabama	7-1-1	
34	Alabama	10-0-0	1
35	Alabama	6-2-1	
36	Alabama	8-0-1	
37	Alabama	9-1-0	2
38	Alabama	7-1-1	
39	Alabama	5-3-1	
40	Alabama	7-2-0	
41	Alabama	9-2-0	3
42	Alabama	8-3-0	4
44	Alabama	5-2-2	5
45	Alabama	10-0-0	6
46	Alabama	7-4-0	
19 yrs.	.795	141-33-9	

Bowl games included above:
1 Stanford 29-13 Rose W
2 California 0-13 Rose L
3 Texas A&M 29-21 Cotton W
4 Boston College 37-21 Orange W
5 Duke 26-29 Sugar L
6 Southern Cal 34-14 Rose W

Bowls W-L-T: 4-2-0

JOHN VAUGHT
(Texas Christian '33)
B 5-6-08 Olney, Texas
Hall of Fame

Yr.	Team	W-L-T	B
47	Mississippi	9-2-0	1
48	Mississippi	8-1-0	
49	Mississippi	4-5-1	
50	Mississippi	5-5-0	
51	Mississippi	6-3-1	
52	Mississippi	8-1-2	2
53	Mississippi	7-2-1	
54	Mississippi	9-2-0	3
55	Mississippi	10-1-0	4
56	Mississippi	7-3-0	
57	Mississippi	9-1-1	5
58	Mississippi	9-2-0	6
59	Mississippi	10-1-0	7
60*	Mississippi	10-0-1	8
61	Mississippi	9-2-0	9
62	Mississippi	10-0-0	10
63	Mississippi	7-1-2	11
64	Mississippi	5-5-1	12
65	Mississippi	7-4-0	13
66	Mississippi	8-3-0	14
67	Mississippi	6-4-1	15
68	Mississippi	7-3-1	16
69	Mississippi	8-3-0	17
70	Mississippi	7-4-0	18
73	Mississippi	5-3-0	

25 yrs. .745 190-61-12

* National Champions

Bowl games included above:
1 Texas Christian 13-9   Delta   W
2 Georgia Tech 7-24   Sugar   L
3 Navy 0-21   Sugar   L
4 Texas Christian 14-21   Cotton   W
5 Texas 39-7   Sugar   W
6 Florida 7-3   Gator   W
7 Louisiana St. 21-0   Sugar   W
8 Rice 14-6   Sugar   W
9 Texas 7-12   Cotton   L
10 Arkansas 17-13   Sugar   W
11 Alabama 7-12   Sugar   L
12 Tulsa 7-14   Bluebonnet L
13 Auburn 13-7   Liberty W
14 Texas 0-19   Bluebonnet L
15 UTEP 7-14   Sun   L
16 Virginia Tech 34-17   Liberty W
17 Arkansas 27-22   Sugar   W
18 Auburn 28-35   Gator   L

Bowls W-L-T: 10-8-0

WALLACE WADE
(Brown '17)
B 6-15-92 Trenton, Tenn.
D 10-7-86
Hall of Fame

Yr.	Team	W-L-T	B
23	Alabama	7-2-1	
24	Alabama	8-1-0	
25	Alabama	10-0-0	1
26	Alabama	9-0-1	2
27	Alabama	5-4-1	
28	Alabama	6-3-0	
29	Alabama	6-3-0	
30	Alabama	10-0-0	3
31	Duke	5-3-2	
32	Duke	7-3-0	
33	Duke	9-1-0	
34	Duke	7-2-0	
35	Duke	8-2-0	
36	Duke	9-1-0	
37	Duke	7-2-1	
38	Duke	9-1-0	4
39	Duke	8-1-0	
40	Duke	7-2-0	
41	Duke	9-1-0	5
46	Duke	4-5-0	
47	Duke	4-3-2	
48	Duke	4-3-2	
49	Duke	6-3-0	
50	Duke	7-3-0	

24 yrs. .765 171-49-10

Bowl games included above:
1 Washington 20-19   Rose   W
2 Stanford 7-7   Rose   T
3 Washington St. 24-0 Rose   W
4 Southern Cal 3-7   Rose   L
5 Oregon St. 16-20   Rose   L

Bowls W-L-T: 2-2-1

GLENN "POP" WARNER
(Cornell '95)
B 4-5-71 Springville, N.Y.
D 9-7-54
Hall of Fame

Yr.	Team	W-L-T	B
95	Georgia	3-4-0	
96	Georgia	4-0-0	
97	Cornell	5-3-1	
98	Cornell	10-2-0	
99	Carlisle	8-2-0	
00	Carlisle	5-4-1	
01	Carlisle	5-7-1	
02	Carlisle	7-3-0	
03	Carlisle	11-2-1	
04	Cornell	7-3-0	
05	Cornell	6-4-0	
06	Cornell	8-1-2	
07	Carlisle	10-1-0	
08	Carlisle	10-2-1	
09	Carlisle	7-3-1	
10	Carlisle	8-6-0	
11	Carlisle	11-1-0	
12	Carlisle	12-1-1	
13	Carlisle	10-1-1	
14	Carlisle	5-9-1	
15	Pittsburgh	8-0-0	
16*	Pittsburgh	8-0-0	
17	Pittsburgh	9-0-0	
18*	Pittsburgh	4-1-0	
19	Pittsburgh	6-2-1	
20	Pittsburgh	6-0-2	
21	Pittsburgh	5-3-1	
22	Pittsburgh	8-2-0	
23	Pittsburgh	5-4-0	
24	Stanford	7-1-1	1
25	Stanford	7-2-0	
26*	Stanford	10-0-1	2
27	Stanford	8-2-1	3
28	Stanford	8-3-1	
29	Stanford	9-2-0	
30	Stanford	9-1-1	
31	Stanford	7-2-2	
32	Stanford	6-4-1	
33	Temple	5-3-0	
34	Temple	7-1-2	4
35	Temple	7-3-0	
36	Temple	6-3-2	
37	Temple	3-2-4	
38	Temple	3-6-1	

44 yrs. .729 313-106-32

* National Champions

Bowl games included above:
1 Notre Dame 10-27   Rose   L
2 Alabama 7-7   Rose   T
3 Pittsburgh 7-6   Rose   W
4 Tulane 14-20   Sugar L

Bowls W-L-T: 1-2-1

BUD WILKINSON
(Minnesota '37)
B 4-23-16 Minneapolis, Minn.
Hall of Fame
Coach of Year 49

Yr.	Team	W-L-T	B
47	Oklahoma	7-2-1	
48	Oklahoma	10-1-0	1
49	Oklahoma	11-0-0	2
50*	Oklahoma	10-1-0	3
51	Oklahoma	8-2-0	
52	Oklahoma	8-1-1	
53	Oklahoma	9-1-1	4
54	Oklahoma	10-0-0	
55*	Oklahoma	11-0-0	5
56*	Oklahoma	10-0-0	
57	Oklahoma	10-1-0	6
58	Oklahoma	10-1-0	7
59	Oklahoma	7-3-0	
60	Oklahoma	3-6-1	
61	Oklahoma	5-5-0	
62	Oklahoma	8-3-0	8
63	Oklahoma	8-2-0	
17 yrs.	.826	145-29-4	

* National Champions

Bowl games included above:
1	North Caro. 14-6	Sugar	W
2	Louisiana St. 35-0	Sugar	W
3	Kentucky 7-13	Sugar	L
4	Maryland 7-0	Orange	W
5	Maryland 20-6	Orange	W
6	Duke 48-21	Orange	W
7	Syracuse 21-6	Orange	W
8	Alabama 0-17	Orange	L

Bowls W-L-T: 6-2-0

HENRY WILLIAMS
(Yale '91)
B 7-26-69 Harford, Conn.
D 6-21-31
Hall of Fame

Yr.	Team	W-L-T
91	Army	4-1-1
00	Minnesota	10-0-2
01	Minnesota	10-1-1
02	Minnesota	9-2-1
03	Minnesota	14-0-1
04	Minnesota	13-0-0
05	Minnesota	10-1-0
06	Minnesota	4-1-0
07	Minnesota	2-2-1
08	Minnesota	3-2-1
09	Minnesota	6-1-0
10	Minnesota	6-1-0
11	Minnesota	6-0-1
12	Minnesota	4-3-0
13	Minnesota	5-2-0
14	Minnesota	6-1-0
15	Minnesota	6-0-1
16	Minnesota	6-1-0
17	Minnesota	4-1-0
18	Minnesota	5-2-1
19	Minnesota	4-2-1
20	Minnesota	1-6-0
21	Minnesota	3-4-0
23 yrs.	.786	141-34-12

GEORGE WOODRUFF
(Yale '89)
B 2-22-64 Dimmock, Pa.
D 3-23-34
Hall of Fame

Yr.	Team	W-L-T
92	Pennsylvania	15-1-0
93	Pennsylvania	12-3-0
94	Pennsylvania	12-0-0
95*	Pennsylvania	14-0-0
96	Pennsylvania	14-1-0
97*	Pennsylvania	15-0-0
98	Pennsylvania	12-1-0
99	Pennsylvania	8-3-2
00	Pennsylvania	12-1-0
01	Pennsylvania	10-5-0
03	Illinois	8-6-0
05	Carlisle	10-4-0
12 yrs.	.846	142-25-2

* National Champions

WARREN WOODSON
(Baylor '24)
B 2-24-03 Fort Worth, Texas
Hall of Fame
College Division Coach of Year 60

Yr.	Team	W-L-T	B
35	Conway State	4-3-0	
36	Conway State	8-0-0	
37	Conway State	8-1-0	
38	Conway State	7-1-0	
39	Conway State	5-2-2	
40	Conway State	8-1-1	
41	Hardin-Simmons	7-3-1	
42	Hardin-Simmons	9-1-1	1
46	Hardin-Simmons	11-0-0	2
47	Hardin-Simmons	8-3-0	3
48	Hardin-Simmons	6-2-3	4,5,6
49	Hardin-Simmons	6-4-1	
50	Hardin-Simmons	5-5-0	
51	Hardin-Simmons	6-6-0	
52	Arizona	6-4-0	
53	Arizona	4-5-1	
54	Arizona	7-3-0	
55	Arizona	5-4-1	
56	Arizona	4-6-0	
58	New Mexico St.	4-6-0	
59	New Mexico St.	8-3-0	7
60	New Mexico St.	11-0-0	8
61	New Mexico St.	5-4-1	
62	New Mexico St.	4-6-0	
63	New Mexico St.	3-6-1	
64	New Mexico St.	6-4-0	
65	New Mexico St.	8-2-0	
66	New Mexico St.	7-3-0	
67	New Mexico St.	7-2-1	
72	Trinity (Tex.)	8-2-0	
73	Trinity (Tex.)	8-3-0	
31 yrs.	.673	203-95-14	

Bowl games included above:
1	2nd Air Force 7-13	Sun	L
2	Denver 20-0	Alamo	W
3	San Diego St. 53-0	Harbor	W
4	Pacific 35-35	Grape	T
5	Ouachita 40-12	Shrine	W
6	Wichita 49-12	Camellia	W
7	North Texas 28-8	Sun	W
8	Utah St. 20-7	Sun	W

Bowls W-L-T: 6-1-1